AMERICAN THOUGHT:
A CRITICAL SKETCH

The long toil of the brave is not quenched in darkness,
Nor hath counting the cost fretted away the zeal of their hopes.

      *   *   *   *   *

For whatsoever one hath well said goeth forth with a voice that never dieth;
And thus, o'er the fruitful earth and athwart the sea hath passed
The light of noble deeds unquenchable forever.

PINDAR, *Isthmian Odes IV, V.*

American Thought

A CRITICAL SKETCH

MORRIS R. COHEN

EDITED AND WITH A FOREWORD BY FELIX S. COHEN

THE FREE PRESS, GLENCOE, ILLINOIS

CONTENTS

FOREWORD

ALMOST THE FIRST BOOK [wrote Morris R. Cohen[1]], I ever rashly promised a publisher was one on contemporary American thought, which was originally planned for publication in 1926 as a volume of the international "Library of Contemporary Thought" that was being published by an English firm. The substance of one of the main chapters in the projected volume, that on American philosophy, had been largely written in instalments for the *New Republic* and published in the *Cambridge History of American Literature* in 1921. But the book I planned would focus not on technical philosophy but rather on the general ideas which are taken for granted in various fields of thought and thus come to constitute the philosophy of a period and a country even before they have been systematically articulated.

Ever since the winter of 1923-24, when Alvin Johnson succeeded in getting the New School for Social Research established and its students elected me to give the first course, I had been lecturing there, off and on, on various aspects of science and philosophy. The course which brought me the keenest response was one on contemporary American thought. I had no difficulty in lecturing on the subject, but the hope that a book could be written from my lecture notes refused to materialize. Perhaps this was because in speaking I could not stop and say, "I'll go and look something up," before continuing, whereas in writing I do that very often. Particularly was this true in a subject like American thought, where meditation cannot take the place of reading, and where the field to be covered grows year by year.

When I retired from undergraduate teaching in 1938, the completion of the volume on American thought was one of the assignments uppermost in my mind. I undertook to lecture on the subject at Chicago in the spring of 1939, and in the course of these lectures managed to get down on paper a series of sketches of American thought on science, history, philosophy, politics, jurisprudence, art, religion, psychology, education, economics, and sociology. These drafts only emphasized the limitations of my knowledge of some of the subjects dealt with. Through the 1939 spring session at Chicago I spent a large amount of time reading up on points in these lectures

[1] M. R. Cohen, *A Dreamer's Journey* (1949), pp. 195-197.

that needed strengthening. Particularly did I seek to remedy the gaps
in my knowledge of early American scientific and economic thought
and of American literary criticism and art criticism generally. Reading in the history of American geology, chemistry, astronomy, and
physics made me realize how much science was cultivated early in
the history of the republic. The work of Franklin in the field of electricity and of Jefferson in geology represented solid scientific research
as well as a striking symbol of the common roots of science and
liberalism.

In my youth, the ascetic and democratic ideas with which I began
to philosophize had predisposed me to view aestheticism as a form of
snobbery. Acquaintance with rare paintings or esoteric music could
not be a prerequisite, I thought, to an understanding of the depths of
human nature or the needs of the human spirit. As a pluralist I could
find plenty of anthropological evidence for the view that talk about
superior taste may mean a blindness to its natural diversity. Later
reflection, however, on the fact that only a few who are highly
trained understand the meaning of such scientific laws as that of
gravitation, suggested that in the field of art, too, training may make
clear what is otherwise vague and indistinct. Later study made it plain
that the enjoyment of nature is largely motivated by art. People see
or hear what great artists have taught them to see and hear. And so
art criticism must be based on understanding of the techniques by
which such results are attained. In this train of thought, discussions
with Edwin Arlington Robinson and other fellow colonists at the
MacDowell and Yaddo colonies proved most stimulating.

The more I read, however, on these themes the wider loomed the
seas of my ignorance. And the more I wrote on contemporary American thought the farther I was from being up to date in all its fields,
much as Tristram Shandy found when it took him seven years to
write the first year of his autobiography. Eventually I had to admit
to myself that if I ever did complete a book on contemporary American thought it would be out of date by the time it was published. It
might be possible, however, to sketch the formative influences or
currents that have entered into American thinking without striving
for contemporaneity. But even with this limitation the task remained
a baffling one.

What was baffling to the author of this volume was even more baffling
to his literary executor. And so the task of putting the vast conglomeration of essays and lecture notes on American thought into book form
was postponed, from year to year, while other simpler editorial tasks
were tackled.[2] The passing years have emphasized some of the gaps in

---

[2] *The Meaning of Human History* (the Carus Lectures delivered in 1945) was
published (Open Court Publishing Co.) in 1947; the *Source Book in Greek Science*
(of which Dr. Israel Edward Drabkin was co-editor) (McGraw-Hill Book Co.) in
1948; *A Dreamer's Journey* (Beacon Press) in 1949; *Studies in Philosophy and Science*
(Henry Holt & Co.) in 1949; *Reason and Law* (The Free Press) in 1950; *Reflections*

the volume but they have not detracted, I think, from the significance of the reflections that are here assembled. For what is most significant in these reflections is that they are the product of a single pioneer mind that has ranged widely on the frontiers of American reflective thought and brought to many diverse fields a unified and unifying perspective. And in a world where academic compartments and other barriers to the free interchange of ideas threaten to make philosophy itself a specialized discipline, there is greater need than ever before for consistent perspectives that range over the broadest horizons of the human mind. The gaps in this volume will be filled, sooner or later, by other writers more expert in one specialty or another. But later writers, whether they agree or disagree with the author's appraisals of particular thinkers or historic events, are likely to profit, I think, by the effort to come to grips with the threads of continuity that Morris R. Cohen found running through the fabric of American thought.

For one who always called himself a pluralist, Morris R. Cohen had a remarkable sense of the inter-relatedness of all the fields of human thought. Always there was the dominating quest for a philosophical outlook to which no honest effort of the human mind would be irrelevant. In his autobiography Morris R. Cohen writes of the dream, kindled by the enthusiasm of his teacher, Thomas Davidson,

"of an Encyclopedia of Philosophy that should do for the culture of the twentieth century what the Brothers of Sincerity did for the tenth, and Diderot and d'Alembert did for the eighteenth. This dream has dominated my whole intellectual life. All my reading somehow or other gets fitted into that scheme. And though I was never to realize that youthful ambition, it has given form to all of my fragmentary efforts at the statement of a philosophical position adequate to the understanding of the problems of modern civilization."[3]

A certain irreverence towards the respectable distances that are supposed to separate one academic domain from another crops up again and again in the titles that Morris R. Cohen chose for his writings: *The Faith of a Liberal; The Faith of a Logician; The Piety of an Agnostic.* How can a liberal or a logician have a faith, or an agnostic a piety? *Legal Theories and Social Science.* Didn't every bar association member who heard this address know that legal doctrines are never theoretical and that social theories are never scientific? *The Process of Judicial*

---

of a Wondering Jew (The Free Press) in 1950; *Readings in Jurisprudence and Legal Philosophy* (with Felix S. Cohen as co-editor) (Prentice-Hall, Inc.) in 1951; *King Saul's Daughter* (The Free Press) in 1952; and a re-issue of *Reason and Nature* (The Free Press) in 1953.

[3] M. R. Cohen, *A Dreamer's Journey* (1949), at p. 109.

Legislation. What business do judges have legislating? *An Introduction to Logic and Scientific Method.* Doesn't every schoolboy know that logic and scientific method are separated by twenty centuries? *Reason and Nature.* Don't we all know that reason is artificial and that nature is irrational? *The Logic of Fiction.* What college courses could be more remote from each other than logic and fiction?

The irreverence of these writings ran deeper than the titles. It was in the coming together of widely diversified ideas that Morris R. Cohen found the promise of American life and the genius of American liberalism. It was in the basic interdependence of opposites, the principle of polarity, that he found a compass for philosophical sanity and a safeguard against all monolithic absolutisms. In such a perspective no field of study can function in complete isolation from other fields, and the task of formulating the seminal ideas of American philosophy must take one on an arduous journey through all the realms of reflective thought.

In a sense, the whole drive of Morris R. Cohen's thinking was towards the breaking down of the petty isolationisms that specialists are so fond of setting up to protect the little domains of their sovereignty from the outsider. During much of the era with which this volume deals, American thought was hopelessly compartmentalized. Each of the natural and social sciences had its own fixed and distinct place in an academic caste world that did not tolerate miscegenation. Economics and politics were regarded as entirely separate and distinct sciences, and the study of law was independent of both. Logic was viewed as dealing with a subject matter that had nothing in common with the subject matter of the mathematical or physical sciences. Philosophy was regarded as essentially other-worldly, and the chasm between American academic thinking and the world of practical affairs reached dimensions which could hardly be matched in any other land. In no other country was technical academic philosophy so far removed from the philosophies of the people. No other country had "more professional teachers of philosophy and proportionately fewer readers of philosophic literature in the general public."[3a] Those phases of philosophy that had traditionally been most closely linked to the affairs of daily life, such as the philosophy of history, of politics, of ethics and aesthetics, were precisely the phases most widely neglected in American academic philosophy down to recent years.

Many of these chasms have been bridged in the past four decades. In the building of these bridges the author of this volume played a significant role. But as a reporter of the currents of American thought,

[3a] M. R. Cohen, "Philosophy in America," in Francis Hackett, *On American Books* (1920), p. 49.

Morris R. Cohen fails to report his own contributions to those currents. This is indeed one of the most serious gaps of the present work.

One must look elsewhere, for example, to find an account of Morris R. Cohen's impact upon the traditional isolationism of American law, the notion as Justice Cardozo once put it, "that law is to be kept in a water-tight compartment and that within that compartment, and no other, is to be found the material by which its growth must be renewed."[4] And Justice Cardozo went on to say: "I can think of no one who has battled against that view more steadily and gallantly than this pseudo-lawyer who has enriched our conception of jurisprudence by the fertilizing waters of a profound and pure philosophy."[5] One may turn to the comments of another brilliant American jurist, Judge Nathan Margold, for an account of the impact upon lawyers and law teachers of "the first American philosopher to interest himself in the law".[6]

"It was back in 1913 that Morris R. Cohen shocked the lawyers and law teachers of America with his epoch-making paper on 'The Process of Judicial Legislation.' What he said then supplied the text to which the most valuable work of progressive jurists since that time has been commentary."

* * * * *

"The non-legal works that now fill the footnotes of Supreme Court opinions, the increasing reliance upon scientific data in the trial and argument of cases of public interest, and the expanding curricula of our more progressive law schools, all bear witness to the breakdown of the old myth of the self-sufficiency of the law. The technique of the 'Brandeis brief,' with its accent on social facts, the tendency of the last twenty years to expand the administrative and investigative side of the judicial process, and the increasing recognition of the role of social outlook in the judicial process, are all indications of the vitality of the philosophy with which Professor Cohen began to break down the walls that separated law from the social sciences. The trumpets still echo and the walls go crumbling down."

* * * * *

"Morris R. Cohen made the phonograph theory of justice intellectually untenable. As judges came to recognize the scope of their creative and responsible role in the legal process, there grew up a more sober attitude of judicial deference to the authority of legislators. At the same time legislators became more aware of the social policy issues involved in constitutional law. There thus arose the practice of including in statutes statements of fact and policy designed to support the constitutionality of the statute. For more than a decade now the Supreme Court has accepted the authority of Congress as

[4] Quoted in *Freedom and Reason: Studies in Philosophy and Jewish Culture in Memory of Morris Raphael Cohen* (edited by S. W. Baron, E. Nagel and K. S. Pinson, 1951), p. 36.

[5] *Ibid.*

[6] Nathan R. Margold, "Morris R. Cohen as a Teacher of Lawyers and Jurists," in *Freedom and Reason*, p. 43.

embodied in such statements. During that period it has refrained from substituting its own judgment for the judgment of Congress on disputed issues of social fact and policy."[7]

"In this change the voice of Morris R. Cohen was the voice of a prophet who first points out that which becomes obvious to all once it has been declared."[8]

The gap between law and philosophy that Morris R. Cohen sought to bridge reflected the prevailing unconcern of philosophers for law no less than the disregard of jurists for philosophy. And so the bridging of this gap involved not only carrying philosophy to lawyers but equally carrying law to philosophers, which was the burden of Morris R. Cohen's 1912 address to the American Philosophical Association on "Jurisprudence as a Philosophical Discipline."[9]

At about the same time, Morris R. Cohen, in collaboration with John Dewey, was organizing the Conference on Legal and Social Philosophy, from which much of the social and philosophical consciousness of modern American jurisprudence derives. It was in this period that Morris R. Cohen introduced courses in legal philosophy into the American philosophical curriculum and began the preparation of a source book for such courses which has only recently been completed.[10] Further assaults upon the philosophical isolationism of the traditional American jurisprudence were made through the translation of modern continental works in legal philosophy in the Modern Legal Philosophy Series, of which Morris R. Cohen was a co-editor. A series of his own lectures, law review articles, and works on legal philosophy that profoundly influenced American law teaching and juristic thinking are not mentioned in the text of Morris R. Cohen's account of American legal thought.

Equally profound and devastating was the isolationism of American instruction in logic when Morris R. Cohen first began to teach that subject in 1912. A tradition almost unchanged since the days of Aristotle regarded logic as a study of syllogisms, without regard for the simple fact that most of mathematics and most scientific reasoning is non-syllogistic. In his teaching, in the essays later collected in *A Preface to Logic,* and in the joint work of Morris R. Cohen and his talented pupil, Ernest Nagel, *Introduction to Logic and Scientific Method,* the old narrow view of logic received its death warrant and the modern conception of logic as identical with mathematics and scientific demonstration came to be a living part of American scientific and philosophic thought. Whereas the

---

[7] *Ibid.,* pp. 38-41.

[8] *Ibid.,* pp. 36-37.

[9] Reprinted in M. R. Cohen, *Reason and Law* (1950), at p. 129.

[10] The volume of *Readings in Jurisprudence and Legal Philosophy,* cited in footnote 2.

traditional logic had seemed to assume a world of hard and fast concepts, a world in which everything is black or white, true or false, modern logic offered a more flexible instrument capable of dealing with the fictions, partial truths, probabilities, uncertainties, and twilight zones which are the true object of science and the material of daily life. "Conceived in these terms," wrote Morris R. Cohen,[11] "logic becomes not a restriction upon the world that science discloses but an indispensable instrument for the exploration of possibilities, and in this sense an indispensable element of liberal civilization and free thought." It will be a long time before any of us can say with certainty how much this broadening of our views of logic has contributed to the widening of American horizons in philosophy and in the natural and the social sciences.

So, too, the divorce between scientific and classical studies that is so deep-seated in the organization of our academic life by degrees, had resulted in a wholly mythical conception of Greek thought as essentially unscientific. Along with this idea went the equally mythical conception of science as a recent product of Baconian empiricism. Both these myths rested largely on the fact that classical scholars did not understand the significance of ancient scientific writings and modern scientists did not understand the language in which they were written. Morris R. Cohen was not content to subject these twin myths to devastating refutations.[12] Rather he went on to arrange, with the collaboration of his brilliant student, Dr. Israel Edward Drabkin, for the compilation of a monumental *Source Book in Greek Science*.[13] Since the publication of that work no literate philosopher or scientist can have any further excuse for believing that the Greeks were mere speculators and that real science begins with Bacon or Galileo.

The philosophy of history,[14] the history of science,[15] the application of scientific method to the social sciences,[16] the intersection of economics and politics in the key concepts of "property"[17] and "contract,"[18] and a dozen other modern developments of what is today called the interdisciplinary approach reflect important contributions to American thought

---

[11] In the foreword to *A Preface to Logic* (1944), p. xi.

[12] See, in particular, "Bacon and the Inductive Method", in M. R. Cohen, *Studies in Philosophy and Science* (1949), p. 99.

[13] Referred to in footnote 2.

[14] See *The Meaning of Human History* (1947).

[15] *Ibid.*, pp. 245-259.

[16] *Cf.* "The Social and the Natural Sciences" in M. R. Cohen, *Reason and Nature*, at p. 333; and "Generalization in the Social Sciences," in *Eleven Twenty-Six, A Decade of Social Science Research* (ed. by L. Wirth, 1940).

[17] *Cf.* "Property and Sovereignty" in M. R. Cohen, *Law and the Social Order* (1933), p. 41.

[18] *Cf.* "The Basis of Contract," *ibid.*, p. 69.

on which the author of this text maintains an over-modest silence. In all these respects Morris R. Cohen's influence upon colleagues and generations of students can best be told by others. My own task as editor of this volume has been restricted, in this respect, to the inclusion of a number of asterisked footnotes pointing to other works of the author in which the unsatisfied reader may find some of these gaps partially filled.

Most serious, perhaps, of all the gaps in American thought to which this volume calls attention is that between academic reflection and the direction of practical affairs. In countless efforts to bridge this gap, Morris R. Cohen played a significant role. The organization in 1899, under the inspiration of Thomas Davidson, of a Breadwinner's College, the first of many significant democratic institutions of adult education for a more enlightened citizenship; the organization of the American Association of University Professors, which did so much to bring a sense of civic responsibility to the ranks of university teachers; the organization of the New School for Social Research; the introduction of scientific team-work into studies of race relations and international tensions; the establishment of two outstanding inter-disciplinary periodicals, *The Journal of the History of Ideas* and *Jewish Social Studies,* these are only a few of the significant developments of organized American thought in which the author participated and which are modestly passed over in these pages.

One result of these omissions is to over-accent the gaps in American thought and to over-emphasize the breach between our academic thinking and our practical life. One needs to remember that constant hammering at the irrationalities and failures of our intellectual life was, for Morris R. Cohen, a part of the process of attaining the richest potentialities of liberal civilization. The faith that is implicit in the critical writing of this volume finds a more positive expression in *The Faith of a Liberal.* And in that volume one finds the author's own criticism of his own earlier critical writing. Republishing, in 1946, an essay written 20 years earlier on the topic, "Have Ideas Prestige Among Us?", Morris R. Cohen added, by way of postscript:

"The twenty years that have passed since this paper was written have witnessed notable advances, I think, in the intellectual life of this country. The development of graduate schools, centers of adult education, and popular forums, the expansion of governmental and private research agencies, the acknowledgment by courts of the relevance of economic and other social studies in the determination of social issues, and the breaking down of barriers against scholarship in Government posts, are tangible signs of intellectual advance. Even more unmistakable is the retrogression of intellectual standards in most of the other nations of the world during these two decades. If, therefore, this paper implies a disparaging comparison, I hope it will be read not against the somber background of Europe today, but against the brighter horizon of what our own resources, natural and human, might produce and cherish."[19]

Apart from those gaps in the present volume which result from the author's failure to report on his own contributions to the development of American thought, there are other gaps resulting from the fact that at the time of the author's death, on January 28, 1947, certain projected chapters of this work had not progressed beyond the form of rough lecture notes. These incomplete chapters, dealing with American thought in psychology, sociology, ethics, education, and literature, and a proposed final chapter on the outlook for American thought, have been entirely omitted from this volume. In addition to these large gaps, there are many smaller lacunae, at points where the author had not completed projected studies of important contemporary thinkers. These are particularly numerous for the period of the late 1930's and 1940's. The careful reader will therefore refrain from drawing any inferences from the fact that some important thinker or writing is not mentioned in the text.

It has been my hope that some day a group of Morris R. Cohen's former students and associates might take up this fragmentary work and, through proper supplementation along the lines which the author laid out for himself, make of this survey a more complete symposium account of American thought in all its significant reaches. But in the absence of such a volume, or even as a prelude to such an enterprise, the gathering of the panoramic views of a single mind may be of some significance in the further development of the groping, hopeful, American thought that this volume sketches.

In order to maintain the character of the present work as the product of a single mind, this volume has been limited to those chapters which were reviewed and approved for publication by the author himself in 1946. Portions of these chapters, however, were then in the form of rough notes, and in editing such notes I cannot hope to have escaped errors that might have been caught and corrected if the author had lived to put the entire manuscript into final form.

Special acknowledgment is owing to those students and friends of Morris R. Cohen who collaborated with him in helping to prepare several chapters of this volume from fragmentary essays and lecture notes. A good deal of the writing and rewriting in Chapters I and VII and in some parts of Chapter IX was done with the assistance of Sidney Hook. Kenneth Arrow helped in the preparation of Chapter IV, and Stanley

[19] M. R. Cohen, *Faith of a Liberal* (1946), p. 287.

K. Nehmer in the preparation of Chapter V. Herman Womack assisted in portions of Chapter VIII. In the final editing of the manuscript, Leonora C. and Harry N. Rosenfield, Lucy M. Kramer, Victor W. Cohen, Charles Biederman, Milton Konvitz, and Maurice J. Goldbloom collaborated. And every chapter bears witness to the contributions of the author's life-time collaborator, Mary Ryshpan Cohen.

FELIX S. COHEN

Washington, D. C.
July 29, 1953.

POSTSCRIPT:

Since neither the author nor the editor saw final page proof of the book, any errors of omission or commission must be charged solely to my inadequacies as literary executor. If the book in final form has technical merit, and if the two indices prove of value, credit must go largely to those friends of Morris R. Cohen and Felix S. Cohen without whose assistance and devotion this work could not have been completed. Particular mention must be made of H. E. Bornstein, Huntington Cairns, William Gerber, Sidney Kramer, David Ryshpan and Patricia Schiller.

To Felix Cohen's daughters, Gene Maura and Karen Ann, I owe a debt not only for active assistance in the menial jobs of proof reading and preparing cards for indexing, but for bearing with a parent whose time and temper were often short. If they in the years to come feel a small sense of pride in having made this publication possible, the debt, I hope, will be forgiven.

LUCY KRAMER COHEN

Washington, D. C.
April 1, 1954

Chapter I

THE BACKGROUND
OF THE
AMERICAN TRADITION

THE THOUGHTS of men and women in America as elsewhere reach after everything under the sun and beyond it. And these thoughts are obviously too multitudinous and too elusive to be encompassed and chronicled by any one writer or group of writers. The best that any attempt at intellectual history can achieve is to indicate some of the traces that the stream of human thought has left in written records. The present book deals only with reflective thought, i.e. with thought that is conscious of its problems, of its methods, and of the widest general bearings of the results obtained so far. We may call it philosophic thought in the generously liberal rather than the narrowly technical denotation of the word.

Men begin to think only after they have learned to talk and their first thought is imitation of what their elders are saying. Indeed, most of what people say and write is dominated by linguistic forms or habits. Thus the dominance of the traditions and habits that make up the English language has been the strongest single influence in fashioning American thought as very largely a province of British thought—despite the Declaration of Independence and two wars.

This is not to deny that French, Dutch, and other Continental influences have played an impressive role in the intellectual history of America, as they have in England itself. Nor is it to minimize the fact that national boundaries have not altogether as yet destroyed the community of thought effected by classical civilization under the Roman Empire. Certainly, in the higher reaches of thought, such as science and philosophy, international cooperation is still an important factor despite linguistic diversity. Indeed human thought on its more reflective levels—and it is to such thought that we address ourselves in this survey—is to a large degree independent of time and place. This is not surprising, for people who really think are seldom absorbed in the affairs of the day; nor are they particularly aware of what is going on about them outside the realm of their special interests. If they were, they would act as people around them act and would not have time to think. And yet even the most original thought finds its starting point within some tradition, just as every journey through the wilderness begins at the edge of some clearing. It is only when the traditional answers fail to satisfy innate curiosity or when a sudden change brings forth problems that cannot be met by the accepted conventional solutions, that thought begins to venture into unexplored regions and attempts to find a more stable intellectual equilibrium. The same traditions, therefore, that confine the currents of prevailing attitudes also provide the starting point for the development of new ideas. Our talking and thinking thus reflect the faiths, habits, and emotional dispositions embodied in the language and culture that we inherit. Any survey of reflective American thought must therefore find its starting points in the prevailing social and intellectual currents within the turbulent stream of American life. And while these currents come to us predominantly from British and European sources there are important differences between the patterns of thought of the Old World and those that have grown up in the New World.

Conquest of the Wilderness

In the first place, what is distinctive about American thought reflects the differences between the men and women who came to America and those who stayed at home. The immigrants who came to America came as to a promised land free from the scourges of persecution and from the oppression of caste. Their coming here was a great adventure. They had to break ties with the past which those who did not immigrate never had occasion to break. They had to tear themselves away from their ancient homes and from those traditions that are deeply rooted in the soil that the immigrant leaves behind. Coming to a New World they had to strike new roots. Of course, not all of our early immigrants were Pilgrims who came here to seek freedom to worship God according to their conscience. Economic motives were always of large importance in the settlement of New England and Virginia as well as in the later currents of immigration. But whether the felt oppression which the immigrant sought to escape was religious or political or economic, the fact of immigration, so long as it remained a dominant fact of American life and development, strengthened the ideals of freedom and equality of opportunity. Through the generations the American dream of a land of freedom has been kept alive by the continued immigration of those who fled tyranny abroad and therefore had good reason to value freedom from tyranny in this country.

The second major factor to which we must turn in order to appreciate the selective shift in the old ideas and the rise of the new is the physical character of the American scene. Now, the great geographic fact of American history has been the physical conquest of the continent —a task which up to a time within the memory of men still living was the major preoccupation of American life.

In the mid-nineteenth century a part of New York State was still referred to as a wilderness, and it is only quite recently that reliable topographical maps of it were first made. Indeed, even in one of the oldest of American cities and the most crowded, New York, there is still virgin land that has not yet been cultivated or built upon. Unlike other countries, the conquest of the new land proceeded without any serious war—from the viewpoint of the white conquerors—with its inhabitants. There was no need to exterminate or absorb the Indians. They were so few and so poor that they could be persuaded to sell their lands or, if persuasion failed, could be driven West by force. The problem of the pioneer was mainly one of conquering the land. The arduous work of clearing forests, opening mines, cultivating fields, building cities, roads, bridges, and harbors, which in Europe had taken many long centuries, was, because of the character of the people, their inventiveness, training and use of machinery, performed here by less numerous people and in much less time.

These strenuous activities generated an atmosphere in which the practical-minded and enterprising flourished more readily than the sensitive and reflective. There was a tremendous strain on people living the frontier life. Pioneers had very little leisure for science, art, philosophy, or general reflection. Since the very life of the community was intimately bound up with economic enterprise, those who took the lead in practical exploitation of nature received not only great material reward but, with it, social prestige and honor.

The clergy was at first the only intellectual class to challenge the prestige of the commercially successful. Early American thought is, therefore, religious in tone or setting (and by religious we must understand Protestant and predominantly Evangelical). The Established Church of England did not take great interest in, or devote any major energies to, maintaining the Episcopal establishment in the United States, and the Methodist movement in the eighteenth century loosened the hold of the Established Church where it had been strongest. Naturally, the political independence of the United States prevented the Episcopal Church from maintaining too close a connection with the Church of England. In addition, the fact that so many of the early and later settlers were dissenters tended to maintain the Evangelical spirit and the consequent independence of the laity. Thus dependent upon the congregation, the clergy sooner or later accommodated themselves to the prevailing attitude, and learned to regard success in this life as the reward of Providence and the best assurance of beatitude in the next.

In short, the struggle of the primitive American community to bring the wilderness under cultivation made the practical-minded entrepreneur, who had no time for leisure and no interest in play or foreign culture, the ideal character for everyone to imitate. It gave a powerful emotional sanction to the ideal of work even when the necessity for work was no longer imperative—an ideal which is still the most influential one in our modern business civilization.

Unfortunately, foreign appraisals of American life frequently fail to appreciate that the American worship of business is not merely the worship of the dollar but rather worship of the active life. In the American view money is apt to be viewed as the measure of a man's productive effort and social worth. This is far removed from the common Old World attitude that a man's wealth is essentially an exemption from the necessity to engage in socially useful labor.

The open frontier has been called the key to American history. Without stopping to consider the extent to which it has entered into our domestic and foreign imbroglios, it cannot be denied that the spirit of the frontier has had a constant and pervasive influence on the social and political traditions of the country. Living in isolated settlements on the fringe of civilization, the pioneer was thrown upon his own resources in organizing his life. He was bound by few irksome administrative regulations. The law he recognized was the spontaneous outgrowth of certain primitive needs of social order and security. As the processes of regular government caught up with him, he chafed in the toils of its red-tape and, often in open resentment, would trek farther West or South. He was aggressively individualistic in social and political matters, naturally suspicious of executive governmental action, and impatient with the slow-moving, authoritative administration of justice. When he felt keenly about a crime that had been committed, he was more likely to mete out summary "justice" by lynch law than to leave matters to courts and constables.

The rigor and monotony of border life far from centers of civilization made any diversion welcome. Trials in the law courts became occasions of public entertainment, in which the audience too had its unwritten privileges. Lawlessness found a natural outlet in the cruel treatment of Negroes and Indians. More significant, however, for its influence on the religious life of the country is the fact that the frontier was peculiarly subject to waves of revivalism. Away from organized forms of worship controlled by a disciplined clergy, the camp-meeting became a social event. It brought contact with the outside world. It offered emotional relief from a socially monotonous environment in an ecstatic rapture over perfervid eloquence. The hysterical contrition of the revival meetings, however, did not make for self-disciplined steadiness. Back-sliding is the other side of conversion, for the frequency of the latter directly depends on the former. To the frontier, America thus owes not only its revivalisms and its "Chautauquas," but also its lynch law and its distrust of the contemplative life.

Though the frontier has passed, these attitudes have become part of the stream of our national life.

Up to the second decade of the twentieth century, agriculture was our predominant occupation. In fact, even today, the United States is more agricultural than Western Europe. Agricultural classes as a rule are extremely conservative in outlook and distrustful of change. Their dependence upon seasonal crops makes them economically less mobile than are traders. Proximity to the soil, a narrow range of social interests, and many years' confinement to the same locality make more for local piety than for the cosmopolitanism of cities open to foreign doctrines. The farmer's dependence upon the financial centers for money and credit and upon the manufacturing regions for finished goods produces a stubborn jealousy of the cities, as well as distrust of highly centralized government, which he regards as the political arm of the financier. Where, as in a country like the United States, large industry and capital are very influential in the government, the farmer, in the absence of a feudal agricultural tradition and large landed estates, may often seem politically more progressive than the city man. But the farmer draws his ideological slogans from the older American philosophy of natural rights rather than from the newer currents of social theory. This political opposition, which is often closely associated with revivalism (as with William Jennings Bryan), intensifies the distrust of whatever city culture there is, so that there is a wider dissemination of the new material goods produced in the city than of ideas. A new toothpaste, or a new form of dress or of wearing the hair, spreads more quickly from coast to coast than a new idea in science or art. The city is imitated in externals; but its sophistication and cultural tendencies represent in the eyes of small townsfolk either effeteness or sinfulness.

The enormous stretches of territory between the ends of the country, broken by rivers, mountain ranges and deserts, made of American life a series of sectional activities. Although sectional isolation served as a check upon the easy circulation of ideas, it also explains why the doctrine of states' rights, as opposed to nationalism, was from the very outset a powerful sentiment in all but the financial centers. This made for a sort of tolerance. The country was so large that the mere knowledge that other groups were different disturbed no one, since there was no forced contact with them. The official attitude to dissenting religious and social groups encouraged European Utopians in the eighteenth and nineteenth centuries to look upon America as the most auspicious place for the establishment of ideal commonwealths.

The emphasis on the practical was strengthened by the successive waves of immigration, almost all bent on securing an economic foothold. The immigrants did not as a rule, with some notable exceptions such as the Germans of 1848, bring strong intellectual traditions with them; and what they brought had difficulty in surviving the hard economic struggle at the beginning, or the prosperity that followed. Whatever influence the culture of the immigrants had was largely restricted to those intellectual centers in and around which they settled. But the solvent of the American school system, long fearful of intellectual differences and unappreciative of the artistic riches of foreign folkways, tended to "Americanize" the younger generations so rapidly as to make them more or less ashamed of the peculiar traditions of their parents.

Opportunities for work and business activity were richly abundant. Idleness and shiftlessness, when associated with poverty, were condemned as moral delinquencies. The resultant mentality developed in this environment was one which glorified the "hustler" and "go-getter" and deprecated devotion to anything which was not immediately practical.

Whatever intellectual traditions the early colonists did have, the Southern Cavalier excepted, were predominantly religious. The strongest of these traditions was Puritanism. The idea that Puritans were generally opposed to religious oppression is, of course, entirely unhistorical. Puritanism had its origins as a middle-class reform movement against the exploitation of the church prelates. The Puritans had tried to force their church organization on the Church of England and had not succeeded;

but the real reason for their immigration was economic. The Puritans adopted a morality which enshrined the economic virtues of industry, thrift, temperance, and the like. They frowned upon luxury, art and expressions of the pure play impulse as deriving from Satan. The Scriptures, as interpreted by individual conscience, gave moral sanction to resistance against governmental authority when it affected the free competition necessary for commercial success. Transplanted to America, the gospel of work fitted in appropriately with the social necessity of building up the country.

For centuries Puritanism helped shape a type of political and legal thinking already congenial to the needs of growing industrial communities. At its heart was the Calvinistic belief in the total depravity of human nature, especially as human nature expressed itself in political legislation. But there was also an abounding grace in man's unrestricted economic activity. All that is valuable in civilization was held to be the result of enlightened and intelligent selfishness working towards ends only partially seen by mortal men. To protect each individual in this right to pursue his happiness in his own way—and in America the pursuit of happiness was most often conceived to be a quest for riches—certain constitutional restraints must be imposed on the majority, and especially on the legislature. From this, and from the fear that disaffected elements would infringe on the rights of property, followed the further political corollary, later drawn on in troubled times, that these restraints could best be enforced by an independent judiciary which, professedly free from passion or interest, decided matters in accordance with "eternal" principles.

A deeply humanistic aspect of Puritanism was hidden in the doctrine of Christian humility. But it was bleached out in the strong sun of economic prosperity. The Puritan who, when he saw a prisoner walking to the gallows, exclaimed, "There, but for the grace of God, go I," showed a sympathetic understanding for the weaknesses of human nature. To regard sin as something which, like all other misfortune, happens to a person, rather than as a result of deliberate choice, could have been developed into a doctrine of social charity to serve as a counterweight to the rampant individualistic tendencies of the pioneer. But the immediate pressure of getting on in the world made evangelical zeal in business and devout meddling in the affairs of one's neighbors an easier form of piety than sustained reflection on religious principles. And so, as saintliness hardened into strenuous asceticism, it was possible for preacher and trader to build up New England and its economic hinterland for the glory of God and a favorable balance sheet.

Two currents in American thought contested the Puritan traditions in religion and morals. These were the eighteenth century Deism, as represented by Benjamin Franklin of cosmopolitan Philadelphia, and the plantation culture of Virginia, where a semi-feudal agricultural economy had kept alive the tradition of the cultured leisure of the English Cavalier. But with the reaction to the French Revolution and the economic bankruptcy of the Old South that set in at the opening of the nineteenth century, these currents lost much of their vitality.

Although New England has maintained a consistent cultural leadership in American life, its efforts at a genuine culture have been seriously hampered by a series of economic catastrophes that have undermined so many of its sources of livelihood—agriculture, whaling, ship-building, and textile manufacture. The historic prerequisites of a profound culture are many generations of leisured ease and social prestige. Where land becomes fully and readily marketable, political and social power passes from the hands of aristocratic families to the families of the industrialist or financier. But it is clear that continued leadership by great families cannot be as well founded on a money as on a land economy, for in the former wealth is essentially mobile and the opportunities and capacities to redistribute it are much wider. The same kind of talent, for example, which enables a Jay Gould to amass a fortune enables a Harriman to take it away from his sons. Now originally the New England aristocracy was not a money aristocracy. It was an aristocracy of the "respectable" families. But with the exhaustion of free land and the hectic commercial activity which followed in the wake of the new immigration, the social prestige of the respectable family was undermined. In an anarchic commercial economy, where the pursuit of wealth is the main absorption, cultural continuity becomes difficult. Having no definite training in matters intellectual, a money aristocracy cannot enforce high standards upon its members. People who become rich are uncritically imitative in manners and thought. Cultivated society demands of them other traits than those that made them rich. Their cultural interests, sometimes frantic, more often apathetic, are thus shadowed by a feeling of insecurity.

The fact that the ruling classes of the country have in the main been composed of successive layers of the *nouveau riche* has strongly contributed to the backwardness of American culture. Continuity of discipline is almost impossible in an unstable environment, and in a commercial economy no group can feel sufficiently secure to disregard new forces in the offing; there is, therefore, no time to acquire an old culture thoroughly. Inwardly uncertain of itself, the dominant group fears independent thought and criticism. It lacks the mentality and taste necessary, in every age of transition, to maintain a straight course between dilettante faddism and narrow conventionalism. Against this background the chaotic, raw-boned insularity of American cultural life, relieved occasionally by evanescent bursts of local color in New England, falls into its proper perspective.

Brief mention should be made of the effects upon contemporary American thought of recent technological and economic developments. The automobile and radio have abolished rural isolation and brought a measure of sophistication to provincial communities. The population is thus becoming citified. More important still are the ties of foreign travel and commerce which have knit America more closely to foreign countries. Since the First World War America has been actively discovering Europe. Whereas European influences were theretofore refracted through a favored few, in the years that followed a great many Americans have been able to familiarize themselves at first hand with at least the externals of European civilization. European books, newspapers and magazines came to be read in ever greater numbers. European lecturers have found more receptive audiences, and a steady infiltration of European currents of thought in art, literature, and even in law has begun to manifest itself in certain quarters.

Despite these promising signs, however, the prevailing temper of American life remains pronouncedly anti-intellectual.

The Evaluation of the Intellect

That the prestige of purely intellectual work is still very low in the United States can hardly be doubted in the face of the comparatively slight social esteem in which those engaged in its pursuit are held. In no other country is the word *intellectual* so often used as a term of derision and opprobrium. This is true not only in the backward rural regions where, under the influence of poverty, ignorance and fundamentalism, intellectual enlightenment is genuinely feared. It is also true in the supposedly more advanced Eastern states where to be called a *mere theorist* is likewise to be damned.

As a people we do not enjoy reflective thinking for its own sake as a noble way of spending our leisure. Such occupation is despised by "serious" souls as an indoor sport. The conditions of scholarship in American universities at first resulted in the selection of teachers predominantly for their orthodox piety or their social acceptability, and today the pressure to publish rather than to engage in fundamental study is hardly favorable to the cultivation of profound scholarship. The economic inequalities in the way of salaries make a mad scramble for promotion occupy a great deal of the attention of younger members of the faculty in those years of their lives in which they can be most productive. The American college has undoubtedly become an object of affection on the part of its students and alumni to an extent unknown in Europe. But this has been largely due to its social features, of which the element of sports is often dominant. Devotion to particular teachers because of the intellectual stimulus which they provide is relatively rare.

The same attitude which makes American business heap its main rewards on the promoter and salesman rather than on the actual producer, makes the American public ignore intellectually productive minds in comparison with popularizers and administrators. Thus, not only are greater material honors bestowed on industrial promoters like Edison or Marconi, but they, rather than men like Willard Gibbs, Edward C. Pickering or Theobald Smith, are generally regarded as the great scientists.

But if any evidence were wanting of the low esteem in which intellectual work is held, the attitude towards it of many who are themselves supposed to be scholars, viz., college and university teachers, would be conclusive. It is hardly necessary to dwell on the responsibility of college teachers for the state of affairs in which students are less genuinely intereted in their studies than in the all too practical business of intercollegiate contests, euphemistically called sports. Teachers themselves often urge that those who manage a track or football team, or who cut a live figure in their social fraternities, learn something of greater importance from doing so than from any of their courses. And we may accept this as unfortunately true. A certain college in a large city in the East used to be regarded with great disfavor in academic circles and its students came to be classified as "grinds" because they were expected above all to devote themselves to their studies. If those who profess the intellectual life do not themselves feel the zest of its high adventure, it is natural for those whom they teach to regard the scholar's life as a pathetic futility.

Even more significant is the way American teachers share without protest the view of the public that to be taken out of teaching and scholarly work and to be put into the administrative post of dean or president is a promotion. Of course it is difficult to resist the temptation of increased pay and greater social prestige. But teachers know that administrative work in education, as in transportation, manufacture, or any other important business, is incompatible with a life of creative scholarship. To give up teaching for business is no uncommon thing in America.

But relatively few business men return the compliment and abandon business for intellectual enjoyments.

It cannot, however, be entirely overlooked that in a country where there are so many opportunities for practical achievement some men of really superior intelligence are not satisfied to remain mere scholars when new worlds may be won in an exacting game of effort and skill. We think it natural that literary men like Disraeli and Morley should find a greater sphere for their activity in the field of statesmanship; but the conduct of great business enterprise offers even greater opportunities for the expression of varied mental gifts than did the old type of statesmanship. As part of his railroad business, James J. Hill built up an empire greater than that created by the Caesars. But the complacent assumption that commercial success always means superior intelligence is peculiarly American, though history shows that our men of wealth have often been distinguished above all for their sheer ruthlessness rather than for versatile intelligence.

The causes of American anti-intellectualism are in part attributable to the physical character of the American scene, and will be further treated when we consider the types of leadership in American life. But the attitude is sufficiently important to warrant an examination of some contributing factors which in indirect ways strengthen it. Despite its boasted educational system, the country has not as yet developed a large liberally educated public—witness, for example, the relatively small number of scholarly books read or published here as compared with Germany, France, England, Holland or Scandinavia. Not so very long ago fewer serious books and fewer *copies* of serious books were published in the United States than in Sweden. In recent years, to be sure, there has been a marked improvement in this respect. But, in the main, serious or "high brow" books find as little genuine welcome among college students as among tired business men. And in a country where time is valued so highly and yet squandered on trivialities, the tendency is manifest to content oneself with excitingly written "romances" of science and outlines of philosophy or art, instead of patiently mastering the elements of any subject.

A large part of the European public that reads serious books consists of business men, who generally retire at what in America is regarded as an early age. The American business man, as a rule, dislikes to retire. He feels more at home in his business than at a concert, art gallery, or lecture. His business, even with all its burdens, fulfills his needs, and assiduous attention to it wins social respect. Since his education has not taught him to find real satisfaction outside of his daily routine, he does not know how to spend his leisure nobly. There has been no training for cultivated enjoyment.

High pressure salesmanship stimulates unnecessary wants and subjects people to a barrage of appeals to vanity and inferiority fears, awakens crazes and phobias, sensations and inflated ambitions, and exploits health, beauty and taste in the interest of money making. Clubs, associations, and orders add to the confusion and complexity of life and diminish its deeper satisfactions. Naturally, where the possession of money of itself gives prestige and a certain field of activity, few are willing to practice economy in order to make possible an early retirement from business into a quiet, contemplative life. Those who would do so would be regarded as queer. Only a few enormously wealthy people can spend the leisure of their advanced years using their money on philanthropic ventures. But the great mass of American practical men are caught in the vicious circle of having to make money to keep up their prestige and of being unable to do anything else the more they devote their energies to the making of money.

A nervous restlessness and an unquenched quest after pleasure set the tone and character of American recreation; the phrase "pursuit of happiness" is typically American. There is an inner shame at reflection for its own sake. And too often does reflection seek justification for itself in its alleged practical uses. Instead of insisting on the obvious truth that the pursuit of useless science and insight, like the pursuit of useless beauty and useless happiness, needs no justification, intellectual workers impoverish the ideal significance of their activity by straining to hitch it to some fancied utility, as if utility were not itself in need of sanctions themselves intrinsic.

The vaunted American love of technique is restricted to practical machines and instruments. It does not embrace a love of the technique of intellectual analysis. Ideas—social, political, or legal—do not receive anything approaching the same analytic attention as a new motor or radio set. They are not refashioned, clarified or developed. They are used for vague conventional purposes and then discarded or forgotten. The American talks more about the technique of autos than about the technique of his thinking.

In the absence of a flexible, critical tradition, mere example becomes a powerful influence both in manners and in thought. Every class imitates the one economically above it. People read and go to see what their neighbors acclaim. Waves of popular sentiment spread like contagions. "Everybody's doing it" becomes a persuasive argument. But nothing holds the popular attention for long. There are always new examples, new styles in dress, speech and interest. The thirst for novelty alone remains constant, because unsatisfied, in the dizzy whirl of change.

The privileged position of women in the United States has also markedly influenced the intellectual life of the country. The American woman has more conveniences, more leisure and more freedom from household cares than her European sister. She more often refuses to take a vicarious glory in the accomplishments of her husband than do women in Europe. She displays greater personal and intellectual independence. Intent upon attaining a social career of her own, she makes greater demands for leisure and means. The husband is induced to work all the harder in order to supply what is requisite. He may be content to let the wife represent the cultural interests of the family. The result is that women make up by far the greater part of the audiences which actively support and give hearing to those who are intellectually and artistically creative in American life.

Since no lecturer or artist can for long go counter to the likes and prejudices of the audience upon whom he is dependent, women have, by virtue of their monopoly of appreciation, conventionalized most forms of contemporary American culture. Women find it difficult to be out of fashion. Averse to facing the darker brutal sides of existence, its uncertainty and irrationality, they prefer the comforting assurance that life is just bitter enough to bring out the flavor of its sugared harmonies. European observers are often highly amused at what feminine taste in America finds "improper," "depressing" or "gruesome." Whatever the causes, women today have little opportunity to cultivate the disinterestedness and objectivity that are necessary for genuine critical appreciation. Feminine tastes are more likely to run to extremes of fear or adoration, under the impact of personal entanglements. Under exclusively feminine standards, conventional forms tend to dominate art and thought, and even the pattern of unreflective nonconformity tends to assume conventional forms.

Intellectual Leadership

The character of the intellectual life of a country may be determined by the kind of leadership it enjoys.

In the beginning, intellectual leadership in America rested with the clergy. While the country was still rural, the clergy represented a certain learning and thus a measure of intellectual authority in the eyes of the populace. The first American colleges were established primarily to train ministers of the gospel, and up to the end of the nineteenth century it was often considered necessary that the head of a college be a clergyman. With the growing importance of industry and commerce, leadership in communal affairs gradually passed to the legal profession. With this there has come about a depression in the intellectual standards of the clergy. There may be more of what currently passes as the milk of human kindness in such books as Peabody's *Jesus Christ and the Social Question* than in Jonathan Edwards' *Freedom of the Will.* But as a food for an adult intellect, the difference is unmistakable. Antics of the revivalists and the ignorance of crude, uneducated fundamentalists help us to understand why the clergy has lost prestige in the intellectual realm.

The organization of the American church also helps to explain the limited influence of the clergy. The churches are not endowed by the state, and are run either by poor communities or by rich men. In either case the clergyman functions like a salaried employee without the authority to enforce his intellectual and moral insights. This is especially true of the ministers of poor parishes, who are generally inadequately trained, for the parish cannot afford to employ others.

Lawyers took government from the hands of the clergy as early as the eighteenth century. In modern times, the influence of lawyers derives from the fact that most business is handled through legal—or illegal—channels—and you need lawyers for both. (In the early history of Indiana almost every prominent official was a lawyer who had been indicted a number of times.)

It is easier for a lawyer than for a business man to leave his business and run the government. Besides, the lawyer can take care of his client in the legislature as well as in his office. Lawyers' leisure and their gift of eloquence supply a national need.

America has for a long time presented the spectacle of a country not only politically but intellectually governed by lawyers. The important political influence of our lawyers is easily understood. Lawyers, until recently, fashioned our social as well as political ideals. This is an anomaly in the world's history. For while the legal profession is one that is constantly making intellectual demands upon its members, its activity is on the whole conditioned by certain practical and technical demands that separate it from the common intellectual life of a nation. The view that the legal profession ought to keep up with the progress of the social sciences, at least to the same extent that the medical profession has to keep in touch with the progress of the natural sciences, has until quite recently been vehemently denied by the claim of most American judges and lawyers that law is law and has nothing to do with economics, politics or ethics.

The bar in America may call itself a learned profession, but it is in the main devoted to business activity. The education of the lawyer was originally based on the model of apprenticeship or trade school training, rather than on the liberal studies of the university. Law schools, almost a century older than real universities, offer a curriculum calculated in the main to train one in the useful art of winning those cases that can be carried to the highest courts. Save in the largest universities, few courses are given on the relation of the law to the general life of the community. Nor are the social standards of the bar conducive to a free intellectual life. As the leaders of the bar have been those who have made most money by the shrewd management of their clients' affairs, they are seldom men of predominantly intellectual interests. The reading of the presidential addresses delivered before the American Bar Association does not impress one with the intellectual power of the American legal guild. Always one finds the same obsolete learning about Anglo-Saxon liberties and Magna Carta, the same eighteenth century *a priori* speculation about liberty, natural rights, the eternal necessity of constitutional restraints on the legislative power, and the like. Sober history may show that trial by jury and other "inalienable" rights are not of Anglo-Saxon origin; or that Magna Carta was of little use to the great mass of the common people; but the historical mis-information of Blackstone is good enough for most leaders of the American bar.*

The legal and political theories maintained by the American bench and bar are still those which were held in Europe in the eighteenth century; but the reasons that have led European thinkers to give up these theories, and, indeed, the very fact that there are civilized peoples who have given them up, seemed until recently quite unknown to provincial-minded American jurists. Although there are some indications that a change has begun to set in, the amount of actual attention to European legal thought is still negligible. The tradition of the isolation of common law still prevails, and a near-sighted nationalism considers it unpatriotic to doubt that the framers of our national Constitution have said the final word in political science.

Many observers of America have remarked on the growing influence of the university professor in national life. But as a class, professors have not yet acquired sufficient self-respect to influence the general currents

---

* *Cf.* "The Conservative Lawyer's Legend of Magna Carta" in M. R. Cohen, *Law and The Social Order* (1933), p. 19; and "The Legend of Magna Charta" in M. R. Cohen, *The Faith of a Liberal* (1946) p. 91.

of American life. They are perhaps gaining in influence. Their achievements, however, are very meagre. In Europe the community looks upon its professors as the lineal descendants of the great teachers of the Middle Ages. In America, the professor is regarded as an advanced type of the elementary school teacher whose business it is to impart to young and immature minds that which is already known. He must also serve as a moral example. The conditions under which university teaching can develop into a truly liberal profession have not yet been realized. And there are many indications that the public at large, as well as university professors themselves, are not aware of what these conditions are.

Unlike any other, the American university is organized on the model of the factory. The board of trustees corresponds to the board of directors, the president is the factory superintendent or manager, and the professors are the hired men or help. But in this case the hired men are genteel. Unkind critics have referred to the American professor as a member of the third sex; but John Jay Chapman puts the case more piquantly when he says: "The average professor in an American college will look on an act of injustice done to a brother professor by their college president with the same unconcern as the rabbit who is not attacked watches the ferret pursue his brother up and down through the warren . . . We know, of course, that it would cost the non-attacked rabbit his place to express sympathy for the martyr; and the non-attacked is poor, and has offspring, and hopes of advancement."

These conditions can in part be explained when we remember that our oldest genuine university (i.e., one affording opportunities for graduate studies) was established only in the 1870's, and that previously our colleges were nearly all, as most of them still are, under denominational control and little above the standard of the European secondary school. The teachers, as a rule, were men who could not be placed as clergymen, or, as Professor Basil Gildersleeve put it, men who, having failed to make good in foreign missions, were permitted to try their hand on the young barbarians at home. Those who wanted to pursue really advanced studies had to go abroad. The generations immediately following the Civil War went to Germany and brought back the outward manners of German scholarship, which obtained great vogue among educated people. The progress away from all this in the development of American universities in the present century has been truly remarkable, but when we contrast the relative salary, the required teaching load, and the general status in the community of the American professor with those of his European confreres we can see how great is the room for improvement. Nowhere else is the scholar subjected to such petty surveillance in both private and public life as in America. Nowhere else has the subservience of all studies to theologic dogmas survived to such an extent that it is thought perfectly proper for a university to be committed in advance, openly or semi-openly, to sectarian teaching. It is taken as a matter of course by most people that an able man should be barred from teaching because of his social manners or because he is not theologically orthodox. Not a stir was raised when Charles Peirce, one of the most fruitful-minded men America has produced—a man whom James and Royce repeatedly acknowledged as the source of their inspiration—was denied opportunity to lecture in any of the buildings controlled by Harvard University because of some overt infraction of conventional morality.

To this very day, the dead hand of the theologic seminary rests heavily on the American college.

A university professor is a person whose business it is to discover or verify truth in a given field and teach or publish it. This obviously carries with it the right to give utterance to that which may disturb established prejudice in the field of religion, economics or politics. So long, therefore, as the professor is not completely free to teach his subject, so long as he can be intimidated by those who control both his salary and his promotion, he will be sadly handicapped in his efforts to lead in the intellectual life of the country.

It is true that many American universities profess to be solicitous about promoting research in the social and cultural sciences, and some have made very liberal provision for research professorships and fellowships. Yet it cannot be denied that the present conception and organization of the universities is profoundly antagonistic to free research. It is not merely that the control of our universities by propertied interests makes a free and radical inquiry into social affairs a risky business for any professor (the cases of Scott Nearing, James McKeen Cattell, Bertrand Russell, and others are in point). Far more serious is the fact that the public at large does not think it is the professor's business to inquire into anything. He is to teach what he is told. Some years ago, when one exceptional president of a large university pointed out the importance of freedom in academic teaching, he was taken to task by a conscientious legalist who pointed out that American universities are endowed institutions, and endowed to teach certain things only.

More than any other country, America has replaced the ancient idea of a university as a society of scholars with the legal idea of so much property administered by trustees. It is not thought at all contrary to public interest that the university should be bound by someone who has made a fortune in oil or on the stock market, to teach forever the virtue of protective tariffs, the eighteenth century philosophy of law or the validity of non-episcopal ordination. Although even the so-called "private" universities are liberally supported by the public through the remission of taxes and in other ways, they remain in law and in public opinion entirely private corporations, with the right to hire and fire professors at pleasure.

Undoubtedly the trustees of American universities are, as a class, public-spirited citizens, desirous of promoting what they conceive to be the public good, and they give freely of their time and wealth to this end. But they are business men and not men of learning; and when they try to manage educational matters, the result cannot be better than if successful scholars were entrusted with the supreme responsibility for the private business of the trustees. It is natural for trustees to carry into the administration of universities the same ideas which they have employed in their industrial and commercial enterprises. At any rate, there can be no doubt that our universities are to some extent run as degree-factories. To standardize the degree business, there has been developed an elaborate machinery of standard courses, hours, marks and credit points, together with a complicated administrative apparatus for compelling attendance at lectures which could not find hearers if attendance were not compulsory. The excuse that these regulations are necessary to compel attendance on the part of the students constitutes a severe arraignment of the effectiveness of the teaching and of the quality of the students permitted to enroll for higher study.

As the "prizes" of the teaching profession—the honors and high salaries of deanships and presidencies—are awarded for administrative ability, they serve as constant and insidious bait to wean ambitious professors from the field of scholarly research. So large a part of a professor's time is occupied with administrative matters that one of America's greatest scholars, George Foot Moore, expressed the view that "the only kind of academic freedom that really matters is freedom from committee meetings." As long as the commercial character of American life reflects itself so literally in the university, and in ideals of the professors themselves, the attempt of the latter to lead in intellectual life will be handicapped.

Mankind has been ruled by soldiers, clergy and lawyers, and now the businessmen control. Not only is the businessman in the ascendant, but he seems to be there to stay. How? Perhaps this is because of his mercenaries—the advertising men who issue propaganda, organize societies, etc., after selling to businessmen the idea that otherwise our prosperity will be endangered!

That the businessmen, as a class, command in all matters the greatest prestige in the American community does not, of course, mean that their influence must always be an unhealthy one. *A priori* one might say that the rule of the captains of industry presents no more danger to art and science than does the rule of those who have preceded them. And when we consider that the problems of modern business are often similar to those of the statesmen—as, e.g., the questions of domestic and foreign markets, the progress of technology, the subtle problems of individual and mass psychology—who can deny that here is a field which not only demands genuine intellectual culture but may contribute to it as well? Yet, as a matter of actual record, the American businessman has, despite our graduate schools of business, produced almost nothing of cultural value, and with well-known exceptions is indifferent, when not hostile, to really intellectual interests. Success in business cannot always be due so much to vision and acumen as to the unparalleled natural resources of the country, which have often been uneconomically exploited for private interests.

In matters intellectual, the typical American businessman, glorifying in the assurance of a very real power, flattered by those who wish to influence his expenditure of money, finds it hard to believe that he is wrong or ignorant in what he says on matters outside of business. Judging worth by wealth, he cannot feel any intellectual humility in the presence of a man whose salary he pays. Especially in the social sciences does he speak with dogmatic authority. He is sure that he knows what is just and practicable because he brings to the consideration of these problems a certain amount of experience.

The successful man of affairs whose mind is not trained to question first principles, his own least of all, is the most likely to be an obstinate doctrinaire. Lacking intellectual discipline, he takes his theories for facts and his limited experience as representative of all life. Fundamental differences on questions of social justice he regards as a sign of overt immorality or sickly Utopianism. Riding roughshod, wherever he can, over opposition, incapable of tasting the joys of creative cultural life, he cannot free himself from the feeling that those who devote themselves to it are either pretentious frauds or deficient in virility. It seems humanly impossible today for the American businessman who has wielded power to defer to the judgment of a person under him, and to refrain from applying analogies to things he knows little about, especially to the running of universities. Illustrations of this may be found on all sides. Some years ago a well-known Eastern railroad executive—President Loree, of the Delaware and Hudson—discovered that the college of which he was a trustee had dropped 20 percent of its freshman class as unprepared to go on; whereupon he indignantly demanded an accounting from both president and faculty, stating that if in his locomotive shops 20 percent of the engines were to be rejected, it would be regarded as scandalous.

The influence of the businessman on the general social life of the country is greatest in a highly developed money economy free from the deep social divisions of Europe. Between a landed aristocracy and its tenants the difference is sharp and fixed, so that imitation of the former's mode of life by the latter is regarded as absurd and even immoral. In the writer's boyhood town, all respectable women wore kerchiefs—all who wore hats were suspect. In a money or commercial economy differences of income and mode of life are more gradual and readily hidden, so that there is great pressure to engage in lavish expenditure in order to appear in a higher class than one's income really allows. Such expenditure may even advance one's business credit. This intensifies not merely the tendency to an ever greater expenditure but more specifically an expenditure for ostentation rather than comfort. Each class zealously copies the habits of the class just above it in the money scale. The captain of industry or finance thus sets the fashion for expenditure.

There are important social and psychological consequences of this imitation in externals. The ideals of success and the models of supreme attainment embodied in the business career are taken over by the community at large. Emphasis on the lives of poor boys who have become rich (in disregard of the many more who have remained poor) has inspired among the young an easy-going faith in the currently accepted ends of life. The working people in America share the ideology of their employers. They have nothing comparable to the theoretical programs of the British Labor Party or of the Socialist parties of Scandinavia, Germany and France.

Compared to the total number of those gainfully employed, the number belonging to trade unions has until recently been small. Many reasons can be assigned for this: In the first place, employers have taken advantage of the differences between white and black labor, between foreign and native born. But in the main it is precisely the freedom of motion, geographic and economic, that prevents the development of the class consciousness of laborers. American labor is to an extraordinary degree mobile, if not migratory. Men are free to move from one place to another to an extent unknown in Europe. In addition, they can move up the social ladder with comparative ease. In this country, the son of a laborer, if unusually gifted, generally looks forward to a career as a lawyer, or even as a capitalist, on his own account. The janitor of one of the Oxford colleges once boasted to me that he held the position of his father and grandfather and that he hoped his son would succeed him. The son of a janitor in an American college does not want to succeed his father. He wants to become president of the college or chairman of the board of trustees, and he sometimes succeeds.

In addition, we must take into account the fact that the American laborer reads the daily newspapers, which are published by rich men, and that he shares the general attitude toward political radicalism. It need not, therefore, be surprising that the official attitude of the leaders of the American Federation of Labor was for a long time favorable to some of the most conservative decisions of the United States Supreme Court. Like the employers, they favored a policy of making the central government relatively powerless. Their naive belief that the interests of business and the community are basically the same has hindered the formation of an American labor party. In no other highly industrialized country is there so little opposition to the business spirit as in America.

Similar considerations explain why, despite waves of populism and progressivism in our Western agrarian states, the American farmer is essentially a property owner, or at any rate has in the past been one, and so has acquired and still possesses the conservatism of the property owner, and precisely because his property is moderate does he cling to it with the greater intensity.

The dominance of business leadership is reflected in the subsidiary field of journalism. It is difficult for American journalists to constitute an intellectual class because the American journal is primarily a business enterprise. It is run under conditions which demand a large circulation, extensive advertisement and a big capital investment. Consequently, the journalist is an employee who has little scope or encouragement for the independent treatment of news or public problems. He finds it difficult to devote himself to themes that are not widely regarded as having news value. He is completely subordinated to the dictates of the publisher who runs the newspaper or magazine for profit and to whom the honest convictions of his employees are less important than the goodwill of advertisers.

Standardizing Education

One of the most serious causes of the present low estate of disinterested intellectual pursuits in American life is to be found in the conditions of democratic education. Democratic education, when uncritically introduced, must inevitably dilute the content and lower the standards of intellectual achievement. A system designed to educate everyone in the same way cannot rigorously pursue high standards of scholarship. It must emphasize the smatterings of literacy open to all, rather than the severe training that can be pursued only by those mentally gifted. Intellectual, like all other, ability is specialized. Nor has everyone the same flair or bent, so that uniform and simplified methods of instruction, modelled on the large-scale factory, cannot do justice to specifically individual talent.

In the past, education has been the possession of those who were especially privileged or especially gifted, and who, if they lacked financial means, had the stamina to make great sacrifices for the sake of the intellectual life. Whatever its defects, the old system did not compromise with mental softness. But today, when large classes must be pushed through the academic mill, the intellectual diet on which students are fed is often reduced to the capacity of those who have no great desire for the mastery of any subject but wish above all "to get through." This is strengthened by the attitude of parents who regard things other than intellectual training (e.g., good fellowship, sports or social connections) as much more important for the development of their children. The result is greater catering to mediocrity. Subjects are broken up into small fragments so as to be more digestible, and knowledge becomes no more than familiarity with conventional labels. Names become fetishes to be feared or reverenced.

College students are looked upon as children who are to be taken gently in hand by men of mellowed conformity, and indoctrinated against radical ideas. Loyalty to the scholar's calling of evaluating lost causes and untried possibilities is regarded as disloyalty to the established order. The freedom of intellectual inquiry, granted in theory, is in practice a freedom to find new justifications for the accepted and orthodox. First principles are to be acquired by authority or habit, never by the outcome of critical intelligence. Consequently, students must be dosed and instructed, rather than puzzled by logical doubts; they must be "sold" ideas, rather than probed as to the basis of the ones they have. The method, content and social background of American education function with admirable efficacy to turn out a standardized product.

I do not wish to extol the continental classical conception of education above the democratic American ideal. The democratic ideal in education is inherently more difficult to put into practice. But, as Spinoza has remarked: All things excellent are as difficult as they are rare.

Perhaps the shortcomings of the old continental idea were best expressed by Mr. Dooley: "I don't care what ye larn thim so long as 'tis onpleasant to them." ("The Education of the Young.") Taken literally, this delight in cruelty to the young is the essence of sadism. But in a more liberal sense, the overcoming of intellectual difficulties is necessary to the growth of intellectual power, just as the overcoming of physical difficulties is necessary to the development of physical strength.

From this point of view it is not impossible to combine the classical idea of discipline in education with the democratic ideal that education should provide the best opportunities for all members of society, provided we recognize the inherent diversities of temperaments and native abilities and aptitudes.

Cross-Currents of American Thought

Any discussion of American thought that can pretend to some degree of accuracy must necessarily consider the diversities of American civilization.

It is obvious that a country almost as large as Europe and containing almost as many diversities of climate and peoples from all countries cannot be treated as if it were a single individual always exercising a unitary point of view. New England is notoriously different from the South and both differ markedly from the West. Some of these sectional diversities, especially in politics, have been studied by Turner and his disciples. Rather obvious also is the difference between rural and urban America, as it shows itself in the greater intensity of so-called Puritan morals and revivalistic religion in the former.

One of the most interesting phenomena in American life is the revival of the South. The Civil War not only was economically devastating to the Southern States, but had a markedly depressing effect upon the intellectual life of the region. The South adopted the attitude that it had a superior civilization and mourned the triumph of the barbarian. Yet those who wished to follow careers in the arts and sciences found greater opportunity in the North, if not in Europe. Recently there has been a good deal of a literary revival in the South, but admittedly Cabell is as near to Paris as to Richmond, to Anatole France as to Lee and Jefferson. Ellen Glasgow's ideas are nearer to those of the New York *Nation* than to those of the good old Southern families. Du Bose Heyward and Paul Green are more like the abolitionists than the typical defender of the peculiar institution of the Old South.

This revival of the South comes in the wake of its industrial resurgence. Under the influence of W. H. Page, we have the New South accepting the new industrial order and trying to take part in it. This shows itself in the rise of North Carolina to be the most populous state in the South outside of Texas,—its university taking the premier position among the educational institutions of the South. The South, hitherto a dominantly agricultural community, is beginning to industrialize itself. It is beginning to spin its own cotton and to manufacture other goods. This shows itself in the relaxation of the hostility of the Democratic Party toward protective tariffs.

But the leisurely rhythm of Southern life and the old traditions do not disappear so readily, and the reaction of the unreconstructed (some would say unregenerated) South is expressed in a volume entitled *I'll Take My Stand*.[1] It defends the spirit of the Old South, agrarian, gallant, anti-industrial, Methodist, frankly provincial and a bit quixotic in its efforts to wave back the movement of industrialism which has swept over the world. The writers attack the use by modern proponents of industry of the term *progress* as a "super-slogan, very efficacious, public and esthetic." They urge that people are frightened into doing what they do not want to do when they are told that it is a demand of progress. But what is this progress? Generally it means the promotion of industrial exploitation,—increased production of material goods. But is this worth while? they ask. Is industrial civilization a means or an end? Industrialism produces art galleries, schools, libraries, etc. But art galleries are not a proper place to see pictures. Pictures should be hung on the walls of homes. Libraries foster superficial rather than intensive reading. One of the writers asserts that industrialism has made our dishes crude in order that we may on solemn occasion enjoy a meal on china of the most delicate design. But did we not go from hovels to cathedrals on solemn occasions in the good old days?

These writers hearken back to the old classic education and thoroughly romantic art as a defense against the sudden arrival of industrialism. Religion, they say, can hardly expect to flourish in an industrial society. Religion is our submission to the general intention of nature that is fairly inscrutable. But nature industrialized is no longer nature.

The authors look to the Democratic Party becoming the organ of agrarianism. But this ignores the fact that actually the Democratic Party largely represents the laborers in all large cities, as is shown by the nomination of Alfred E. Smith in 1928 and by the policies of President Franklin Delano Roosevelt.

Why deny the existence of, and the legitimate demand for, articles

---

[1] *I'll Take My Stand; the South and the Agrarian Tradition*, by *Twelve Southerners* (1930). Among the authors are Allen Tate, Stark Young, J. C. Ransom.

that industrialists offer for sale, such as silk stockings, combs or face powder? Apparently these writers expect people to throw out the radio, forsake the movies, abandon the automobile, renounce science and research and appeal to the word of authority. Apparently they do not believe that time brings about changes.

Standardization and Intolerance

Despite local diversities, the most impressive feature of American civilization is its ever-growing standardization. The great rolling plain and the emphasis on machine production lead to indefinite repetition.

Indeed, one of the complaints that Europeans make of American life is its excessive standardization. Every city is like every other, they say, and houses are all of the same pattern, as if they came out of the same machine. Our newspapers and magazines all seem to be machine products.

One of the consequences of this standardization is a profoundly contemptuous attitude toward the individual who ventures to think for himself on any question. Nowhere else does the standard or mould of the average man dominate more as a categorical imperative. Great achievement in itself receives little recognition. It is this, perhaps, which has led so many artists to make their home abroad.

In the absence of cultivated taste, mere quantity, size and volume function as marks of quality; "bigger" and "better" become synonymous terms even where they are of dubious application as in schools and families. The attractions of material comforts, from breakfast foods to the latest automobile, have better sales value when they are advertised with a high numerical coefficient of distribution. Action and thought fall into certain simple grooves. A rather childish preoccupation with quantity and novelty helps to produce a mode of life too uneventful to leave behind much that is significantly unique or rich in common memory.

With increasing standardization in the modes of living we have the disappearance of the old-fashioned tolerance. Traditions of federalism were necessarily strong in a country created by Catholics in Maryland, Puritans in Massachusetts, Quakers in Pennsylvania, broad Churchmen in Virginia and numerous sects scattered throughout the land. Today no community feels sufficiently secure by itself. The development of the means of communication and facilities for organization have wiped out the security of distance. Differences that were innocent tend to become obtrusive. We allowed polygamy in Utah only until we were asked to grant statehood. Then we objected. When we have to mix we enforce sameness. The up-state farmer who formerly was not disturbed by consciousness of alien stock inhabiting the cities fears their presence in his immediate vicinity. Those whose ancestors fought in the Revolution fear lest recent arrivals endanger their social preeminence by bringing about another revolution. And in their opposition they echo the new, particularistic nationalism of Europe and the general decline of humane thought throughout the world.

This intolerance is often called Puritanism. Actually it has nothing to do with that. There was excessive interference with people's opinions and conduct in all the colonies. Catholic Maryland had the same blue laws as Plymouth in colonial days. Our prohibition and blue laws emanate from backwoods sections. There, sociability and conformity are insisted on (witness the white-caps of a generation ago, and the K.K.K. of our time). It is characteristic of the rural mind, which is a large part of the American mind. We have less insistence on conformity in a city, where there is more freedom of motion.

Since the First World War, American life has been marked by a revival of unabashed egoism—by an appeal to self-interest similar to that of the Reconstruction period. Wars not only let loose mob violence and official lawlessness but make them respectable. In times of passion it is natural that the ruffians should get to the top, for where there is noise and confusion only the loudest are heard. But even in times of peace a herd-minded and standardized community can be stampeded into excesses unless a strong liberal and critical spirit can make itself felt in strategic places.

Recent years have witnessed a remarkable transformation in the intellectual life of this country. Socialists and other radicals who used to fulminate against our Constitution as an eighteenth century document are invoking the Bill of Rights and appealing to individual rights, while the conservatives who used to insist somewhat monotonously on the sacred rights of minorities and the necessity of an appeal from mob violence and passion (the organized appeal from Philip drunk to Philip sober) have been willing to justify the most ruthless suppression of freedom of utterance.

The doctrinaire anti-intellectualist may insist that this is but an illustration of how lightly general doctrines rest on the shoulders of their adherents and how readily they are changed in response to changing conditions. This, however, need not deter us from observing how anomalous and confused have been the lines of intellectual conflict in this country. Our national system having been organized as the result of a revolution, our conservative classes continue to profess a revolutionary philosophy out of sheer habit; while the Socialists, obsessed by the fact that constitutional rights were invoked to protect property, lost sight of the fact that the Jeffersonian elements in our Bill of Rights were intended to protect human freedom against tyrannical government in the fight against the power of the least democratic branch of the government, the judiciary. And in their insistence on leaving everything to majority decision, the Socialists forgot the impatience of majorities who are traditionally averse to allowing any agitation for a change of law. Unless the minority has the right to agitate for a change of law, and that right is protected in times of popular passion, all Socialistic and reformist efforts will be in vain. War, after all, has put our radicals and conservatives in the same relative position which they occupy in Europe. At the turn of the century William James, speaking to the Anti-Imperialist League, told them to accept the defeat of 1900 as final. "America," he said, "has outlived its traditional liberalism. We Americans have embarked on commercial relations with the rest of the world. Henceforth, the situation in this country will become the same as in Western Europe and our liberals must ally themselves with their liberals just as our conservatives will ally themselves with their conservatives."

This prophetic insight has since become clear to thoughtful men and is illustrated by the growth of Socialism in the United States in the twentieth century, with Americans like Eugene V. Debs and Norman Thomas assuming the leadership of an active movement which has supplied the philosophic justification for most of the practical social reform of the century. In the nineteenth century the Socialist wave was largely confined to foreigners and literati like Albert Brisbane and the others who organized Brook Farm. But these communistic experiments made little impression on American life and thought. In the early part of the nineteenth century there was a native labor movement led by Robert Dale Owen, George Henry Evans, Thomas Skidmore and Fanny Wright, whose ideas anticipated those of Marx and De Leon; but there can be no strong labor movement where the opportunities for the more able laborers and labor leaders to enter a more remunerative life are as great as they were in nineteenth century America.

For this reason Chartism and the radical European movements of 1848 found no response in this country, though our people generally sympathized with European republican leaders like Kossuth. The enthusiastic reception given to Kossuth when he visited this country in 1854 stands out in striking contrast with our refusal to admit the second Republican President of Hungary, Count Karolyi. The contrast is a significant indication of the change in American sentiment towards monarchy and republicanism.

While our aristocrats have generally been favorable to intellectual freedom so long as their power was unquestioned, the traditional attitude of conservatives has been the distrust of principles and arguments. Here we are in the established order. It is up to the radical to prove that a change is necessary; and can he prove it to unwilling ears? The conservative naturally prefers to rely on authority and tradition. As Balfour said when Welsh dis-establishment was proposed on the ground that the majority of the people in Wales did not belong to the Established Church: "The Established Church is good enough for us; why isn't it good enough for the people of Wales?"

American liberalism in the nineteenth century was based on the absence of besetting fear. We had thrown off the yoke and we entertained a contempt for the effete monarchies of Europe. The continual immigration of those who escaped tyranny abroad and who valued the absence of it in this country tended to keep alive throughout the nineteenth century the idea of America as a land of promise where the mistakes of the Old World were not to be repeated. This stream of immigration has reinforced two cardinal points of the traditional American liberalism: first, that America is a land where the people rather than kings and privileged classes rule; and second, that America would never allow itself to be drawn into the sordid struggle for foreign lands and new markets. The Germans who came to this country after the failure of the revolution of 1848 contributed much to American liberalism. Men like Carl Schurz liberalized our ideas of education, of art and even of politics, as is shown by the pronounced anti-slavery attitude of the German settlers, which helped to win states like Missouri to the Union cause.

American latter-day nationalism is not a product of economic jealousy. By and large, the United States is confident that its commercial supremacy is assured, and that its methods of production can only be imitated, not excelled, in Europe. We can therefore afford to be tolerant and helpful, especially in so far as we are financially involved in the reconstruction of European industry. But our nationalism is due to fear—fear of new political and social doctrines abroad in the world today. Shall experiments now being made in foreign countries invade the United States? Shall principles of social philosophy other than those of a strictly business civilization flash upon American minds and grip American hearts?

Fear of the unfamiliar is not something new in human history. Rather it is the most universal form which the force of inertia assumes in the social world. But what has been most distinctive about American civilization down to our own generation has been the extraordinary degree to which the American people have risen above such fears.

The dominant forces that have produced whatever is distinctive in American thought have reflected, in one way or another, the conquest of such fears. The frontier is not simply a stretch of physical wilderness. One may find wilderness aplenty in Brazil, Siberia, or Central Africa without finding the social repercussions that our historians since Turner have ascribed to the frontier. The frontier is a social fact created when men and women freely confront the challenge of a life not dominated by established local traditions.

So, too, the process of immigration which has so largely moulded the differences between American and European life has historically reflected a dual conquest of man's ancient fear of the unfamiliar. On the one hand, immigration demands of the immigrant a type of courage that is not often found among the peoples of the world. The overwhelming majority of men and women have always preferred to accept the privations and oppressions with which they were familiar rather than break the ties that bind them to the soil of their childhood and of their ancestors. The courage that leads people to look to a better future in a new world has been a vital factor in building the distinctive institutions of American life. And conversely, immigration has been a vital force in American history because until fairly recently the American people have not succumbed to prevalent Old World fears of alien faces, strange accents, and novel ideas. Typically American has been the confidence that our way of life is so clearly preferable to any other way of life that any immigrant could be turned into a useful American citizen in the space of a few years. If that confidence and courage now wane—as they seem to have been waning since the days of the First World War—the basic factors which have made American thought distinctive for three centuries will have ceased to exist.*

---

* Cf. "The Future of American Liberalism" in M. R. Cohen, *The Faith of a Liberal* (1946), pp. 437-469.

Chapter II

AMERICAN IDEAS
ON HISTORY

ARE AMERICANS ON THE WHOLE greatly interested in history and what is the direction of their historical thought?

It has been remarked by many observers that for a young country ours is already overcrowded with monuments. But monuments once erected are soon forgotten, and the over-population of stone and concrete applies only to limited sections. Our various local historical societies are largely supported by the pride of the older families, who look anxiously at the new forces in our public life and seek through the recital of ancestral deeds to instil respect and reverence for things they hold dear. Thus, in the old South, cultivated pride in the past served at first as a consolation to offset the long period of distress following the defeat in the Civil War; now it has come to serve as a spiritual refuge to those who see the destruction of the old order in the vise of the new industrialism. In the main, however, the appeal to history is of minor interest; for Americans are characteristically more preoccupied with the present and the immediate future than with the past.

There are obvious reasons for this. In the first place, ours is still a new land. After we leave the Atlantic seaboard we build, for the most part, on relatively virgin soil, and we are faced with few obstructing views to remind us of the past. Secondly, our era is absorbed in questions of machinery, and that is a theme on which ancient history offers little direct help. What can a young contemporary American learn from those who lived prior to the advent of the modern age of subways, telephones, automobiles, radios, and other mechanical innovations of a like nature? The very fact, thirdly, that most of the peoples who have come to America have done so to escape some political, economic, or religious difficulty abroad has naturally weakened their attachment to the traditions of the countries abandoned. Moreover, whatever traditions they have brought with them have been largely disintegrated by the mixing of peoples which has resulted from a free immigration unprecedented in the history of the world.

It is often easily—too easily—assumed that the culture which the English colonists brought with them in the seventeenth century has been imposed upon all subsequent newcomers. This seems true in language, literature, and law. It is not so true of art, religion, or our system of education. Cultural relations between the older and more recent immigrants involve interaction—a give and take on both sides. Our educational system is certainly more Scotch and German than English; our music is more Celtic and German; and the English elements in our household manners and ecclesiastical institutions, in our industrial and fine arts, and even in our political organizations, have departed beyond recognition from their English origins. The separation from the English Church and State brought about by Colonial conditions, the irritations of the War of 1812, and the prevailingly hostile attitude of Great Britain to the North in the Civil War brought about anti-English feelings which were accentuated by the Irish and later by the German elements of our population. On the other hand, the American school system and the general feeling of superiority with which those who have been in this country for any length of time look down upon more recent arrivals, have tended to make the children of Germans, Italians, and Jews ashamed of their parents' peculiar customs and institutions, such as singing societies, domestic arts, interest in learning for its own sake and the like.

All these factors, together with the prevailing absorption in economic enterprise and our extraordinary freedom in moving from place to place, tend to lessen interest in history. We revere, to be sure, certain names and documents of the past; and since World War I, various chambers of commerce, the American Legion, the Sons and Daughters of the American Revolution, and others have rather loudly insisted that in our schools only approved patriotic legends be taught as history. But our practice can be symbolized by the fact that no country destroys so many old buildings and landmarks to make place for new structures. And when that typical American, Henry Ford, declared that "history is bunk," he did not altogether lose his representative character. He was only stating in a crude way a traditional attitude which had been more nobly expressed by Emerson and Walt Whitman when they advised men to turn their backs on the past and their faces to the future; and in our own day a distinguished historian, in a book which has had an amazing and unprecedented popular appeal, has preached the same gospel. The Greeks, he told us, accomplished as much as they did because they did not know much history. In the great sciences of today, such as psychology and sociology, history, he maintained, is of no use for we can get no light on them from the past! No wonder that his book, *Mind in the Making*,[1] proved a best seller.

This prevailing popular indifference to history, and the relative absence of powerful passions centering on long-fought but as yet unsettled issues, has given a definite academic stamp to the body of our historical writings. The latter have not, of course, escaped partisan and especially geographic bias—witness the peculiar blindness of New England historians to the achievements of the South. But our writers of history have been markedly subject to the winds of doctrine that prevail in the world of scholarship. Thus, despite the fact that an unusually large number of our historians have been independent gentlemen, unconnected with our universities, the German conception of historical scholarship came, in the early part of the nineteenth century, to exert a pronounced influence. Even Bancroft was unable completely to escape the impact of his study in Germany under Heeren.

The Religious Interpretation

As our earliest historians were clergymen, or else absorbed in ecclesiastical struggles, it was natural for American philosophy of history to be at first theologic. Its fullest and most urbane expression is to be found in Bancroft—a statesman or man of affairs with European experience, but still laboring under the Old Testament conception of history as an account of a chosen people. God got tired of the mess that princes and prelates had made of the Old World, so he picked out the best seed— God-fearing, but freedom-loving Englishmen—who had fought kings and bishops—and he planted them in a new land where the difficulties of climate and savage Indians were only such as to draw out the virtues of the chosen people. When the colonies were young, they were protected by British suzerainty against the Spanish, the French, and others. But when they attained sufficient strength Providence led them to overthrow the oppressive rule of King and Parliament and gave them inspired leaders, like the fathers of the Declaration of Independence and the Federal Constitution, and has since blessed them and made them spiritually and materially prosperous beyond any other people before them.

This is, I believe, a fairly accurate sketch, as far as it goes, and if it sounds somewhat ironic, it is because we no longer speak that language. But the substance of this view has not disappeared. It will be found

---

[1] By James Harvey Robinson.

involved in the Presidential address of Simeon Baldwin before the American Historical Association in 1908 and in the writings of Professor Burgess, according to which the American form of government (up to the end of the nineteenth century) is the absolute perfection for which all previous nations had vainly striven, so that all previous political experience was only a *preparatio evangelica*. I might even suggest that a good deal of the substance of this view is also to be found in the progressive, or evolutionary, philosophy of history.

"What," we may well ask, "has caused the decline of the old Providential philosophy of American history?" One might urge that this philosophy did not offer any real explanation of such phenomena as the inglorious events of the War of 1812, or that it led to a somewhat distorted view of the character of American colonization. For it is simply not true that the colonists came here solely to find religious freedom from the oppression they suffered in their old homeland. Even the Puritans, like others, came here primarily to improve their economic condition, and this is shown by their colonization of other places,—for example, the Barbados. In general, the theologic interpretation not only attributes decidedly variable human strategy to Providence, but by centering on one people it necessarily takes a somewhat limited and provincial view. When the history of the American colonies began to be studied by Osgood, Beer, and others, as a part of the British colonial empire, and thereafter part of an international situation, Providence could no longer be represented as interested primarily in any one chosen people. And with the disappearance of the latter concept, the theologic interpretation of the history of any one group or period becomes amorphous and loses itself in the vague phraseology of the spiritual interpretation of history advocated by Dean Shailer Mathews. No intellectually sensitive mind can be entirely impervious to the appeal of the religious interpretation of the world. But in regard to history it has so far proved itself barren. It has been of no aid in helping us to understand the specific character of the historic process at any time or place.

We find a somewhat inverted theologic view in those American historians who, following the philosophy of the Enlightenment, see in human history the gradual removal of the superstitious influence of the church, that thus changes places with Satan in the Augustinian historic drama. We can see this in the works of John W. Draper[2] and Andrew D. White[3] on the conflict between religion and science. It appears as well in many of the current expressions by men of science, when they

---

[2] *History of the Intellectual Development of Europe* (1863); *History of the Conflict between Religion and Science* (1874).
[3] *A History of the Warfare of Science with Theology* (1896).

take vacations from the fields of their competence to instruct the world at large in the meaning of history, religion and politics. Let me mention as one of many examples the book of the zoologist W. C. Curtis, *Science and Human Affairs from the Viewpoint of Biology*. Now it is true, as Lea[4] and others have shown, that the Inquisition did, on certain occasions, repress free scientific curiosity. But this is unwarrantedly exaggerated in the popular anti-theologic accounts. The great fact is that the periods of prosperity in theology are also periods of prosperity in science; and in periods of depression all human activities and knowledge languish. Indeed, throughout many centuries clerics were the only ones who had any opportunity to cultivate science. And this applies not only to the theoretic, but also to the applied sciences. For it must not be forgotten that the Church did more than any other agency during the Middle Ages to cultivate rational knowledge concerning agriculture in accordance with the Benedictine motto, *ora et labora*.[5]

The Racial Interpretation

A new form of Calvinistic predestinarianism and the notion of an elect or chosen people appears in the racial interpretation of history. In imitation of Gobineau and Chamberlain, men like Madison Grant and Lothrop Stoddard have tried to explain American history in terms of the inherent superiority of the Nordic stock. But ironic fate has brought forth a Southern writer, Eckenrode, who contends that it was Jefferson Davis who fought for a Nordic America, and that it was the defeat of the Southern cause and the triumph of the industrial North which opened the gates to the non-Nordic peoples of Eastern and Southern Europe to invade America and mix their blood with the pure Nordic stock. Little need be said about this theory. The verifiable fact is that America has almost from the beginning been colonized by diverse peoples—Huguenots, Palatinate Germans, Irish and Welsh, whose Nordicity is dubious and of no verifiable significance. It may also be said that the Teutonic view of the early Johns Hopkins School,—particularly that of H. B. Adams, and J. W. Burgess,—that all our free institutions come from the

---

[4] Henry C. Lea, *A History of the Inquisition of the Middle Ages* (3 vol., 1888); *A History of the Inquisition of Spain* (4 vol., 1906-7).

[5] To characterize this view as inverted theology is not to deny the great intellectual services of its faith in liberal ideals and in progress. But the latter can be more adequately dealt with in connection with the evolutionary philosophy of history.

German forests—a view for which Douglas Southall Freeman is largely responsible—is now generally regarded as a baseless myth. Real freedom, as Freeman himself was forced to recognize in his history of Federal Government, is far more rooted in the traditions we derive from the Mediterranean Greeks than in the practices of the Anglo-Saxons, whether the latter are Nordic or Alpine.

From a strictly logical point of view, race is a constant factor which cannot by itself explain the variations of history. We require some other factor to explain the different traits which any race displays at different times.*

The Geographic Interpretation

The geographic interpretation of history can be traced back to the Hippocratic treatises on Airs, Waters and Places and to some pregnant comments by Plato and Aristotle. It has been employed in modern times by thinkers as diverse as Montesquieu and Hegel, Buckle and Taine. The last named, recognizing that geographic, as well as racial, factors, are relatively permanent, invokes the Epoch (a positivistic ghost of the romantic *Zeitgeist*) as a factor to explain historic changes. But it is not at all clear how time itself can be a cause of historic change if the other factors are constant. Nevertheless, at least one American, Simon Patten, has followed Taine in trying to represent romantic poetry as the necessary outcome of a successful adaptation to the weather.

In general, the earlier American attempts in this direction start with an *a priori* determinism that there must be a causal relation between climate or topography and the general character of a people. But this assumption does not in fact lead to any significant progress in the understanding of history. For it is not true that the presence of certain natural resources has invariably led to their exploitation. Human and cultural factors are also necessary to determine such facts. Thus, the Hudson-Mohawk Valley did not become a highway to the West until the Erie Canal, and later the railroads, made it so. Nor did the great Kanawha River become a historic highway from the Alleghany Valleys of Virginia to the rich grassy lands of Kentucky. As Professor G. B. Adams puts it, "Waterfalls do not grind wheat." It requires the erection of mills to which men are willing to bring their

---

* *Cf.* Chapter 6 ("The Biologic Element in History") in M. R. Cohen, *The Meaning of Human History* (1947).

grain. The rich limestone soil of Eastern Pennsylvania was abandoned by the hardy Scotch-Irish pioneers and remained relatively unoccupied until the Palatinate Germans came, (at the end of the seventeenth century), and found its soil like that of their native home and made a granary of it. The Scotch-Irish, having different habits, could do nothing with such dry soil so readily subject to frosts. But the influence of their neighbors led them to learn this type of agriculture in the Shenandoah Valley, and this proved an important factor in the conquest of the Alleghany valleys and the opening up of the West.

Considerations of this sort have led writers like Ellen Semple to apply Ratzel's anthropo-geographic approach to the interpretation of history. Miss Semple's methods of interpretation, however, are still somewhat too abstract. They do not take into account the many variable factors which are sometimes indiscriminately lumped together under the heading of geography. These should include not only such pure topographic factors as mountains and valleys, but also such geologic and geo-physical considerations as the formation of soil and its relation to plant and animal life, considerations as to tides, river and air currents, as well as temperature and rainfall. All these are not only connected with man's daily occupation but also directly affect his health and capacity for work. Thus, there seems to be a direct connection between the character of the soil and certain diseases endemic to given regions, as shown by the fact that the virus of enteric and typhoid fever prospers in some soils more than in others. Miss Semple's methods have also proved to be too abstract in not taking sufficient account of the subtler and intangible factors, such, for instance, as, those which prevented foreign stocks as the Scotch-Irish, from taking root in New England in the seventeenth and eighteenth centuries (except in certain patches of New Hampshire, around Londonderry, Dublin, and Antrim). Studies by Hulbert on American highways have taught us to distrust simple geographic generalizations and to recognize the complex conditions under which rivers, for instance, become avenues of transportation. Thus, the Southern rivers at first attracted commerce because their ports were free from ice during the winter, but their warm climate proved injurious to the shipment of grain, and the cooler, more northerly routes gained the advantage.

In the main, American geographers like Hurlburt have recently been following the more concrete historic methods of the French, LePlay and Vidal de La Blache, rather than the German school.

An important contribution to the geographic interpretation of history has been made by American botanists in supplying us with a chronology of rainfall for the past few thousand years through the study of the annual rings shown by old trees. On the basis of this, Huntington has tried to correlate periods of prosperity in the last two thousand years with increased rainfall. Without accepting his results, there can be no doubt that we have here an additional key for the exploration of past life.

Americans like Dexter and Huntington have also tried to utilize statistical and experimental methods to establish correlations between certain meteorologic phases, such as changes of temperature and frequency of wind, and social phenomena, such as relative activity and frequency of crime. While many of these results are subject to obvious criticism, it is certainly useful to have some empirical check on *a priori* assumptions as to the relation between climatic and social phenomena. The subject teems with interesting logical problems, especially as to the nature of social causation.*

The Economic Interpretation

As Marxism is not respectable in American academic circles, the economic interpretation of history has been vigorously criticized by our professional historians. Algie M. Simons' *Social Forces in American History* was criticized as a Socialistic book, and Gustavus Myers' volume on the Supreme Court was considered even worse for its suggestion that the justices of our highest court are just human beings, subject to the same class bias and prejudice as the rest of us. But it was a Brahmin of New England, Brooks Adams, who applied economic interpretation in a very suggestive, if not always accurate, way to the effect of trade routes on the course of empire.[6] (Later he became much more doctrinaire and monistic.) Applying this view to legal history, he maintained that the law is nothing but the will of the dominant or victorious class, just as the falling of a stone is the result of the force of gravitation. This was attacked by orthodox legal scholars as if it charged our judges with dishonesty. More serious, however, have been the logical objections—that no social arrangement can be the result of a single force,—indeed, that no physical system can possibly be so constituted. There can be no force without resistance, no action without reaction. Laws are rather like treaties of peace, where the victor may dictate terms, but only those that the conquered or defeated party will accept in preference to fur-

* Cf. Chapter 5 ("The Geographic Factor in History") in M. R. Cohen, *The Meaning of Human History* (1947).
[6] *The Law of Civilization and Decay* (1900).

ther resistance. If the defeated party were completely wiped out, there would be no need for any law. Modern society, in fact, is divided into classes in many different ways, not only between capitalists and workers, and between urban and rural interests, but in many other ways, e.g., along religious lines. The great pieces of legislation, such as our constitutional amendments, are always the result of a union of the activities of several classes. It was the union of manufacturers and the Women's Christian Temperance Union that was responsible for prohibition, and it was the union of manufacturers, farmers, and the Catholic Church that defeated the Child Labor Amendment. These obvious objections to the Marxian interpretation seem to me to be avoided in the works of Beard and James T. Adams which explore the economic foundations of New England, of the Revolution, of the United States Constitution, and of Jeffersonian Democracy.

In his *Theory of the Leisure Class*, Veblen has in a striking way united the Marxian interpretation of history with the Aristotelian conception of the aristocrat or gentleman. But his attempt to interpret the higher education in America from this point of view lacks sufficient scholarly detachment. Upton Sinclair's economic interpretation of American education, as well as of art, is characterized by a preternatural capacity for inaccuracy, even when he happens to be right in his main point.

Of course, it may be contended that the objections against the one-sidedness of the economic interpretation of history are valid only if we operate with a narrow conception of economics; that the objections disappear if, following Veblen and others, we make economics a concrete study of social behavior in its evolutionary and psychologic setting. But rather than ask whether such a unitary social science covering the whole of social life cannot just as appropriately be called social psychology or sociology as economics or political science, let us inquire whether such a science can be created by definition and what its relation to history may be.

Scientific History

If history is concerned with actual (particular) events, no science can exhaust it, because every science must, to verify its propositions, limit itself to abstract or repeatable aspects of the phenomena. Whatever progress the various social studies have made in the use of scientific method has been made along this line. That is why specialization or division of the social sciences has been so helpful. Now a unitary social science may be either the sum of the actual social sciences or some abstract phase of all of them. The first implies that the historian must be careful not to be too one-sided, not to restrict himself to the political, economic, religious, or other phase of the social life of the community, but to include them all. This, however, is a counsel of perfection which has been followed in the past as often as it is likely to be followed in the future. If, on the other hand, we consider a unitary social science as abstract, such as social psychology, it can only be partially verifiable. It must, if it is to be applied to history, be largely dialectical; and to guard against the danger of such abstract dialectics, it must seek comprehensiveness, which is philosophy by whatever other name you may choose to call it.

The realization that history dominated by science must necessarily be abstract—which is true of the history of sciences or special arts—has caused a revolt against the scientific attitude, and we have men like James Harvey Robinson, in a presidential address before the American Historical Association, urging that the historian must seek to be more like the historical novelist who conveys the genuine spirit of the past rather than the painstaking annalist who seeks only the phenomenal side, "the face and the appearance." This is parallel to the suggestion that the man of affairs,—the lawyer, the physician, the teacher, or the businessman,— may be helped more by an observation of Molière or Balzac than by a treatise on physiologic psychology. But poetry is not science and the intuitive observation of men of genius may persuade us without being true. When a proposition is verified as generally true it becomes science no matter who suggested it. The feeling of reality, of the concrete, is more satisfactory than that of the abstract, not because it is more true but because it is more familiar. Progress in truth requires, therefore, the breaking up of the concrete and the familiar.

Technical Philosophy and History

On the technical side few American philosophers have dealt explicitly with the problems of the philosophy of history. Dean Woodbridge has formulated some weighty aphorisms on purpose in history which are highly suggestive but do not pretend to any systematic treatment. De Witt Parker has written a thesis on the *Metaphysics of History*, in which he has made an acute analysis of the nature of our knowledge of the past. Around the turn of the century Alfred H. Lloyd wrote a little book on the philosophy of history which tried to analyze some of the leading categories of social process.[7] Professor Münsterberg, following Windelband and Rickert, developed some of their ideas in his book on *Psychology and Life,* as well as in his distinctively German *Philosophie der Werte.* But no one would claim that any of these efforts are fully commensurate with the importance of the subject or what the writers could have done if they had treated this theme as their major enterprise. Nevertheless there are certain currents in American philosophy which bear definitely on the nature and meaning of history.

The Evolutionary Philosophy of History

Belief in evolution seems to be a characteristic of almost all American philosophers—idealists, pragmatists, and realists—and this profoundly influences the conception of history. First in the field was the Hegelian form of dialectic evolution. It was a natural successor to the theologic interpretation. Providence, instead of revealing itself in miraculous interventions, shows itself in a logical development which is also a progress in the consciousness of freedom. This latter phase explains why the Hegelian philosophy of evolution appealed so to liberal Protestants. It made possible the combination of the old religion with the newer evolutionary ideas which were sweeping over the scientific world. Hegel himself certainly viewed his philosophy of history, and indeed his logic, as but a development and clarification of the content of Protestant religion. But the progress of the Hegelian, or neo-Hegelian, philosophy made it throw little light upon the specific facts of history, despite many acute observations on the part of Hegel himself, which were really independent of his philosophy. Indeed, neo-Hegelians like F. H. Bradley realized that Hegel's idealism left little reality to time in the temporal process, since for the Absolute all is actual. Little real historical content can, therefore, remain in such a philosophy. It has become merely a method according to which every period represents an idea, and as each idea generates its opposite, every period is succeeded by a reaction. This became a popular way of playing with history. The only serious attempt on the part of an American to organize some actual branch of history in accordance with this Hegelian method is Roscoe Pound's construction of legal history, wherein, however, he follows Kohler more than Hegel.

[7] *Citizenship and Salvation, or Greek and Jew: A Study in the Philosophy of History* (1897).

Imaginative and stimulating is Alfred North Whitehead's view of human history as an evolutionary development of the idea of freedom.[7a] Although not avowedly Hegelian, Whitehead's vision is largely the vision of Hegel, modified by the Victorian version of idealistic liberal Christianity made a little more pungent by dashes of Bergson's romantic intuitionism. Without using Hegel's terminology or dialectic method, Whitehead accepts Hegel's view of history as essentially a development of ideas, more especially of progress in freedom.

Whitehead's insistence on the effectiveness of ideas, not only in transforming society but also in conserving our human gains, does not prevent him from recognizing the primacy of the organic and emotional life of which mentality is an outgrowth. He rightly emphasizes the importance of custom and routine and admits that in the end nothing is effective except "massively co-ordinated inheritance." In specific situations he recognizes the controlling influence of geographical and economic factors, such as trade routes, the opening of new continents, and so on. But as a philosopher he is naturally and emphatically interested in the Platonic and Christian idea of the soul, which he thinks is the key to the progress from slavery to freedom and from force to persuasion that has characterized West European history for the last two millennia.

Unfortunately Whitehead does not offer very much evidence in support of these appealing doctrines. Is the progress from slavery to freedom a historical fact? Even if we take slavery in the conventional legal sense, the question may well be raised whether there were not proportionately more slaves in the Southern States of this country in the middle of the nineteenth century than in Periclean Athens. In any case, one may well deny that the abolition of slavery can properly be attributed to the Platonic and Christian traditions. The chief disciple of the former explicitly justified slavery, and the greatest of the Apostles preached that servants should obey their masters. The Christian fathers and the great teachers like Saint Thomas did not protest against slavery. For a long time Christianity refused to admit the children of serfs to the priesthood. In fact, the practical enslavement of free land-owners into serfs in Russia and in the rest of Europe came after the introduction of Christianity, and in our Southern States the Methodist Church and other Christian denominations defended slavery as a divine institution until 1865.

It would be pleasant to believe that we rely today more on persuasion than on force. But is there sufficient evidence to prove that this is so? Possibly we differ from the ancients in the fact that in our modern complex society the exertion of force is much more indirect. But ultimately economic and political force cannot exist without physical force.

[7a] Developed particularly in his *Adventures of Ideas* (1933).

The revival of dictatorship in Twentieth Century Europe only emphasizes in a brutal way the force with which no government can completely dispense.

There seems no evidence to support Whitehead's contention that Eastern civilization declined through "the stoppage of the growth of persuasive intercourse." In general, it seems rather strange to deduce the specific traits of Western civilization from the Platonic and Christian view of the soul, when the latter is essentially Oriental—that is, Egyptian, Persian, and Semitic.

Whitehead speaks of the sense of unity promoted by Christian ethics. Not only does this unity seem noticeably absent in the world today, but one finds little trace of it in the entire history of the last eighteen centuries. Division among Christians was a notable cause of the triumph of Arabs and Turks in Eastern Europe, Asia, Africa, and Spain. Can we say that there was less sense of human unity before the triumph of the Christian Church in the fourth century A.D.?

Despite Whitehead's rather cavalier treatment of historic evidence, his writing on historical themes is full of provocative insights and his recognition that no metaphysics can be complete without a philosophy of history—that is without applying ideas to the interpretation of the temporal process of human civilization—is a distinct conribution to American philosophy.

The most popular American attitude towards history is the evolutionism of Herbert Spencer. Nowhere else, with the possible exception of Russia, has Spencer had the influence and vogue that he has had in America. And many philosophers, despite his agnosticism and his crude ideas on metaphysics, are still under the domination of his conception of social evolution as a law of nature, according to which all history shows, and must show, progress. Though our leading American anthropologists, like Franz Boas and his students, have shown ample ground for questioning the adequacy of the Spencerian conception of social evolution, and though John Dewey has indicated the viciousness of Spencer's method of trying to prove his thesis, it still largely holds the field; and not to believe in evolution is to put oneself down as an obscurantist, fit only for backwoods Tennessee. Now, in point of fact, the concept of evolution has for some time been really eliminated from natural science (witness Jacques Loeb, who called attention to the meaninglessness of the concept "evolution" in experimental biology). But men of science, no less than other men, have certain verbal pieties, and will not talk freely to the public in the face of hostile legislation. Nevertheless, if social evolution means anything definite, it means not only that things change but that they change in a definite direction, and Spencer is the only one who has tried to formulate that direction as one from the simple to the complex, from the homogeneous to the heterogeneous. The philosophic test of this is to ask, "What is inherently simple? Shall we deny that legal procedure today is simpler than in the barbarian codes, with their very elaborate and complicated rules? Shall we say that English syntax today is more complex than that of inflected Anglo-Saxon?" To ask these questions is to show the vagueness, if not the falsity, of the Spencerian formula. In the end, the adherents of the evolutionary philosophy of history justify themselves by saying that they mean only that everything in human affairs has a cause. But if this is so, what philosophy of history is not evolutionary?

The truth is that the evolutionary philosophy grips us because it is optimistic and leads us to expect progress. According to this view, science and technology have developed in this country, unhindered by European traditions and privilege, and are bound to make for a newer and higher type of civilization. Capital and labor will harmonize their conflicting interests by the use of intelligence and we shall not have the class struggle which has embittered life elsewhere. The errors of democracy will be corrected by education or by new types of intelligent leadership. Professor James Harvey Robinson has preached the gospel of evolution and progress as the greatest single idea in all the history of mankind. It is thus a sin against the Holy Ghost to refuse to cooperate with the meliorative principle inherent in the nature of things. If conditions today are unprecedented, we can, by humanizing knowledge and democratizing education, meet the new situation. To call attention to the vagueness and question-begging use of the terms *education* and *democracy*, or to express a doubt whether increased schooling will enable us to solve our complicated problems of today, is to proclaim oneself an infidel.

One of the most striking outer manifestations of what is generally viewed as progress is the increased use of machinery, which is said to give men greater control of nature, and thus to insure an ever more glorious future. Among some of our poets (Gerald Stanley Lee, *The Voice of the Machine;* Carl Sandburg, *Smoke and Steel;* McKnight, Black and others) there has been a rather strained effort to see in the machine, not only an aid to economy, but an object of intrinsic beauty. This is in accordance with Santayana's view that every vital impulse or organized form of life will develop its own ethics and esthetics.

Nevertheless, there has recently developed in America considerable doubt about progress and an uneasiness about machinery. Even before the First World War, which brought so much disillusion to American liberals,

Henry Adams expressed a deep distrust of our jaunty historical optimism —apart from his attempt to apply the second law of thermodynamics to history. "He was morbidly curious to see some light at the end of the passage,"[8] but alas, there is no end. Some of our present distrust of machine civilization comes from those who are sentimentally stirred by the modernized, if not Westernized, representatives of Hindu philosophy, Tagore and Gandhi. Some of it comes from the pre-industrial, unrecon-structed South, that is beginning to find a voice in our national life. Some of our Southern writers contend that machinery and industrialism are inherently opposed to art and spirituality, and that agrarian, or Jeffer-sonian, democracy is still the proper path for our country. This view is shared by some Western progressives, like Parrington, the author of the most significant history of American literature. Others, somewhat less discriminating, lump together machinery and physical science, and wish us to return to what they call humanism. This is often but a new name for the old authoritarian supernaturalism, though its advocates have no definite authority to appeal to other than their own superrational intuitions, which to an outsider seem decidedly romantic in their capri-ciousness.

The most philosophic member of this school, Paul Elmer More, has tried to write the history of Christianity from this point of view. And its leader, Professor Babbitt, seeing nothing but romantic degradation in modern spiritual history, out-Rousseau's Rousseau in asking us to return to an entirely mythical human nature that consists solely of an inner check that says "no" to all our animal, if not our vegetative, nature. As an authority for this, he invokes an entirely apocryphal Aristotle. (I might add that Babbitt's Rousseau is also largely a figment of the imagina-tion, for the actual Rousseau possessed a large element of the classic spirit current in the eighteenth century and imbibed it directly from Plutarch, according to his own testimony.)

Nevertheless, despite all the vagaries of those who oppose the Utopias of the future by putting theirs into the past, there is a real basis for the fear lest humanity perish spiritually from the consequences of the ma-chinery which is its own creation. Nothing highly useful can be free from danger. And the danger is that man using machines will acquire their rhythm and thus become mechanized. This process manifests itself in our excessive standardization of life, as well as in our inability to rest and contemplate. It produces our intolerance of all diversity in clothes, manners and real opinions. This is shown by our progressive schools and parents, who talk constantly about developing the individuality of the

[8] *The Education of Henry Adams*, p. 396.

child, but fear most to leave the child alone to think for himself or to find amusement through his own resources. Machine civilization makes for a dense population, which demands standardized life. This cannot be easily exorcised by glib phrases about individuality or personality.

Determinism and Tychism

The philosophies thus far discussed have been European in origin, though American in development and emphasis. A relatively original American philosophy, though somewhat parallel to the thought of Cournot and in some points Bergson, is the tychism evolved by Peirce and in part applied to history by William James. Peirce had many novel ideas on history and cyclical changes in it. But his leading idea, the primacy of chance, makes novelty and time real and history truly autonomous. If all temporal changes involve elements of genuine novelty, then no laws of any kind can completely explain individual events, though they may greatly aid in making certain phases of them intelligible.

James, with his eye always on the colorful and the concrete, has developed this view by emphasizing the importance of unique or great men as primary determinants in history. This view has been vehemently "pooh-poohed" by so-called scientific determinists.[9] And it must be admitted that James leaves out of account the determinant conditions under which great men *can* be highly influential. No one can well deny that the remarkable increase of population in European and American countries during the nineteenth century is of primary importance in determining the direction of history. To what extent is that the result of great men suddenly appearing by chance? Unusual men like Franklin, Napoleon, or Bismarck may influence battles or diplomatic and economic policies which set nations going in certain directions. But they can be said to do so only if certain social conditions are assumed to be connected with others in definite ways. The growth of population which determines the power of a nation depends in part on increased food supply, but also on other factors which increase the birth rate and decrease the death rate. Individual men, no matter how distinguished, count relatively little in determining such general currents. Thus, the most significant factors in the amazing increase of European and American population in the nineteenth century and of the radical transformation of life resulting therefrom were the discovery of the steam engine and vaccination against

---

[9] See Seligman's *Economic Interpretation of History*.

smallpox. Here the work of Watt and Jenner seems of utmost importance,—much greater than that of Napoleon or Bismarck. Yet, where so
many men were laboring independently in the same direction, it is not
unreasonable to suppose that the perfection of the steam engine and of
vaccination would sooner or later have been achieved by others. Such
postponement would, to be sure, have made a tremendous difference in
the history of Europe. Yet, in the end, we are bound to admit that we
call men great only to the extent that they take advantage of, or come to
signify, the great streams of influence which modify the conduct of large
numbers. We cannot read mass phenomena out of history, no matter how
dull and uninteresting they appear. This is not to deny the importance of
great men in setting patterns of conduct, but these patterns are significant
only when there are multitudes who imitate them and mechanisms for
spreading such influence.

History versus Value

Two doctrines are current on this point—the idealists claim that any
coherent history pre-supposes a system of values, while the realists insist
that any theory of value that is not arbitrary must be based on actual
experience, which, as past, is the object of history. Both of these theories
need critical examination if we are to separate their elements of truth from
the confusion in which they are generally involved.

Pragmatists as well as idealists, such as neo-Kantians, insist that our
valuations, what we regard as worthwhile, give direction to human effort,
and that the historian must have a theory of value to understand human
conduct; otherwise, he would have no principle of selection to enable him
to decide what is significant or relevant to his inquiry. But to admit this
does not mean that the system of values in the mind of the historian must
be the same as that of the people for whom he writes. One does not have
to be a Puritan or share the political philosophy of Madison and James
Wilson to write the history of Puritanism or of the Federal Convention
of 1787. The historian can take a point of view as to economic causes and
spiritual values which presents these events to us in a light that they did
not have to their contemporaries, just as our own youthful deeds may in
retrospect possess a significance that we did not see earlier. The historian's
sense of value molds his interpretation of past events, but does not create
them. A new interpretation of the character of Washington or Jefferson
does not change the past facts. Does the idealist mean to deny that the
past did exist before and apart from our present interpretation? To admit

that Washington did exist independently of our present knowledge of him enables us to deal with certain hard facts, e.g., his house at Mt. Vernon, the existing documents bearing his signature, and various references to him in English and American archives. Unless we are to say that all these facts come into existence only when any one of us learns about them—which assertion makes their existence arbitrary and entirely mysterious— then their significance as the consequences of Washington's existence must be recognized by us as independent of our own existence and acts. Our judgments on Washington and on his acts could not be true if these acts were not prior in time to judgments passed on them. If this seems too elementary or rudimentary, I must reply that idealists and pragmatists sometimes speak as if the opposite were true.

The realistic theory insists that a true valuation of anything depends on its real nature and that to know the latter you must know its history. For history shows us the nature of things as they unfold in time. But when all this is fully admitted, it still remains true that the common insistence that our social problems are to be solved by studying their history is a snare and a delusion. The history of war or of labor will not of itself solve our contemporary difficulties in regard to these matters. For the past did not solve them either. Knowledge of the past may be useful and at times necessary, but it is seldom sufficient. If it is true that we must know the past in order to know the present, the reverse is even more true. We must know something of the present before we can understand anything of the past. Truly, no one ignorant of physics or medicine can understand its history. Similarly, we must know something of our present economic life in order to understand the economics of Greece, Rome, Feudal Europe, or of the England of the Industrial Revolution.

Those who readily draw moral or political lessons from history are apt to overlook the difference in historic conditions and to forget the relativity (which is not subjectivity) of political and ethical values. In general, all parties or sects draw from history their partisan or sectarian lessons because they read history in the light of their peculiar assumptions. This does not make history entirely vain. It is a necessary way of extending our experience by discovering the meaning of things in their past connection. But to do this we must be both docile and energetic, admit existing truth and insist on pursuing our own ideals, checking our ideas by facts and testing the significance of facts by clarifying ideas. Historic investigation and philosophic reflection are distinguishable, but complementary and inseparable.*

---

* Cf. M. R. Cohen, *Reason and Nature* (1931), Book III, Chap. 2 ("History versus Value").

Chapter III

SCIENTIFIC
THOUGHT

ONE MIGHT MAINTAIN THE THESIS that science in America is both too much honored and too little appreciated. There is no doubt that the prestige of science today is pre-eminent. No one dares openly to disparage it, and the amount of money we spend for the promotion of science and scientific research is truly unprecedented. So far as outer manifestations go, more attention is paid to science in America than in any other country. There are more scientific museums, laboratories, and endowments in this country than in any other. Moreover, in many quarters science has taken the place of religion as the support for the hope of an earthly paradise or heaven on earth. Through the progress of mechanical inventions and scientific education all the evils of human life will, it is hoped, be gradually eliminated. In the popular mind and in the view of many men of science, the scientist has become a priest to deliver of his special oracle which tells the truth that will make men free from the ills which an unscientific world has suffered. Nothing is more familiar than the phrase "science has proved" or "science teaches us so-and-so."

Behind this prestige there is a general apathy if not positive distrust of science itself as a search for truth; for, to the ordinary American, science is identified with mechanical inventions. Ask an American to name the greatest scientist of this country and he will very likely reply, "Edison." As a nation, we respect only the practical applications of science and have regard for the efforts of inventors and promoters rather than those of the scientific discoverers. Scientists are not held in as great repute here as abroad. For a thousand men who have heard of the names of Marconi and Edison there is probably not more than one who has heard the names of Willard Gibbs, Theobald Smith, Henry A. Rowland or G. W. Hill. The endowments for science are largely for buildings, administrative purposes and laboratories in those fields in which some material profit is expected, that is, in technology and medicine. (Only recently has private industry realized the importance of research in pure science.) Science, then, is regarded as of purely instrumental value, useful because of its practical application. The notion that science might be a valuable activity for its own sake, like religion or art, appears strange to most Americans. Why?

Among the many reasons that can be set forth, perhaps the following are the most significant: (1) This country was originally settled by middle class people not scientifically trained or intellectually curious. Benjamin Franklin was an exception *sui generis*. (2) The first genuine university in America, Johns Hopkins, was founded in 1876. Until the end of the nineteenth century most of our distinguished scientists were trained abroad. (3) The business tradition has diverted attention from the ideals of free curiosity and knowledge for its own sake. (4) The Puritan tradition bolsters up the business idea and the hostility to idle speculation.

The colonists who came here in the seventeenth and eighteenth centuries, and even the immigrants of the nineteenth century, for the most part, did not bring with them the traditions of scientific research. We must remember that little of what is modern science was taught in the English or European Universities in the seventeenth century. There were some beginnings of the new learning in Cambridge, England, in the latter half of the seventeenth century, but this did not reach America until much later. Scientific learning was under the patronage of princes, great merchants, and special academies founded for that purpose, generally with the aid of governments. Thus, the Royal Society of London had much more to do with the advancement of science than the universities, and the galaxy of stars of which Newton was the greatest luminary was not succeeded by any of equal magnitude before the nineteenth century. The immigrants who came to this country were, by and large, cultivators of the soil, or men of the lower middle classes, and did not bring with them the traditions of higher learning. Nevertheless, we find, as early as 1706, Thomas Brattle of Massachusetts writing for the Philosophical Transactions of the Royal Society on the eclipses of 1692 and 1706.[1] The study of nature was developed here in the eighteenth century, and the founding of the American Philosophical Society at Philadelphia in 1743 by Benjamin Franklin may be said to be the beginning of organized science in this country. One might mention other names, such as those

---

[1] Solon I. Bailey, in his *History and Work of the Harvard Observatory: 1839-1927* (at p. 5), tells us that Newton in the *Principia Mathematica* refers to Brattle's observation of the comet in 1680.

of Cadwallader Colden (1688-1776), Robert Hare (1781-1858), Benjamin Silliman (1779-1864), Edward W. Morley (1838-1923) and Simon Newcomb (1835-1909). But though interest in the observation of nature was not lacking in the eighteenth or early nineteenth century, continuous organized scientific research did not exist. By the beginning of the nineteenth century, however, we find a number of societies for the promotion of scientific studies, notably the American Philosophical Society, the Philadelphia Academy of Natural Sciences, and the American Academy of Arts and Sciences with its headquarters in Boston.

The proceedings of these societies show considerable attention to what used to be called natural history, that is, mineralogy, botany, and zoology, and especially ornithology. It is well to note that Franklin's contributions in the field of electricity were regarded as epoch-making by all European scientists. It is also well to note that Franklin had many original and penetrating ideas on geology. So far as I know, he was one of the earliest to conceive that the earth may not be solid in its interior, but be constituted rather of a condensed though highly heated fluid or gas, with a relatively thin shell of matter on the exterior. In this way he thought the various disturbances on the surface of the earth could be explained. However, the great achievements of Benjamin Franklin in natural science should not blind us to the fact that from the beginning of our history up to the days of Joseph Henry we have had no other great contributor to physics.

It is interesting to note that in the fall and winter of 1800 and 1801, when the question whether Burr or Jefferson should be made president arose, Jefferson was entirely absorbed in certain geologic studies, as he was in the summer of 1808 when the question of the Embargo was stirring the people of the United States to such an extent that New England threatened secession. (Jefferson was president of the American Philosophical Society in 1817.) Outside of the colleges we find also a man like Bowditch, whose great treatise on navigation is still in use and whose translation of Laplace's *Mécanique Céleste* showed such profound knowledge of the subject that he was elected a corresponding member of the French Academy of Science.

Popular Interest in Science

A genuine interest in science develops in the early part of the nineteenth century and is attested by our first successful scientific journal, which was founded by Silliman in 1819 and has continued ever since (at first under the title of "The American Journal of Science and Arts" and since 1880 as the "American Journal of Science"). A few years earlier McClure had published his great treatise on the *Geology of the United States*. Silliman's son-in-law and successor as editor of the Journal was the geologist Dana whose work may be put beside the classics of that science, the works of Lyell. The founding of the Smithsonian Institution gave great impetus to the study of natural history, and the collection of fossils for the National Museum added richly to the material of the science of paleontology.

The coming of many cultivated Germans to the United States after 1848 accelerated the study of science and philosophy, and the generation which came to maturity at the time of the Civil War and immediately thereafter was greatly stirred by the works of Spencer and Darwin. Justice Holmes once told me that the rift between his generation and that of his father was, in his judgment, greater than any previous separation between two generations.*

The effects of the doctrine of evolution have been most curious. Contrary to the usual impression, the doctrine of evolution did not come to this country through Darwin. It came through the New England movement of transcendentalism, which emanates from the philosophy of Schelling through Coleridge.** We must also remember that the philosophy of Lamarck found great favor in this country. The popular version of that will be found in Chambers' *Vestiges of Creation*. The nature philosophy of Schelling and Oken was available to Americans in the English translation of Oken's work. The application of the evolutionary concept to human history and institutions, the great work of Hegel, influenced Spencer considerably. And its effects on Protestant theology can be seen in the lectures of Professor Shedd of the Presbyterian Union Theological Seminary.

The advent of Spencer's new work, however, took the American public by storm. There was in this country in the period after the Civil War a great mass of people who had become fairly prosperous, but who had not acquired much of a classical education. They were avid, as many people are today, for culture on easy terms, and Herbert Spencer offered them a vest pocket guide to all problems of philosophy and science. Thus one who did not know what life is might read in Spencer that it is the sum of all vital activities and feel that he had acquired the essence of philosophical knowledge thereby. Philosophy, indeed, may

---

* Cf. "The Holmes-Cohen Correspondence," ed. by F. S. Cohen, in *Journal of the History of Ideas*, Vol. 9, p. 14 (1948).

** Cf. Marsh's introduction to the 1829 American edition of Coleridge's *Aids to Reflection*.

be defined as the unity of all the sciences. Mill had made popular the theory of science as empirical. Spencer put content into this empirical view. Moreover, Spencer gave men a vista into infinite time and space. He really replaced the old religion since he told us where we come from, how we have developed, and what is the ultimate goal of civilization. In addition, he found in this country enthusiastic disciples. And John Fiske made the gospel of evolution respectable with his two heavy tomes on *Cosmic Philosophy* (1874) and his repeated exposition of that gospel.

But the orthodox felt that their prestige was being challenged by the unacademic apostles. At Harvard Professor Bowen, head of the department of philosophy, thundered against the "mud philosophers." At Princeton one of the professors thundered against the new heresy: If evolution is true then Christianity is a fraud. President McCosh, a canny Scot, would not go so far. But the resistance to evolution explains why the crusading enthusiasm for it has persisted so long. It has dominated sociologic thinking with the various conventional stages and the theory of survivals. It dominated the economic theories of Veblen and the epistemology and ethics of John Dewey. In the course of its development, however, it has become quite orthodox. Natural selection has functioned very much as the old providence.

Yet, peculiarly enough, the notion of evolution, as conceived in popular thought, is merely a tremendous dramatization of scientific ideas.

Spencer, with his great popular appeal, accelerated its spread with his presentation of the nebular hypothesis. Laplace, the physicist, and one of the protagonists of this hypothesis, stated that there was not enough mathematical proof to substantiate the theory. Later, it was actually observed that certain satellites retrogressed and did not build up. Chauncey Wright, in 1865, showed that the evolutionary concept of the nebular hypothesis was a myth and that there was nothing scientific about extending the idea of evolution beyond the organic world.

Moreover, the unicellular and lower animals have remained the same since geologic time, indicating no evidence of change at all. Darwin was aware of this and in no way was he disconcerted. He knew that there was no universal law of change. There are some species that do change and there are some that do not. In addition, the notion that ontogeny recapitulates phylogeny seems pleasant to believe, but we know that we change embryological development by changing the embryo's environment. Thus, it appears that the ideas of evolution are not always scientific.

However, the scientific philosophy of Spencer, with its distrust of theology and its emphasis on factual study, appealed more to Americans than to any other people with the possible exception of the Russians, who were culturally in somewhat the same undeveloped state. This was the period in which Draper published his *Intellectual Development of Europe* and *History of the Conflict Between Religion and Science*, and White his *Warfare of Science with Theology*. It was the period when Youmans founded the *Popular Science Monthly* and the imagination of America was captured by the mechanical inventions of Thomas Edison. Still, the amount of first rate scientific work cannot be said to have been very large. Of the outstanding men one may mention Benjamin Peirce in mathematics, Willard Gibbs, who worked at chemistry in utter obscurity at Yale, tolerated only because of his wealth and pious family connections, and Henry A. Rowland in physics at Johns Hopkins. Possibly we should add Edward C. Pickering in astronomy. But even these men can hardly compare with the foremost ranks of European scientists.

The subject of astronomy, because of its bearing on navigation and the support of the government, has naturally been one of the first to produce a line of first-rate men, and of these one may mention Simon Newcomb and especially G. W. Hill. When George Darwin and Poincaré came to this country in 1904 they both paid tribute to Hill, whom they regarded as their master. However, Hill was not very well known in this country. Since the construction of the Mount Wilson and Yerkes Observatories we have had in this country the best of the world's equipment, and the men engaged in this field will compare favorably with their European colleagues.

With the development of our universities, since the close of the nineteenth century, research in the physical sciences has been rapidly expanding. In recent years the prestige of our scientific journals and the increasing number of our Nobel Prize winners, beginning with Albert A. Michelson, Theodore W. Richards, Robert A. Millikan, and Arthur H. Compton, indicate that leadership in science is passing to this side of the Atlantic.

Still, it must be remembered that the great new and fruitful ideas, such as the theory of relativity, the earlier and later quantum mechanics theories, and the newer form of statistical mechanics, have been mainly European in origin. Americans have been devoting more energy to detailed experiments and less to the larger issues. When Professor Ehrenfest of Leyden visited this country he commented as others have on the superior equipment of American laboratories, but on the relative paucity of American physicists who command a knowledge of the mathematical instruments of their field. This is not to disparage the work done in pure mathematics at Chicago, Princeton, and Harvard in recent years, but the fact still remains that we have too narrow a conception of specialization and the popularizing of research.

We, in America, have inherited a peculiar attitude toward the significance of any enterprise, whether it be scientific or otherwise. This attitude which is embodied in the Puritan tradition is reflected in the European's acknowledgment of "Americanism" as synonymous with the subordination of pure science to practical science, or of the theoretic to the concrete. The Puritan tradition of hostility to games and pure enjoyment is hostile to the satisfaction of that disinterested curiosity or wonder which is one of the basic drives that make science possible. And this is reenforced by the practical businessman's aversion for speculation, the outcome of which he cannot tell in advance. The man in the street tends to look upon science as a practical kind of trade or business, concerned with the dissemination of useful information.

The general literary attitude toward science is that while science may be sovereign in limited fields, e.g., when dealing with electrons or museum specimens, it cannot give us insight into important human affairs, so that there is an inevitable gulf between humanism and science. In an article on Tolstoy, which Theodore Roosevelt wrote after leaving the presidency, he bluntly put the acid test of the value of all spiritual reflection by the appeal to the market-place in the literal sense: What has it to offer to the man of affairs?[2]

However, all of these tests and attitudes serve only to lose sight of the nature, function and roots of science. Science has two roots: first, the native desire to know, to satisfy what Aristotle calls "wonder" and what we may call "curiosity"; and second, the desire to get information that will help us to achieve other ends, such as the practical or economic ones. The general tendency in this country has been to underestimate the former and over-estimate the latter.

In a book called *Science, the False Messiah,* Professor Clarence E. Ayres, in the manner of Veblen, gave expression to some bitter truths in regard to the false speculations on the benefits derived from science. Back of this wholesome recall to sobriety, however, was the naively confident but altogether baseless assumption that science originates from and is subordinate to machine industry. The latter thesis, despite the lack of any foundation for it, seems to be generally accepted.

Now it is inconceivable that even in the applied sciences any progress can be made except by those who are animated by a keen interest in the intellectual solution of problems. For the solutions are not found by intensive devotion to social or individual utility but by the capacity for concentrating on the problems and unraveling the conditions of their solution. Moreover, the keen enjoyment and delight in the exercise of

---

[2] *The Works of Theodore Roosevelt, National Edition,* Vol. XII, pp. 319-24.

intellectual faculties will always attract certain individuals to the problems of pure science. Nevertheless, by and large, the general esteem with which any pursuit is held determines, in large measure, its attraction for ambitious youths. In a country where the achievements in pure science are not held in great repute few men will be drawn to it, and the result will be a relative paucity and poverty in achievement. Whereas in pre-Hitler Germany the precarious post of *Privatdozent* was the object of some aspiration and regard, the pursuit of science in America is not so honored as to make men willing to incur the necessary sacrifices or to be supported by their families. They prefer to engage in pursuits which offer immediate gain and financial independence. Moreover, the lack of dignity and self-confidence of science is manifest in the manner in which the leaders of science have bent their knee to those who are hostile to freedom.

Science, Religion and Philosophy

The attitude of religious leaders to science has generally been either avowedly or implicitly hostile. In the middle of the nineteenth century, the works of Voltaire and Diderot affected the intellectual climate of the United States. Thereupon the warfare between science and religion developed. In England the Seven Clergymen answered Darwin and Huxley. Rationalism reached its high-water mark in the eastern centers of this country with the publication of the works of Spencer. It was only natural that ministers who lost their intellectual prestige with the rise of science should regard scientists as presumptuous, and should endeavor to delimit the field of science so as to exclude it from the "important" realms of knowledge and experience.

When in certain quarters of the country the hostility to certain biologic theories was expressed in legislation, because of their failure to harmonize with the old Biblical theology, the leaders of science did not take the position that the search for truth must be unhampered, regardless of the scientific evidential weight in favor or disfavor of the theory; rather did they try to prove the very dubious proposition that all the advances of science only repeated the old truths of the Christian religion. And even among our philosophers, both of the idealistic and the modern schools, there is what Santayana calls a malicious view according to which science is damned with faint praise as something which has to do with mere practical affairs and does not give us truth. The idealists urge that science deals only with phenomena, while philosophy gives us intuitions of reality. The pragmatists, such as James, and at times Dewey, regard science as merely instrumental for man's practical activities. Dewey's philosophy is definitely practical and his entire conception of knowledge is utilitarian in nature. James once said that pure science was pure "bosh," and at the end of his life plumped straight for Bergson's view that immediate experience rather than science gives us the truth; but this experience is one which lacks all discrimination and is indistinguishable from Bradley's ineffable absolute. James' contention that, since science cannot demonstrate eternal verities, therefore we should believe what we like, is indicative of the extent of this reaction from the philosophy of the Enlightenment. The God of Science now bends his knee to the God of Theology. Even our positivistic schools, pushing the modern doctrine of fictionalism, minimize the value of the laws or principles which science reveals as a characteristic of the actual world.

In brief, the philosophic attitude toward science in America has been either one of open hostility, advising scientists to keep within their own domain, or one of apparent acceptance but implicit hostility. Of the latter type is the pragmatic attitude today, which is based upon the popular theory that science deals in "fictions." Science is simply a device for classifying our knowledge of phenomena for practical purposes. It requires no theory and gives no insight. Experience is basic, and electrons, atoms, etc., are mere tools of manipulation. This theory of fictions was developed in Germany by Mach, Ostwald, *et. al.* of whom James was a follower. Recent physics shows the absurdity of this position by weighing, counting, finding the electrical charges of, and otherwise examining, atoms and electrons. The fictionalists have withdrawn their argument but they have retained their attitude. Science is still said to be a "mere description and not an explanation," as if there were any other sort of explanation. Mystic insight is not more important than the elaboration of what we really know. The view that philosophy deals with reality and science with phenomena is that of traditional idealism. James and Bergson hold to this mnemonic theory of science. But what the inner reality is, which science misses, is left uncertain.

There is one exception to this indictment of science by American idealist philosophy,—Josiah Royce, who was influenced by Peirce and by Russell's *Principles of Mathematics*. The philosophy of Royce endeavors to assimilate the general results of modern logical and mathematical studies. The realistic arguments as to the nature of mathematics were first advanced by Royce in his *World and the Individual*, several years before the appearance of Russell's *Principles of Mathematics*. The mathematician, we are told, is as much a student of given facts as is the chemist, astronomer, or businessman. The results of his observations abound in the unexpected as much as do the facts of any other field of research. Royce adds that the mathematician watches the result of his own activity, in a sense, but this "sense" is made clear by the example of the diagram. The mathematician makes his diagram or set of postulates, but he cannot wilfully alter the consequences which alone are, after all, specifically mathematical facts. This purely realistic account of mathematics was developed by Royce in his St. Louis address, "The Sciences of the Ideal," in his monograph, *Relations of the Principles of Logic to the Foundations of Geometry,* and in his essay on "Logic" in the volume entitled *Encyclopedia of the Philosophical Sciences.* The fruitful character of deductive reasoning as a source of truth appears even in his *Sources of Religious Insight.*

Sheffer and Lewis have continued the tradition of respect for science and especially for mathematical logic at Harvard. Santayana, in the last chapter of *Reason in Science,* offers a sharp criticism of the traditional attitude of contempt on the part of American philosophers toward science (regarded as "mere materialism"). The view that facts are for the vulgar minds is characteristic. This view was reinforced by the transcendental philosophies imported from Germany. Santayana regards this point of view as "malicious," since it throws doubt on the deliverances of science because they do not support religious superstitions and themselves throw doubt upon the procedure of reasoning *a priori* from superficially plausible principles erected into eternal truths. Santayana admits that science is fragmentary, but holds that the proper attitude is to recognize the limitations of knowledge. He has no coherent philosophy of science although he makes some illuminating remarks, e.g., in regard to physics, mechanics and psycho-physics. Santayana has a positive attitude towards science, but it is literary rather than scientific.

Charles Peirce of all American philosophers has shown the greatest insight into science. The son of a great mathematician and himself experienced in actual scientific work (geodetic survey), he understood what it was to engage in scientific measurements. With Chauncey Wright and other members of a philosophical club he worked out a substantial theory of science, analyzing the nature of law, predictability, and other basic scientific concepts. Fundamentally, he regarded science as a method rather than a bundle of laws.

Peirce attacked these problems entirely in the interests of exact logic and a rational account of the physical universe. As a rigorous logician familiar with the actual procedures by which our knowledge of the various laws of nature is obtained, he could not admit that experience could prove the claim of any physical law to absoluteness. All the physical laws actually known, like Boyle's law or the law of gravitation, involve excessive simplification of the phenomenal course of events, and thus a large element of empirical inaccuracy. But for Peirce a more positive objection against the traditional assumption of absolute or invariable laws of nature, is the fact that such assumption makes the regularities of the universe ultimate, and thus cuts us off from the possibility of ever explaining them or how there comes to be as much regularity in the universe as there is. In ordinary affairs, the occurrence of any regularity is the very thing to be explained. Every explanation of the moon's path, for example, must take particular existences for granted. Such original or underived individuality and diversity is precisely what Peirce means by chance; and from this point of view chance is prior to law.

James and Royce have called attention to the similarity between Peirce's doctrine of tychistic-agapism (chance and love)* and the creative evolution of Bergson. But while both philosophies aim to restore life and growth in their account of the nature of things, Peirce's approach has the advantage of being in close conformity with the outlook of modern physics. Bergson's procedure is based largely on the contention that mechanics cannot explain certain empirical facts. Peirce's account involves no rejection of the possibility of mechanical explanations. Not only has Peirce a greater regard than even Bergson for the actual diversity and spontaneity of things, but he is perhaps in a much better position than any other modern philosopher to explain the order and coherence of the world. This he effects by uniting the medieval regard for the reality of universals with the modern scientific use of the concept of continuity. For those who have faith in the ancient and fruitful approach of philosophy through the doors of mathematics and physics, the writings of Peirce are full of suggestions which can throw light on the vexed problem of scientific knowledge.

In the period of American philosophy, which began with the publication of Dewey's *Studies in Logical Theory* (1903-1909), the old idea of philosophy as a critique of the special sciences was abandoned in favor of the more modest effort to make philosophic discussion itself scientific, i.e., to narrow it down to certain definite and decidable issues.

Dewey's philosophy may be viewed as one of the many efforts since Hume to introduce the experimental method of the physical sciences into philosophy and moral subjects. However, except for the important fact that Dewey substitutes a theory of active experience for the psychology

* Peirce, Charles S., *Chance, Love and Logic* (edited by Morris R. Cohen, 1923).

of sensations and their association, he belongs to the Lockian tradition that almost banishes the cosmologic interest from philosophy. For instance, concentration upon practical or social applications have led him to belittle, if not ignore, the interest in physical or cosmic issues.

While thus minimizing the relations between philosophy and the physical sciences, Dewey has sought to make social philosophy more rigorously scientific in its methods and generalizations. Valuable as this effort has been, it is often vitiated by the naive assumption that social philosophers in all prior ages failed to utilize scientific method only because they did not think of such a course or were prevented from moving in this direction by sheer prejudice or by Aristotle. The outstanding fact is that we cannot experiment on human beings as freely as we can on hydrogen gas or guinea pigs. Moreover, Dewey minimizes the significance of precise quantitative thought, which has done so much to advance physics, when he says "the domination of man by reverie and desire is as pertinent for the philosophic theory of nature as is mathematical physics."[3] No one doubts that human reverie is a natural event, but surely it is not one of the great controlling forces of nature that science uses to explain phenomena. It illumines the human scene to understand the desire which made men refuse to accept the Copernican astronomy, but it gives us no light on the nature of planetary motion. The solution of human problems depends upon a knowledge of physiology, chemistry, and inorganic physics, not vice versa.

Dewey strains the facts when he contends "that philosophy originated not out of intellectual but out of social and emotional material."[4] The origin of Greek philosophy is certainly connected with the interest in abstract mathematics and cosmology as distinguished from any technical or social applications. Great philosophers speak to all time; only the minor ones are dated.

Dewey calls his philosophy humanistic naturalism; more properly it could be called anthropomorphic naturalism. In it the central role is played, not by physical cosmology, but by social anthropology or a doctrine of human experience. In general, it is a denigration of the symbiotic relationship between the natural and physical sciences and philosophy. It offers no vistas of nature beyond the human scene, and manifests no interest in such questions as the origin and future of our solar system or of life on our earth, or even in the natural conditions which are likely to bring about the disappearance of the human species. Unlike Peirce's orientation, for example, Dewey's perspective is essentially

[3] *Experience and Nature* (1925), 1st ed., p. 6.
[4] *Reconstruction in Philosophy* (1920), p. 25.

that of a moralist, moving in the humanistic tradition. In this, there is a subordination of cosmic to moral considerations, to the hurt of both.

Scientific Method

The refusal to recognize that the strength and source of science lies in its methodology has led to some interesting and confusing notions of what science is, both among laymen and among scientific workers. It is generally assumed that ours is an "age of science," and the terms "science" and "scientific" are bandied about in a rather glib fashion. But there is always a danger when a word becomes honorific that it will cease to be descriptive, and that when it is applied to anything and everything that we approve, it will thus cease to have any discriminatory denotation. It is well therefore to ask at the outset: What is science? When some people talk of Christian Science or the science of theology, others of the science of archaeology, heraldry or numismatics, while still others use the authority of Thomas Huxley to deny that mathematics is a science, and interminable controversies rage as to whether history and other social studies can be sciences—surely we are dealing with a word whose meaning is by no means clear or definite.

The word "science" originally meant knowledge, but though everyone has some knowledge no one is willing to say that everyone is a scientist. On the contrary, Americans use the word "scientist" much more than the English to denote a special group of people whose business it is to pursue science.

The identification of science with the individuals who work within the field has led to several misleading notions as to the body of knowledge which is called scientific and as to the status and worth of those scientists who venture into fields other than those in which they reign supreme or at least have established their reputations. This tendency to view the pronouncements of the scientist with awe and reverence, in domains other than those of his special pursuit, has encouraged the notion that the scientist of today is the real priest and the genuine disseminator of truth. Formerly we went to the theologians for the truth and now we go to the scientists for the truth. We confuse and generalize to the extent of asking a great engineer or physicist his opinion on the education of girls, immortality, or the existence of God.

Eddington tries to make weighty issues rest on weak foundations. The fact that Heisenberg finds a quantum missing from the atom gives us no reason to believe in the existence of God. The existence of a curvature in the world's circumference is no better proof of the existence of God. God needs no such basis upon which to stand. The scientist who claims to have seen God in the laboratory is subject to the same scepticism as the one who claims to have discovered an element which no one other than he can see. Scientists who constitute themselves as authorities on religion only serve to aggrandize the confusion. Millikan, for instance, is ill-informed when he states that the essence of science is the same as that of religion. All of this is symptomatic of the reaction from the philosophy of the Enlightenment.

In a somewhat similar manner, the answer to the question, "What is science?" has been impeded by the tendency of Americans to confuse science with "popular science." The prevalence and the popularity of such titles as "Physics for the Layman" and "Astronomy for the Hundred Thousand" in the book mart has given to the people of our generation the illusion that they are living in the "Age of Science." Science is available to everyone who cares to spend a few free hours every day or month. In this fashion science has replaced ancient mythology.

"Popular Science" publications are not science. They are conventionalizations of true science, stripped bare and dressed up in lurid clothes. The notions of science derived from these myths of popularized publications are, however, a genuine part of popular American thought. Typical of these myths are the views that the world is a machine and that the apple falls to the earth because the earth pulls it. The scientist who works in the laboratory knows that the world is not a machine any more than it is a tree. As far as the popular notion of gravitation is concerned, it was ruled out of pure science by the time of Galileo. The true scientific idea of gravitation is a set of mathematical rules. The reporters of science, whether laymen or temporary excursionists from the fields of science, have offered the tinsel and have neglected the core.

The body of knowledge which we identify as science is the outcome of a specific methodology in terms of which we test and verify our assumptions and hypotheses. The items of knowledge which survive these tests are incorporated in the *corpus* of science. This method is characterized by universality and objectivity. It legislates the conditions under which the terms *evidence* and *proof* are meaningful and significant. Moreover, it functions as a guide to the discovery of the invariant relationships which are found in the universe. Science, in brief, is the method of verification and points to the paths wherein systematic knowledge is to be sought. The distinguishing traits of this method may be best indicated by a comparison with alternative methods of attaining stability of ideas.

1. The method of iteration is the most common method of learning, especially in those fields where we are most certain of our knowledge. The Mohammedan does not doubt the existence of Allah after praying to him every day. The modern American does not think of doubting the existence of electricity. This method requires an acceptance of authority. Doubts suggested by contact with other ideas are insulated as much as possible. They may, however, rankle and create more disturbances. Especially is this so in complex societies where no simple authority is all-powerful. In general, the method of authority requires the suppression of divergent opinions, since they cannot be assimilated. This, in turn, increases the needed scope of the authority and the intensity of its affirmation, so that the new doubts are strengthened, extended and organized, and this finally may lead to active rebellion.

2. The appeal to self-evident principles is another method of attaining stability of ideas. Americans customarily appeal to ideas in question as self-evident. The Greeks based geometry on self-evident principles, using the method of mathematics to deduce the necessary consequences. But the appeal to self-evident principles is apt to be broken down by contact with diverse cultures. Thus Xenophanes found that, while the Ethiopians had Gods with snub noses and dark hair, the Thracians worshipped fair-headed Gods and he concluded that if oxen made Gods they would have the shape of oxen. This idea, of course, would not have occurred to a peasant, habituated to a traditional view. Modern mathematics has made great progress by questioning self-evident principles, e.g., that two points determine a line, or that the whole is greater than any of its parts. Thus the classical Greek method of self-evidence breaks down.

3. The method of science according to Peirce tries to attain stability of ideas by encouraging doubt and attempting to undermine every hypothesis. This sounds paradoxical. But it is impossible to question everything at once, since to question any proposition involves the setting up of the possibility of contrary or contradictory propositions. This is impossible in logic itself. That the conclusion of a syllogism is true if the premise is true cannot be questioned. Nor can we question the proposition that there are propositions. But any material proposition can be questioned, and some can be shown to be improbable in the actual world. Thus the assertion that through a point outside a line only one line can be drawn parallel to the given line, as applied to the physical world, can be and has been questioned, by setting up and considering two alternative negatives of this proposition (a) that more than one such line can be drawn, and (b) that no such line can be drawn. Thus the scientific method enables us to consider all possibilities and build upon a

foundation that cannot be overthrown. Science is not a form of despotism tempered with anarchy, as is religion in its ordinary conception, but rather a self-corrective system, like a constitutional government which allows for its own amendment. In science, where every theory is provisional, we have progress and liberalism, which is impossible in religious realms where everything is regarded as certain and dogmatic. The inability to provide for their own correction is the chief difficulty with the methods of authority and self-evident principles.

The Greeks developed science in protest against the oriental view of authority which was dominated by the fear of God. The Greeks ignored the Gods and asked, "What do I see?" They arranged their answers in orderly patterns.

How do we get hypotheses? They occur to people who think. Logic is the science of possibilities and enables us to multiply hypotheses. Peirce was worried by the problem of accounting for the large number of true hypotheses that we attain, when the mere mathematical probability is against any such result. Dewey attempts to explain the difficulty by environmental selection, that is, that the environment supports true hypotheses and eliminates others. The analogy to biological selection has a limited application. False ideas also maintain themselves. History is full of instances where truth "gets it in the neck." False ideas are not necessarily biologically harmful—or true ideas beneficial.

For Einstein, the discovery of scientific truths is seen as a sort of divination. Faith is important in so far as it is necessary for the pursuit of the consequences of an idea past points where apparent improbability develops. Fundamentally the scientist's faith is a faith in the intelligibility of physical events, a faith that beneath the apparent confusion and chaos of the world we live in there are underlying invariant relations.

Without abating an iota from the recognition that the laws or general assertions of science must be experimentally verifiable, Einstein rightly insists that science has not actually been built up by the process of induction or empirical generalization, which plays a necessary but subordinate role and often comes to a dead stop. Real progress, he insists, comes when one fortunately hits on some great unifying idea from which one can deduce consequences that can ultimately be brought into agreement (through elaborate mathematical processes) with observed and measurable phenomena.

In the main Einstein stays in the Platonic tradition of Kepler, Galileo, and Newton: that "nature is the realization of the simplest conceivable mathematical ideas." As a follower of Mach, however, he is inclined at times to give a subjective interpretation to mathematical-physical theories and to refer to them as fictions. But how does it happen that these fictions turn out to be such powerful clues to the nature of the physical world? There is no mystery in the case if we regard physical axioms or principles as hypotheses (in plain language, guesses) concerning the nature of things, and mathematics as an accurate analysis of what is contained or involved in these hypotheses. If our guess happens to be true, its mathematical consequences will be in agreement with experience; if not, our mathematics will sooner or later show that our guess is not compatible with the world of empirical existence. Assuredly the mind is active or creative in the construction of physical theory, but when this construction is properly conducted it is found to be a process of exploration and discovery.

That there is an independent reality, which the physicist seeks to discover and understand rather than to create, is indeed the essence not only of Einstein's theory of science but of his theory of religion as well. While fully realizing the value of science as an aid in advancing the practical interests of the community, and also as a natural field of human activity wherein some can best exercise their intellectual energies, Einstein insists that the temple of science did not originate in the utilitarian way, and that it could not continue to exist if it were not for those to whom science has a religious value. It is a way of salvation, i.e., an escape from the life of purely personal concerns into a world of objective reality, revealed to thought as a vision—even if but a fragmentary glimpse—of the world as a whole. For though the rigorously accurate methods of physics enable us to grasp only a small and thin part of the cosmos, still, since all that truly exists contains physical elements, the physicist can feel that he has some grasp of the totality, which grasp the progress of science can and does enlarge.

It is instructive to reflect on Einstein's position in the history of science. Hailed at first as a great revolutionary who overthrew the classical Newtonian system, we now see him rather as at heart a staunch representative of the classic tradition of the unity of nature—so poignantly expressed by Spinoza and Kant—trying, by introducing certain needed changes in the Newtonian system, to defend it against the purely statistical or probabilistic view which the younger revolutionaries are advancing.*

Now we may, as I for one do, share Einstein's conviction or faith that behind all the statistical variations there are ultimate invariant relations, and yet feel more of the difficulties in the way of our *ever* attaining a systematic account of nature in terms of simple laws. Nature, according

---

* Cf. "Einstein's Theory of Relativity" and "Roads to Einstein" in M. R. Cohen, *Studies in Philosophy and Science* (1949) at pp. 215-242.

to Fresnel, does not care about our mathematical difficulties; and one may well suspect that it contains a good deal of brute irrationality or lack of intelligible order. At any rate our descriptions of nature always have contained and probably always will contain an arbitrary element determined by human history rather than by the object studied.

The traditional conception of scientific method, held alike by philosophers and scientists, is the Baconian.* One is to begin by observing facts and classifying them; then one is to formulate hypotheses to explain them. Evidently we do not need any special genius to develop ideas. We do not have to think to find out. If we are sufficiently industrious and gather enough facts the idea will come of itself. Induction thus conceived seems truly a democratic idea. However, science does not progress in this way. Scientific activity does not begin when man is a baby without previous ideas. The scientist begins when he already has knowledge and ideas derived from authority, experience, and earlier background. Science begins with common knowledge. But common sense is not something apart from philosophy. The common sense of today is old scholastic metaphysics hardened with age. Science tries to make common knowledge systematic. It applies the method of questioning. Its ideals are consistency, accuracy, universality and abstractness. As we substitute for everyday description more and more abstract and systematic knowledge, our science gets further from the familiar, but the latter is full of illusion.

A due regard for the essential role which mathematical or theoretical development plays in experimental work is not only necessary to explain the growth of science, modern or ancient, but also to remove the false dualism between experiment and rational determination. Scientific progress depends on considering only the relevant circumstances, which depends upon prior knowledge. Hence scientific discoveries are not made by those who begin with an unbiased mind in the form of a *tabula rasa*, but by those who have derived fruitful ideas from the study of previous science.

The notion that great scientific discoveries are made by accident, which appears in so many conventional history books, is highly mythical. Take, for example, the oft cited case of Roentgen's discovery of X-rays. It is said that he discovered X-rays by accident—just picked up a photographic plate, and finding a picture of a key, naturally concluded that a new kind of radiation must have produced it. But, in point of fact, Roentgen had previously devoted years of study to the different kinds of

---

* Bacon's view of scientific method is set forth and criticized in the essay, "Bacon and the Inductive Method" in M. R. Cohen, *Studies in Philosophy and Science* (1949) at pp. 99-106.

radiation, so that the accident was the kind that could happen only to one who had thought as much about the subject as he had. It was only because he was ready to see the importance of that particular picture that he discovered the rays that caused it. Poincaré used to say that science is built with facts as a house is with bricks, but a collection of facts is no more science than a pile of bricks is a house. The role of previous assumption is a crucial one in determining the course of scientific research.*

Science does not function in all human domains. We cannot control the factors of certain situations. Besides, most people do not want certain beliefs questioned. Science demands reference to objective evidence and regards as irrelevant the moral terms in which philosophers, theologians, and popular writers value propositions.

Philosophy is often an apology for the opinions or attitudes that philosophers have held. Science makes no apologies. It subjects all views to the same objective tests. Whether truth has any value is a question that is irrelevant to the scientist's task. Perhaps ignorance is bliss, although in that event it seems that people should be much happier than they are now, being born with enough of it to last many lifetimes. At any rate, the activity of science considered merely as play, the search for truth, is a liberating activity and makes life worthwhile apart from any utilitarian values that the discovery of truth may serve. Liberalism and the method of science are closely interwoven. Liberalism paves the way for science by removing obstacles to the development of human energy. Science, in turn, affords greater opportunity for the liberation of human energy.

It is the custom today to belittle the people of ancient Greece because they placed little emphasis on application, feeling that the pursuit of science and the satisfaction of curiosity were enough for them. We are prone to forget that science is a kind of intellectual energy, as valuable to human life as pleasing people. To regard it in any other way is to misunderstand the source from which it emanates and the function which it serves in the affairs of men.

We live in a paradoxical world in which it happens to be true as a matter of historic fact that the men who have most deeply affected human weal and woe have been precisely those who have pursued pure science as a pastime or as an escape from the monotony of empty life. Not a single advance in man's control over nature in modern times but is based on the work of men like Galileo, Newton or Lagrange, whose predominant passion was to find the simplest mathematical expression in which,

---

* *Cf.* "Philosophy and Scientific Methods" in M. R. Cohen, *Studies in Philosophy and Science* (1949) at pp. 48-49.

they believed, the book of nature was written. We should never have had wireless electricity and the consequent saving—or destruction—of life, if Maxwell had devoted himself to the promotion of human welfare instead of speculating about the ether—which may not exist at all—and about the purely mathematical properties of electro-magnetic equations.

There is the final paradox that science, by seeking the truth in a dis-interested manner, regardless of moral issues, may achieve its most useful results, just as the artist may please not by trying to please people but by expressing his own vision of beauty.

Chapter IV

ECONOMIC
THOUGHT

General Background

It is curious to note the difference between our own and foreign estimates as to our intellectual achievements. Thus histories of political science written by Europeans pay scant attention to any of our political theorists. But hardly any history of economic thought fails to mention a relatively large number of American economists. We, however, have devoted a large literature to the history of American political thought but on the whole relatively little to the history of American economic thought. I shall not pursue any inquiry as to the cause of this disparity except to comment on one suggestion, namely, that while European economic conditions are very much like our own, their political situation is quite different. I do not think that we can accept this explanation as adequate in view of the close connection between economics and politics. For the great fact about American political life—the absence of feudal class distinctions—is also the dominant note of our economic life.

The settlers who came to this country in the 17th, 18th and 19th centuries brought with them European ideas on economic as well as on political issues. America, it must be remembered, despite our Declaration of Independence and the War with England in 1812, has up to very recently remained intellectually a province of England. English books, extensively reprinted in this country, had a greater prestige in the main than those produced in America, for the intellectual standards of education and culture were higher in England than in the United States. But the conditions of a cheap land economy developed a mode of thought that was quite distinctive.

Professor E. A. J. Johnson of Cornell has done a pioneer work in

American Economic Thought in the 17th Century.[1] He has analyzed the content of 17th Century American writings in the South as well as the North, seeking to bring out their general views. The result is interesting in several respects, but above all in showing how similar experience developed similar attitudes in Puritan Plymouth and in Cavalier Virginia. Thus, for instance, Governor Bradford of the Plymouth Colony and John Smith of Virginia are both convinced that communism, or, as we would say today, cooperative work on the land, is not as efficient as is a system in which every family cultivates its own field. And this has become a permanent note in American economic thought. Another characteristic in American economic thought in the 17th Century is the insistence on enlarging the amount of money or currency. It is curious to note the continual recurrence of this demand.

The notion that wealth is to be held in trust for good purposes (or for God's glory) is another constant note in the thinking of 17th Century New England.[2]

By and large, we can say that American colonists in the 17th Century at first accepted the mercantilist theory of economics. The Colonies were settled largely as a product of English imperial ambition. Their justification was that they were to supply raw materials to the mother country and provide a market for English manufactures. Accordingly, they were not to engage in manufacture. But this limitation was not feasible if the Colonies were to have a normal economic development. A source of irritation was thus present from the beginning. The efforts of England to discourage manufacture and commerce on any extensive scale were felt to be a serious handicap when the population of the Colonies began to grow in density. The practical experience of the Colonists thus made them reject the mercantilism of England as they became progressively conscious of the ways in which they suffered from its application.

It is a curious coincidence that the year of the American Declaration of Independence, 1776, is also the year of the publication of Adam Smith's *Wealth of Nations*. Both are significant documents of what might be considered the liberal thought of the 18th Century, technically known as the philosophy of the Enlightenment. Its fundamental categories, reason and natural human rights, represent in the economic world an attempt to abolish all privileges, such as monopolies, and restrictions on manufacture and exports.

[1] E. A. J. Johnson, *American Economic Thought in the 17th Century* (1932), pp. 93 ff.

[2] See Roger Williams, *Bloody Tenant* (1647); Cotton Mather, *Durable Riches* (1695); and *cf.* John Woodbridge, *General Relation to the Fund* (1682).

Scientific thought on economics may be said to have begun, in America as in England, substantially with Adam Smith, who argued that the wealth of nations consists principally in goods produced and exchanged freely, i.e., without government bounties, monopolies, or restrictions of any kind. The defense of freedom to manufacture and freedom to export and import was popularly expressed in the French motto, "*Laissez faire, laissez passer.*" In England this view eventually triumphed with the repeal of the Corn Laws (1846) despite the opposition of the landed aristocracy. Adam Smith was concerned with the wealth of nations, but not with that which increases the wealth of one nation at the expense of another. He thus gives little attention to robbery and conquest as ways of increasing national wealth. He devotes his attention to what happens in a peaceful commercial economy, involving relatively large-scale production for a mercantile market. He emphasizes the importance of an increasing division in labor and the advantages of free trade. His arguments, however, are consistently cast in materialistic terms. The wealth of a nation is restricted to its material goods. Favorable dispositions and moral attitudes which make for human happiness are hardly taken into account in Smith's economic theory, although they figure largely in his *Theory of Moral Sentiments*. These basic attitudes, and the limitations of outlook that attended them, formed the starting point of American economic theory.

Here, as elsewhere, Calvinism was a major source of inspiration. Our whole conception of government is the pessimistic Calvinistic one of the total corruption of all mankind and particularly of government officials; but there was, alongside this notion, a notion of the "elect." And one became a member of the elect by faith—according to the Protestant doctrine. This was a revolt against government by the Universal Church and was the religion expressive of the individualistic doctrine. Economically, the growing bourgeois class wanted to escape regulation of its industries. There was an economic demand for individualism, which was consonant with the doctrine of the "elect" or of grace, a positive contribution of Puritanism which grew from an earlier negative admonition—"Do not interfere with the business man."

The Colonies had chafed under the commercial and financial restrictions of the English colonial system—in fact, the Revolution was in large part caused by the commercial restrictions placed upon colonial trade and the financial maladjustments resulting from English mercantilism. Thus the fathers of the Revolution, when they faced the problems of a national economy, came to respect Adam Smith with the reverence due to an oracle. Absolutely free trade, however, was never adopted. Indeed,

Smith himself recognized and justified exceptions to the theory. There was need to raise revenue for the expenses of the national administration, and above all for the development of the country with roads and highways. In view of the unpopularity of domestic excises, as witness the Whiskey Rebellion, general acquiescence in a tariff only for revenue seemed to fix the keynote of our tariff policy in the early days of the Republic.

Washington and Hamilton may be said to have been the founders of the Federalist party, which stood, among other things, for the development of the commerce of the United States. In this regard there was a general agreement among all parts of the country, especially after the War of 1812, that, to keep this country independent, some protective tariff was needed to enable us to produce as much as we could of the manufactured goods that we consumed, instead of having to import such goods from England. Clay and Calhoun both supported this policy. But a rift gradually developed between the manufacturing interests, that profited by the tariff, and the agricultural interests, mainly in the South, who felt that a protective tariff only served to enrich the Northern manufacturer. The old American Whig Party, supported by the growing West, stood for the policy of developing the roads and highways of the country, which depended on the revenue derived from a tariff. But the agricultural South was jealous of the growing power of the national government controlled by the free states.

The Tariff of Abominations of 1828 marked the triumph of the combination of the commercial North and the agricultural West, a triumph which, despite the setbacks of 1846 and 1857, became more or less permanent as a result of the Civil War. The Civil War was won more by the Western states than by the industrial North. The states of Indiana, Illinois, and Iowa sent an almost unbelievable proportion of their men to the armies of General Grant. At any rate, when the Civil War was over and the South was defeated, the government of the country was controlled by this combination of the West and the North. Almost the first important result of the Republican victory of 1860 was the National Homestead Law, which provided access to the western lands to all who would work them. The building of transcontinental railways followed as a natural consequence.

Although the West continued to be predominantly agricultural, it remained wedded to the Republican Party, due partly to the memory of the war for a free, as opposed to a slave, economy, and partly to the dependence of the newer Western states on the industrial North for the financing of their local improvements and of their party organization.

This combination tended to break up when the interest of the Western farmers in cheaper currency came into sharp conflict with Northern financial interests. The Republican Party came to be predominantly one controlled by the manufacturing and commercial interests, and when the Western states showed signs of revolt, joining the solid South in the formation of the Populist Party, the greater strength of the North in population as well as financial power resulted in the decisive defeat of Bryan, the standard bearer of the South as well as of the Populist West. In this the Republicans were helped by the growing intellectual classes, which consisted in large part of people such as teachers and other civil servants who depended principally on their salaries, which, it was generally feared, free coinage of silver would serve to depreciate.

During this period the adherents of a protective tariff had their way almost completely. The protective tariff was originally invoked for America's infant industries. (Like Peter Pan, they never grew up.) This was to be temporary, but, in fact, the United States never has had free trade. The protectionists consolidated their position when they succeeded in persuading the working men of the country that they would lose their jobs unless the tariff were maintained and even strengthened. This explains the fact that the Democratic Party, which traditionally advocated free trade, or at least a "tariff for revenue only," practically capitulated on the tariff issue when it won power under Cleveland and dropped the tariff even as a campaign issue when Governor Smith ran for the presidency in 1928.

While the major cleavage has thus been mainly between the industrial North, represented by the Republican Party, and the general agricultural interests, there were other currents of influence which must not be overlooked. Thus, for example, Theodore Roosevelt swept the West by espousing a policy of land reclamation, which served the interests of Western farmers.

The Development of
Classical Economic Theory

HENRY CAREY

The intellectual revolution brought about by Bentham, the Mills, and their followers in England naturally made its impression on American thought. Especially is this true of the influence of John Stuart Mill, who has continued up to our own day to be regarded as a beacon of light to all who view themselves as liberal. In logic he stood for freedom from old traditions which could not maintain themselves by the light of common experience, and his general human sympathy, candor, and openmindedness made his economic views attractive to all those who wanted to liberate themselves from old prejudices and authorities. Mill softened the rigor of Ricardo by expressions casting doubt upon the Benthamite assumption that unrestricted competition is bound to produce a maximum of human happiness. He became the principal source of subsequent orthodox and authoritative economic thought in America. His utilitarianism fitted in with American liberalism in politics, with the motto which regards the promotion of the pursuit of happiness as one of the principal ends of government.

The American pattern of economic thought found its first systematic intellectual expression in the work of Henry C. Carey (1793-1879), who at his death was regarded abroad as the best known citizen of the United States. Carey treated the subject of economics as part of social science, or what we call today sociology. Beginning as an admirer of Adam Smith, his characteristic American optimism and his subordination of theory to practical application led him to reject the darker side of classical British economic theory as developed by Ricardo. As against the Malthusian law of population, the law of diminishing returns, the "iron law of wages," and the Ricardian law of distribution with reference to rent, wages and property—which were earning economics the name of the "dismal science" in England—Carey made the starting point of his thought the optimistic idea that a divine harmony of interest made high wages and high returns on land and capital natural concomitants to increased production. This approach found some justification in the economic development of the 86 years through which Carey lived. Like most of his contemporaries, Carey looked upon the increase of population as a blessing in an expanding economy. The value of land was viewed not as a function of scarcity but rather as something determined by the labor expended on it to clear it, to improve it, and to make it accessible, i.e., by the building of roads and other means of transportation. Value in general Carey viewed as equivalent to the social cost of the labor necessary to reproduce a given article or an equivalent satisfaction.

Increased production became the key to economic prosperity. Improved machinery, diversification of employment, education, and the elimination of misgovernment were viewed as the essential prerequisites to increased production. The only competition that the United States need fear, in Carey's view, was that of Great Britain or Holland, not of

India or Poland. After 1842 Carey became a prominent supporter of the tariff. A protective tariff, he thought, would tend to unite the South and the North, making the South less dependent on England for imports of machinery and other industrial supplies. It would also, he thought, by encouraging the industrialization of the South, lead to the peaceful elimination of slavery. Within the nation he consistently urged the importance of decentralized concentration or economic federalism, under which each region or district would have a local market.

Carey, in contrast with the contemporary British economists, stressed the importance of the farmer as the backbone of the nation. The suffering of the farmers from the low prices prevailing after the Civil War with its consequent impairment of the home market for manufactures, strengthened his emphasis on the importance of a plentiful supply of money. This, he felt, would promote the interests of both labor and capital. Towards the end of his life he joined the Greenback party, opposing paying the national debt of the Civil War in specie. He constantly opposed the export of the precious metals.

In all of his work Carey makes the principle of association (which later came to be called the principle of sociability) basic. The law of association or molecular attraction he regards as parallel to the law of gravitation. The force of local attraction to centers separated by large distances prevents the formation of too large masses.

Carey's generally optimistic outlook on economic development and his agrarian slant left a permanent impress on popular as well as academic economic thought.

DANIEL RAYMOND

Daniel Raymond (1786-1849), too, raised the standard of revolt against British economic theory, as expounded by Adam Smith, Say, Ricardo and Malthus. He held that the dissimilarity of their government to ours renders their observations unsuited to our country.

He distinguishes between private riches and national wealth. The national wealth is not confined to commodities privately owned, but includes, besides national domain, non-material factors such as the character and skill of the people and the ability of the government to stimulate enterprise and equable distribution of the national income.

Like Carey, he differs from the British economists on the tariff and on rent. In encouraging agriculture and manufacture, tariffs are held to be necessary. He refuses to accept the views of Malthus. He sees no difference between rent paid for the use of land and money paid for the use of any other commodity.

Raymond had little taste for sustained theoretic analysis. Hence he ignores the question of the nature of value and is rather hostile to paper money and banks of credit, whose workings he does not understand. But there runs throughout his work an ethical fervor (e.g. for free labor against slavery) which is a persistent trait of non-academic economics in the United States.

WILLARD PHILLIPS

Willard Phillips (1784-1873),[3] takes a dynamic view, emphasizing economic progress. He insists that capital and industry are not stationary or of fixed amount. He, too, denies the existence of "no rent" land and denies that rent arises from the necessity to cultivate inferior soil.

J. B. CLARK

John Bates Clark, professor at Columbia, and author of the *Philosophy of Wealth* (1886) and the *Distribution of Wealth* (1899), is regarded in some quarters as the one great American economist of the calibre of Smith and Mill.

Clark was influenced by ethical notions like those of Henry George; but in some respects he plays fast and loose with ethics. Thus, he assumes that ethics is irrelevant to property; but elsewhere he insists that moral ideas are relevant to economics. These ethical notions make him reject Marxian economics. He dislikes both the hard non-ethical laws of classical economics and the use to which Karl Marx put those iron laws. He recoiled from rigid Newtonian formulae, and tried to inject ethical ideas into economic theories as to the value of labor. He rejects the notion of an "iron law" of wages in favor of ethical notions that human beings can change their income, and denies that value is determined by cost of production or labor. It is more natural to suppose that value depends on utility. Clark's views in this regard are derived from hedonism; he regards utilities as quantities of pleasure rationally expressed. Clark is one of the founders of both the marginal utility theory of value and the marginal productivity theory of wages, both of which became widely accepted. Capital he regards as simply the savings of labor.

The effect of Clark's theories is to make him concentrate on the total equilibrium or harmony between production and distribution. An industrial society can under competition and in the absence of interference absorb any amount of labor and capital, so that there is no unemployment. Clark thus fails to account for the existence of unemployment in a com-

---

[3] *A Manual of Political Economy with particular reference to the Institutions, Resources, and Condition of the United States* (1828).

petitive system such as we have today. "One effect of competition is to insure to the public the utmost that the existing power of man can give in the way of efficient service."[4] The worker gets the value of his product, and natural law prevents all exploitation or spoliation. Tied in with this is the Spencerian theory of indefinite progress. "If nothing suppresses competition, progress will continue forever."[5] He believed, therefore, in private property and individual freedom in the pursuit of gain, and opposed both socialism and "trustification"; but he admitted that the government might be needed to regulate competition. In the *Philosophy of Wealth* he noted the decline of competition; in the *Distribution of Wealth* he held that competition was inextinguishable, but that it sometimes breaks down, and that the government should then regulate trade so as to preserve competition.

The method of equilibrium analysis is a natural one and represents a good functional approach. Whenever Clark finds inequality, he studies the reasons for this lack of harmony and attributes it to inefficient productivity, for, in his view, the laws of economics agree with morality. His view is one that leads to a generally static outlook, in that he assumes equilibrium or cycles which are equivalent i.e., always return to the normal when disturbed. He believes, however, in both statics and dynamics; but both are laws of a mechanical analysis, (such as the hedonistic calculus). His dynamic factors include changes of population, increase of capital, improvements of technique and machinery of production, improved organization, changes in the standards of taste, and such matters as immigration laws, taxation, tariffs, government regulation of banking, labor unions and the effect of education, travel, etc.

Clark's results can well be questioned. His conclusions leave no ground for—indeed are contrary to—facts that can be historically established. (1) increasing profits; (2) economic conflict; (3) immobility of capital and labor; (4) unemployment (his economic laws preclude widespread unemployment); and (5) the reduction or raising of real wages by social pressure.

In answer to the question. "What is the fair price in a given market?" Clark says, "The prevailing price is the only possible answer if we consider the individuals involved." But this is unsatisfactory. I want to sell my corn, and no one wants to buy it. I am willing to lose money but those who have money do not need my corn. But A is willing to invest some of his money and no more in a gamble—perhaps he can sell this corn at a profit if he buys it at 10 percent of the last announced market

---

[4] *Distribution of Wealth*, p. 77.
[5] *Essentials of Economic Theory*, p. 374.

price. What is the fair market price in this situation? The fair price should be adjusted to the several needs of society; it is such a price as will adjust the processes of production to social needs. Without the social element, there is no way of fixing an equivalent.

Clark and his followers (such as Fetter and Davenport), called marginalists, therefore do not greatly change the results of the classical school and in fact merged with the classical doctrines to form modern orthodox economics. His dryness led to a reaction against theory in favor of description or practical reform.

THE HISTORICAL SCHOOL

This reaction, taking form in the historical school, was led by a group of young men who had studied in Germany. In the last quarter of the 19th Century students generally went abroad for graduate studies, especially to Germany. There such men as Richard T. Ely, Henry C. Adams, and Edwin R. A. Seligman came under the influence of the German historical school, the so-called "socialism of the chair," led by Schmoller and Wagner. This group arose as a reaction against the Manchester school of individualism. Man, it was held, was, from the historic viewpoint, not a purely economic animal.

The historical school, both in Germany and in the United States, was not strong on theory—understandably in view of its origins as a protest against abstractions—but was interested in social legislation. Professor J. Laurence Laughlin referred to the historical school as having an exceptional development of the heart without a corresponding development of the head. Its adherents regarded the positive assistance of the state in industrial life as one of the indispensable conditions of human progress.

In this respect, the views of the historical school ran counter to the popular tendency in the United States at that time and were not popular in college and university circles. Though the members of the historical school were instrumental in the founding of the American Economic Association, its first president, Francis A. Walker (the author of the leading economics textbook at the end of the Nineteenth Century) led the reaction against the pseudo-socialism of the historical economists, which appeared to him threatening and even appalling.

VEBLEN AND MORE RECENT ECONOMISTS

The strongest objections to the classical view voiced in America were those of Thorstein Veblen. He studied philosophy but could not teach it as he was not a clergyman (a standard prerequisite in the 1880's). Later he became professor of economics at Chicago, and then at Stanford. His first book, *The Theory of the Leisure Class,* which appeared in 1899, was not on economics—it was inspired by Aristotle's conception of the gentleman. A Greek gentleman was a man with an income who did not work. That is the classical conception of the gentleman through the ages. The sculptor and the musician were not gentlemen, as they worked for money. Veblen poked fun at these "gentlemen" and their waste. He made a sharp differentiation between productivity and income. Non-producers with income he refers to as endowed spenders. In his later works (such as *The Engineers and the Price System*) he points out that profit often comes from reducing productivity, e.g., buying up patents in order to continue the use of old machinery. He draws a distinction between business and industry, between the *financier* and the *engineer* (similar to that existing in educational administration). The continued specialization of the engineer leaves control in the hands of financiers who distrust experts on subjects on which the directors are ignorant.

The point of view of Veblen was well expressed in a remark of Colonel George E. Waring, a somewhat scholarly Newport resident, who cleaned up New York streets when it was thought impossible and died in the attempt to do the same for Cuba. He was told, "Your neighbors go in for enjoyment regardless of expense." He answered, "On the contrary, they go in for expense regardless of enjoyment." This is true in a large area of American life. Our rich are not respected, as an ancient aristocracy is, for what they are—so they can enjoy their wealth only by lavish expenditure and display. There is a very strong difference between lavish expenditures in our money economy, and the lavish expenditures in a land-economy or a fixed class economy. In our money economy, all go in for money expenditure in order to get prestige. So we have increased demands for luxuries (to advertise our wealth) like cars or jewelry, and we disregard necessities for this purpose.

The pressure to buy things for which we cannot pay results in a very elaborate and fragile credit structure. Recurrent depressions have been caused in part by a production not geared properly to our real purchasing power. Classical economics cannot solve our depressions, since its champions say that labor should get only enough to stay alive, while the rest goes into capital for increased productivity.

Veblen was much interested in problems of scientific method. Thus, he asks how the classical economists prove that our system is best. The only proof they have is its existence, which is not good proof. The older physics looked for "final purposes." Now, we look for "causes" in science. Veblen associates this with Darwin, and it is true that up to

Darwin, biologists had a conception of nature as purposive, just as science before Galileo had ascribed purpose to physics. Darwin helped to eliminate teleology and brought about insistence on cause. To Darwin, evolution was a blind mechanical relation of cause and effect with no trend and no final term. Veblen insisted that economics, too, should investigate *changes* and their *causes*—not their purposes. Economics must then be an evolutionary science (though he recognizes that economic activities are teleological). In his view that causation has no plan or order, there seems to be no basis for the idea of a definite direction to economic evolution. He even identifies science with a philosophy of history or historic change. Despite his emphasis on change, his extreme mechanistic views leave scant room for human planning. What is most "characteristic of western civilization comes to a head in modern science, and finds its highest material expression in the technology of the machine industry. In these things, modern culture is creative and self-sufficient; and these being given, the rest of what may seem characteristic of western civilization follows by easy consequence."[6]

To Veblen, economics necessarily involves social institutions. His work and that of his followers, commonly known as institutional economics, is essentially sociological economics, i.e., a study of economic phenomena in their interrelation with other social factors (law, government, religion, morals, family organization, etc.) which condition economic phenomena and which are in turn modified by them. Veblen here borrows greatly from the German economists of the historical school, especially Schmoller. An example of this viewpoint applied to economic theory is Walton H. Hamilton's "A Theory of the Rate of Wages."[7] No mathematical formula is adduced, but instead a searching inquiry into the various forces involved is made. This does not enable us to predict phenomena at once but gives us points of view for further study.

Veblen's views are strongly contrasted with the hedonistic views of classical economics, as unfolded by Bentham and Ricardo. These assume that all seek pleasure and absence of pain. Under free trade we all sell what we need least and buy what we want most. We all know better than anyone else what we want. It follows, obviously, that all regulation by government is bad. This is the background of our classical system of economics and emphasizes production of goods for purposes of sale. When we sell, we get cash and buy what we want with it. And so we achieve a calculus of pleasure from these goods. Veblen abandons the hedonistic psychology for the psychology of instincts of William James

[6] *The Place of Science in Modern Civilisation* (1919), p. 2.
[7] *Quarterly Journal of Economics*, Vol. 36, No. 4, Aug. 1922, pp. 581-625.

and McDougall. It is not the calculus of pleasure but rather the instincts and habits of mankind that must be tackled. Instincts are the stable element in human nature. Concomitant with this, the "ideal situation" method of analysis must be abandoned when the ideal (of free competition) is no longer visible. There was a basic shift from a physical to a biological and psychological method of analysis.

In refuting the utilitarian view of labor as only a means to an end (pecuniary reward), Veblen assumed that men labor not only to produce certain commodities, but also because they are organisms that are essentially active. We see this in the misery of men out of work who are not lacking in the necessities of life. Of course, work is a habit, and we are miserable when we can no longer continue our habitual ways. But it is also obvious that sheer inactivity is not the ideal mode, that, on the contrary, some activity is a necessity and habit merely fixes the kind of activity to which we get accustomed.

But when you press Veblen's idea more closely, you find it difficult to see that he explains any specific development of industry or economic activity. We may pass over the Rousseauistic crude mythologic character of Veblen's idea of instinct as if it were something divorced from the social milieu or life in which men find themselves. But the specific ways in which Veblen or his followers work out the theory of instincts in industry certainly cannot be regarded as scientific. Most of Veblen's notions of scientific method are hazy, as are those of most critics of scientific method who are not scientists. His concept of scientific laws is drawn from a misunderstood Darwinism, which is really the Spencerian law of evolution. He fails to recognize the difference between Mendel and DeVries, identifying both with the theory of fixity of types. Contrary to Veblen, Darwin was not interested in the causes of variations. Veblen confuses cause and effect with teleological purposes and logical necessity.

His economics represents a point of view or attitude rather than anything worked through, an emphatic protest rather than a coherent achievement. There is little sense of what men are doing daily in the market but a vivid perception of what the drones are not doing in their clubs. Though he preaches scientific verification, little of the actualities of economic life gets into Veblen's writing.

Notwithstanding the weakness of Veblen's economic and general scientific theory, he succeeded in arousing an interest in the economic functioning of social institutions which has profoundly affected American economic thought. Veblen's satire effectively undermined the apologetic use of economic laws as a general justification for all of mankind's economic ills, and focused attention on the alternatives to the classical *laissez faire* pattern. Veblen's influence has been particularly fruitful in the work of Wesley Mitchell, Walton Hamilton, J. R. Commons, and J. M. Clark.

Wesley C. Mitchell, one of the outstanding economists of the twentieth century, a pupil of Veblen at Chicago, follows Veblen in many of his views. "The human nature which men inherit remains substantially the same over milleniums," and the changes are due mainly to the evolution of culture. He agrees with Veblen that in our economy money profits predominate; production is subordinated to profit (instead of subordinating profit to productivity and productivity to welfare). Mitchell's chief work has been in statistical economics. His principal interest has been the theory of business cycles and the forecasting of markets. In this, he has stressed the lack of effective cooperation between independent enterprises—there is no controlling director, no common end, and no common good.

Walton H. Hamilton did not leave the field of economics when he began to teach law at Yale, where he did much to break down the academic separation between law and economics. Economists, he insisted, must tackle the problem of poverty, which is a legal problem. Hamilton, however, distrusts all simple solutions of social problems. Rather he tends to look upon each industry as presenting a unique set of problems. These problems can be solved only as our legal and economic analyses reveal how the technological and human organization of an industry and its relation to financial practices determine its actual workings.

Professor J. R. Commons of Wisconsin also agrees that economics is to be studied in its actual workings in concrete cases. The categories used, he insists, should be volitional rather than mechanistic. In his *Legal Foundations of Capitalism* (1924), he stresses the effects of law on the distribution of wealth and analyzes decisions of the United States Supreme Court to see their conception of property.

J. M. Clark is especially concerned with the problem of social control. He feels that social control should extend not only over competition but also over excessive production.

All of these economists reflect Veblen's ideology in leaning away from pure economic laws and towards inductive and statistical work.

GENERAL REFLECTIONS

American economics has differed in certain characteristic ways from that of the Europeans. The American temper in economics, as well as in other fields, is social, and has little regard for privacy. We do not as a rule surround our houses with hedges. We do not even always put the blinds down before turning on the lights in the evening as is *de rigueur* in England. So our men of science want to publish their ideas as soon as they occur and before they ripen. We thus have droves of brilliant ideas which never mature and proposals for reform and even elaborate programs which are never carried out. There are also doctrinal characteristics of American economics. We in America have a more individualistic attitude, with greater stress on natural rights. Besides, our "institutionalists" have developed their monographs differently. They are liberals and eclectics rather than extremists like the Europeans, who are either out-and-out radicals or conservatives. The empirical, pragmatic view dominates in the United States.

Theoretical economics must necessarily deal with indefinitely repeatable units—processes of production (not from their physical but from their social aspects), the universal relation between purchaser and vendor, between employer and employee, etc. The subject must be simplified in order to act on it; we need, not perfect pictures, but maps and charts. Prices and index numbers wipe out the individual elements, e.g., the man who sells his house because he cannot pay his mortgage, the man who sells his produce or services, the man who sells stocks and bonds are all involved in transactions which are reduced to the common denominator of dollar value. The social differences are not only significant for the individuals involved but often determine the direction of future economic activity of the entire community.

Thus, the United States was in a period of prosperity between 1921 and 1929, if we lump together all classes and all sections of the country. The amount of production and the demand for goods was large. But analysis showed that clothing workers, farmers, and coal miners were not sharing in the prosperity. The demand for goods was thus too largely at the top for luxury goods, a demand which can be more readily reduced than the large demand for goods like food by the great masses. There was thus great danger that any financial disturbance would throw the whole order out of gear. This actually happened—for one reason because so much of what we produced went on credit to South America and Europe which we financed, so that we received paper but not anything of real value in return; and when this process ceased, we found no more market for much of our goods. We likewise stimulated installment buying which made people buy goods that they could not afford to pay for (since real wages were not rising proportionately). When the crash came, there was little to stop the deflation.

Theoretical economics must deal with the universal, but actual economic life is part of the here and now. We want to know what are the interests now of producers of America as against Great Britain or of our company as against our competitors. The contrast might be put most sharply by saying that economics does not take into account local differences to the extent that economic geography does.

Many of the limitations of classical economics are revealed in the thinking of Justice Oliver Wendell Holmes. His reputation as a liberal must be corrected by a realization of the backwardness of his economic views, which he inherited from the classical economists, and more fundamental illiberality of his race theories, which he got from his too uncritical acceptance of Malthus.

In point of fact, Holmes was an extreme conservative. He said in substance:[8] "Never mind profits and unequal distribution of wealth—they're matters of bookkeeping. What about a realistic study of what our capitalists actually consume? They consume a tiny amount. What does ownership mean? Ownership, in a competitive system, goes to the man who can anticipate the effective demands of the people. So our competitive system brings to the fore the man who knows what the people want and who can produce it at the lowest cost." This is very plausible, because if we contrast this attitude with Russian Communism we find that, in fact, man has to work definite hours, on machines, for wages, in both cases. Whether an individual of the state pays may make no difference. Who controls production? Men, again. All systems are governments of men—even when they arrogate to themselves the power to govern in the name of God.

A realistic analysis shows that any form of government is by men—even when the men are called Commissars. So the difference between the competitive system and the Communist system is not as great as it may seem. The question is, how are our *governors* picked? In our system, the governors are chosen, according to Holmes, by "survival of the fittest," for the one who can anticipate and provide for the effective demand makes good in America. Contemporary economists in America still maintain this theory—with modifications.

The classical economic theory which Holmes accepted makes three basic assumptions: (1) that the profit motive produces a maximum of productivity; (2) that maximum productivity is a proper social objective; and (3) that human energies are in fact dominated by the profit motive. No one of these assumptions can withstand rational scrutiny.

The assumption of Holmes, as of the classical economists generally, that private profit leads to maximum productivity is not in accord with

---

[8] "Law and the Court", in Holmes, *Collected Legal Papers*, pp. 291 ,293.

economic facts. Farmers are told to reduce their acreage to increase their income. Everybody has heard of fishermen who, when they make a big haul, dump a large part of their catch into the ocean, lest the news of their great success depress the price. Publishers frequently find more profit in limited editions. This is not exceptional; in general, whenever monopoly considerations enter, Holmes's general thesis fails in application, for then there may be more profit in a smaller turnover. Worse yet, there are many cases where it is more profitable to wreck an enterprise than to use it for constructive purposes. The example of Jay Gould and his fellow-pirates, as described by Charles Francis Adams "A Chapter of Erie,"[9] illustrates this. But this is by no means exceptional. The history of inventions shows how many labor-saving devices have their patents bought up and "frozen" because it is not profitable to shift to the more economical process. Then, too, profits are the reward of a genius for money-making; they go, not to the inventor, but to the financier. But the issue has deeper implications for a social philosophy. Why, we ask, have so many natural resources of the country been wasted? The answer is: Because the desire for profit does not make for economy in the long run. Water power, timber resources, and other gifts of nature have been unconscionably squandered because the desire for immediate profit will not allow private owners to husband these resources for the benefit of posterity. This is typical of a large number of cases. It is more profitable to build a large number of cheap houses, the useful life of which terminates in a short time, than it is to build substantial houses that endure.

On this matter, as others, classical economics is closely akin to natural theology. The natural order is asserted to be one of pre-established harmony. "Nature does nothing in vain." Hence the existing order is right; every man is productive and gets the equivalent of his labor. Every man is entitled to enjoy the fruit of his labor, and interference with his liberty to do so is a violation of natural rights. Hence, when anyone is rewarded by gaining money, he must have rendered service. Though machine technology has affected most sciences, old aristocratic notions of invidious merit still prevail in economics. The optimistic assumption as to the harmony of interests is strengthened by fixing attention on ideal equilibrium conditions and omitting changes. Yet the view of rewards for productivity is upset by the consideration of activities which are nonproductive (in the industrial sense) but remunerative, e.g., the activities of clergy, actors, musicians, entrepreneurs, promoters.

Society has been compelled to recognize the bankruptcy of the old

---

[9] First published in 1869 in the *North American Review;* reprinted in 1871 in volume titled *Chapters of Erie and other Essays,* with Henry Adams as co-author.

laissez-faire viewpoint. Competition and "free" contract ruin the men, women and children of a nation. Our usury laws never were abolished, though they certainly restrict the freedom of the lender to get his reward.

There is a more fundamental error that is involved in the classical position. Is material productivity always good? Obviously the answer to this question depends upon the cost of production. Now if the cost of production is measured not only in material goods but in human values, the case for material productivity becomes more than questionable. Consider, for instance, the production of phosphorus matches. Their production subjected the workers to a terrible disease popularly known as "phossy jaw." Very few people would vote for continuing the production of these matches simply because they were cheaper. The human cost was too great. This analysis can be extended indefinitely. Many things which can be produced at a saving of material cost can be obtained only with social consequences which no humane person will approve on reflection. In general, we may say that many things which can be produced economically from a material point of view are not worth producing from a broad social point of view. Indeed, there is a recurrent incompatibility between making labor more productive in material services and securing the greater interests in life, dignity and richer and nobler leisure. Increasing the number of hours and increasing efficiency by elimination of waste movements do not make for *total* productivity. Activity is not merely a means but a part of life, so that planning for consumption and the good life must take account of the physiology and morale of machine rhythm. Increased productivity must be used to increase the opportunity for more and better leisure, if we are to avoid the vicious cycle of seeking increased productivity to maintain increased consumption and then increased consumption to maintain increased productivity.

This general principle is applied by all civilized people and many others in limiting the hours of labor. For of what use is it to increase material goods if thereby the opportunities for human enjoyment are diminished and human life itself is shortened?*

Finally, in accepting the classical doctrine that, by gratifying their selfish desire for profit, our captains of industry set in motion the productive forces that increase the supply of goods consumed by the masses, there is the assumption of the motive power of individual profit. But strong as that motive undeniably is, it has many well-known limitations, which even the defenders of capitalism such as Justice Holmes fully recognize on occasion. For example, the motive to obtain social esteem

---

* Cf. "The Industrial Discipline and the Governmental Arts" in M. R. Cohen, *The Faith of a Liberal* (1946), p. 148.

by distinguished service frequently runs counter to it and exceeds it in potency. It would be interesting to inquire how much human activity is motivated by love, by religious devotion, by the desire to receive recognition or acclaim. Surely, the possession of money is most often only a means to attain other ends. Some amount of money, to be sure, is always necessary to attain our general objectives. But people continue in business, especially in America, after they have made sufficient money to live comfortably for the rest of their lives. Why do they do that? Because business itself is an activity and those who get used to it do not know what else to do. Also, where the mere possession of money is a distinction, everyone wants to be more distinguished by possessing more of it.

In general, what means anyone would choose for gaining desired profits depends upon general social conditions, in which the activities that receive social approval are, as a general rule, more likely to prevail. In certain fields, such as the church, the army, and art, non-pecuniary motives are definitely predominant. The classical theory is too hedonistic and utilitarian. It stresses enjoyment of the product rather than the process; yet process is a most important part of life.

Moreover, the motive power of individual profit may be strongest in individuals who lack the intellectual competence to overcome the technical difficulties in the way of increased production and distribution. And, conversely, individuals with great competence to solve technical problems of production and distribution may be more interested in their work than in financial rewards.

Applied Economics

SCIENTIFIC MANAGEMENT

One of the most distinctive American contributions in the field of economic thought is the idea of scientific management, of which the late Frederick Winslow Taylor is the prophet and apostle. The concept appeared as early as 1886.[10] The manager, according to Towne, must not only have familiarity with the goods produced and the process employed but also and equally have a practical knowledge of how to observe, record, analyze, and compare essential facts in relation to wages, supplies, expense accounts, and all else that enters into or affects the economy of production and the use of the finished goods. Management is an art of which the science (i.e., the cumulative wisdom) should be developed. No

---

[10] H. R. Towne, "The Engineer as an Economist," in *Transactions of the American Society of Mechanical Engineers,* Vol. VII, pp. 425-432.

record is available to the world in general, so that each enterprise has to start *de novo* and learn by its own experience without benefiting from the experience of others.

Strictly speaking, we must discriminate between two elements in Taylor's thought. The first is directed to the problem how to increase production by minimizing the number of motions necessary to produce any given result. This is a purely technical problem of what might be called applied physiology, how to make the human organism fit into the modern machinery of production. This phase of his work (which was by no means entirely original with him) has appealed to men as diverse as Justice Brandeis and Nicolai Lenin. Louis D. Brandeis, as counsel for the shippers, thought that railroads could save a good deal of money by introducing these labor-saving devices; and Lenin favored the Taylor plan because it would increase Russian productivity.

The other phase of Taylor's plan is a system of payments of bounties which will speed up production. This last, almost strictly economic, scheme is neither very distinctive of Taylor, nor has it had any marked success in practice, in view of the objections of workers to pressures for overwork, which in the end often reduce the effective life-span of the worker by increasing the number of serious accidents. The objections of labor are that scientific managers rely on their own ideas as to what is best for labor rather than find out exactly what labor wants, that efficiency of production is preferred to the standard of living of the workers; and that there is no opportunity for industrial democracy.

There is a basic divergence between the two objectives of making labor effective and making labor happy. Modern labor demands intensely hard effort, which leaves one devitalized, and intensifies the uncertainty of life by adding the uncertainty of employment. But labor is necessary to make enjoyment possible.

Scientific management is the human side of mechanization. It seeks to increase the output of material things, which increase the comforts of life, and to decrease the actual amount of labor by eliminating waste motions. It increases differences of pay and the competitive spirit. Now the advocates of speeding up production generally assume that production of goods is an end in itself, and this, I submit, may be regarded as a mania. A great deal of the scientific management in use at the present day "is similar to the situation in which a great deal of money might be spent in curing of flat foot a person who had some disease of the knee which might lead to amputation."[11]

Mere productivity is of no value unless the goods produced are worth

[11] Robert G. Valentine in Edward E. Hunt, *Scientific Management since Taylor*, p. 203.

while at the cost of production, and unless the people can buy them or consume them. Nietzsche asserts that the characteristic form of human stupidity is to become so absorbed in the means that we forget what is the end. Now, the production of commodities is often a necessary means to make life liveable. There is no doubt, however, that over-production is far from a blessing. In the depression of 1929 the fact that our industries were all geared up for the production of goods for which there was no market was, undoubtedly, a primary factor in throwing our economic machinery out of gear. Increased productivity has not caused increased consumption of goods, for it has not brought with it increased purchasing power. Overproduction causes glut, bankruptcy of the farmer, and unemployment in the city. The surplus of food cannot be used to feed the hungry. Wheat and corn are fed to cattle and even burned. Fruit is allowed to rot, and carloads of food are dumped to prevent a drop in prices. A reduction in labor's share occurs if wages are not increased or prices decreased proportionately to output; and there is no advantage to an individual employer to raise salaries or wages because only a small part of the goods he produces can be bought by his own men. (The charge that high wages would demoralize the workers was already refuted by Adam Smith; on the contrary, high wages tend to raise the workers' productivity and industry.)

Scientific management may increase the nominal wages of the more skillful and stronger workers. But if prices have not fallen, this gain is at least partly offset. (Increased output may not lower prices because of increased costs of marketing and advertising.) Further, the lower brackets of wage-earners are positively penalized by not sharing in the rise of wages and even being permanently depressed by lower wages; also their work is mechanized unduly. To be sure, it is only increased output that makes a permanent increase in real wages possible. Richard Feiss, indeed, claims that scientific management is the best preventive against cutting wages and laying off men.[12] But to be able to produce more cheaply (because of greater efficiency of labor) does not in itself prevent unemployment. Of course, with credit, a community can buy more of a cheaper product. But efficiency of labor cannot create "effective" demand (i.e., demand based on purchasing power), or overcome the inability to buy by the mass of workers.

Taylor's own idea of "solving the wages problem" is, according to a writer in sympathy with his system, that management should "so fix the rates in the first place that * * * no man could by virtue of any effort

---

[12] Hunt, *op. cit.*, p. 167.

attain to an excessive income."[13] Taylor himself said, "The lower differential rate should be fixed at a figure which will allow the workman to earn scarcely an ordinary day's pay when he falls off from his maximum pace. * * * Mr. Halsey is in error in his assumption that my system involves paying a higher price per piece than is paid under the ordinary system. On the contrary, with the differential rate the price will, in nine cases out of ten, be much lower than would be paid per piece either under the ordinary piece-work plan or on day's work."[14]

But much more significant is the fact that to speed up production beyond a certain point results in the end in a waste of our human resources. The number of men, for instance, who break down in working in certain factories is tremendously large. If we view the life-span as a whole, it is obvious that physiologically it is not economical to run the human organism at too rapid a pace. You may in five or ten years increase its productivity fifty or even one hundred percent, and yet by exhausting a man's vitality make the total production of his lifetime much smaller than if he were allowed to work at a more uniform but less rapid rate. According to Taylor's own testimony, in the Bethlehem steel works, he found only one pig-iron worker out of eight physically capable of maintaining the pace set under scientific management.[15] There is a distinction between long-term efficiency by planning industry, e.g., by avoiding unnecessary travel and freight charges, storing of material, etc., and short-term efficiency by saving the movements of the individual employee. In scientific management, the engineer, when in the employ of the capitalist, must subordinate long-term productivity to short-term productivity, for the employer has no interest in the whole life of the worker. The average period during which any workingman is employed by any one employer is limited, and it is uneconomic to think of the employee's life beyond that period. Management may prevent immediate loss through fatigue resulting from overspeeding, as in the Bethlehem plan; but, in the long run, the factory manager cares for the immediate product and not for the greater efficiency of the total life of the worker.

Increased mechanization is an advantage to men in that it saves them the trouble of thinking but a disadvantage in that it leads to atrophy, as if a man were to lie in bed a major part of the day. In the Tabor Manufacturing Company there were employed five office men against 105 shop men. After the introduction of scientific management, the ratio became

[13] Horace B. Drury, *Scientific Management*, p. 55.
[14] "A Piece-Rate System" in *Transactions of the American Society of Mechanical Engineers*, Volume XVI, pp. 873, 887.
[15] Drury, *op. cit.*, p. 79.

twenty to seventy-five.[16] "All possible brain work should be removed from the shop and centred in the planning or laying-out department."[17] Under the mechanization of men under private capitalism, "scientific management, at its best, furthers the modern tendency toward the special-ization of the workers."[18] Taylor, in his effort to take from the latter many of the activities which they were formerly obliged to perform, makes a man a machine feeder without incentive to think or experiment. The system—functional foremanship, time study, the method of pay-ment, etc.—tends to make the work mechanical and monotonous and to eliminate the skilled laborer. The worker is an animated tool in the hands of management. The study and experimentation leading to changes in the method of work are carried on by observers, and the worker only knows that he must change his motions. Further, if work becomes more mechanical, men are more readily replaceable, i.e., more readily dis-charged, like the parts of a standardized machine, and have little more to say about the conduct of the industry to which they give the larger part of their lives. Industrial democracy cannot flourish in such a con-dition.

From a philosophic point of view, it is not wise to keep on producing without knowing what advantage the articles we produce will give. There are many things which are being produced today which have questionable value for the life of civilization. The ancient ideal of a wise man is one who makes less demands on nature and more on his own self-control. But whether we accept this or not, history shows that there is a vicious cycle when we go in for increasing production and increased consumption without limit.

These and similar issues raise the general problem of the relation of material goods and their consumption to the life of civilization, and I know of no American philosopher who has considered this matter except Santayana, who harks back to the classic conception that unregulated consumption is barbaric, that indiscriminate amassing of goods is precisely what is meant by barbaric opulence, and that the Greeks were wise in their conception of pleasure and harmony in the economic as in other realms.

But while America has not produced a philosophic critique of what might be called Taylorism, it has displayed two practical objections to it, and those have come from the two parties to the process of production,

---

[16] Drury, *op. cit.*, p. 83.

[17] Taylor, "Shop Management" in *Transactions of the Amer. Soc. of Mech. Engineers*, Vol. XXIV, p. 1390.

[18] R. F. Hoxie, *Scientific Management and Labor*, pp. 123 ff.

namely, capital and labor. It is a curious fact that Taylor himself could not get along well with his employers[19] and struggled with his men.[20]

(1) One of his employers, William C. Whitney, formerly Secretary of the Navy and a man who amassed a fortune in business, told Taylor bluntly, "Fred, you don't understand the first element of business. Business exists for profit, not for the sake of indefinite production." It is the great merit of Veblen, not to have discovered this ancient truth, on which the socialist Fourier harped, but to have given this an emphasis which has made even American economists recognize it.

(2) Nor did Taylor get along well with his employees. They respected him as a man, but recognized that his system would not only wear them out individually, but be in the end destructive to labor unions. The process of over-mechanization of industry not only impoverishes the life of the workers but hinders the integration of the various laborers into effective union. This was shown very clearly before a Congressional committee and has been quite definitely explained by Robert F. Hoxie.[21] In general, Taylor's schemes are an attempt to dehumanize industry, and the limitations of the manager's knowledge of the human elements in industry have been admitted by the leaders of the Taylor Society.

SOCIAL PLANNING

One of the economic problems which has agitated the American mind in recent years is the problem of economic planning.

In our responses to this problem we have thus developed three points of view. (1) Those who wish to develop some kind of central direct government control over all the processes of production, so that goods will be produced to meet the known need of our population; (2) those who rebel against this and wish that all production should remain in the anarchic form of individual enterprise and free competition, and (3) those who draw a distinction between government ownership and government regulation, accepting the latter but opposing the former.

(1) The first school have been called Socialists or Social Democrats. Stuart Chase and George Soule have noted the breakdown of individualism and competition. Their great argument is drawn from wartime organization. During a war period, the various boards and commissions of the government actually run the country as to production, railroad service, and consumption. The result of the system of planning was to support many millions of people in a non-productive enterprise (the

---

[19] F. B. Copley, *Frederick W. Taylor*, Vol. I.
[20] H. S. Person in Hunt, *op. cit.*, p. 7.
[21] Hoxie, *op. cit. supra.*

army and the manufacture of ammunition and other means of war).

Private business, according to this school of thought, cannot plan for several reasons. Planning in the absence of government control requires unanimous consent; if one wants to stay out, others fear his competition. Business thus has no adequate power to plan. Further, private business, especially in its corporate form, cannot sacrifice the present for the distant future.

In this connection we must consider the fact that private capital cannot generally afford to withhold profits for any considerable period from its stockholders. It therefore goes through our natural resources at too rapid a rate, so that we soon find ourselves bereft of natural wealth. The profit of today may prevent the production of tomorrow. The waste of American resources is well exemplified by the destruction of our forests. Lumbering is generally done without regard to the future. Our consumption of lumber is wasteful. The destruction of forests diminishes the steady water supply and we have rivers which are sometimes torrents and at other times almost dry, thus interfering with navigation. The improper care of the forests also results in waste of soil. There is also a waste of our natural resources of coal, oil, etc. The need of profit makes it uneconomic to mine all the coal, so that a good deal is left, often in a way to make future mining impossible. Similarly, following the pay streak in ores is a wasteful method.

Larger enterprises under national control can make production and employment steadier and labor turnover less than under private capitalism. The individual employer fires or lays off employees without being responsible for what happens to them. No one is responsible for helping adjust the labor of the community to the need. The government cannot find employment if it has no direct power over industry. A community must regulate industrial relations if it wants to prevent the exploitation and starvation of labor. And how can it possibly meet its obligations to do so unless it has the power to initiate and regulate industry to that end? It is not enough to tax people or to ask them to contribute voluntarily to charity. The industries of a nation, it is urged, should be planned as a whole as they are during war time—to keep up the strength of the whole nation. Only so is it possible to keep everyone employed, and if there is a slack, reduce everyone's time equally. The community can plan various enterprises and adjust them so as to absorb surplus or unused labor. The larger the volume of an enterprise, the easier it is to make employment steady, provided good management is used to prevent unnecessary turnover.

A planned social economy can take advantage of improved machinery and increased productivity to lessen the hours of labor, and, by means of education, to make the leisure worth while. It can also reduce the effect of inequality and autocracy, which arise because of the separation of interests of the employees and the directors of industry.*

(2) The opponents of government planning urge that even if government control were more economical and more productive, the bureaucratic feature of it would abridge our liberties, and that this is too high a price to pay for the result, even though the vast majority do prefer security and are daily selling their freedom in order to secure jobs where they serve others. It is argued that government is influenced by popular passion, while business is dictated by deliberate judgment. But the passion may be generous, and the deliberate judgment of business men directed to pecuniary profit may have evil consequences.

The opponents of governmental planning generally argue that such planning is inconsistent with our constitutional form of government. Yet the fact remains that for many decades before the adoption of our Federal Constitution and our earliest state constitutions, wages, food prices, interest rates, and other incidents of the economy were normally controlled, in England and in the Colonies, by government. Not until the last decades of the nineteenth century did our judges interpret the due process clauses in the Fifth and Fourteenth Amendments as guaranteeing theoretical free competition and prohibiting social control and protection. And this interpretation of the Constitution was renounced even by conservative judges when the Depression of the 1930's demonstrated the practical consequences of governmental non-intervention in economic crises. There followed a widespread acceptance of the practical necessity of public control of wages, hours, working conditions, farm prices, transportation, and other utility charges, foreign trade, and various other aspects of our economic life. Yet the theoretical opposition to these "socialistic" developments continues to be proclaimed on all sorts of ceremonial occasions.

The chief argument of the surviving champions of "free private enterprise" is the argument from communism. Indeed, it is very doubtful that the introduction of the Soviet system of centralization would produce greater productivity here in America. We human beings are often foolish and stupid. Our essential weakness—that of making mistakes—will not be eradicated by having a central agency. Educated men are not free from error. Often, error comes from physical causes. All governments make mistakes, and the more power a government has, the worse the mistakes it may make. In our Federal Government, such mistakes are not

---

* *Cf.* "Socialism and Capitalism" in M. R. Cohen, *The Faith of a Liberal* (1946), p. 93.

so dangerous. An analysis of our capitalistic system (which is not really a system) shows its defects, but does not point to the validity of the opposite extreme. This might be worse.*

Our problems would not be solved by the elimination of profits. We would still have an important set of problems left under centralized administration, which could prevent unemployment but might bring about slavery or the absence of freedom. Freedom of thought and a critical type of mind are needed here as everywhere else.

(3) Midway between the advocates of socialist reforms and the champions of free private enterprise, are those who admit the need for government regulation of the economic life but oppose government ownership. Much of the traditional strength of this position comes from the distrust of bigness, which is so vigorously expressed in the views of Justice Louis D. Brandeis. But the nostalgic longing for a return to an economy of small units, extensive competition, and widespread opportunity throws little light on the actualities of contemporary economic life.

The obvious fact, of course, is that the increased size of our industrial enterprises is the result of such factors as modern machinery, the integration of all parts of our country into one market, and the accumulation of the savings of the many made available through banks and insurance companies to finance the bonds and preferred stock of concentrated enterprises. The hope, therefore, of a return to a Jeffersonian state of free competition among small producers is as Utopian or Quixotic as a restoration of Medieval knighthood. Nor is it really desirable. In a country in which mutual interdependence is so great, the industrial anarchy or warfare called competition is as wasteful and out of place as dueling. Surely, no one can seriously propose today that our farmers or business men extricate themselves from their sad plight by increased competition, or that our railways improve their position by breaking up into smaller and competing units.

The real difficulty with the old fashioned economic liberalism championed by Justice Brandeis is that there is really no intelligible line between government regulation and government ownership, that the concept of ownership is an obsolete one in modern society, where no one can do what the law calls "his own business." For no one can act without affecting his neighbors, and the regulation of what you may do is supreme sovereignty, of which ownership is only an incident. In peacetime, competition is modified by factory legislation, child labor and minimum wage laws, anti-trust laws, laws governing trade unions, and the regula-

---

* Cf. "Why I Am Not a Communist" in M. R. Cohen, *The Faith of a Liberal* (1946), p. 110.

tion of public utilities. In war, competition is virtually abolished. Raw materials are controlled, labor turnover reduced, rational priorities established, consumption restricted, and luxuries largely abolished.

The great liberal tradition of 1776 and 1848 which is so gloriously expressed in many of the opinions of Justice Brandeis will be strengthened, I think, if it is divorced from the antiquated and a priori economic individualism which Justice Brandeis never questioned.

Liberalism is older than modern capitalistic economics. It has its roots in the Hellenic spirit of free critical inquiry which laid the foundations of the sciences on which modern civilization rests. Only fanatical ignorance can deny the services of liberalism to all classes of people. It banished the Inquisition, persecution for heresy and witchcraft, and all kinds of cruelties which made life horrible. Even economically, while it has emphasized differences of wealth, it has brought to the meanest peasant and tenement dweller comforts which formerly monarchs could not enjoy. Why then has liberalism been steadily losing ground? Why are its characteristic institutions—representative government, toleration of religious and political differences, free thought and free discussion—so successfully attacked today from the right and from the left? The answer is to be found in the way liberals have clung to the economics of free competition, to the dogma of a pre-established harmony such that if everyone seeks individual profit the greatest good of all will be assured. This dogma was useful in destroying the older abuses of crown-granted privileges and monopolies. It satisfied, in a way, the needs of a predominantly agricultural people as in the United States during the nineteenth century. But it has led to unconscionable exploitation of men, women, and children in industry; and the opposition of liberals since Bright to needed factory legislation has alienated the laboring classes and strengthened the Tories in industrial countries like England and Germany. Thoughtful people today can no longer hope for salvation through economic warfare and anarchy. There is a general consensus that some social plan of production for the needs of a community, rather than for individual profit, is necessary if the routine of civilized life is to continue. The real question is: shall the planning be done by some irresponsible dictatorship or by democratic representatives whose acts are subject to discussion and criticism?

This is the question which we must face if we are to stop the flood of fanaticism and barbarism which has already swept over parts of the world formerly cradles of enlightenment.

This is the problem we must solve if we are to maintain the old ideals of liberal democracy, enlightenment, toleration, and respect for civil rights, in which all the benefits we have inherited from the liberal tradition and all the essential values of our American civilization are centered.

Perhaps the most significant outcome of the economic controversy that has raged for some decades now over the idea of planning against poverty and unemployment is the fact that on all sides the terms of discussion have shifted from abstract economic questions to issues of practical politics. Opposing spokesmen of labor and industry, conservatives and radicals alike, have abandoned in fact, if not always in theory, the traditional idea that government and business are separate realms of human activity. The walls that once seemed to separate property as an economic fact from sovereignty as a political fact have turned out to be misty illusions.* Today, therefore, every economic controversy demands consideration in the context of a comprehensive view of political realities.

---

*Cf. "Property and Sovereignty" in M. R. Cohen, *Law and the Social Order* (1933), p. 41.

Chapter V

POLITICAL
THOUGHT

Since the United States had its beginning as a group of English colonies, its thought in political as in other fields naturally began in the English tradition. Other European influences, however, were not lacking. The English, after all, were not the only people who supplied colonists for America. In the seventeenth and eighteenth centuries there was considerable Dutch, French, and German influence, which continued into the nineteenth century. Besides, we must not forget that the tradition of Western Europe, the foundations of which were laid in the Roman Empire, continued in the form of the classical tradition of education to influence all peoples who pretended to civilization.

American political thought has been marked by three more or less distinct periods, each of which has left its impress in the strata of contemporary politics,—periods dominated successively by the clergy, the lawyers, and the university professors.

The Religious Heritage

In the English-speaking colonies, we may distinguish three waves of religious opinion which colored political thought. The first, which may be called, in general, Calvinistic, was pre-eminent in New England, but also existed in a measure in other colonies. Its dour temperament fitted in with the conditions which encouraged hard work and left little room for play.

The second wave of religious thought that influenced our political life was the movement known as Deism, the English form of the philosophy of the Enlightenment. Its principal exponents were Locke and Tindal, the author of *Christianity as Old as the Creation*. This movement was a form of natural religion, i.e., religion without authority of supernatural revelation. It fitted in with the liberal spirit of the late eighteenth century and its commercial and cosmopolitan economy. In America, Benjamin Franklin was a typical representative of this attitude. But even before his time the commercial people of Holland developed a liberal attitude to all dissenters or people of different faiths. This attitude was well expressed in words of advice that the directors of the New Netherlands Company in Amsterdam sent to a New York governor who had been accused of persecuting Quakers. Tolerance, they said, had "always been the guide of our Magistrates in this City [Amsterdam] and the consequence has been that people have flocked from every land to this Asylum. Tread, then, in their steps and we doubt not you will be blest."[1]

Transcendentalism, the third wave of religious thought that left its mark upon our political life, was a movement in which Unitarian ministers played a leading role. Most notable was the influence of Emerson, who, although a friend of Carlyle, did not fall entirely for Carlyle's worship of German culture, which at that time was romantic and was represented principally by Schelling. Emerson himself harked back to the Cambridge Platonists (More and Cudworth). While the movements of Deism and Transcendentalism eventually served to diminish the rigor of Puritan attitudes and to strengthen the note of tolerance in our political philosophy, the early development of American political thought began with the heritage of Puritanism, which remained dominant as long as the church was the center of intellectual life in the colonies. Four fruits of this dominance command attention.

In the first place, democratic representation appeared in the church. The Geneva plan of electing ministers to represent the congregation before God was easily transferred to the political field. Every congregation chose its own ministers, instead of taking them from above with the other graces of God. The custom of each congregation choosing its own minister naturally continued in a country where, owing to free land, there were no landed barons to nominate the clergymen. As waves of settlement spread over the continent, the conditions that made for local autonomy were intensified. When the seat of government, either ecclesiastical or political, is far away and not always readily accessible, what we call home rule naturally flourishes. Political decentralization, therefore has become a tradition.

---

[1] Horatio Seymour, *Lecture on the Topography and History of New York* (1856), p. 22.

The second result of theocratic dominance was the excessive regulation of man's personal affairs. Traces of this are apparent even in our present-day legislation. In the popular mind, only Puritanism is associated with blue laws and excessive regulation of personal morals. There is no doubt that the Puritan opposition to the luxuries of the richer classes did in this country strengthen the tendency to excessive regulation of moral conduct. It is well, however, to recognize that this so-called Puritan trait characterized Cavalier or Episcopalian Virginia, Quaker Pennsylvania, Catholic Maryland, and easy-going Dutch Reform New York. To this day it seems to be a characteristic of rural society.

Here again, the conditions of American life reenforced Calvin's teaching and his practice at Geneva. Innovations in fashions and morals find free entrance in commercial and cosmopolitan cities, whose inhabitants have traveled or have had the opportunity of noting some of the world's vast diversity of moral feeling and practice. But not only has America, as a predominantly agricultural country—until recently—been extremely conservative in morals, but the conditions of village life in New England, the West and the South make it difficult for people to tolerate departures from the accepted moral code. As the rural population is still the dominant political power even in industrial states like Massachusetts, Rhode Island, New York, Pennsylvania and Illinois—the city population being partially disfranchised by political gerrymanders—our legislators and our courts are much more under the influence of the Puritan agricultural tradition than prevailing talk about capitalist rule recognizes. Such constitutional amendments as the popular election of United States senators, the income tax, woman suffrage, and prohibition are predominantly due to our farmer population, who were among the effective agents in defeating the child labor amendment. In any case, there can be no doubt that the mania for regulating the private morals of our neighbors is a tradition that finds a congenial home in the rural mind. In small communities, where friendship is less a matter of choice than of proximity, there is always an intolerance of deviations from the social norm, against which, if social pressure is insufficient, legislation is brought to bear. Villages are not as favorable to social freedom as are cities. Only the advent of the automobile and the radio has precipitated in some measure the breakdown of the Puritanic code of morals.

A third contribution of the Calvinistic philosophy to political thought is the basic idea of the depravity of government. It is a peculiar paradox that Puritanic America, so bent upon minute regulations of the individual's daily life, is also the last stronghold of the view that all government is an evil, necessary at times, but an evil nevertheless: thus, that government is best which governs least. This essentially anarchistic theory was largely conditioned by the sparsely settled communities of this country. When people are far from the seat of government they resent direction. Expressive of this attitude was the Jacksonian Revolution, i.e., the revolt of the backwoods farmers who elected their own kind to office. This theory found its sanction or justification in the Calvinistic conception of the corruption of human nature. So certain is man to sin that to give governors any powers will certainly lead to the abuse of those powers. John Marshall summed up this attitude succinctly when he said that the men of the eighteenth century believed that the mere fact of the possession of power by the government was certain to bring about its misuse. George Bernard Shaw, in his characteristic way, comments that the United States Constitution is a conspiracy against government. In this respect, it is well to remember that the Bill of Rights was put into our Federal as well as our State constitutions by Jeffersonian democrats, who had had the experience of being dominated by squirearchies which controlled the state governments, and who considered that the only safe way to prevent abuse of political authority was to limit the powers of government.

Finally, it must be recognized that the democratic temper of American political thinking owes much to the religious impress of its infancy. Whether we call it Calvinism, Puritanism, or English Non-Conformism, the Protestant doctrines of salvation by faith and the sovereignty of God,—the thesis that in the eyes of God all of us are but worms of the dust made for a democratic attitude. Opposition to bishops is only part of the hostility to intermediaries between the individual man and God. In God's vision none of our achievements can amount to much.

The Influence of the Lawyers

The intellectual center of gravity in this country shifted, in the latter part of the eighteenth century and the early nineteenth century, from theological dominance to dominance by the class of lawyers.

The lawyers in this country were not professionally trained in the universities; for that matter English lawyers were not either, due to the fact that the English universities founded in the Middle Ages were genuine universities and taught the law of mankind, namely, civil and canon law, but not the local laws of England. Hence, the Norman barons, who clung to their feudal privileges, organized the professional Inns of Court, and legal studies were largely a matter of what we should call today office training, together with professional discussions. When the colonists came to this country, they generally adopted the law of Moses as the rule of common life, but with the development of industry, trade and commerce, and dealings with England, the English common law naturally began to assert itself. From the largest of our colonial cities, Philadelphia, many lawyers went to London to receive their training in the Inns of Court, and hence the phrase "as sharp as a Philadelphia lawyer." For the most part, however, colonial and early nineteenth century lawyers relied largely on text-books of natural law. Some of our early state legislatures, indeed, passed statutes against citing English law, and Jefferson was very hostile to the innovations of Lord Mansfield, which favored the commercial interests. By and large, doctrines of natural law controlled our legal thought throughout the eighteenth and nineteenth centuries, and remnants of them still are implicit in the doctrines of constitutional law.*

The philosophy of lawyers is still that of natural rights; hence their advocacy of free competition and their strenuous opposition to government regulation of industry. For many years the conflict in industrial control has been waged between the lawyers, manufacturers, and farmers, on the one hand, and the laboring classes, on the other. Judges are ordinarily chosen from successful lawyers who are subject to business psychology. It is not therefore surprising that the American judiciary as well as the American bar should have clung so long to the old eighteenth century conception of law—especially constitutional law—as a body of absolutely fixed principles hovering over and above human affairs, and so constituted that the judge need only know these principles to deduce just decisions in all possible cases that may come before him.

The United States is perhaps the only country that looks to private lawyers to settle problems of the constitution of its government. Lawyers have framed our political theory, which accordingly abounds in fictions. There is, for instance, the fiction that the people make the law. But obviously law is made by legislatures that are frequently elected by minorities. Our government is not, therefore, strictly a democracy, but it differs from other non-democratic republics in that it does not possess permanent class distinctions. The cause of this lack is the commercial nature of our economy, which, in the absence of any monopoly of land, makes social differentiation depend upon the adroitness and talent of individuals rather than upon the tenaciousness of family groups. Freedom of passage from one class to another and a diffused adoration of the

* Cf. "Constitutional and Natural Rights in 1789 and Since" in M. R. Cohen, *The Faith of a Liberal* (1946), p. 175.

business magnate helps to explain the present status of the American labor movement.

Today we are still living on a revolutionary philosophy professed by conservatives. In Europe, people are building on traditions that antedate their revolutions, which are looked upon as accidents. The strange state of affairs in American politics, whereby it is possible for two conflicting parties to have the same philosophical basis, is an outgrowth of the fundamental lack of hereditary class distinctions in a primitive pioneer community. Divisions in American society are still based upon financial differences which are being continually upset.

As the lawyers' philosophy of natural rights is now professed by American conservatives, it is well to remember that originally it was part of a movement of general enlightenment and liberation. In general morals, eighteenth century liberalism stood for a restoration of the rights of natural man against superstitious taboos, the fear of witchcraft, and the like. In economics and in politics, it meant the removal of arbitrary restraints, of monopolies and special privileges. Previous to and during the American Revolution a theory of natural rights based upon freedom and the belief in perfectibility was the chief weapon in the battle against the Crown's excessive interference with industry and trade. In the religious realm, this liberal movement took the form of natural religion, i.e., religion based on reason independent of special revelation and ecclesiastical authority. The movement of Deism and its implicated belief in man's perfectibility (the basis of the modern theory of evolution) provided an instrument to free men from excessive regulation. Just as Deism was a protest against privilege in the realm of religion, so the doctrine of natural rights was a protest against privilege in the political as well as in the economic realm. This finds expression in our Declaration of Independence. The traditional prerogatives of the Crown, and the legal obligation to obey the laws duly enacted by Parliament, are not primary. They must justify themselves before the conscience of mankind. It is assumed, of course, that the conscience of mankind is rational and always gives the same answer, just as the moral conscience of the individual is supposed to do.

In Europe, this philosophy of the Enlightenment was overwhelmed in the period following the French Revolution by the romantic reaction against universalism, humanity, and reason, in favor of particularism, nationalism, and irrational emotion or intuition. In England this liberal wave gathered momentum at the end of the seventeenth century, partly by way of reaction against the reign of Puritanism under Oliver Cromwell, and partly as a result of increased intercourse between the court of the later Stuarts and that of France. But the material foundation for this liberal movement came from the development of British overseas commerce, financed originally from the surplus revenue of the land. The American colonies imitated English fashions of thought in the eighteenth century, just as much as their descendants did in the nineteenth. In this respect, the development of colonial commerce and the rise of a class of lawyers must have exercised a contributing influence. American political theory in the eighteenth century goes back to Dutch and French writers—Grotius, Pufendorf, and Montesquieu—just as the political theory of Puritanism had its roots in the view of continental religious reformers. The typical form of eighteenth century liberalism, however, is the doctrine of natural rights as expounded by Locke and continued by such men as Thomas Paine. (Rousseau does not seem to have been extensively known in the Colonies.)

The Bills of Rights (1785-87) in the various states were the results of this liberal movement and they are still its best monuments. The Federal Constitution was a compromise between those who favored states' rights and those who wanted a strong national government. The latter party was dominated by the propertied classes, who had lost heavily during the Revolution and were afraid of a democratic government in the hands of farmers and small tradesmen. This split has continued throughout most of our political history, the Federalists being succeeded by the Whigs, and the Whigs by the Republicans.

The theory of natural rights turned the Calvinistic doctrine of the essential depravity of the human flesh against the claims of all governments. Unfortunately, a government that cannot do much harm is also incapable of doing much good. However, the conditions of American life, especially in the more thinly settled portions of the country, made for local self-reliance and for impatience with central control by a government not always geographically accessible. It is only at the end of the nineteenth century that the great industrialists and capitalists, afraid of state intervention on behalf of the workers in industry, began to harp on the theory of natural rights and the necessary limitations of the functions of government. Government, under this view, must protect property from all attacks; it must not do anything positive to promote the welfare of the downtrodden. This union of what might be called capitalistic philosophy with the philosophy of small agricultural landowners—than whom there is no more conservative class in society—made the theory of natural rights all-powerful in America at a time when it had lost all prestige in Europe.

Underlying the Bills of Rights and the Declaration of Independence is the theory that men have certain inalienable rights, and from this it follows that no government, state or federal, has unlimited sovereignty; it has only those rights which the people grant it in order to avoid certain mischiefs which result from the state of nature. Under this theory it has been contended that there is no need to find a specific prohibition in the Constitution against certain kinds of legislation. If a law violated natural rights, it had no justification and the citizen was under no obligation to obey it. If the theory were taken literally, then judges would also have the right to disregard any law, even if written into the Constitution, as void and contrary to natural right. This, indeed, was the position of Justice Chase in one of the early cases in the Federal Supreme Court.[2] Certainly, many of the Federal judges used to lecture to juries from that point of view. Federalists like Marshall, especially after the Democratic victory in 1800, took a more cautious view. As a nationalist, Marshall believed in enlarging the power of the Federal Government, and as an anti-democrat, he wished to restrain the states from exercising certain rights over private corporations; but he tried to achieve these results by finding skilful interpretations of the Constitution, that is, finding meanings in it which had never been thought of by those who drew it up, or by the people who adopted it. Throughout the early part of the nineteenth century we meet with occasional claims on the part of judges to set aside various statutes as void for being contrary to the principles of natural right or the spirit of free republican government. But in the main, the method of Marshall,—what has been called loose interpretation, —has prevailed. This has especially been the case since the work of Thomas Cooley, who, in his book on *Constitutional Limitations*, skilfully discovered implied limitations on the power of the states even apart from the Fourteenth Amendment, which as construed by his brethren on the bench, has been characterized by Justice Holmes as a free license to judges to throw out any state act which does not appeal to them as the right kind of law.

Thus, while we continue to profess the democratic doctrine that our law is the will of the people, we also have the strictly legal doctrine that law is the expression of eternal principles, or at any rate, of principles of common law discovered by our Anglo-Saxon ancestors in the German forests, so that he would be a bold man who should set his individual opinion against the principles that allegedly have prevailed throughout these ages.

The notion that the Constitution represents only the will of the

---

[2] *Calder* v. *Bull*, 3 Dall. 386 (1798). And see *Vanhorne's Lessee* v. *Dorrance*, 2 Dall. 304 (1795).

people is in the first place false in fact, since constitutional law is actually made by the courts. In the second place, it is inconsistent with the theory of the American legal writers who reject the right of a majority to make the law in accordance with their will. Law is not the will of the people, but the regime of legal rights; and the majority does not, as such, have inherent rights—as the judges decided in Dorr's case.[3] On the other hand, a minority opinion is enforceable if embodied in legal form.

The confusion between these two theories of supreme law—first, that it is the will of the people, and second, that it is the expression of eternal reason—has been strengthened in this country by the vogue of Blackstone's *Commentaries*. Blackstone, like a good many facile writers, was not a clear and precise thinker. He had before him two views of the nature of law: Coke had said that law was reason; Hobbes that Coke's decisions were law, not because Coke had more reason than any one else, but only because the King had made him a judge, and the power of the King rested upon the force of the Great Leviathan or the community. Thus, in law "when nothing else turns up clubs are trumps." Blackstone gently combined these opposing views and made law a command,— commanding, however, what was right. As to the possibility of the law commanding something which is not right, nothing was said.

The real nature of American government has been obscured by the dogma of the separation of powers, and the even more ancient dogma that judges do not make the law, but only declare what has been the law. It would take us far afield to explain the error of the latter doctrine, both logically and historically. But the point is brought out concretely in the famous case of *Marbury v. Madison*, which was long supposed to have proved beyond any rational doubt the right of judges to set aside statutes as unconstitutional. Marshall's opinion rests upon the argument that judges are sworn to obey the law and must rely on their conscience in declaring it. But the President and Congress are also sworn to enforce the law. So the argument amounts to a question-begging assumption that only judges are competent to declare law. The real fact is that if the executive and the legislative organs, which theoretically are independent, were to exercise such independence, we would not have unitary government, and so the custom has arisen in the case of conflict to defer to the judgment of the courts.

The philosophy of natural rights did not die at the end of the nineteenth century, but continues to play a prominent role in our present-day

---

[3] See *Luther v. Borden*, 7 How. 1, 12 L. ed. 581 (1849), and especially the argument of Daniel Webster as counsel (17 How. 29-33; 12 L. ed. 593-595) in opposing the validity of a popular gubernatorial election not authorized by the Charter of Rhode Island.

political thought. No other conceptions of political theory arose to challenge it until the arrival of the theories derived from German models by the university professors.

The doctrine of natural rights has had so much scorn heaped upon it by professors of history and political science in recent decades, that the American educated public has lost all perspective, not only of the great amount of truth in it, but also of the tremendous amount of influence which it has exercised in the development of American law and popular political theory. The great argument, which in the minds of most of our teachers of political science seems to have eliminated the doctrine of natural rights completely, is the altogether gratuitous charge that the doctrine was unhistorical,—that it assumed an original state of nature and a social contract for which history showed no justification. In answer to these points it must be noted, in the first place, that none of the authors who most influenced American political theory—Grotius, Rutherford, Vattel, or Burlamaqui—consider the state of nature to be something in the remote past. The state of nature is the state in which individuals are not governed by positive law, and the state in which nations still exist relative to each other. Natural law, then, is simply social ethics, and the arguments as to its content (except for a few references in Locke) do not rest upon history.

The second point to note is that American experience does to some extent illustrate historic occasions of the social contract. It was by a social compact that the Pilgrims established Plymouth Colony, and it was by a social compact of some sort that the thirteen colonies voluntarily united to form the United States.

The main point to note, however, is that the theory of natural rights was the form which liberalism, or if you like, humanism, took in Europe in the latter part of the seventeenth century and throughout the eighteenth century against the Jesuit contention that the Catholic monarchs had no obligations to heretical princes—not even obligations to keep their word. Grotius, following the Spanish theological jurist Victoria, developed the theory that the obligation of contract,—of keeping one's promise,—which is the essence of commercial life, would remain even if we did not know God's law. But in the main, the appeal to reason or nature is simply the effort of liberal thought to examine all traditional institutions; to bring them before the bar of reason to justify themselves.

The Declaration of Independence formulated the essence of the old-fashioned liberalism and its conception that government derives its just powers from the consent of the governed. No nation therefore had a right to govern any other people without the consent of the latter. This was in line with the traditional liberal conception which dates back to the Greeks. Indeed, many of the phrases of the Declaration of Independence are derived from the speeches of Isocrates. The Greeks were a very loosely federated group of city-states, each jealously guarding its own liberties; and these they tried to maintain until overpowered by the brute force of Macedon and Rome, which they might have successfully resisted if they had united. But to have united would have meant to them the wilful abandonment of the life which they desired. They preferred to go down struggling for what they wanted rather than take a chance in a struggle for what they did not want. They did not want an empire. They wanted a democracy in which all freemen took part. Hence the city-state was maintained and attempts at confederation failed.

The liberal conception of government held by the Greeks is the basis of the Declaration of Independence. It is the city-state wherein all have a voice in a government which exists by consent of the governed. The American conception continues the classical tradition represented by the civic virtue of Plutarch. This Greek ideal then remained as the beacon of liberty and something of the vitality of this tradition can be seen in Machiavelli's *Discourses on Livy*. In the eighteenth century this was the ideal professed by every enlightened thinker, and it found its extreme expression in Kant's *Essay on Perpetual Peace*, in which he pointed out that the object of government is to assure moral freedom. With freedom necessarily arise limitations fixed by laws. Therefore, the whole world must become a federation of republics to get rid of wars.

The nature of the constitutional solutions found in the creation of the Republic both exemplified contemporaneous political philosophy and set the framework for further political and legal theorizing. One of the touchiest problems before the Constitutional Convention involved the political concept of sovereignty. Vigorous forces contended for a strong central government; equally powerful groups insisted upon decentralized sovereignty. The solution was a reconciliation of these sovereignties in federalism.

The characteristic American approach inherent in this compromise was the principle of checks and balances. Much has been written of the application of this principle to the relations of the various organs of Federal government to each other. In the long run, however, the most important application of this principle is to be found in the double sovereignty that results from dividing authority between the states and the central government.

The United States was created as a federated republic, a group of individual states, each with two ambassadors in the Senate—in line with the classical tradition. It was not a nation but a federal republic. It boasted of the fact that it had no subjects, just as it had no monarchs. The territories were admitted into the partnership as equals. This federal concept extended to religion. European countries, for political reasons, each had to have a strong national church, which, however, did not prevent those that controlled the church from being Catholic atheists. But the numerous churches in this country gave no hope of dominance for any one and the states allowed all churches.

Federalism is more than a political or legal philosophy. It is one of the basic elements of American liberalism. The United States is the only great power that has flourished under a federal system of government, and this has been profoundly reflected in our whole life. As a free federation we have never worshipped the monarchic uniformity which is jealous of all diversity. Instead our political philosophy has sought a unity which encourages the free development of the component states, and has emphasized the value of local autonomy and self-expression.

The theory of the limited powers of the central government is inconsistent with the sentiment of nationalism. Alexander Hamilton seems to have perceived this and to have organized the Federalist Party to make the national government workable. In this he was powerfully aided by John Marshall, who used his office as Chief Justice of the United States to give the Constitution a liberal interpretation in the way of making necessary national enterprises possible. Circumstances fought on the side of the Federalists. Thomas Jefferson, the apostle of anti-nationalism and state's rights, thought at one time that a revolution would be necessary every generation. But the ease with which his party gained control of the Federal Government dispelled that notion, and, despite his leaning toward state's rights, conditions forced him into an extreme nationalistic policy, as in the purchase of Louisiana and the Embargo policy. The Whig Party, however, could not make much headway against the Democratic Party as reorganized by Andrew Jackson—a party that stood for the removal of all the remaining political privileges and that also ministered to the pride of the Southern states.

The problem of striking a generally acceptable balance in the equilibrium of forces set up by our federalism presented a persistent challenge to American political thinking. Popular political controversy focused on the doctrine of state's rights even before slavery became the specific issue upon which that doctrine was first tested.

The greatest political thinker of the first half of the nineteenth century was probably John Calhoun. Calhoun had the misfortune of fighting on the side that was ultimately defeated in the Civil War. But the superior force of arms of the more populous and industrially more developed North cannot take away the intellectual force of Calhoun's arguments. Calhoun assailed the eighteenth century liberal doctrine that all men are born free and equal, arguing that no men are free when they are born, and that there is no sense in calling them naturally equal. Calhoun was also emphatically clear when he indicated that the Federal Constitution was a compact between sovereign states that never completely abandoned their sovereignty. The outcome of the Civil War, however, put a quietus on such arguments.

The Republican Party continued the tradition of the Federalists and the Whigs. One of its first tasks when it obtained power was to plan for a transcontinental railroad to unite the far West with the East. The nationalism of the Republican Party, however, has been tempered by the fact that it has been largely controlled by the New England industrialists and the descendants of New Englanders who populated western states like Kansas, Nebraska and Iowa. This political union between New England industrialists and western farmers has been intensified by the effects of the Civil War and the reconstruction of the South, which until recently forced the Southern states into a sort of permanent opposition. The Democratic Party is thus largely sectional and this tends to make the Republican Party sectional as well. Nevertheless, populism, insurgency, and progressivism occasionally appear within the Republican Party, especially in the West.

To a certain extent, political differences on the issue of federalism have been reflected in the field of international policy.

In foreign relations the great enemy of liberalism has been nationalism (with imperialism as its concomitant). Nationalism is a modern concept. Tribalism did not conceive of the sovereign state with its organized machinery and territorial limits. In medieval times there existed a conception of divided sovereignty. There were two rulers—one temporal, the other spiritual. The Reformation brought, or coincided with, a rise in the power of the temporal ruler, and with that came nationalism. The King of the English People gave way to the King of England. Nationalism was a concomitant of a growing commerce and a response to the need for liberation from the oppression of the guilds and other local tyrants.

Jefferson's party called for sympathy with the liberalism of the French Revolution and this became a part of the Democratic tradition. However, the Federalist party of Washington and Hamilton did not share this sympathy. They maintained that since the country was young its commerce should be developed, and that it would be safer not to become involved in foreign affairs. America for Americans—the keynote of Washington's farewell address—remained the Magna Carta of our foreign policy to the end of the nineteenth century. This was not only the maxim of prudence but also the expression of the feeling of the American people. They had washed their hands of the great mess of dynastic wars. Of course, we were on the verge of war with France in 1798 and did go to war with England in 1812. But these were, in the main, expressions of resentment at insults and injustices. The war with Mexico was indeed as brazen a bit of imperialism as can be found in the history of any nation and it was so characterized by the conscience of New England. It was denounced by Lowell (in his *Biglow Papers*) and other liberals of New England. Yet these acts did not involve imperialism in the sense that our government was imposed upon an unwilling people. There were relatively few foreign people in the territories we acquired and soon there was a large American population. The territories acquired by purchase—Louisiana, Florida, and Alaska—were all obtained from foreign powers which in accordance with the Monroe Doctrine we regarded as dangerous to the American people. In brief, splendid isolation, freedom from entanglements with European nations, was the dominant ideal to the end of the nineteenth century and was an integral part of the American ethos. It was a policy which appealed to the ordinary American. The feeling was that we were trying an experiment in which there were to be no subject peoples, but government was to derive its powers from the consent of the governed. Every territory was sooner or later to be admitted as a sovereign state into full partnership in the Union.

Imperialistic nationalism for the United States is a comparatively recent phenomenon and has always met with opposition. When Harrison sent to the Senate a treaty for the annexation of the Hawaiian Islands, one of the first acts of his successor, Cleveland, was to void the treaty on the ground that it had been improperly negotiated. And when as a result of the Spanish-American War the United States did annex these islands along with other territories, there was considerable opposition, organized in the Anti-Imperialist League, which felt that America was deserting its old moorings. William James was one of the first thinkers to realize the full significance of this for the liberal temper of America.

America after the First World War was still unprepared for the full abandonment of its traditional policy, as was shown by its refusal to join the League of Nations and the World Court. Opposition as voiced by Borah and Johnson was traditional Americanism. Not being acquainted with Europe, as are the Atlantic seaboard intellectuals and cosmopolitans, the majority of the American people felt that we had to let Europe fry in its own fat.

Under the weight of the failure to join the League and the Court and because of the inadequacy of its philosophy, the traditional American form of liberalism broke down. The philosophy of national isolation is an impossible ideal, for if we wish to grow in material and cultural resources, we must have commerce with other nations, and this involves in essence the European game. The problem of liberalism in international relations is not to be solved by fear of entanglements, but by the much more difficult enterprise of adjusting international relations in some rational manner. The notion of isolation, sovereignty, no meddling, must go by the board when men are so closely interrelated by modern communication and thought. There is still the issue of Greece vs. Rome, isolation vs. interdependence. We still need something of the vision of Rome, of Kant, and of Tennyson. With James we must adopt the European attitude of collaboration among liberals and seek schemes for world cooperation.

The Role of the Professors

Thus far we have considered the general thoughts about the political outlook current among the great mass of the American people. What about learned or philosophic reflection in politics? One would suppose that a country having such a rich and unique political experience would generate a distinctive political philosophy. This, however, is not the case.

It is significant that substantially the only early synoptic views of the American political scene were written by foreigners, the Frenchman De Tocqueville's *Democracy in America* (1835) and the Englishman James Bryce's *The American Commonwealth* (1888). In general, American political thought has not been related to any broad philosophic vision but has rather tended to concentrate on specific institutions (such as slavery or revolution) or particular subjects of immediate controversy (such as tariffs or foreign affairs).

Legal political theory down to very recently was insular, uninfluenced by the current of European thought or experience, and on the whole uncontested in this country, because up to the end of the nineteenth century we had no real universities where law and politics could be studied as sciences. Our first genuine university, Johns Hopkins, when it was established in 1876, had only one professor of history and politics.

Moreover, the teaching in the universities which bore upon political theory was largely in the hands of the professors of philosophy, who, with very few exceptions, were dominated by Scotch intuitional or common-sense philosophy. This philosophy sanctioned all the traditional opinions as fundamental intuitions of the mind, which could not be questioned without risk of losing the claim to rationality as well as orthodoxy. Until very recently we could find many judges displaying the influence of this Scotch philosophy in judicial opinions that declare, "We need no elaborate arguments, since common sense or the recognition of fundamental principles shows beyond doubt" something—which is generally a proposition that a great many people question.

The rapid development of our educational system with the rise of American universities and the great need for teachers, technically trained, made a number of our young men go to Germany to study political science. These young men came back and developed the teaching of political science in this country. They brought back with them the German worship of the state. Especially after Bismarck, this led to a glorification of governmental efficiency, and an antagonism to the American theory of necessary restraints on government as a protection for natural rights. For this and for other reasons they have had very little contact with the general political thought of this country. Under the circumstances it was natural for these men to conceive of the American political system in terms of continental theories. Thus, the concept of sovereignty, which Austin had brought into Anglo-American legal theory, was developed by Burgess who in the last decade of the nineteenth and the first decade of the twentieth century trained most of our leaders of political science.

The United States presented a peculiar and interesting field of study for political science, in that it partook simultaneously of the nature of monarchy, aristocracy, and democracy. The country is monarchical in the literal sense that more power is concentrated in the president than in any of the present-day European kings. It is at the same time an aristocracy of the robe,—the Supreme Court wields more power than any similar body in Europe. Yet it is a democracy in the sense that almost all its citizens are able to participate in the determination of fundamental policies through popular elections.

There is no necessary connection between elective and representative government, but in spite of its monarchic and aristocratic tendencies, the government of this country is to a large degree representative. The Supreme Court, for instance, although not elected, may reflect the opinions of the public. A majority of the representatives in our govern-

ment are lawyers, who have not in all cases broken their connections
with their clients.

Separation of powers is looked upon as a prime characteristic of this
government. This is due largely to the theories of Montesquieu, derived
from erroneous observation of the political structure of England. Actually, of course, a government consisting of three separate powers would
get no farther than a span of three horses without a driver. Unity in our
government is achieved by means of the extra-legal party system. The
President is responsible to the same constituency as Congress, and generally belongs to the party with a majority in that body.

Against this background Professor Burgess developed the Hegelian
or classical Aristotelian doctrine of the sovereignty of the state. By an
elaborate intellectual machinery the state is distinguished from the
government, which must be subject to enlightened limitations as under the
traditional political theory of the lawyers and businessmen. The German
political scientists devoted much of their attention to the origin of state
sovereignty and to its theoretical justification, frequently confusing the
two issues. American teachers, like Lowell, leaned very strongly towards
the historical method in political science. Explaining origins and thereby
justifying existent institutions is a much safer course for teachers to
pursue than criticism or independent judgment as to the most desirable
forms or policies of government.

Lowell, however, provided us with a realistic criticism of the German
theory of sovereignty. According to him sovereignty is not absolute, as
lawyers frequently claim, without noting the implications of their claim,
but rather correlative with actual obedience. The grounds of obedience
are deep in human nature. It is easier to obey than to think independently.
American thinkers have had experience with this limited and un-unified
sovereignty. The most obvious example of this is the power of the
Supreme Court to declare unconstitutional a law passed by Congress and
approved by the President.

Laski and some of his American followers have developed the theory
of multiple sovereignty, without, however, adequately considering the
experience of the guild system of medieval times with its incessant civil
strife.*

The hallowed traditions surrounding the constitutional tri-partite
separation of powers have had little if any influence upon the actual
development of our governmental institutions. At least since the 1880's,

---

* A more detailed criticism of Laski's pluralism is contained in the essay "On
Three Political Scientists" in M. R. Cohen, *Law and the Social Order* (1933) at
pp. 323-326.

the increasing complexity of our industrial economy has brought forth a series of administrative agencies, in which executive, legislative, and judicial functions have been inextricably intertwined. Not even the appointment of a conservative constitutional lawyer, Thomas M. Cooley, as first chairman of the Interstate Commerce Commission could make these administrative agencies operate in accordance with the American political axiom of the separation of powers. Instead, while lip service is still paid to the traditional doctrine, the works of such law teachers as Frank J. Goodnow, Ernst Freund, and Felix Frankfurter have helped to provide a consistent rationale for the newer developments in administrative law.

One of the characteristic contributions of the professors in the field of American political philosophy is the systematic study of specific aspects of our political tradition and patterns. An example of this is the analysis of political parties and pressure groups.

Contrary to the English tradition, our Constitution makes no provision for political parties. In fact, Washington and Madison warned their countrymen against such "factions" and did not consider political parties to be necessary for the democratic system. Nevertheless, such parties developed early. To some extent parties provided a means of taking sides in the great controversies over political philosophy which divided Hamilton and his Federalists from Jefferson and his Anti-Federalists. But what was even more important to the functioning of our federal system was the role of party organization in achieving political responsibility by cutting across the separation of powers.

The universities have given extensive study to the part political parties have played in the American democracy. Such consideration has involved not only the practical involvement of parties as a bridge between the electorate and the government, or as a unifying force between the legislative and executive branches or between the central government and the states, but also the role of parties in the formulation of political policies and goals.

Dominant today in this country are two theories as to the function of government which, while not logically incompatible with each other, point in different directions. One is the *laissez faire* theory; the other, the theory of democracy. Locke, Bentham, Mill, and Jefferson were the exponents of the theory that that government is best which governs least. This doctrine eventually came to be used mainly to justify the opposition to legislation favorable to labor. The right of the employer to hire men and the right of workers to accept starvation wages must not be curtailed.

The *laissez faire* arguments that had been used by John Bright and other British manufacturers against factory legislation in the first half of the nineteenth century continued to dominate American thinking long after they had ceased to convince in England. In fact, it was not until the 1930's that these arguments ceased to control our economic life as a result of the yielding of the Supreme Court to the pressure of public opinion. Yet there remains a solid element of value in the approach of Locke and Jefferson to the problem of the proper scope of government. A wise government will not attempt to do too much. Law enforcement depends upon machinery which in turn depends upon people. If the people object the machinery ceases to work, and as a result the power behind the law is not effective.

The popular theory of democracy makes the will of the majority supreme, irrespective of natural or theoretical limits upon governmental authority. The notion of democracy is so deeply ingrained in the national culture that a large literature has grown up about it. Writers like Herbert Croly and Walter Weyl have tried to grapple with the problems of progressive democracy. Despite, however, the widespread feeling that the word "democracy" covers a good deal of loose talk and intellectual "bunk," this country has not yet produced a thorough criticism of the fundamental assumptions of the democratic theory comparable to the work of the Italian Pareto or the German Michels. If the contention of the latter be sound, all governments—even the government of the Socialist Party,—must be by experts and therefore necessarily oligarchic.*

Perhaps the most trenchant criticism of democracy formulated on this side of the Atlantic is that of Santayana, for whom the life of the spirit is the ideal, in subservience to which social life must be regulated. For Santayana, an aristocracy of the spirit must not be oppressed by the mob. This is a challenge to the conventional American political theory which the theory is sooner or later bound to meet. Already many have arisen to disparage faith in democracy on the ground that the majority of the people are ignorant, and that if the unenlightened rule corruption must ensue.

There are several defenses open against this charge. In the first place, while people may be ignorant it is possible for them to choose wise rulers, just as people may select physicians wiser than themselves to treat their physical ills. In the second place, the average person without detailed knowledge necessary to construct government policies may nevertheless

---

* *Cf.* "Democracy Inspected" in M. R. Cohen, *The Faith of a Liberal* (1946), p. 155.

be competent to pass judgments of right and wrong upon policies presented to him. In the third place, people know their own interests and are best able to guard them.

Beyond these specific answers to specific criticisms of the theory of political democracy there remains the perennial American faith in the heroic potentialities of ordinary mortals. In the philosophies of James and Dewey this faith achieves new philosophic dimensions.

To John Dewey democracy is less a political philosophy than a way of life and a release of vast human powers that are suppressed by all restraints on free inquiry. He is fundamentally opposed to class distinctions because of the consequent exclusion from others' experiences. In this he formulates the American valuation of sociability, cooperation and the dignity of labor, to the disparagement of privacy, aristocracy, and caste. But to do justice to this democratic philosophy of life, it is necessary to go beyond the limits of political theorizing and to consider more broadly the problems of legal philosophy and moral philosophy with which American thought has wrestled.

Chapter VI

LEGAL
THOUGHT

THOUGH AMERICAN EXPERIENCE in lawmaking (and lawbreaking) has been extraordinarily rich in novelty and diversity, our contributions to legal philosophy have been impressive neither in quality nor in quantity. Wealth of practical experience does not always bring about great achievements in the field of thought. Still, if we take the term philosophy of law not in its technical but in its wider sense, as general reflection on the nature of legal institutions, it has not been completely absent here, though it came near its nadir in the nineteenth century. Such reflection was in fact provoked by the Revolution, and later stimulated by controversies on the nature of the Constitution in its relation to the states and the Union. Also, as a nation we have had an unprecedentedly large diversity not only in the legislation of the different states, but as well in the interpretations of the "common law"; and in a few states elements of the (Roman) civil law have entered. The problem of codifying the enormous and growing mass of this judge-made law aroused a good deal of discussion in the middle of the nineteenth century, and the topic is now revived in the attempt by the American Law Institute at a Restatement of the Law. In recent times, prohibition has provided a new and emphatic illustration of the difference between law that is formally enacted and law that is actually enforced, and has brought back the issue of natural rights as limits not only of legislative power but also of the people's right to amend the Constitution. Indeed, since Theodore Roosevelt, in his message to Congress in 1908, stated bluntly that our unsatisfactory judicial decisions have resulted from the antiquated philosophy held by our judges, leaders of the American bar have entered on a campaign of "education" to convince the people of the theory that the decisions of the courts are completely predetermined by the law and that judges have nothing to do with making or changing it. Though the agitation for the recall of judges or judicial decisions subsided after triumphing in a few states, we still have wide dissatisfaction with the power of our courts to declare legislation unconstitutional. Granting, therefore, that we do not have many works expressly devoted to juristic philosophy, we may still trace the history of the general ideas about the nature of law which have dominated American thought.

The Classic Tradition

A follower of Auguste Comte could probably find no better illustration of his law of the three stages than the development of legal thought in America. The latter, he might contend, began in Puritan theology, passed on through the eighteenth-century metaphysical stage of natural rights, and is now entering upon the positive stage of realistic jurisprudence. Like other sweeping generalizations, this is more suggestive for purposes of analysis than accurate as a historic description. While a theocracy did prevail in Massachusetts up to the end of the seventeenth century, this can hardly be said to have been the case in Virginia, New York, and other Colonies. It is tempting to trace our traditional distrust of legislatures and of human nature in public office to the Calvinistic belief in the total depravity of the human flesh. But the most extreme proponents of this political pessimism are also most optimistic concerning the outcome of human nature in the "free" economic arena.

In any case, it is true that as soon as the Colonies developed extensive commercial relations, lawyers began to take the leading role in formulating our political and legal ideas, and, naturally, they followed the English tradition current in their day. In the period following the Revolution, the intellectual leaders of the bar, men like James Wilson, John Adams, and James Madison, were also acquainted directly or indirectly with such Continental writers on law as Grotius, Pufendorf, Montesquieu, Mably, Vattel, Bynkershoek, Beccaria, Domat, and Pothier. But the main body of our legal thought took its departure from Blackstone. From the beginning his *Commentaries on the Laws of England* found a remarkably wide public in this country. It was reprinted here five years before the Declaration of Independence, and, up to the end of the nineteenth century, it was the *pièce de résistance* of whatever legal education most lawyers received before admission to the bar. Many, in fact, received little more, except acquaintance with the management of a legal office. Though the influence of Maine and historical jurisprudence cannot be ignored, the fact remains that the Blackstonian view of law—the confused compromise or conglomeration of law as eternal reason and law as the will of the supreme power in the State—still prevails. Blackstone with characteristic complacency juxtaposed the two elements without bothering to try to indicate how the rational and imperative elements could be combined, how the absolute supremacy of Parliament could be compatible with absolute natural (individual) rights. Substitute the will of the people for the absolute power of Parliament and you have the essence of the prevalent American view.

The view of law as dictated by eternal reason took, in the seventeenth and eighteenth centuries, the form of a doctrine of natural rights. The idea of a paramount law of nature goes back to antiquity, and has had a continuous history from the days of Aristotle, the Stoics, Cicero, the Roman jurists, and the scholastic philosophers, to our own day. The Stoics used it to mitigate the rigor of laws such as those of slavery, and medieval theologians used it against the kings and emperors who tried to interfere with the established privileges of the Church. What was novel in the modern form of it was the individualistic or contractualistic emphasis, used in the interest of free commercial enterprise, against the established privileges of kings and feudal barons, lords temporal and spiritual. It was, therefore, an especially fitting and attractive doctrine for a country characterized by a (predominantly) free-land economy where the spirit of individual adventure in exploiting the natural resources of a vast continent seemed to yield the best visible results. After the French Revolution, Europe experienced a reaction against this philosophy. This reaction came at first from the old aristocracy (Burke, De Maistre, etc.) and from the rising spirit of nationalism, and was soon reinforced by the clear revelation of the utter degradation of the lives of men, women, and children through free competition's becoming a free exploitation of the economically weaker members of society. This recognition of the evils of "free" or unregulated industrialism and commercialism came very much later in this country, partly because up to the end of the nineteenth century we remained predominantly an agricultural people, and partly because the heavy work in our industries was largely taken over by immigrant and foreign laborers. The individualistic *laissez faire* philosophy, therefore, remained regnant in this country for a longer period than anywhere else.

Another feature that tended to strengthen the conception of law as resting upon eternal natural rights was, paradoxically enough, the fluid character of our law in the face of changing conditions of life. The English common law which the colonists brought with them never fitted

American conditions completely. Almost from the beginning, therefore, American courts had to exercise discretion in discarding some of it. In this fluid state of the law, courts necessarily appealed to principles of justice or of ultimate social policy, *i.e.*, to the principles that ought to prevail in the law. And that is, after all, the essence of the traditional doctrine of natural rights. Now, in the old rationalistic philosophy and in the Scotch intuitionalism, which prevailed in America almost to the end of the nineteenth century, the principles of political ethics and justice were regarded like the principles of Euclidean geometry or Newtonian mechanics—simple, self-evident, and forever unchanging. For this reason, men as different as Locke and Napoleon could believe it to be a very simple task to formulate a code of laws according to nature which would need no change and no commentary. Such a view was applied to the Constitution alike by Federalists and Democrat-Republicans, though the two parties naturally drew different implications from this assumption. The Jeffersonians wanted to limit not only the power of the national government by bills of rights but also the power of the state governments over the rural population; for experience had shown that the people, *e.g.*, of central and western Virginia, could not hope to get fair treatment from the eastern squirearchy that controlled the state government. So long as this country remained predominantly agricultural and rather thinly settled, with large distances from the state capitols, the Jeffersonian philosophy conformed to a social reality which no dissatisfaction with eighteenth-century ideology can well ignore. On the other hand, the Federalists (and Whigs and Republicans after them), while more realistic in stretching the Constitution for nationalistic purposes, held to the classical conception of the Constitution as a fixed code in order to block popular legislation inimical to the interests of the propertied classes. It thus came to pass that the two major parts of our population clung to the view of the Constitution as expressive of eternal unchanging principles of public morality.

On the other hand, the tradition of the Declaration of Independence and our Revolution, with the background of the English struggle against the Stuart kings and of the Colonial struggle against the royal governors, strengthened the democratic tendency to regard law as naught but the will of the people, and this democratic faith was strengthened through the overthrow of the old squirearchy by the farmers of the western border and of the newer states, who were not tenants but freely owned their own land. Anti-aristocratic feelings were strengthened also by the continual arrival of immigrants who had fought for liberal ideals in Europe.

The foundation and most of the superstructure of the classical American attempt to harmonize eternal natural rights and the will of the people can be found in the lectures on law delivered by James Wilson in 1790-1791. In trying to combine democratic ideas of liberty and equality with the idea of restraints on popular will by a system of checks and balances, Wilson had, indeed, been preceded by John Adams's *Thoughts on Government*, published in the very year of the Declaration of Independence. But Adams's subsequent extreme and somewhat tactless antidemocratic utterances (of which indications were already found in his *Defence of the Constitutions of Government of the United States of America*) and his inordinately diffuse and unfortunate mode of exposition prevented his thought from becoming generally acceptable. Wilson was much better equipped. Well trained in Scotch universities, he had a fair acquaintance with European juristic literature, and as a follower of Reid he, more than any American before him or for a generation after him, seems to have been familiar with the main currents of British philosophy. This and his wide legal experience in the service of our Revolution, of the French government, and of the state of Pennsylvania helped to free his mind from provincialism. As one of the most influential men in framing the Federal Constitution he could speak with great intimacy of what it established. And with his pious and moderate temper he had a modest but disarming way of presenting his ideas. As nationalistically inclined as Marshall or any Federalist (witness his opinion in *Chisholm* v. *Georgia*), he was devoid of the latter's distrust of the popular will. Rejecting the theory of sovereignty propounded by Hobbes, Pufendorf, and Blackstone (*viz.*, that law is a rule laid down by a superior), Wilson went as far as Jefferson in insisting on the great vital principle "that the supreme or sovereign power of the society resides in the citizens at large; and that, therefore, they always retain the right of abolishing, altering or amending their constitution, at whatever time, and in whatever manner, they shall deem it expedient."[1] Though he was one of the founders of the Bank of North America, he insisted that "property, highly deserving security, is, however, not an end but a means."[2]

Wilson starts from the classical view of natural law as emanating from God and manifesting itself to the universal conscience of mankind in simple, eternal, and self-evident principles. Though as a good Protestant he invokes the support of special revelation through the Bible, it is the classical Ciceronian form of the doctrine which he develops. In accordance with his intuitionalism, "the first principles of morals . . . are discov-

---

[1] *The Works of James Wilson* (1804), Vol. 1, p. 17. *Cf. id.*, Vol. 3, p. 292.
[2] *Id.*, Vol. 1, p. 30.

ered in a manner more analogous to the perceptions of sense than to the conclusions of reasoning."[3] These principles, however, govern the more important part but not the whole of life. Something is left to man-made law, and on this the majority expresses the general will. Laws are not commands but contracts. Where, in the interests of natural rights, the powers of legislatures are limited by written constitutions, the courts must necessarily have the power to declare certain legislation void. But Wilson recognizes that the judiciary and other branches of the government must be mutually dependent as well as independent. The limits to the sovereignty of Parliament or of any other legislature are to be found not only in natural rights but in the division of legislative chambers and the existence of common or customary law. He shares the general fear of turning over our rights to other human beings, but recognizes that it is in fact inevitable, as, for instance, in a jury trial. Our safety consists in relying on generally or popularly accepted rules.

Wilson succeeded in expressing what became the classic American view on the nature of law and its role in the human scene against its cosmic background. But his own prestige declined rapidly when, in the bitter political fight after the election of 1800, neither Federalists nor Democrats could find complete satisfaction in his writings. He had no successors. Down to the period of our Civil War, philosophy was at an unusually low ebb in this country. The so-called common sense or Scotch intuitionalism, of which Wilson was an adherent, developed into hardly more than a turgid exposition of sectarian theologic doctrines and dogmas concerning personal morals. The academic German philosophy which replaced it at the end of the nineteenth century devoted itself almost entirely to points in the theory of knowledge, and showed little interest in the underlying principles of man's legal experience. On the other hand, the legal profession became more absorbed in practical affairs and less interested in theoretic or philosophic issues. The American public came to regard the practice of law as a business and was jealous of any attempt to exclude people, by scholastic prescriptions, from earning a living. The vast majority of our lawyers came to the bar through the apprentice method, and with very few exceptions our law schools up to recently were hardly better than trade schools. In the absence of real university traditions, their connections with our colleges were administrative and financial rather than educational. We must remember that even in England the training of lawyers was carried on in the professional Inns of Court rather than in connection with the arts and sciences taught in the universities. In addition, the separation of barristers from solicitors,

---

[3] *Id.*, Vol. 1, p. 126.

which fosters certain intellectual standards in the former, was abandoned here. It was, therefore, rare indeed to find a lawyer like Holmes with an interest in, and genius for, juristic philosophy. This does not deny that some of our keenest minds went into the legal profession or that our courts have shown great acuteness and ingenuity in adapting the law to actual but temporary and local conditions. But there can be no great or vital contribution to any field of general thought without free and sustained reflection, and, for the latter, conditions in America were not favorable.

The situation has changed markedly in the life of the present generation through the expansion of our universities and the development of law teaching as an independent profession. The legal profession as a whole, however, still proudly professes to despise theorists and doctrinaires, and for that very reason still naïvely clings to the old legal theories that prevailed in Europe before the French Revolution.

When, in the latter part of the nineteenth century, American students of history and political science began in larger numbers to go to Europe and to establish closer contact with its thought and scholarship, the doctrine of the social contract naturally fell into disrepute even here, where people had actually seen commonwealths established and their laws framed by general agreement. It is well to note, however, that as late as 1874 the United States Supreme Court still spoke[4] of "implied reservations of individual rights, without which the social compact could not exist, and which are respected by all governments entitled to the name. No court, for instance, would hesitate to declare void a statute which enacted that A and B who were husband and wife to each other should be no longer, but that A should thereafter be the husband of C, and B the wife of D." Apparently this mode of thought and speech was so ingrained in the American tradition that the justices of our Supreme Court could not see that our divorce statutes did exactly that on a whole-sale scale, and that acts of Parliament and of our state legislatures had done it in individual cases. Nor has there since been any general recognition of the fact that another principle of natural law invoked in that and other cases, *viz.*, that property may not be taken from A and given to B, is consistently disregarded by all government subsidies, protective tariffs, and pension or bonus laws in which the funds are raised by taxing others than the beneficiaries.

After phrases about the social compact became obsolete and judges gave up the claim of being authorized to set aside statutes that conflicted with their opinion of what constitutes natural right, our courts neverthe-

---

[4] *Loan Association* v. *Topeka*, 20 Wall. (87 U.S.) 655, 663 (1874).

less continued in fact to exercise this claim, first under the guise of enforcing on the legislatures the "inherent limitations of free government," and later by stretching the terms "property," "liberty," "due process," and "equal protection of the laws" in our constitutions, so that Judge Andrews could well say:[5]

". . . under the broad and liberal interpretation now given to constitutional guaranties, there can be no violation of fundamental rights by legislation which will not fall within the express or implied prohibition and restraints of the Constitution, and it is unnecessary to seek for principles outside of the Constitution, under which such legislation may be condemned. . . ."

Other countries have adopted written constitutions which are political documents setting up a plan or framework of government. What is characteristically American is the notion of limiting the powers of the legislature, and leaving it to the judiciary to determine whether any statute goes beyond such powers. Ideologically, this rests on the old eighteenth-century rationalistic view that we know certain self-evident principles concerning the just powers of government, from which the decision of every case can be rigidly deduced, just as propositions of geometry are deduced from Euclidean axioms. This view is logically necessary to justify the claim that our judges have no part in creating our constitutional law, but only declare the solemn will of the people who adopted the Constitution.

The currents of thought in modern logic as well as in history and political science have turned against this classical doctrine.

In view of the limitations of human knowledge, of our imperfect knowledge of the future, we cannot logically suppose that all the subtle distinctions which make up our present constitutional law were actually in the minds of the people in 1789 or when, after the Civil War, they adopted the Fourteenth Amendment. The people could not have intended to prohibit the specific legislative regulation of affairs of which they could not have had any idea. As conditions change, the law must be changed, and the judiciary will necessarily play a part in this change. But the pretension that what they declare is only the preëxisting will of the people or is logically necessitated by the language of the Constitution is too absurd to deserve serious attention. It is a fiction and not a truth. In fact, no one pretends that our system of government today is precisely what those who framed or adopted our Constitution really intended or anticipated. Not only have our electoral system and the relation of the president to the voters been radically changed, but there have been all sorts of shifting of power between the states and the federal government

---

[5] *Berthold* v. *O'Reilly*, 74 N. Y. 509, 515 (1878).

and between the executive and the legislature. Our Constitution is rigid
only if the judges choose to make it so and if the people are satisfied with
the results. Actually, this rigidity has been balanced by remarkably
flexible methods of interpretation whereby entirely unexpected meanings
have been found in the terms of our Bill of Rights. Thus the terms
"property" and "liberty" have been stretched to include the freedom or
the right to contract, and to prevent legislative regulations of such contracts in behalf of such public interests as the preservation of the standard
of living.

The notion of a government of limited power—certain rights being
reserved to the people—is undoubtedly derived from the notion of a social
contract in which people give up to the government some of their rights
and reserve others as inalienable. But historians now insist that such
social contract is a pure fiction and that men in a state of nature without
government would be like beasts and have no rights—certainly no real
liberty or power to do what they wanted. It is only through social rules
and regulations that real freedom can be achieved, as can be seen in our
traffic rules. More recently, some students of political theory have come
to recognize that the essence of the theory of natural rights is not the
historical existence of a state of nature but rather the appeal to an ideal to
which the law should conform.* Certainly, unless we are prepared to
deny that legislation can ever be unjust and oppressive, some appeal from
it to natural law, political or public morality, or the principles of sound
social policy and public welfare—call it what you will—is unavoidable.
But this is an appeal in the moral forum, and in other countries it takes
the form of a solemn declaration addressed to the conscience of the
legislature and of the people at large. The courts' function is limited to
the enforcement of the enacted law. It has been characteristic of the
American system to confuse the legal and the moral and, in effect, to
make the judges' view of public morality the law of the land. Not only
Democrats like Jefferson but Federalists like James Wilson, living at a
time when the Revolutionary tradition was vivid, found it easy to think
that the people had a right to disregard the law when it seemed to them
unjust or contrary to conscience. The development of our constitutional
law has changed this moral right of the people into a legal right of the
judiciary. From the anarchy that would follow if every individual felt
free to disobey what seemed to him an unjust law, we have been saved
by a doctrine of judicial absolutism or infallibility. Presumably whatever
a majority of the Supreme Court decides not only is the law but is also

---

*Cf. Book III, Chapter 4 ("Natural Rights and Positive Law") in M. R. Cohen,
Reason and Nature (1931), p. 401.

the original intention of the people, and conforms to the eternal principles of justice, or at any rate to the principles recognized by Anglo-Saxons since they roamed in the German forests.

The attitude of more recent political writers is not that we should not apply principles of justice to the law, but rather that judges are not the most competent to do so because the judiciary is not properly constituted to institute investigations to ascertain the actual social facts of contemporary life. In a homogeneous and stable society, courts may be relied on to take judicial notice of the prevailing morality. But living as we do in a most heterogeneous society, spread over the whole continent and undergoing very rapid changes, the work of judges in putting their view of justice or the rights of men above that of the legislature has in fact made very arbitrary opinions the law of the land, thus impairing that certainty and definiteness which are claimed to be the requisite characteristics of justice administered according to law. Even the most orthodox defenders of our established system have to admit that there is no certain way of determining whether a law is constitutional or not before the courts have actually ruled. And the only guide thereto is our knowledge of the personal inclinations of the judges.

The practical workings of this tradition in the law answered, on the whole, the needs of our free-land economy which prevailed to the end of the nineteenth century. It led to the abolition of entailed estates and to the greater freedom of testamentary disposition. Commercial ideas favored more liberal bankruptcy laws to encourage enterprise by doing away with the old-fashioned imprisonment for debt. The need for laborers to develop the land and natural resources made for free immigration, religious tolerance, and liberal suffrage laws. The relative scarcity of women in the Western states made for woman suffrage—though in the early part of the nineteenth century the American courts were exceedingly backward in recognizing the separate property rights of married women. Possibly the untrained character of most members of the bar aided the early abolition of the old technical forms of action and helped to enact the laws that allowed amended pleadings. America also took the lead in allowing those charged with felony the right to be represented by counsel and to appeal. Somewhat similar motives may have led American courts to give greater freedom to the jury and to limit the power of the judge. The supernaturalistic fear of perjury, which had led to the absolute exclusion from the witness chair of interested parties, was softened by the demands of justice and humanity into more generous rules about the admissibility of testimony, with extension of the privilege not to be compelled to answer certain questions. Indeed, the Fourth and

Fifth Amendments to the Constitution at one time threatened to serve as an "immunity bath" for all corporate wrongdoers. But there can be no doubt that the original intention was in the interest of humanity against torture. In the international field, America has contributed the recognition of the right of expatriation.

On the whole, the American legal tradition in our courts has been dominated by regard for "individual" property and freedom of enterprise as well as by certain traditional morals. It has not been so zealous for the interests of family continuity and has had little regard for the laborer who is at the mercy of superior economic forces. A money economy naturally tends to identify virtue with monetary success, so that it is only the exceptional poor who are worthy or honest, and this view is strengthened when the economically weaker members are largely foreign born.

The Beginnings of Systematic Jurisprudence

In the light of the foregoing sketch of the dominant ideas around which our legal thought has moved, we can see the position of men like Marshall, Kent, Story, Cooley, and those who have followed them.

MARSHALL

There can be no question about John Marshall's great service in giving the Constitution an interpretation that enabled the federal government to serve our national interests. In this respect, however, it is well to remember that his arch-opponent, Thomas Jefferson, when faced with the facts necessitating the Louisiana Purchase, equally served national interests, despite his theories of strict contruction of the Constitution. Indeed, on the question of protecting American commerce against England, Jefferson and Madison were even more nationalistic. Marshall was a great politician. He combined the gifts of a persuasive personality and seductively convincing utterance with a marked shrewdness concerning what was feasible under the circumstances. Thus he was willing to forego the supremacy of the Supreme Court in constitutional interpretation when it looked for a while as if the power of impeachment might become an effective weapon of the legislature against the judiciary.[6] He was not,

---

[6] A. J. Beveridge, *Life of Marshall* (1916-1919).

however, either widely informed or a great original thinker. When he was not following such models as *The Federalist* or did not have the aid of counsel at the bar, his writings—witness his *Life of Washington*—lacked real intellectual distinction. When today we examine his naïve reliance on very questionable principles[7] as if they were self-evident, we cannot rank his contributions to legal science as highly as was the fashion till recently. The doctrine of the judicial power over unconstitutional legislation was, of course, not his invention. From a strictly intellectual point of view his arguments in *Marbury* v. *Madison* were effectually refuted by Gibson of Pennsylvania.[8] President Jackson also disposed of Marshall's argument that the judges swear to obey the Constitution, by pointing out that members of Congress and the executive also swear to obey the Constitution and must therefore follow their own conscience regarding what the Constitution means. From time immemorial it has been recognized that the interpretation of law cannot be restricted to the judiciary, but must necessarily be exercised also by the executive and the legislature. Indeed, our own Supreme Court has since recognized that what the Constitution means by "a republican form of government" must be determined not by the courts, but by Congress and the executive. The historic fact that the American people have grown accustomed to allowing the interpre-

---

[7] Thus, if he had known the constitution of the French Republic, he could not have argued that all written constitutions must give judges power to disregard a legislative enactment that they deem unconstitutional.

[8] No scholar today will defend either on historical or on logical grounds Marshall's argument in *Marbury* v. *Madison*, 1 Cranch. (5 U. S.) 137 (1803) that the section of the Judicature Act of 1789 was unconstitutional. That Act was drawn by several framers of the Constitution and one of them, Ellsworth, became Marshall's predecessor as chief justice of the United States. It would certainly require very cogent arguments to prove that these men, the members of the First Congress who passed the Act, and President Washington, who presided at the deliberations of the Constitutional Convention and signed the Act, either were all ignorant of the Constitution or wilfully disregarded it. Logically, Marshall's argument that Congress could not give the Supreme Court original jursidiction in mandamus proceedings, because this was not mentioned in the second clause of Section 2 of Article III of the Constitution, rests on the untenable assumption that grants of jurisdiction must be exclusive and that otherwise the clause would have no meaning. But this is quite fallacious. An affirmative grant of jurisdiction to the court may mean that Congress cannot take away that jurisdiction. It does not mean that Congress may not add to it. In fact, the Supreme Court subsequently ruled that the grant of original jurisdiction to it was not exclusive and that it could also be conferred on district courts (in the case of consuls). Marshall's decision in *Marbury* v. *Madison, supra,* was a clever trick for escaping from an embarrassing situation, into which the federal courts had become involved when the Federalist Party created judicial offices for its followers after it was defeated in the election of 1800. The trick is obvious when we note that in quoting the Constitution Marshall left out the concluding words of the second clause of Section 2, Article III, which gives Congress express power to make exceptions to the appellate jurisdiction of the Supreme Court. For a clear indication of the unfortunate logic of *Marbury* v. *Madison,* see Ernst Freund, *Standards of American Legislation* (1917) 276-277.

tation of the Constitution by the judiciary to prevail has been due not to Marshall's very questionable arguments but to the fact that a government of three *independent* departments according to the classical theory would inevitably fail to function; and it is only by some process of mutual deference and compromise, or by the extra-legal method of a political party controlling all three, that effective government has been made possible.

It is often claimed that Marshall rendered a great service to the development of our country by his *Dartmouth College* decision; that this decision made franchises and corporations more secure and thereby facilitated the flow of funds for the development of industry and commerce. This is at best a debatable issue. It may well be contended that our overdeveloped corporation has become a Frankenstein monster, and that a slower development in this respect might have been much more favorable to our general welfare—might have led to a less hurried and wasteful exploitation of our natural resources and not stimulated such unprecedented corruption of our franchise-granting bodies. But be that as it may, one cannot read the opinion of Chief Justice Richardson of the New Hampshire court in the *Dartmouth College* case without feeling that it was legally a much sounder view, more in accordance with the general principles of the power of States and with the proper distinction between a public charter and a private contract. The undue extension of the notion of contract to government relations, begun by Marshall, has in fact worked havoc in American jurisprudence. Instead of making legal transactions secure, it has, actually, made them most insecure because no one can tell how far the courts will go in limiting the power of the government.

Marshall also rendered some vigorous and sound opinions in matters of international law. His essential limitations, however, his narrow sympathies, and the absence of a sense of the really larger issues can be seen in his opposition to the right of expatriation—a view that, if strictly adhered to, would certainly have hindered the free development of this country. In this respect he certainly failed to appreciate the wisdom of James Wilson.

Nor has time served to enhance the great reputation of our three classic legal writers of the nineteenth century—Kent, Story, and T. M. Cooley.

KENT

James Kent had an undoubtedly vigorous mind and a rather wider legal learning than was prevalent in his day. He made some notable decisions as an equity chancellor. But in his general legal views he never got beyond Blackstone; and his anti-democratic views made him devoid of sympathy for, and understanding of, many actual developments of American law.

STORY

Joseph Story also possessed a good deal of miscellaneous learning which he used to support Marshall and to enhance the prestige of the English common law. But he was a voluminous rather than a penetrating writer or clear thinker. His great, outstanding contributions in the field of conflict of laws no one can deny, but his conception of general jurisprudence was a confusion that has plagued American law. And while he rendered some important decisions in admiralty, some of them showed astounding intellectual confusion. He created a tradition of legal scholarship at the Harvard Law School, which resulted in useful voluminous treatises by Washburn, Parsons, Greenleaf, and others. But the scholarship was narrowly technical along the old beaten paths and made no contribution to our store of general ideas.

COOLEY

T. M. Cooley's great achievement in legal theory was to have reformulated the doctrine of the inherent limitation of legislative power, without explicit recourse to the senescent doctrine of natural rights or the social contract. The Civil War had weakened the powers of the states and the Democratic influence on the Supreme Court which had come with Chief Justice Taney. The country was, therefore, ripe for a new extension of nationalism at the expense of the states, and Cooley's work was essentially directed to the limitation of the powers of state legislatures, even in matters of taxation. The Republican party, as the union of western farmers and eastern manufacturers, was a nationalist party interested in tariffs, transcontinental railroads, industrial development, and the like. And the Fourteenth Amendment to the Federal Constitution, by subordinating the legislation of the various states to the veto power of the federal courts, was a great step in the direction of nationalism. It also tended to take the ultimate decision of social-economic issues out of the political into the legal forum, where property interests could be better represented and protected. It is interesting in this connection to note that Cooley became the first chairman of the Interstate Commerce Commission—a commission that opened the door for joining executive and judicial functions, in flat contradiction to the professed doctrine of the separation of powers as the condition of liberty.

Historical Jurisprudence

It may be, at first, somewhat surprising that Bentham exercised so little direct influence on the legal thought of this country—that most of his ideas came to us rather through Austin. But it must be remembered that he wrote at a time when revolutionary ideology and the phraseology of natural rights were in the ascendant in this country. Moreover, the specific evils against which Bentham fought, for example, remnants of feudalism, were not serious matters in our economy; and the commercial interests in this country did not then need his support as they did in England. Similar reasons will explain the later influence of the conservative, Henry Sumner Maine, and, indirectly, of the German historical school; for the former gave a new and positive sanction to the doctrine of *laissez faire* and contractualism, and the latter strengthened the prejudice against codification or attempts to change or reform the law by popularly elected legislatures.

POMEROY

The writer who first showed the marked influence of this historical school of jurisprudence was John N. Pomeroy. The fusion—an ungenerous critic might say the confusion—of ethical and historical considerations in the law is perhaps best illustrated in his work *An Introduction to Municipal Law*. He defines law as the body of rules by which the supreme power in a State is guided in its governing actions. From this it logically follows that there may be laws that are unjust. Indeed, Pomeroy explicitly recognizes that rules interfering with natural rights may still be positive laws. But the clear distinction between what is in fact law and what on ethical grounds we think ought to be the law is not a pleasant one to face. And so Pomeroy, like others before and after him, tries to identify the actual with the ethical by means of the dubious historical generalization that, as nations develop, laws become more ethical and are imbued more and more with those "innate principles of natural justice common to all times and peoples which the Romans called *Jus Gentium.*"[9]

In line with the general attitude of the historical school, Pomeroy opposed the adoption of a code and regarded that as equivalent to abolishing our traditional system of jurisprudence. In insisting that the present system is more elastic, he glides over the implication that the judges must engage in the process of supplementary legislation in order to enable them to meet new situations in a progressive society. Pomeroy, however,

---

[9] J. N. Pomeroy, *Municipal Law* (1864), §12.

seems to have had too much good sense not to recognize the advantages of codifying the criminal law and also parts of the law of political conduct, where the need of clarity and certainty is supreme. Against the fashionable indulgence in panegyrics on *written* constitutions, he pointed out that some of our constitutions contain a good deal of evil. He also expressly recognized that rigid constitutions are unworkable in times of crisis and tend to disappear in the mass of judicial interpretations. He regarded our disastrous Civil War as the "inevitable consequences of an organic law, rigid and inflexible . . . framed for one generation and so quickly outgrown by the progress of ideas in another."[10]

Complete nationalism, however, was still foreign to America, and Pomeroy recognizes that a large part of the law cannot be national, since reason and justice are not restrained by the boundaries of different lands or the divisions of different races. In opposition to those who would put the common law beyond all legislative changes, he contends that it is not a complete system, "existing partly in actual precepts, and partly in an undefined or cloudy state, ready to have the curtain rolled back and the law discovered by judicial action. . . . it is, rather, a power continually reproducing itself, taking up fresh material and converting it into new regulations, new maxims, new applications, in short, a new code."[11] "Religion, philosophy, letters, arts, trade, commerce, government and above all, the ethnic life of a people, enter into and shape their Law."[12] A detailed analysis, however, of how this actually takes place, and of the relative weight of different elements of society in the final determination or making of the law, was not forthcoming from this school of legal thought.

CARTER

A later but more uncompromising representative of the philosophy of the German historical school was J. C. Carter, who opposed the introduction of the Field Code for reasons somewhat similar to that which led Savigny to oppose a German code, *viz.*, that law must grow and cannot be made. Carter, however, did not have Savigny's learning or philosophic outlook. He, therefore, quite naïvely took the view that law is nothing but custom, and that judges are simply experts on the various customs that they enforce. His book is a remarkable example of the limitations of a great lawyer and an earnest, devout soul seeking to come to grips with the fundamental questions on the nature of law. Carter left

[10] *Id.*, §353.
[11] *Id.*, §38.
[12] *Id.*, §286.

a large legacy to Harvard University for a chair in the Law School, piously hoping that the occupant would continue his views, but he was liberal and generous enough not to restrict the University in any way. It is a tribute to this liberality and to the enlightenment of Harvard University that the first man to occupy that chair was Roscoe Pound, a pioneer in the effort to show that legislation may be a legitimate source of legal principles.

Langdell and his School

Frederick Pollock in his inaugural lecture[13] remarks on the absence of positive and analytic method in American works on the general theory of jurisprudence. "Their theoretic work is mostly akin to that of the German philosophical and historical schools." Yet even before these remarks were made there was growing up at Harvard University a vigorous school of positive and analytic jurisprudence led by Dean Langdell, whose Christian name, Christopher Columbus, some regarded as prophetic of his achievement.

The great prestige that the case method of law teaching has achieved—in large part due to the ease with which it can be employed—has not been conducive to a right appreciation of Langdell's views on the nature of law or to a just estimate of his position in American legal thought. The widespread notion that by the case system he introduced scientific method into legal studies is based on the prevalent ignorance of the history both of law and of science. The case system was in vogue in the Inns of Courts centuries ago. Indeed, it was a lawyer, Francis Bacon, who was so carried away by it that he arrived at the fantastic idea that it was *the* proper method for making scientific discoveries, and that by means of it he could soon build up all the sciences. This was made plausible by the traditional Neoplatonic notion that nature was constructed on the basis of a few simple forms, so that by the observation of a limited number of instances all of these forms could soon be brought to light. Similarly did Langdell believe that a few principles were at the basis of all law, and that it did not require the analysis of very many cases to get at these fixed or invariant principles which no human agency such as courts or legislatures could change. Few men ever showed so much concentration and keenness in trying to reduce the whole law to a few simple principles.

---

[13] Introductory Lecture delivered at University College, London, October 31, 1882, "The Methods of Jurisprudence," in *Oxford Lectures and Other Discourses* (1890), p. 1, 33.

He was thus a vigorously traditional rationalist. And while he ignored the political theory of sovereignty, neither he nor any of his followers went beyond the Austinian system of legal categories.

Though Langdell paid some attention to legal history, *e.g.*, that of equity pleading, neither he nor his immediate followers had Austin's familiarity with the substance and form of Roman law and with its modern institutional writers. Hence they tended to conceive of the "common law" as it existed in England at the end of the eighteenth century as the perfect embodiment of a completely rational legal system. Unsympathetic critics suggested that this was an excuse for teaching diverse students what was not the actual law in any of their native states. The reply which James Barr Ames and other followers of Langdell made was that the object of a law school was not to teach the substance of the law that prevailed in any one jurisdiction but the method of legal thought. But this distinction is not as clear as it sounds, because Langdell and his followers failed to indicate the precise relation between the logical and the historical elements in legal systems. They could not, therefore, separate legal method from the historical substance of the law. The common law is, after all, not a purely timeless logical system but merely a body of rules that historically grew up under definite social conditions in England. Why, therefore, should not the laws of New York, New Jersey, Pennsylvania, Wisconsin, Texas, or Louisiana, and their variations, be entitled to similar historical and systematic study? To restrict the student to the conventional common law of England as if it had become an eternal, unchanging pattern can, therefore, be defended only on the ground of pedagogic economy rather than of scientific adequacy. Moreover, it may well be urged that the Harvard school has envisaged legal history as a chronicle of judicial decisions with some reference to their logical connection rather than as a branch of social history. Roscoe Pound later defended this conception of legal history on the ground that the greatest single factor in molding any judicial decision is the logical force of the best available analogy that counsel suggests. But though this may be true if we take a short-span view of time and substance, taken over a longer time and range of interests the history of law needs a knowledge of social and economic, as well as of political, conditions to make it fully intelligible. This does not, of course, deny the value of the contributions to legal history made in such articles as those of Ames on the history of assumpsit or in Thayer's illuminating remarks on the history of the law of evidence. But this conception of legal history indicates a limitation in the conception of law and of the influences which modify it.

The neglect of the social-economic factors that actually mold legal as well as other institutions naturally went together with the tendency to elevate into the rank of fixed principles legal rules that are by no means universally valid but can be more appropriately explained by reference to specific historical conditions. Thus Langdell argues that it is "impossible" for creditors' rights to survive the death of the debtor, but admits that legislation sometimes "interposes" to bring about this impossibility—an impossibility which is alleged to be as old as the law. Similarly does Ames explain why certain claims (choses in action) cannot be transferred, on the ground that personal relations, in the very nature of things, cannot be assigned. He himself, however, goes on to show how this is actually done by various devices and by the fiction of "the obligor's consent given in advance." Clearly the "impossibility" in such cases follows from a dogmatic assumption which may be very useful in building up a teachable doctrine, but which does not correspond to the full historical actualities. Among the Romans such a personal relation as that of the wife's or son's duties to the husband or father could be transferred to others by sale, but this could not be done with ordinary debts, for the latter involved danger to the life of the debtor. The question which personal claims can be transferred and which cannot be thus depends upon historical conditions. The inherent inalienability of "personal claims" is thus not an eternal principle but a dogmatic fiction, a useful device for building up a serviceable account of the law, but sheer error when set up as something "as old as the law," "a rule of universal law," or "a working principle for the determination of controversies for all time."[14]

WILLISTON

Professor Samuel Williston elaborated and applied Langdell's idea of contracts into what is, from the analytic point of view, the classic treatment of the subject today. The traditional idea of the meeting of minds, or of an expression justifying such an interpretation, and the classic conception of consideration, here received their definitive form by the aid of very ingenious technical refinements. Williston's work must command respect from all those who value coherence and thoroughness; but it is meeting with an ever increasing volume of discontent from those who wish to understand how the law actually works and what social realities determine its development. Professor Williston has also made substantial contributions to the law of sales and negotiable instruments, in which

[14] J. B. Ames, *Lectures on Legal History* (1913), Chap. 18, p. 218.

he shows himself shrewdly appreciative of practical convenience in commercial transactions but hardly in a mood to question the adequacy of traditional ideas.

BEALE

Langdell's point of view was faithfully carried on by Joseph H. Beale, to whom the law is a system of fixed legal concepts, so that a judicial decision is correct or incorrect according to whether it does or does not conform to them. Professor Beale has worked in many fields with admirable intellectual tenacity. His main field, however, has been that of the conflict of laws (private international law) for which the wealth of American experience with forty-nine different jurisdictions offers rich material. The newer so-called realistic writers on jurisprudence frequently call him a legal fundamentalist. It is characteristic of the present American temper that this is not generally regarded as having a eulogistic connotation.

THAYER AND WIGMORE

Associated with Langdell, but somewhat independent of him, is the work of James Bradley Thayer in the fields of constitutional law and of the law of evidence. In the former field Thayer was one of the first legal scholars to approach the matter without the rhetorical ceremonies that Story had made fashionable. Thayer attributed the origin of the power of our courts to declare statutes unconstitutional to the fact that the King's Privy Council declared some legislative acts beyond the powers granted in the colonial charters. But he did not give any evidence that our own colonial judges ever did so, and it is unthinkable that our post-Revolutionary judges would have dared to follow the practice of the hated King's Privy Council if it were not that the prevalent doctrine of natural rights and of a social compact supported the idea of a government of enumerated powers.

Thayer was more fortunate in his contribution to the theory of the law of evidence. Here he had the advantage of building on the work of Brunner. He analyzed the ideas of rationality and evidence in the English common law, and introduced order in what had been an arid labyrinth of technical rules. His analysis of the nature of presumptions and other fictions in the law of evidence showed a real grasp of realities behind ceremonial expressions.

Thayer sketched his views of the history and nature of the law of evidence in his *Preliminary Treatise on Evidence at the Common Law.*

He did not live to do any more, but his ideas were adopted and elaborated with acumen and extraordinary industry by J. H. Wigmore, whose treatise on evidence represents the high-water mark of analytic jurisprudence. It will probably be a long time before any one produces a legal treatise of such dimension and competence. Wigmore shows a catholic spirit and an acquaintance with varied sources of culture. His hardheadedness in refusing to accept on faith the deliverances even of psychologists such as Münsterberg on the nature of testimony has become classic.

The newer tendency among the younger teachers of law today is to pay somewhat more attention to newer psychologic movements and to question the soundness and adequacy of traditional rules about hearsay testimony and the like. Professors Jerome Michael and Mortimer Adler have done significant work in introducing modern logistical methods into the law of evidence.

Langdell and his followers, especially Dean Ames, laid a broad foundation for legal scholarship in this country not only by their insistence on examining all the cases but by making law teaching a dignified profession, and by training a group of scholars to regard the study of law as a worthy field of human interest apart from its aid to successful practice. Ames devoted all of his life to law study and law teaching, and he did this with a nobility that won the veneration of his pupils, who later became our leading practitioners, so that he who had never practised law was shortly before his death considered for the presidency of the American Bar Association—a remarkable achievement when we remember the great prejudice of the practical lawyer against the theoretical teacher. But the Langdell school as a whole did not make any substantial contribution to the growing movement for social legislation, such as was represented by Workmen's Compensation Acts. And while its members did not go as far as President Eliot in regarding the scab or strikebreaker as a hero, they did cling to the old *laissez faire* notions in the law of torts. Today the most significant effect of its lack of any coherent philosophy is shown by its influence in the restatement of the law. The doctrine of *stare decisis* and the empiricist living from hand to mouth that is called "deciding each case on its merits" (without any guide on how to evaluate these merits) have made our actual law a hopeless labyrinth. Clearly, there is no way out except by some process of selecting some rulings and rejecting those that conflict with them. This, however, requires conscious examination and evaluation of the policy of the law, for which there is no room in the tradition of the Langdell school. The law is viewed as a perfect system, even though in practice it cannot be so. How, then, can a restatement be made when in fact the laws of different states actually conflict and it is not always clear how to reconcile different rulings in any one state? Unless the restatement is backed by cogent considerations of public policy or social utility as a basis of selection, it merely adds one dogmatic statement (*i.e.*, the opinion of the writers) to those of diverse judges in different jurisdictions. There is doubtless a vast amount of agreement in the laws of the various states, but to the extent that this agreement holds, there is no problem. The difficulty arises when we ask how to choose between different rulings, and for this purpose the principle on which the restatement is made cannot be of aid.

Gray and Judicial Legislation

Associated with Harvard University—but hardly followers of Langdell—were Holmes, Gray, and Pound. Holmes was by far the greatest legal historian that this country has produced and one to be counted among the foremost masters of all countries for substance and for the penetrating insight that illumines and fuses otherwise miscellaneous information. As his work has been made the starting point of the recent realistic movements in jurisprudence, I shall refer to him later. Here, however, we cannot pass over the work of his friend, J. C. Gray, whose *Nature and Sources of the Law* is one of the first American books devoted explicitly to the theory of the law. Gray was a practising lawyer as well as a professor, and his treatises on the law of real property, *Restraints on the Alienation of Property* and *The Rule Against Perpetuities*, follow the conventional individualism as well as the traditional conception of legal history. But he had an honest and robust mind that liked to face difficulties which others evaded by smooth phrases, and he seems to have taken a proper delight in confronting legal fiction with the actualities of social life. This gives unusual value to his treatment of the general theory of the law. He showed with irresistible force that judges not merely declare what the law was before they ruled, but that their ruling actually makes law. In thus making new law, courts are limited by their material or sources, such as opinions of authorities and their own previous decisions.

Gray has been severely criticized from two different points of view. The traditionalists have urged that if the judges make the law, then there is no law before they make it, and this they regard as a *reductio ad absurdum*. The absurdity, however, is in the traditional assumption that the law is a closed system which has a determinate answer for every question that can come up, so that the judge has nothing to do but to declare what the fixed law is. If that were so, all growth or change of the legal system would be impossible. But if the law is like an organism that grows without losing all continuity with the past, then there is no reason for denying that judicial decision is one of the ways through which it is changed and made to assume the form that it actually has at any time.

Another criticism of Gray is made by the nominalists, who object to his defining the law of a country, or other organized body of men, as composed of the rules of conduct that its courts follow and that it holds itself ready to enforce.[15] They argue that what a court does is only to decide a given case before it, and that, so far as such a decision serves as a precedent in future cases, it is as Gray himself characterized, not law but a source of law. And, indeed, precedents are sometimes disregarded. This argument, however, ignores the actualities of the case. No case is so unusual that no other is like it. Whenever a court makes a decision it implicitly (and sometimes explicitly) decides a class of cases. While the exact limits of the class may not be precisely defined, we do not find closely similar cases constantly brought before the appellate courts. Lawyers recognize that the case has been decided on some abstractly relevant circumstance and the formulation of this is what we call the rule. Such rules change as the number of cases widens, but this does not deny the reality or relevance of the rules as guides for lawyers in their advice to clients or for courts in their actual decisions.

It is sometimes asserted that Gray regards law and morals as altogether distinct. This is not accurate. What he does assert is that they are not identical, but that law in fact does and must draw freely on the moral ideas of the community and of the individual judge. Not only does moral feeling serve as a source of law when other factors fail, but it largely influences the direction and effect of other factors: "Whether a statute shall be interpreted one way or another is often determined by the moral character which the one or the other interpretation will give to it; and there are few judicial precedents or professional opinions or customs whose position as sources of Law is not strengthened or weakened by the fact of their agreeing or disagreeing with sound ethical principles."[16]

The real difficulty, however, is that Gray assumes that moral ideas are

---

[15] J. C. Gray, *Nature and Sources of the Law* (1909), §656.
[16] *Id.*, §645.

uniform, and therefore does not in fact raise the question of what makes judges decide on some one view of morality rather than another.*

The Sociologic Jurisprudence
of Roscoe Pound

Though associated for the greater part of his professional career with Harvard University as a teacher and dean, Roscoe Pound is not entirely of the Harvard tradition. He started life as a western progressive influenced more by German jurists, such as Kohler, and by the Chicago school of sociologists, especially A. W. Small. His sociologic jurisprudence began as a determined effort to view the law as a social institution —how it actually operates in the life of men. To this task he brought not only a prodigious amount of learning in regard to the different branches of the common law, equity and their history, as well as the actual course of American legislation, but also a remarkably wide acquaintance with Roman and other systems of law and their literature. To this he added considerable familiarity with the course of the history of philosophy as viewed by Erdmann and other Neo-Hegelians. This learning was used to explain and make intelligible many dark corners of the legal world, and, in general, to enable us to see some order in the bewildering multitude of legal facts. At the very beginning of his career he preached the necessity of a philosophy of law—that unless our legal doctrines are united by some coherent system of fundamental ideas, we must continue to wander aimlessly and get nowhere.

It is easy today to forget the stimulating effect of Pound's early writings, coming at a time when philosophy of law was at a very low ebb. The present writer is glad here to acknowledge his own obligation to these writings.**

---

* *Cf.* "John Chipman Gray" in M. R. Cohen, *Law and the Social Order* (1933), p. 352.

** "Roscoe Pound helped me to discover that though the stage of American legal philosophy was nearly empty, vigorous thinking and writing in Germany, France and Italy had much to offer towards an understanding of the underlying issues of the American scene. For by and large, the 'standpat' philosophy of our own legal conservatives followed ideas developed by Savigny and other Continental opponents of law reform a century ago. The criticisms which had been directed against these musty champions of European conservatism over many decades offered a good deal of light on the weaknesses of American legal thought." M. R. Cohen, *A Dreamer's Journey* (1949), p. 177. These comments are part of an account of

1. Pound liberalized the study of law in America by his insistence on what Holmes had emphasized—that law is part of human life and therefore subject to the same winds of doctrine and climate of opinion that prevail in our political, economic, religious, and other social views and activities; that our legal experience could be illumined if we studied other legal systems and the writings of those who had reflected upon them. One has but to glance at comments of his contemporaries, expressing indignation that any one should read foreign legal writings, to appreciate the significance of this.[17]

2. Not only did he emphasize in general the social function of the law and its history, but he pointed out the need of distinguishing between law in books and law in action; that the former has to do for the most part with arguments before our appellate courts, while in actual life the law and justice which most people receive are meted out by justices of the peace, city magistrates, or municipal judges, and that the expense of an appeal makes it generally unavailable to most people. Among other human factors in the law he called attention to the fact that there is a sporting element in judicial procedure which is a source of entertainment to the public.

3. He sought to break down the sharp distinction between common law and legislative enactments, indicating how the former grew out of statutes such as the Statutes *quia emptores, de Donis conditionalibus,* the Statute of Frauds, etc., and that there was no reason why modern statutes should not be used as sources of legal analogies in the adjudication of cases.

4. Finally, he emphasized the importance of rendering justice in the given case before the court by appreciating the social factors that enter into it as opposed to mechanical manipulation of legal concepts. Unfortunately, however, he has not elaborated any definite ideas or methods by which such justice can be secured.

It is amazing that, despite such an equipment of ideas and learning, and a most influential position as dean of one of our leading law schools, Pound has found so few disciples or direct followers. Part of the explana-

---

the Conference on Legal and Social Philosophy, organized in 1913, of which John Dewey was chairman and Morris R. Cohen was secretary and in which Roscoe Pound, Felix Adler, John Wigmore, Ernst Freund, Louis D. Brandeis, Felix Frankfurter, William Draper Lewis and William Ernest Hocking, and other philosophers, jurists, and social scientists delivered papers in which some of the more significant trends of modern American juristic philosophy find their earliest expression.

[17] Robert L. Fowler, "The New Philosophies of Law" (1914), 27 *Harvard Law Review* 718.

tion, it seems to me, is to be found in the absence of a coherent philosophy or in a certain lack of constructive intellectual energy.[18]

It is not merely that Pound fails to attain a high degree of consistency —perfect consistency in human affairs is an unattainable as well as an unavoidable ideal, and a narrow consistency often shows lack of perception of diverse and opposing considerations—but that one does not gather whither in the long run he is driving or how he can fruitfully marry the ideas of Small and Dewey to those of Stammler and Kohler, Coke and Marshall. On the one hand, we have a persistent opposition to mechanical jurisprudence of concepts or fixed rules, and a devastating criticism of our courts' uncritical reliance on such principles as the freedom of contract. On the other hand there is a naïve clinging to the fiction of the division of power between the judiciary and the executive, against those who favor the fusion of judicial and administrative functions in commissions. He insists that only rules and principles interpreted by courts can stand between the citizen and official incompetence, caprice, or corruption, as if principles and rules could enforce themselves without human—all too human—judges. Courts, he insists, decide on principles. Yet no one has pointed so emphatically to the fact of judicial empiricism, that principles are empty and misleading unless we know all the relevant social facts to which they are to be applied. And how can any one doubt that our courts have less opportunity than commissions have to institute researches and factual inquiries even before disputes arise? He denounces law without rules as cadi justice (which ignores the fact that in a simple community, governed by custom and the Koran, the rules are well known). Yet, in insisting on the element of judicial discretion and on the presence in the law of standards, he admits elements other than rules or principles. It is, therefore, hard to see the difference between cadi justice and a judge or juryman exercising his discretion. No doubt wisdom consists in avoiding easy opposite extremes, but Pound fails to indicate

---

[18] A certain hesitancy in carrying out ideas is perhaps responsible for an excessive tendency to taxonomy, a fondness for classifying thinkers or doctrines without regard to whether such classification is really helpfully promoting a better understanding or how they actually function. Thus the classification of jurists into analytic, historic, philosophic, and sociologic is neither logically satisfactory (because overlapping) nor very fruitful in promoting an understanding of such radical differences as those between men like von Jhering and Gierke. On the other hand, Pound's account of the stages of legal development tends to set up as rigid historical periods what were at first only stages of discourse; that is, points of logical analysis in what is perhaps nothing more than the general rhythm between the forces of growth or expansion and the forces of organization which dominate the law as well as other social institutions at all times.

the *via media*. Though he insists on a balancing of interests, he does not give us any guidance on how that is to be effected.

Lovers of truth are properly jealous of the popular demand that the work of scholarship should justify itself by immediately practical applications. But it is disheartening to find so much thought, learning, and zeal for the better administration of justice leaving us so bereft of any new outlook on our legal institutions. From the whole enterprise of sociologic jurisprudence there has not come, so far as we know, a single suggestion for the modification of the traditional law-school curriculum or of our judicial system.

Though Pound recognizes that judges have a large part in making the law and that some of the results have been bad because based on an outworn individualistic philosophy, and indeed on inadequate knowledge and appreciation of the history of the law as well as of modern industrial conditions, he opposes any popular control over courts and repeats with approval Lord Coke's dictum that law is an artificial reason and that judges are answerable only to God. Why judges should be more answerable to God than are presidents and congressmen and not at all to the community in whose services they are employed we are not told. Pound seems to be aware that irresponsibility is not altogether desirable in human affairs and he tries to mitigate it by claiming that professional opinion of the bar is a sufficient check against unwise or unjust decisions. But history hardly supports this. Moreover, the opinion of the bar is class opinion, controlled largely by a few leaders who may have acquired prestige by defending the interests of wealthy clients.

It is clearly a case of what James and Dewey have called vicious intellectualism to argue as if the presence of a good logical reason for a rule of law excludes a social or economic motive for it.* In the case of the limitation of the master's liability for injuries by a fellow servant, Pound has himself shown that there were within the legal system logical analogies to the contrary. The actual result was, therefore, certainly not uninfluenced by the considerations of social economic policy as viewed from the point of view of the possessing class—as is, indeed, unmistakably indicated in the opinions of Lord Abinger, Chief Justice Shaw, and others —which established the "fellow servant" rule.**

In general one misses in Pound's later writings a realistic appreciation of human motives in the law. In arguing for the certainty of justice

---

* *Cf.* " 'Real' and 'Ideal' Forces in Civil Law", in M. R. Cohen, *Law and the Social Order* (1933), p. 248.

** See M. R. Cohen, *ibid.*, pp. 327-351.

according to law, he ignores the sources of our actual uncertainty, such as the diversity of political and economic opinions among our judges or their different degrees of sympathy for those who are economically oppressed and whose sufferings our more sensitive and responsive legislatures try to alleviate. Nor does Pound stop to analyze the meaning of "reason" as a "standard" when he defends the transparent fiction to which courts resort when they say that they do not declare a statute unconstitutional except when it is so beyond any rational doubt. When in fact the president, a majority of the members of the House of Representatives, of the Senate, and a minority or perhaps even a majority of all the judges who have passed on the act, have expressed a contrary view, one would think that a sense of humor as well as of courtesy would prevent even a majority of a court from setting up their own opinion as the only rational one.

The Influence of
Justices Brandeis and Cardozo

Closely related to Pound's effort to view "law in action" as it actually operates in the life of men was the development of a new attitude of judicial respect for social and economic facts. That attitude is inseparably associated with the names of Louis D. Brandeis and Benjamin N. Cardozo. It was these two men who, more than anyone else, gave currency to the idea that judicial decisions inevitably turn on basic questions of economics, politics and sociology, and that judges can rise above their own limitations and prejudices in these fields only by opening their minds to the progress of research and the testing of old and new theories.

The idea that judges can learn something about their business from economists and other non-lawyers had shocking overtones. In the established American hierarchy of values the so-called "theoretician" is a lowly figure, and there is no class that occupies a higher status than the judiciary. Indeed, according to the current tradition, it is proper to criticize all public officials, including the President, and it is considered an act of superior political wisdom and virtue to disparage the work of our legislators, but any disrespect to the judiciary is regarded as evidencing lack of patriotism.

In no other country has the power and prestige of the judiciary been so great. Ancient as well as contemporary history is, of course, familiar

with the persistent view that the established system of government rests
on divine sanction and that, therefore, any critical attitude to it is
evidence of an evil disposition. We have, however, since our Declaration
of Independence rejected the doctrine of the divine right of kings and
with it the maxim that the king can do no wrong. We are committed to
the view that the basis of good government is an enlightened public
opinion, and that our security consists in realizing that all officials are
fallible human beings and therefore open to criticism, if we are to guard
against their errors proving fatal. Why should judges be beyond the scope
of this democratic faith? They are, in fact, predominantly lawyers, largely
drawn from the same class who serve in our legislatures or occupy the
major political offices. Does a man lose his human frailty when he mounts
the judicial bench? In the early days of the Republic, people did not
think so. The number of indictments against judges in the territories of
Indiana and Illinois in the early part of the 19th Century is astounding.
The beginnings of the movement to impeach high Federal judges scared
John Marshall so that he was willing at one time to advocate something
like a legislative recall of judicial decisions.

The conservative public was shocked when Theodore Roosevelt, in a
message to Congress, said: "The decisions of the courts on economic and
social questions depend upon their economic and social philosophy." Yet
he was but repeating the homely wisdom of Jefferson. "All know the
influence of interest on the mind of man and how unconsciously his judgment is warped by that influence." Judge Edward A. Parry's volume,
The Law and the Poor, shows how humanly impossible it is for judges
to get away from the bias of their limited experience and class feeling.*

It would be absurd to press such an obvious fact if it were not for
the generally accepted, persistent, and vehement assertion that our judges
speak only what the law has solemnly declared, and that their personal
bias has nothing to do with their actual decisions.

The pretense that our courts are not expressing the personal opinion
of the judges, but only obeying the solemn will of the people as expressed
in the law, would be as ridiculous as the pretensions of the Roman augurs,
were it not for the fact that it is far more tragic to our people.

The American people has been accused, not unfairly, of lacking a
due respect for law. In part, our judges are responsible for this fault
through their failure to correct their personal opinions by objective tests
and factual information. This failure is not primarily a personal one, since
all of us find such an effort difficult. The fault is, in the main, with our

---

* Judge Parry's thesis is discussed in detail in Morris R. Cohen's *Law and the
Social Order,* at pp. 3-6.

judicial system, which is intellectually the weakest part of our government. It has the least opportunity to get adequate information on the
issues which it has to decide. Which of us who wants to inform himself
on one of the principal current issues will be satisfied with listening for a
few hours to a couple of lawyers and reading their briefs? Much is said
about the calm atmosphere of the courts in contrast with the passionate
attitudes which exist in the legislative and executive branches of the
government. The truth of this is very dubious. Certainly our courts are
less in contact with the actual facts of our complicated economic and
social life, have no power to initiate investigations, and, by pretending to
pass only on the law and not on the facts, leave the door open to most
uncritical opinions.

It is against this background of legal practice and theory that the
influence of Justices Brandeis and Cardozo must be appraised.

Although Justice Brandeis can hardly be called a legal philosopher,
he came very close to embodying the ideal of what a great judge should
be, combining broad human sympathies with thorough knowledge of all
the relevant factors of the case before him. The very strength of Justice
Brandeis' mind in concentrating on the facts of a concrete case is naturally
associated with an absence of what is generally called "the philosophic
mind," the gift of clearly grasping ultimate issues, so beautifully exemplified by Justice Holmes. Nevertheless, there is implicit in the enormous
energy and painstaking thoroughness of Brandeis' work, first as a lawyer
and later as a judge, a certain humility in the face of facts which shows
signs of profoundly influencing American legal philosophy.

On the bench, Brandeis pursued the practice of making independent
researches not only on the strictly legal but also on the social and economic aspects of the cases. By dint of his liberal experience and painstaking research, he was able to master the social and economic incidence
of the great cases that make the work of the Supreme Court of fateful
significance. Unlike his colleague Holmes, Brandeis had the patience to
acquaint himself with the hard facts of current economic life. His pro-
clivities towards independent research on the bench stemmed from a
conviction that he had consistently followed in the practice of the law.
What has since become known as the "Brandeis brief" placed special
accent on the social facts that give human meaning to legal decisions.
The most famous example was his brief in *Muller* v. *Oregon*.[19] Today
briefs before courts, as well as opinions of the courts themselves, are
filled with references to non-legal data.

Justice Brandeis never succeeded in freeing himself from the old-

---

[19] 208 U. S. 412 (1918).

fashioned idealization of free competition, which was always associated in his mind with a general fear of bigness in other fields than industry and finance. Having been brought up on the continental liberalism of 1848, which was also the liberalism of Jeffersonian democracy, Justice Brandeis continued throughout his judicial career to speak in its individualistic terms. Nevertheless, his sensitiveness to the actual demands of new economic situations made him ready to sacrifice the dogma of free enterprise or competition to the need of social regulation, as is beautifully illustrated in his dissent in the Oklahoma Ice Case.[20]

Justice Cardozo was one of the few of our judges who, like Justice Holmes, thought it important to *have* a philosophy. In the forefront of humanity's most cherished heroes, among prophets, saints, philosophers, scientists, poets, artists and inspiring national leaders, the number of lawyers does not loom large. Mankind as a whole cannot well live by bread alone, but needs sustaining and directing vision. It is hard for lawyers, bent on the affairs of the market place, to look up and see the heavens above, or to grasp entire the scheme of things in which they move. This is especially difficult in a country or epoch which, under the leadership of captains of industry and finance, worships a narrow practicality and acts as if theory could be safely ignored, if not despised. It requires, therefore, a high order of intellectual and moral energy for one who has been immersed almost all his life in the business of the law to avow and pursue an interest in its general backgrounds and ultimate outcome, following the maxim of the old Talmudic sages that he who would deal justly with the law must contemplate the eternal issues of life and death.

The main features of Cardozo's philosophy, like those of any sound philosophy, are essentially simple, though it needs genius and energy to trace their implications and to carry them out consistently.

The first point is that law is not an isolated technique, of interest only to lawyers and to litigants, but that it is an essential part of the process of adjusting human relations in organized society.

The second point is that the law of a growing society cannot all be contained in established precedents or any written documents, important as are continuity with the past and loyalty to the recorded will of the people. In the law as a social process, the judges play a determining role, having the sovereign power of choice in their decisions. It was in this emphasis on the judicial process as selective and creative that Cardozo's thought centered.

The third point, the logical corollary to the foregoing, is that to meet

---

[20] *New State Ice Co.* v. *Liebmann,* 285 U. S. 262 (1932).

his responsibility for making the law serve human needs the judge cannot rely on legal authorities alone, but must know the actual facts of the life about him, the psychologic and economic factors that determine its manifestations, and must thus keep abreast of the best available knowledge which those engaged in various social studies, researches, or investigations can supply.

The prevailing orthodoxy expressed some years ago by Senator Elihu Root* and still passing as authoritative insists that the duty of the judge is simply to read and obey the statute or the Constitution and that it is no part of his business to make or change the law in any way. This assumes that the framers of a law or constitution can foresee all possible future contingencies and make definite provisions for meeting them, so that the judge can be merely a logical automaton, a sort of phonograph repeating exactly what the law had definitely declared.** But this is a childish view which no student of law can maintain. The whole common law has grown out of judicial decisions, and in our constitutional law the meaning of such phrases as "due process," "equal protection of the laws," "interstate commerce," and the like is precisely that which the courts have assigned to them.

The fundamental fallacy in the "phonograph theory" of the judicial functions, against which Justice Cardozo's entire career was an eloquent protest, is the illogical view that general principles alone can determine individual decisions. Modern logic and modern science alike demonstrate the untenability of this conception.*** Established legal principles may supply guiding analogies, but the decision of any individual case depends on an understanding of the actual social conditions, and of the consequences of the decision, as well as on the judge's view as to which of these consequences are best or most important. Elevation to the bench does not make a man omniscient, and the obvious fiction that courts decide only points of law prevents us from giving them adequate facilities for investigation into the relevant facts of the case, and into the larger social consequences of their decisions. In our anxiety to make judges independent of the popular will we are making them independent of the knowledge necessary to make their work satisfactory.

The consequence of judicial recognition that the judges make law is the responsibility of making it in accordance with existing conditions. Now, for judges who are intelligent enough to recognize the inadequacy

---

* Cf. "The Legal Calvinism of Elihu Root", in M. R. Cohen, *Law and the Social Order* (1933), p. 12.

** Cf. "The Process of Judicial Legislation," *ibid.*, p. 112.

*** Cf. "The Place of Logic in the Law", *ibid.*, p. 165.

of their own training in economic and social studies, it is easy to take refuge in the thought, "We are judges of the law and have nothing to do with economic or social theories." But the refuge is illusory. Those who are not aware of theory assume as facts the theories of an older generation.

A great lawyer preparing a brief in the Consolidated Gas Case told his clerks not to quote any economists later than John Stuart Mill—the judges wouldn't have heard of them. The philosophy of Cardozo makes this position impossible. Not only is law connected with other phases of human life, but human life is changing and the content of certain abstract principles must change. The principles of economics formulated two generations ago can no longer be relied on today. They must be corrected by the best available knowledge. Absolute finality is not to be found in human affairs.

It was Justice Cardozo's essential humility which made it possible for him to recognize what many of his brethren on the Bench found it intolerable to admit, that he as a judge had to rely not only on past judicial decisions but on developments in the various fields of social study. He was indeed criticized for quoting nonlegal authorities in some of his judicial opinions. But the sharp distinction between legal and non-legal authorities is an arbitrary one which no serious philosophy of law can well maintain. History celebrates the occasion when thought is wedded to fact. This is the philosophy which has made modern science so fruitful in the field of technology, and that is the philosophy which makes possible the progress of the spirit and the life of society.

The Legal Philosophy of Justice Holmes

Holmes was not only a legal historian, the author of the greatest legal classic that this country has produced, but essentially a man of a philosophic turn of mind. He did not, to be sure, have an extensive or close familiarity with technical philosophy and did not seem to enjoy the process of building up systems of thought by long and closely articulated reasoning. But he had a genuine desire for getting at fundamentals and seeing details *sub specie aeternitatis*. He belonged to none of the traditional schools but, coming to manhood in New England when the ideas of Darwin, Spencer, and the higher critics of the Bible were shaking the foundations of the older orthodoxy, Holmes developed a unique combination of skepticism and mysticism which enabled him to formulate for himself a modernized version of Calvinism. We do not and cannot know the ultimate nature of things but we are controlled by forces bigger than ourselves, and it is the part of wisdom to accept our lot and heroically strive to do our best. Accepting the old concept of destiny, he liberalizes it with the addition that effort is one of the ways through which the inevitable comes to pass. The legal philosophy that results from this is realistic in the modern sense in that it is distrustful of ideas or principles that are not embodied in actual decisions of courts enforced by the power of the State. But he is also a realist in the ancient sense of recognizing the reality of ideals which mold the policy of the law. Though distrustful of mere logic-chopping, he constantly preached the importance of theory, of critically examining the grounds of social policy.*

In his economic and political views Justice Holmes remained personally faithful to the classical tradition of individualism and *laissez faire,* and this showed itself in the extreme harshness of his legal opinions in cases of tort and in his faith in economic competition as bringing to the fore the most capable directors of economic production. His extraordinarily keen intellectuality, however, made him realize the limitations of his personal knowledge of these matters. His conception of chivalry also enabled him to appreciate that the laboring people were entitled to more consideration than his less imaginative and more traditionally minded colleagues would grant. His great dissenting opinions thus gave him a reputation for radicalism. This was not at all an accurate appreciation of his position, except to the extent that radicalism may denote the position of the liberal evolutionist who recognizes that it is impossible to fix in advance for all times what governments may or may not do, and that the pretense of courts to find in the Fourteenth Amendment all the restraints on popular legislation which they have read into it is intellectually indefensible.

Though Holmes was always a gallant figure and greatly admired, he has until recently had very little influence.** His great decisions were those in dissent. No branch of American law can be said to have been molded by him. He was an intellectual aristocrat and was not disturbed by the fact that the legal profession did not take the trouble to under-

---

* *Cf.* "Oliver Wendell Holmes" in M. R. Cohen, *Law and the Social Order* (1933), p. 363.

** Since the considerable changes in the personnel and fundamental attitude of the Supreme Court in the later 1930's, "Holmes's views on constitutional law have been pretty generally followed by the majority of the court, and expressed with particular clarity by Justices Black and-Douglas." M. R. Cohen, *The Faith of a Liberal* (1946), p. 21.

stand him. It might also be added that his preference for pregnant, pithy utterances rather than for systematically articulated arguments did not make it easy for the neophyte to get the full bearings of this thought. His utterances came like streaks of lightning that illumined the whole scene but left us with little guidance on how to manage the vexatious details. In this respect he was the direct antithesis of his dear friend and colleague, Justice Brandeis, whose strength is almost entirely in his acute perception of the relevant economic details rather than in the fundamental principles involved.

Still, the essential soundness of Holmes' main views on the nature of law, the thorough though unpretentious scholarship, give his work an enduring quality, so that it seems unquestionable that future students of the law will come back to his writings as to those of no other American jurist. At any rate, the latest school of American jurisprudence seems to start from one of his dicta: to wit, that the law is not a brooding omnipresence in the sky but our prediction of what courts will decide—a dictum which some have taken too literally.*

Holmes showed the keenness of his independent mind by expressing the opinion that he would not be afraid if the veto power of the federal courts over Congressional legislation were done away with. In his insistence, however, on maintaining the power of the courts to declare state laws unconstitutional, he ignores the fact that in a changing society the relations between the states and the nation are essentially political, *i.e.,* determined on grounds of social policy, and that it is only by an intellectually indefensible fiction that they can be deduced from a written document such as our Federal Constitution. Justice Holmes' own repeated protests against the unconscionable stretching of such terms as *liberty* in the Fourteenth Amendment to void laws that a majority of the judges do not approve offer some evidence that a federal council, as in the case of the Swiss Confederation, could adjust state and federal relations on taxation and the like in a manner no worse than we do by giving the last word to judges who are trained and think in terms of private law.

The Realistic School

While the term *realistic* is now extensively applied to a number of recent juristic writers, it is rather difficult to formulate any positive doctrine on which they all agree. Some of them, indeed, profess a deep

---

* Cf. "Justice Holmes and the Nature of Law" in M. R. Cohen, *Law and the Social Order* (1933), p. 198.

distrust of all doctrines. Yet, it is clear, they all reject the classical view that the law consists of fixed principles and that cases are actually decided by purely logical deduction from them.

There certainly is no connection between the realistic movement in law and the two forms of realism (neo and critical realism) in recent American philosophy; for the latter emphasize the reality of universals or essences, while the legal movement is decidedly hostile to that, and most of its members seem inclined to nominalism.[21] It uses the term *realism* in the sense in which it is used in literature; namely, true to actualities as opposed to ideals. Some hostility to idealism is already implicit in Holmes. Contemporary legal realists, however, have not shown much interest in the philosophic foundations of their point of view.* One must stand outside to discover the intellectual currents that have taken them up.

BIGELOW AND BROOKS ADAMS

The first pronouncement of this school came in the volume entitled *Centralization and the Law,* to which the venerable Melville Bigelow and Brooks Adams were the principal contributors. Dean Bigelow, who had done splendid pioneer work in the field of legal history, came out strongly for the view that the law is something that actually holds sway in human society and that the rights of individuals must be judged entirely in terms of social effects. Brooks Adams dealt with the law on the principle of a monistic economic determinism, without mentioning Marx or any of his followers. Despite the great eminence of its contributors, and the obvious relevance of its ideas to the progressive movement which had begun about that time, the volume failed to stir effectively the current of American legal thought—though it would be hard to assert that the tenth edition of Bigelow's book on *The Elements of the Law of Torts,* in which some of these ideas were applied, exerted no influence.

BENTLEY

On a somewhat wider philosophic basis was Arthur F. Bentley's *The Process of Government,* in some respects still the most vigorous expression

---

[21] The nominalistic note was first struck by Professor Bingham who, starting from the assumption that there are no universals in nature, insisted that the law consists of actual decisions in individual cases, and that legal rules or principles are merely opinions in the minds of those who think about the law.

Bingham's articles were published at a time when the classical theory was otherwise unquestioned and, though they drew a reply from Kocourek, they continued to be ignored until attention was called to them two decades later by Frank and Llewellyn.

* Cf. "Philosophy and Legal Science" in M. R. Cohen, *Law and the Social Order* (1933), p. 219.

of legal realism in America. Some time before behavioristic psychology came into its vogue, but shortly after William James' attack on consciousness as a substance, Bentley opened a vigorous war against mind stuff or mental qualities as an explanation of social phenomena, and particularly against the use of emotions, instincts, and ideals as if they were separate substantial entities acting as causes. From this point of view, he submitted to drastic criticism not only all the regnant sociologists, but also jurists like von Jhering and Dicey. Von Jhering's interests or ends (*Zwecke*) and Dicey's ideas, such as individualism and collectivism, are not in themselves social realities. They are nothing apart from certain factual contents, the explanation or mechanism of which they in no way describe or indicate.

In accordance with the current distrust of the abstract as unreal and preference for dealing with the totality of things (common to Neo-Hegelians like Bradley and Bosanquet, and instrumentalists like Dewey), Bentley views the law not as an abstract system of principles but as an actual social process. It is not merely what judges do or will do, but what happens in a society in which various groups seek to control certain transactions or forms of conduct. From this point of view he saw what had previously been expressed by H. J. Ford, to wit, that political organs and divisions are not absolutely rigid and fixed, but are to some extent plastic, and that they shift their function under the pressure of diverse groups. Bentley thus laid the foundation of the study of what later came to be called "pressure-politics."

Bentley deflates the metaphoric or fictional element in the usual talk about the social will. The actual fact before us is that of action and reaction between classes and groups. In this view there is no denying or even minimizing the importance of documents, precedents, doctrines, judicial attitudes, and the like. But these things are the raw material of the legal process.

When we thus view the law socially, the differences between public and private law and between criminal and civil law cease to be of great importance. The smallest dispute between two parties involves questions of general import to classes of people. We try not the particular individual but the *murderer* (and thus introduce the abstract conception). "It is impossible to try a murderer purely as an individual. Actually the murderer, that is the murdering activity, is just as much generalized, just as much 'social' as is the rule."[22] Bentley thus distinguishes between formal and actual law. An unenforced statute may more readily become law, because the group that brought about its enactment is likely to insist that

---

[22] Arthur F. Bentley, *The Process of Government* (1908), p. 280.

the government machinery enforce it; but the actual enforcement is the social fact.

Bentley recognizes, as every honest thinker must, that law is made in the course of administration by the process of filling in details, and that all the various portions of the governing body, judiciary as well as executive, participate in this process. Although the law is developed by individual judges, it is misleading so to overemphasize that fact as to lose sight of the interconnection which gives us a system instead of merely diverse judgments like disconnected pebbles. To be sure, not the whole of society but definite groups favor any specific law to the extent of pushing its claims. Still there is the great reality of social inertia which tends to create respect for the judiciary, so that the fact that judges have ruled in certain ways itself becomes a determining factor.

Groups tend to unite on common interests, and to that extent the content of the law spreads. While laws come into being to meet certain specific difficulties—*e.g.*, the laws of quarantine—once a law exists many interests will seek to avail themselves of it and thus spread its influence.

In determining the various groups that make the law, we need not ignore the interests of the lawyers and of the court itself. They are interested in precedents and technicalities, which save them the labor of having to think long before deciding. Out of this develop general doctrines. In the conflict between group interests before the court, advocates base their claims on general reasons. These reasons tend to form a rational system and constitute a legal theory. The theory may then become a philosophy of law.

Bentley's book fell on a deaf world. There were few members of the legal public to pay attention to it, and leading sociologists like Small could not understand it. But in the 1920's behavioristic psychology attained great vogue and its influence spread into all the social sciences. Possibly the forms of anti-rationalism that came to the front (described in Aliotta's *The Idealistic Reaction Against Science*) were a factor in the situation. At any rate, we notice economists, sociologists, and political scientists abandoning the old classical methods and aiming instead to describe institutional behavior rather than the logical consequences of assumed laws. It was, therefore, to be expected that a revolt against the traditional ideology of the law should turn to the positivistic view of scientific method prevailing in neighboring fields.

OLIPHANT

The influence of behaviorism in legal thought, or at any rate in its formulation, is shown in the writings of Herman Oliphant, and even more characteristically in those of Underhill Moore. Oliphant is rightly impressed with the untenability of the classical view that every case decides a principle; for, obviously, many principles of diverse generality can be adduced in support of any particular decision. Hence, to argue that any particular case determines a principle as its *ratio decidendi* is clearly fallacious. Oliphant is also impressed with the fact that the course of actual decisions does not coincide with the reasons stated in the judicial opinions that accompany and justify them. He wishes, therefore, to disregard the written opinion ("vocal behavior") and study what the judge actually does ("subvocal behavior"). He does not, however, give us any clue as to what part of the judge's behavior is relevant to a course of decisions. Suppose, for instance, that for several years the courts of one or more states continue to extend the liability of railroads or banks. It would seem clearly irrelevant to consider as a cause any physiologic factor or temperament that either varies with different judges who participate in this movement or is common to judges who do not. A variable factor cannot possibly explain a constant effect. Moreover, though the reasons judges give for their decisions may sometimes be but a "rationalization" or afterthought and not a real determinant, still it would be strange if ideas that recur in discourse had no influence at all on the course of decisions. It would seem, therefore, that the expression of judicial opinion cannot be neglected by one who wishes to understand the actual course of the law. To determine *all* the different ideas that move a judge to decide any one case seems hopeless. But, if we take a series of cases, we can eliminate variable factors and discover constant ideas or patterns, such as political or economic convictions or bias.*

UNDERHILL MOORE

Even more consistently behavioristic is Underhill Moore, who conceives the law to be the behavior not of the judge but of all the parties to any social transaction. Law, therefore, becomes identical with custom, and jurisprudence is replaced by descriptive sociology. The law of checks is simply what happens in the various transactions in which the check enters. Professor Moore has ingeniously worked out a number of categories to describe these transactions, but in the end he has no consistent and coherent test whereby to distinguish the legal from the illegal.

In modern heterogeneous and rapidly changing society the legal cannot be identified with the customary—indeed, it is the diversity of

---

* A more detailed analysis and critique of Oliphant's views will be found in "Justice Holmes and the Nature of Law", in M. R. Cohen, *Law and the Social Order* (1933), especially at pp. 216-218.

customs and their uncertainty under changing conditions that largely necessitate modern lawmaking. At any rate, there can be no doubt that the usual practices of modern business are largely determined not only by legislative enactments but also by what courts have thought the law is or should be. There is, therefore, no way of drawing the distinction between legal and illegal behavior without reference to the system of ideas which authoritatively prescribe what we should and what we should not do.

Other realists have, therefore, made the concept of legal behavior refer to the conduct of government officials. Taking a phrase of Justice Holmes out of its contextual limitations, the realistic doctrine becomes: Law is the prediction of what judges will decide. But who is properly a judge, or when is he acting within his legal power, itself depends upon our system of legal ideas. To define the law as what the courts will decide is, as others have pointed out, like defining medicine as what the doctor will prescribe—it misses the question which faces the doctor or the judge, *viz.*, what he *should* prescribe or how he *should* rule. The lawyers arguing a case are not merely predicting what the court will decide. Judges of a court in conference or individual judges deliberating how they should rule are not concerned with predicting the future. And surely the legal critic pointing out the merits or demerits of any ruling is not engaged in the process of prediction. Yet obviously lawyers, judges, and writers who are systematic critics of the law do play a large part in making the law according to their ideas. We cannot, therefore, understand the process of lawmaking without taking account of the prevailing system of legal ideas and principles. But the nominalistic bias is hostile to the patient analysis of legal ideas and to the logical methods thus involved.

FRANK

The question of logic becomes crucial in the discussion of the element of certainty in the law. So far as the law does proceed from definite rules in a rigorously deductive way there can be no more uncertainty in it than in mathematics. The actual uncertainty arises from the fact that when we try to apply legal principles to an actual situation we generally find them either meaningless or else discover that other principles leading to different results seem equally applicable. Now in many regions (though not in all) the content of a rule is not as important as that the rule be as certain as is humanly possible; and in the natural confusion between what *is* and what *ought to be* our traditionalists tend to exaggerate the extent to which the law actually is certain. Using a method that has been most useful in the natural sciences, namely, ignoring perturbations or disturbances caused by other factors and describing the ideal condition of our system when such disturbances are ignored, one can describe the ideal of the law as perfect certainty. Now such an ideal is something which every lawyer, judge, or systematic jurist must employ if he is to find or make any order, system, or meaning in the law. Those, however, who are not interested in intellectual processes, which make science or system possible, and notice how often the expectation of litigants is frustrated, are naturally unsympathetic with the effort to find any certainty at all in the law. This is one of the main points of Jerome Frank's book, *Law and the Modern Mind.** Relying on psychoanalysis, which had been introduced into the field of politics and law by Harold D. Lasswell and Hugh Goitein, Mr. Frank traces this demand for certainty to the child's reliance on the authority of the father, and, with a logic characteristic of psychoanalysis, concludes that those who insist on as much certainty as is attainable are childish.

Mr. Frank's book made a great impression among the legal modernists, though the psychoanalytic explanation of what he calls the great myth has not proved very persuasive. His subsequent work was directed toward calling attention to the disturbing factors which prevent legal rules from operating under certain conditions, for example, moving judges or juries by passion or bribery—the possibility of which no systematic jurist denies. The mere fact, however, that there are disturbances, that some people bribe juries, shows that there are recognizable legal rules which we normally expect to prevail.

ARNOLD

A somewhat more trenchant use of psychoanalysis to discredit legal rationalism is Arnold's *The Symbols of Government.*** Classical jurists, such as Dernburg, von Jhering, Tourtoulon, and Holmes, had called attention to the fact that as men live by symbols, the legal realm could not be an exception, and that, therefore, many legal rules and ceremonies must be studied from that point of view. Thurman Arnold, however, seems less interested in developing the positive content of this approach to the law than in its polemic use to show the absurdity or irrationality of our legal institutions by viewing the striking disparities between the rational principles which we profess and the courses of conduct which we actually follow. He also takes delight in showing what practical inconvenience and inhumanity follow from such devotion to ideals, principles, or theories, somewhat as the author of *Don Quixote* might have done.

* Reviewed in M. R. Cohen, *Law and the Social Order* (1933), p. 357.
** Reviewed in M. R. Cohen, *The Faith of a Liberal* (1946), p. 136.

Yet Professor Arnold does not want to be merely critical. He thinks of psychiatry as a science and that the law would become more humane if people were treated as they are in a lunatic asylum—though he recognizes that this is hardly an attainable ideal. (This is worth noting, in passing, as an interesting indication of the reaction against the legal and practical notion of responsibility.)

Professor Arnold assumes that psychiatry is a science and that it knows how to cure people. But he does not ask, When is a man cured of other than recognizable physical disease? Reflection might show that the only criterion we have of normality is the ability to behave in accordance with the prevailing ways of our community, and that is largely a moral standard. The only other test actually used is the patient's own belief that he is cured and that, of course, is affected by all sorts of faiths that do not rest on natural science.

ROBINSON

A companion volume to Arnold's book, and sharing its nearsighted craving for the method of the natural sciences in legal studies, is Edward S. Robinson's *Law and the Lawyers*.* Like other positivists, Robinson starts with the assumption that science must restrict itself to the study of the facts of existence and concludes that we must, therefore, get rid of all ethical ideals about what law ought to be. This, however, ignores the fact that all developed sciences proceed from theories and the consideration of ideal conditions, *e.g.*, rational mechanics, thermodynamics, physical chemistry, and the like. Moreover, Professor Robinson himself views the law as a form of social engineering. But how can we engage in any form of engineering without some idea of what is worthwhile achieving? We must, of course, recognize the facts of existence, which are often, alas, not as we should like them to be. But that, however, is only a necessary and not a sufficient condition. Ideas of the desirable social aim in the law are indispensable. And if we do not subject these ideals to a critical study, we continue to use them in traditional and superstitious ways.

Functionalism

Less anti-rationalistic, though still vigorously opposed to the traditional, logical methods of the fundamentalists of the Harvard school, are a group of writers who call themselves functionalists. The chief objective

---

* Reviewed in M. R. Cohen, *Reason and Law* (1950), p. 173.

of this group is the study of the law as it actually operates in the social milieu. Pound had already included this in sociologic jurisprudence, but these writers are more emphatic and make it their primary objective. The functional approach is distinguished from the historical, which describes how rules originated, and from the analytical, which is interested in the internal logical structure of legal doctrines. The meaning of a penal law, according to this view, is the set of social processes which it starts in operation. Justice Holmes had already indicated that we do not know but only guess how much actual good or evil the criminal law brings about. The functionalists stress the importance of taking pains to find this out. So far, this seems to be mainly a program, and it is curious to note that the principal factual inquiry along this line has been made by Professor and Mrs. Sheldon Glueck who seem to be much more under the influence of the Harvard school than of the functionalists.

COOK

The leadership of this functional school may well be attributed to Professor W. W. Cook, who seems to have exerted considerable influence on his colleagues at Yale and at Columbia. Professor Cook was trained as a mathematical physicist and, unlike most law professors, he has had some firsthand knowledge of the methods of the natural sciences. Adding to this some familiarity with the trends of modern logic, Cook has been able to bring effective criticism against the traditional assumption of self-evident principles. The school of jurisprudence that he organized at Johns Hopkins and which seems to have devoted itself mainly to statistical studies was not, unfortunately, able to carry its work far enough to show significant results.

CORBIN AND CLARK

With somewhat less regard for theoretical programs but with admirable persistence in applying these new ideas to legal material are the studies of Arthur L. Corbin in the field of contracts and those of Dean Charles E. Clark in the field of pleading.

LLEWELLYN

Starting from a sociologic point of view, in many respects similar to those of Ehrlich, Karl N. Llewellyn's conception of jurisprudence is that of a study of the typical modes of conduct which the law regulates. At times he conceives the law also as the conduct of government officials, which is, of course, not quite the same as the conduct, let us say, of merchants in buying and selling. Like Ehrlich, Llewellyn tends to underemphasize the logic of litigation, for it is the atypical case that gets into court. The question, however, what effect a court decision will have upon the general practice cannot be ignored by one interested in the interaction between law and general economic activity, for business practices are framed with a view to their legal obligations. Explicit recognition of ethical issues does not seem to find favor in contemporary legal realism.

F. S. COHEN

It is the merit of Dr. F. S. Cohen's work, especially of his *Ethical Systems and Legal Ideals*, to have attempted this task on a broad philosophic basis and on adequate legal knowledge. It is not at all certain that he has succeeded in combining the "intrinsic goodness" of G. E. Moore with the stark hedonistic utilitarianism of Bentham; for the former is essentially objective, independent of human preference, and indeed of human existence, which pleasure and happiness certainly are not. In view of the insuperable difficulties of finding a common denominator for all forms of happiness or of arriving at any objective process of measuring or weighing heterogeneous pleasures against each other, we cannot expect this kind of work to be available for the immediate settling of actual legal cases. In the end, however, such analysis clarifies our ideas on the relation between law and the various human values that are set up as its goal, and this is a necessary first step for dealing with legal issues intelligently and honestly.

The Outlook

The liberalization of legal studies is likely to be aided by movements in three allied fields; to wit, economics, political science, and philosophy.

The emphasis by writers like Commons, Veblen, and others on the actual institutions which control economic activity is bound to call attention to the more intimate relations between law and economics. There is a possibility, however, that institutional economics may become purely descriptive and devoid of significant ideas, just as happened in the previous reaction against pure economic theory by the historical school.

While political theory seems to be passing through a singularly unpromising period, it has liberated itself in large part at least from the scholastic constitutionalism of the late Professor Burgess, and in the treatment of administrative law it seems to have already opened the way for a more realistic and constructive mode of study.

Traditional American legal thought not only directed its energy primarily to private and commercial transactions, but it took a certain pride in minimizing administrative law. This, of course, followed from the dogma of the supremacy of the civil courts and the subordination of all public law to the forum dominated by lawyers representing private clients. But with the expansion of government machinery, the growth of administrative law could not be stopped. Courts might theoretically control the administration of public office, but in fact this is not feasible beyond a limited extent; and the absence of administrative courts thus actually serves to give practically unlimited discretion to the official. For technical reasons also, special administrative courts to determine questions of customs duties and various issues in other departments of the government arose, and various industrial and public-service commissions began to exercise governmental duties that could not be split up into executive and judicial. The two men who had the wisdom to see the growing importance of administrative law and to consider closely its nature and relation to other departments of jurisprudence were Frank J. Goodnow and Ernst Freund. Goodnow began with the study of municipal government and went on to the wider study of comparative administrative law. He realized the inadequacy of our blind rejection of the Continental system, according to which centrally appointed officials administer locally enacted laws, instead of locally elected officials administering centrally enacted laws, which is the American way. Coming to his subject from the point of view of political science rather than from the orthodox teaching of law, Goodnow shared the aversion of historicists to the natural-rights philosophy. This made him sympathetic to the movement for social reform and opposed to a narrow interpretation of the Constitution.

It is characteristic that when Burgess retired as Ruggles Professor of Constitutional Law at Columbia, Goodnow was passed over and a conservative "common-law" lawyer of little if any scholarly achievements was appointed. The latter, however, lectured only in the Law School and in the end scholarship triumphed through the appointment of Howard L. McBain, a careful and conscientious student of constitutional and municipal law as they actually operate under our political institutions.

The doctrine of natural rights and the traditional theory of a division of powers strictly limited by what is found in a written Constitution would have made actual government impossible had not our courts found the device of a police power inherent in the states to protect public safety, health, and morals. What is within the police power and what is not has never been definitely determined, being in fact largely dependent on the personal opinions of the judges about what states and municipalities should or should not do. Professor Freund, however, has dealt with this problem in a courageous, scholarly manner and has sought to clarify the actual body of American decisions in some rational way. Despite a good deal of natural revulsion against the nebulous speculation that often passes as legal philosophy, he was never quite satisfied merely with digesting the actual decisions, but always sought to find a genuinely rational pattern which should aid us not only to harmonize the actual decisions but to supply illuminating ideas on the direction in which the law can wisely be pushed. There seems to be a good deal of promise that work along this line will help to clear the ground of much legal superstition.

On the part of our professional philosophers there is still little attention to political and legal philosophy. William Ernest Hocking of Harvard has written on the state and on rights, but he has been a lone voice in the idealistic camp. This is rather surprising, for Josiah Royce had developed the organic view of federalism by emphasizing the dangers both of too much centralization and of provincialism or separateness. But the idealistic school of philosophy has made no attempt to work along this line. It must be added that, if pragmatic philosophers were to follow William James, their interests in political philosophy would be small and their views predominantly and conservatively individualistic. James, however, did strengthen utilitarianism, which may again become a dominant note in legal philosophy if traditional liberalism can recover some of its old force. More important, however, is the vital sense of justice and sympathy with human needs shown by John Dewey and J. H. Tufts in their great textbook on *Ethics* and in other of their individual writings. Perhaps the union of this tendency with the growing interest among younger American philosophers in logic and rigorous scientific procedure may lead to a genuinely realistic philosophy of law—realistic not only in recognizing what actually exists but also in perceiving the finer possibilities which are worth achieving.

Chapter VII

RELIGIOUS
THOUGHT

Popular Attitudes Towards Religion

THE POSITION OF RELIGION in America seems anomalous. Nowhere do educated people speak of religion with more general respect. The number of our outspoken atheists is negligible and even to call oneself a free-thinker is considered "bad form." Nowhere else does the classical tradition which goes back to Lucretius and which makes religion and superstition synonymous seem to have so completely disappeared. But on the other hand it may also be contended that though we use the word *religion* in an honorific sense, its old content or meaning is all gone, and we now apply it vaguely to any generous emotion, especially about social or political reform. This appears clearly in the voluminous writings of that most typical American, Theodore Roosevelt. Though he often speaks of religion, it is never of its mysteries, sacraments, beliefs or virtues, never of Christian humility, faith, hope, charity or love. Religion to him means good deeds, like the acquisition and building of the Panama Canal—and it has nothing to do with other-worldiness, spirituality, or organized divine worship. In his own estimation and in the public eye, Theodore Roosevelt was a religious man. No general protest greeted his reference to Tom Paine, one of the authors of the American Revolution, as a "filthy little atheist." Yet the fact is that Tom Paine, the friend of Washington and Jefferson, not only represented the liberal thought of most of the founders of our republic, but professed quite definite beliefs in God, in the immortality of the soul, and in rewards and punishments as a consequence of the moral government of the universe. How did Theodore Roosevelt stand on these issues? One looks in vain for any indications of such beliefs in the writings of our national hero who was the wielder of the "Big

Stick." I have not found in any of his writings any trace of what used to be regarded as the essentials of Christian belief, the Trinity, the Incarnation, the need of atonement, or faith in the sacraments of a church. Practical, worldly morality and an occasional attendance at some church seem to have been sufficient to make Theodore Roosevelt generally acceptable as a type of the religious citizen. Surely it would be difficult to find a better example of continued honor to the word *religion,* coupled with disregard of all that it has historically denoted.[1]

THE DIVERSITIES OF RELIGIOUS ATTITUDES

We can better understand this paradoxical position of religion in our life if we bear in mind not only the separation of church and state, but also the differences between our rural and urban life.

The great diversity of sects in our cities, and the fact that all are free and that no one is sufficiently powerful to have its church "established" and supported by direct taxation, remove most of the traditional sources of fear, irritation and conflict in regard to organized religion. Atheists, to be sure, sometimes complain against the remission of taxes on church property; but as their own buildings, devoted to educational work, are similarly privileged, their complaint arouses no great popular indignation. Thus, not only do American cities breed the indifference to religion characteristic of modern cities generally, but the absence of fear or feeling of religious oppression promotes a prevailing attitude of benevolent neutrality.

This attitude towards religion is to be explained by the absence of any one sect sufficiently powerful by itself to control the state, rather than by any attitude of general tolerance. If Roman Catholicism were to become the faith of a predominant part of the population, its rejection of the doctrine of the separation of church and state could certainly lead its adherents to demand greater secular sanctions for its views on education, marriage and divorce, greater respect for the hierarchy, etc.[2] The close connection between some of our rural Protestant churches and the Anti-Saloon League, and the part played by churchmen like the Methodist Bishop Cannon in opposing the election of Governor Smith in 1928, indicate other limitations of the desire to keep church and state entirely apart.

---

[1] See his *Fear God and Take Your Own Part* (1916); also the William Belden Noble lecture on "Applied Ethics" delivered at Harvard Univ., December 14, 1910. (Reprinted in *Works of Theodore Roosevelt,* National Edition, Vol. XIII, pp. 596-610).

[2] See *The State and the Church* (1937), ed. by John A. Ryan and M. F. X. Millar.

There is nothing, indeed, in the Protestant tradition or in the language of our Federal Constitution hostile to an established religion in any of our states.

It is often asserted that one of the great contributions of America to the civilized thought of mankind is the notion of a free church in a free society: that is, a society in which everyone is free to develop his own religious conscience without any group controlling the state so as to interfere with the freedom of others. In this respect the complete separation of church and state in America is supposed to be an ideal achievement, and we Americans are sorry for those peoples who have no such advantage as we have in this respect.

Now while it is true that we have no established church, and that our political life is relatively free from religious warfare, it is a great mistake to think that religious toleration or complete freedom is an achievement based upon the liberal attitude of the American mind. It is important to examine this matter more closely in order to understand what has happened, and what is likely to happen in the future.

In the first place, it is well to note that the American Constitution does not guarantee complete religious liberty to every citizen. Our Federal Constitution prohibits Congress from establishing a church, but it puts no express restrictions on the states.

In fact, at the time of our American Revolution nine of the thirteen colonies had established churches supported by public taxes. It was not until 1833 that the Congregational Church was finally disestablished in Massachusetts. Non-conformists were persecuted in most of our colonies, where for a long time only orthodox church members could exercise the right of political suffrage. And states like Maryland have an even longer unenviable record of intolerance to those outside of the Trinitarian Christian churches.

In view of this history we can understand the tacit but widespread assumption, especially in rural America, that ours is not only a Christian but also a Protestant country. Many well-established practices (perhaps vestiges of an order which has been outgrown) agree with this, e.g., our Sunday legislation, the prayers which open our legislative and even some judicial sessions, the laws against blasphemy, the reading of the Bible in schools, the oath on the Bible demanded of witnesses in courts, etc. In some of our states it is still possible to discredit a witness, or the declaration of a man about to die, on the ground that if he does not believe in a future life he has no motive for telling the truth.

It is not surprising to find in rural American communities strong feelings against Catholics, Jews, or infidels. This prejudice often takes the form of social and even economic discrimination. Church membership is likely to improve one's business credit as well as social respectability. Disbelief, openly avowed, disqualifies one for a political career. Ingersoll's free-thought killed his political prospects. The depth of our intolerance is shown by the reaction to the candidacy of Governor Smith for the presidency of the United States, especially among Southerners, who preferred to vote even for a Republican rather than for a Catholic. In a very large part of our country the same attitude would be maintained against a Jew.*

That the churches have not kept out of politics, is attested by our national experience in regard to prohibition. The defeat of the Child Labor Amendment to the Constitution, the defeat of the plan for a Federal Department of Education, and even the defeat of the President's Court Plan, were largely due to the influence of the Catholic Church; and the influence of Protestantism in our educational institutions is not confined to anti-evolution laws.

It is doubtless true, that compared to other countries we are relatively free from religious controversies in our political life; but it would be a great mistake to suppose that the progress has been due to an original demand, on the part of the American people, for freedom in the field of religion. The history of religious thought in this country shows no such simple demand for general religious freedom.

It has frequently been alleged that the Puritans came to this country to secure religious freedom. But this assertion, depite repetition, is contrary to fact. The Puritans were not persecuted in England because of their religious views; on the contrary, it was they who tried to upset the form of government which had prevailed in the English church. When they came here they had no desire to permit any other form of worship than their own, and they, in fact, persecuted Quakers and others, who tried to settle within their domain. The actual growth of tolerance in this country came through the need of inviting emigrants and through the actual diversity of the different religious sects who took advantage of the opportunities thus extended to them in the new world. Out of this diversity there gradually emerged the concept of the separation of church and state which has become so important a part of our liberal civilization.

Another feature which has dominated American religious thought has been the tremendous role of the laity in the government of American churches. This, again, was originally an outgrowth of local conditions.

---

* See "Jews in Commerce and the Professions" in M. R. Cohen, *Reflections of a Wondering Jew* (1950), p. 34.

Theoretically the colonists of Massachusetts and Virginia were subject to the Bishop of London, but there was not sufficient revenue to make the matter one of great importance to the governors of the Church of England. It was purely local conditions which led originally to the separation of the Congregationalists from the Church of England.

The Anglican churches (Episcopal and Methodist) had to overcome the shock of the Revolution: the revolution against English rule necessarily denied the right of the English hierarchy to govern in American religious communities. And when the Episcopal Church was reorganized here it had to assume the right to change the prayer book, since it had to eliminate prayers for the King and introduce instead prayers for the President of the United States.

The domination of church organizations by the lay community was vastly strengthened by the character of American immigration. Those colonies, especially the proprietary colonies, that were most anxious to attract settlers were relatively liberal in their immigration policies. In order to attract more tenants they had to relax religious discriminations. Thus they came to offer religious autonomy to many diverse groups and sects, each of which was likely to set up its own religious structure. The need of settlers and the wide spaces between settlements made this tolerance and departure from uniformity acceptable first to the Crown and later to most of the States.

Further strength was given to the pattern of local lay control by the fact that our religious communities have always engaged so heavily in activities not strictly ecclesiastical. Properties used for educational and other social services are commonly held by lay trustees. It was thus very hard to fit the old pattern of hierarchical governmental control of religious institutions into the conditions of American life. Even the Roman Catholic Church has not completely escaped the American tendency towards domination by the laity. Lay trustees exercise a large control over property and purse strings.

The American ideal of a community of free-willing souls arranging their own religious affairs carries with it, as an obverse side of the coin, a certain restriction upon the authority of the ministry. This has been poignantly put in the columns of the *Christian Century*:

"There is a tyranny of the pew over the pulpit in America which is not paralleled in other protestant nations and which only the stoutest heart can defy."[3]

Lay control of religion proved to be both a cause and a consequence

[3] July 15, 1926.

of the relatively backward character of our religious leadership in large areas.

The conditions of a sparsely settled people, prevented, in colonial times, as well as today in large parts of the country, the employment of any trained clergy. Hence, not only was the property of the church held by laymen, but lay preachers played a dominant role in many religious communities. This was reenforced by the growth of Methodism and the Baptist Churches, which led to systematic disparagement of learned theology and excessive emphasis on the type of emotional religious experience that is associated with revivalism in the camp meeting. Indeed, revivalism, with its recrudescence of the most primitive forms of religious frenzy, is essentially a phenomenon of the influx of groups that have no trained authoritative religious leaders. It is when new countries are opened, or new classes come into their own in times of rapid change, that revivalist forms of religion spread.

MODERNISM AND FUNDAMENTALISM

With this background we can better understand the conflict between modernism and fundamentalism in the Protestant churches.

The efforts on the part of Tennessee and other states to prohibit the teaching of evolution have seemed to some observers to be a recrudescence of an attitude generally supposed to have disappeared long ago. This view is a mistake. Fundamentalism is not a recrudescence. Its adherents never accepted anything else. Their alarm is rather an indication that modernism is for the first time knocking at the gates of rural, provincial America.

Until quite recently those regions of the West in which fundamentalism now flourishes were practically cut off from all centers of liberal culture. The people who flocked to the territories were land-hungry, and they were subjected to an environment that made no call on, and left little time for, refinement of thought. Between clearing fields and fighting Indians, cultivated interest in free religious ideas could take little root. The religious life of the open frontier consisted largely of occasional revival meetings, swept into emotional orgies by itinerant preachers. In sparsely settled communities, struggling for economic necessities, the regular minister had not a parish but a circuit. These clergymen themselves had received little academic schooling; and whatever religious training they possessed had been acquired in Bible institutes which intellect-fearing Methodists substituted for regular theological seminaries. All this, together with the absence of universities and of an intellectual class, prevented the infiltration of any modern ideas about science. The effect was that the traditional religious conceptions, fortified by a crude emotionalism, remained unmodified and unchallenged in such communities.

Matters have been only a little different in the South. It is true that the South, which today is the stronghold of fundamentalism, was during the eighteenth century much more liberal than was Calvinistic New England. Middle class bourgeois asceticism had never dominated the plantation culture of the Southern squirearchy in the time of Jefferson. At the beginning of the nineteenth century, the old culture of the South still continued the liberal eighteenth century tradition, which flourished in England and which was represented in this country by Benjamin Franklin, Jefferson and Tom Paine. The New England theology of Jonathan Edwards and of Timothy Dwight, was regarded as chill blast from the northern barbarians. But the opening up of new land in the West led, in the first quarter of the nineteenth century, to the economic bankruptcy of the old Southern aristocracy and to the decline of its intellectual traditions. As the Southern liberal tradition broke down, the wave of revivalism spread from Kentucky and Tennessee to the Atlantic seaboard. The North, with its greater variations of religious belief, due to the demand for Northern labor for its manufacturing enterprises, then became the religiously liberal part of the country. Thereafter, the Civil War impoverished the South and numbed its culture. Proud of its past, it despised the progressiveness of the North. Thus conservatism in religion, as in politics and social life, tended to replace free intelligence. Newer scientific doctrines had to overcome the double disadvantage of being irreligious and Northern. The intensely evangelical character of Southern Methodism was hardly conducive to the development of reasoned religion. Emotionalism fortified by ignorance is immune to new ideas.

Religion in the small towns of the South and West, while social in organization, is narrowly theologic in conception. The church functions as a local "natural" society. It is the center of the "legitimate" social life of the community; it supports Sunday schools, a branch of the Women's Christian Temperance Union, and other popular religious causes. In the absence of any dangerous opposition from competing faiths or active disbelief, there is no stimulus to reexamine the religious doctrines professed. Religious teaching becomes primarily an emphasis on traditional supernaturalism, on the hereafter as a moral sanction, and on the Bible, literally interpreted as God's word. No need is felt to adapt religion to the progress of modern thought.

In the industrial North and East a different situation exists. In these regions there is a much greater diversity of religions, a wider knowledge of popular science and a freer system of education. Not only do many churches exist in the same community, but, what is worse, there are good citizens who belong to none, and the city churches cannot, therefore, generally depend upon direct *social pressure* to fill their organizations. To attract new members they thus must resort to sundry devices. They must engage in apologetics, and in doing so they try to adjust themselves to whatever scientific currents are prevalent in the intellectual atmosphere. They cannot merely thunder against non-believers: men must be persuaded to come into the church before they can be threatened with hell-fire. This has gradually led to the subordination of the strictly theological aspects of thought to social organization and to the substitution of a vague social idealism for a definitely formulated creed.

Even in the Roman Catholic Church, which as an international faith claiming universal truth cannot have a separate American Catholic philosophy and has probably been less influenced by the American scene than most of our Protestant sects, the American emphasis on social reform and progress has proved a significant force. What used to be called "Americanism" in the Catholic Church embodied an emphasis on liberal social thought and piecemeal reform that would scarcely be found a dominant note in the Catholicism of most other lands. To some extent this tendency in American Catholicism may be attributed to the fact that American Catholics are predominantly urban and largely involved in the struggles of labor and in the efforts of underprivileged immigrant groups to achieve equality of rights. It is reasonable to expect that the contributions of American Catholics to Catholic philosophy, which are just beginning, will eventually assume large proportions. All the indications to date make it probable that the contributions of American Catholics to social ethics will be more American than Catholic.

A church, like any other social organization, puts its own existence first. No compromise seems unjustified when the basis of its very existence is threatened. And at all times the desire to exercise power and influence is stronger than the desire for doctrinal purity. A modern city clergyman can attract an audience by preaching on some contemporary social or political problem; he can hold the young with movies and dances; he can present the women with noble occasions for their teas and bridge parties. City churches have become neighborhood clubs interested in those social sides of religion which the adherents of the old faith were wont to call *worldliness*.

Hitherto, so long as the city and the country had not achieved the same standard of social living, and so long as the means of communication were undeveloped, the country remained practically indifferent to the religious life of the city. But today our rural sections have become acutely aware of what is going on in metropolitan centers. The automobile and the radio have brought some of the ideas and facilities of the city to the youth of the village and small town. But the rural church cannot imitate the many enterprises of the city church. Feeling that they are being outdone, they sense a threat to their own security in the loose manner in which the historical teachings of Christianity are being diluted. Fundamentalism is the response of rural America to the swelling tide of new modes of thought and action which threaten to engulf it and upset its fancied security.

The main points at issue between the fundamentalist and modernist may be stated simply. The fundamentalist maintains that Christianity is an historical religion centering around certain *beliefs,* such as the Trinity, the Divinity of Christ, His Virgin Birth and Resurrection, and the absolute literal truth of the Bible. He protests against the modernist practice of denying these facts and yet continuing to use the traditional concepts and phrases which imply them. He insists that to substitute a vague faith for a definite theology is to abandon the Christian religion. "The liberal attempt at reconciling Christianity with modern science," writes one of the fundamentalist leaders, "has really relinquished everything distinctive of Christianity, so that what remains is in essentials only that same indefinite type of religious aspiration which was in the world before Christianity came upon the scene."[4] The struggle, then, is conceived to be between the redemptive religion of Christianity and a naturalistic paganism disguised under the name of Christian liberalism.

Having abandoned the central doctrines of historic Christianity, the modernist should, according to his opponents, withdraw from the church. No one has a right to enter or remain within a church in order to overthrow its doctrines. To the charge of intellectual dishonesty in the ambiguous use of traditional symbols is thus added the charge of personal immorality involved in accepting financial support from an institution whose doctrines modernists are undermining.[5]

The modernist, however, points first, to the impossibility of a literal interpretation of the Bible. Not even the most rabid fundamentalist believes that the hare chews the cud (Lev. XI, 6). But if the Bible is mistaken in this, as it clearly is also in various geological and astronomical matters, the doctrine of plenary inspiration must be reinterpreted. In view of the progress of modern science and the revelation of new truth,

---

[4] John G. Machen, *Christianity and Liberalism* (1923), p. 7.
[5] *Cf.* Machen's *What is Faith?* (1925), pp. 102ff.

no friend of religion should interpret its doctrines in such a way as to make them inconsistent with demonstrable truth. "Why may not the Holy Ghost have spoken in ancient times through parables?"

The question whether we can have religion without any creed or definite intellectual content, comes up acutely in connection with the struggle between religion and modern science. The Christian religion, for instance was organized in the definite belief that salvation was restricted to those who believed in certain historical propositions, namely, that in Adam the whole human race fell into mortal sin, that to atone for it God assumed human form in Jesus Christ, was crucified in the governorship of Pilate, rose up on the third day, etc. These facts were recorded in the Bible, which was thus regarded as a supremely authoritative source of truth. Modern astronomy, biology and history have been forced to reject many Biblical propositions as inconsistent with verifiable truth, e.g., the account of creation, the chronology and genealogy from Adam to Jesus, that Jesus drove devils out of human beings into swine. From time to time various churches fought against the Copernican astronomy, againt the higher criticism of the Bible, against the doctrine of organic evolution, as well as against the denial of witchcraft. In this struggle the opponents of science have, in the intellectual field, been ignominiously defeated.*

The modernist seeks to avoid the ignominy of past and future defeats in the struggle against science by relocating religion in a world where there are no disprovable propositions. In this view of religion it is not necessary for the church to have a *common* faith or doctrine or belief. Christianity for the modernist is a life, not a doctrine, and must be understood in terms of personal experience and social evolution. The conception of absoluteness or finality for any religion must be abandoned. Jesus is not an object of belief but an ideal inspiration of faith. On this view even God "ceases to be a principle of explanation. His existence then becomes necessary only for religious experience."[6]

It is curious to note that so far as consistency is concerned, the simple-minded fundamentalists occupy much the stronger position. So much is this the case that the sophisticated modernist often resorts to dangerouly obscurantist, anti-intellectualist arguments. In thinking of the church, not as a body committed to a certain belief, but rather as a body of friends that can share their beliefs at will, modernists fail to indicate

---

* *Cf.* "The Dark Side of Religion" in M. R. Cohen, *The Faith of a Liberal* (1946), p. 337.

[6] Gerald Birney Smith, *Religious Thought in the Last Quarter Century* (1927), p. 112.

how we can have any common program demanding our supreme loyalty, if there is no common body of belief as a basis of action or aspiration. Doubtless people may change their religious beliefs, and they are within their rights to form churches of their own. But they cannot, without loss of intellectual integrity, abandon the historic doctrines of their church and at the same time claim that their new beliefs do not differ from those of the traditional founders.

The attempts, for instance, to harmonize the Bible with modern thought can only result in methods of interpretations so loose as to make it possible to prove that anything can mean anything else. Modernists generally abandon the attempt to harmonize the Biblical cosmology with our scientific geology. But can they harmonize alike the Old and New Testament commandments with our modern moral conscience? The moment, however, we begin to pick and choose amidst the various elements in the heterogeneous mass of the Biblical books, how does the Bible differ from other ancient and modern books? The logic of modernism cuts at the root not only of Christianity but of all revealed religion. Indeed the religious creeds of modernists can hardly be distinguished from those of men who used to be characterized as infidels. Few modernists, indeed, show as much positive belief in one God and in happiness beyond the grave as does Tom Paine.

THE SCIENTIST-THEOLOGIANS

Few events are so characteristic of American intellectual life as the reply of the leaders of American science to the fundamentalists' attempt at prohibition of the teaching of evolution in schools supported by state funds. Instead of taking the honest and dignified position that science as the pursuit of truth cannot pledge itself to respect any particular dogma in the Bible or elsewhere, the leaders of the American Association for the Advancement of Science (men like Pupin, Conklin, Millikan and Osborn) turned amateur theologians and tried to prove that science and religion are essentially in harmony—that even St. Thomas was an evolutionist. In order to make this reconciliation possible, both science and religion were emasculated of definite meaning. The conception of religion turns out to be such a vague altruism that it cannot possibly be identified with the historical teachings of any Christian church. They talk of a religion without theology; but when pressed as to what that means, they offer a diffuse romantic sentimentalism, with rhapsodies over a pursuit of goodness—which refers to nothing in particular; and at last to a sort of perpetual motion ever "upward and onward" but with no indication of any specific direction. Instead of pointing to any instance of a vital religion without a definite body of belief, these men of science ignore, or lightly brush aside as mere theology, all the distinctive religious doctrines which have organized and disciplined the lives of hundreds of millions of people for thousands of years. An orthodox Christian might well pray for deliverance from friends who show so little respect for the dogmas which distinguish his from other religions.

And similarly genuine friends of science have reason to be concerned at the conception of scientific method which those harmonizers assume. Instead of trying to define what precisely is meant by evolution—a word so vague that a great biologist like Jacques Loeb avoided using it—the term is used to prove that the universe is the result "of an omnipresent beauty and order, attributed in the Old Testament to Jehovah, in our language to God."[7] This, of course, ignores the fact that science deals not with the universe as a whole but with certain specific questions within it, which it solves without reference to beauty, order, Jehovah or God.[8]

The outstanding leader of these theologians of science, Robert A. Millikan, is one of the great figures in modern physics. His passionate utterances on religion show such an amazing indifference to the facts of the history of Christianity as to confirm the ancient insight that aptitudes are highly specialized and that there is little transference of training from one discipline to another. Millikan tries to prove the truth of Christian religion by identifying God with the rational order and orderly development. But such order does not differ from the necessity ($\dot{\alpha}\nu\alpha\gamma\kappa\eta$) of Democritus, or the *nature* of Spinoza and Shelley, which the orthodox have regarded as atheistic. For the Christian God is a triune person, incarnated in Jesus who suffered the crucifixion and established a church to remit the sins of those who believe in Him. From this point of view Millikan is a sheer atheist, or at best a pantheist, but surely not a Christian. The fact, therefore, that so many of our churchmen welcome his message is a most significant indication of the real status of religious thought in America. Illuminating also is his contention that ". . . The practical preaching of modern science—and it is the most insistent and effective preacher in the world today—is extraordinarily like the preaching of Jesus. Its keynote is service, the subordination of the individual to the good of the whole. Jesus preached it as a duty—for the sake of world salvation. Science preaches it as a duty—for the sake of world progress . . .

----

[7] Henry F. Osborn, *Evolution and Religion in Education* (1926), p. 34.

[8] For, as Millikan rightly admits, the universe is not yet comprehensible. *Evolution in Science and Religion* (1927), p. 28.

It would be hard to find a closer parallel."[9] It is interesting to note how many Americans make the Rotarian cant of "service" the essence of the Christian faith. They fail to note that salvation, for historical Christianity, was otherworldly in intent: deliverance from the mortal sin of birth in this world and from punishment in the next. It was clearly supernatural; and in its highest form it regarded celibacy and withdrawal from social life as supreme goods.*

Nor do all men of science admit that the technological improvements which have resulted from modern science represent the highest achievement of scientific method. Genuine science, a few still contend, is interested in discovering the truth and not in the extra-scientific uses to which the truth is put.[10] In fact, Millikan's own special accomplishments in astro-physics have contributed nothing to the control of the physical environment and have no relevance to his theologic formulation of science.

Philosophies of Religion

Reflective thought in this country on the nature and problems of religion does not seem to have been marked on the whole by great vigor and originality. There are several reasons for this: (1) The development of social Christianity in America has transferred attention from traditional questions of belief to current industrial and social practices. Labor, peace and similar matters are engrossing the interests of churchmen more and more. This attitude has been reinforced by the attitude of many social workers, who are largely drawn from the class of persons of benevolent disposition who formerly would have gone into the ministry and sought to save human souls from perdition; now they seek to save human beings from a certain temporal distress and carry over into their work a diffuse social mysticism—a feeling that by rubbing elbows with one's neighbors,

---

[9] *Ibid.*, p. 83.

* *Cf.* "A Note on Rabbi Joshua of Nazareth" in M. R. Cohen, *The Faith of a Liberal* (1946), p. 320.

[10] *Cf.* "Science Bends the Knee," *New Republic*, August 5, 1925, p. 281. Commenting on efforts to control scientific teaching in the interests of religious orthodoxy, the anthropologist, Robert H. Lowie, asserts:

> "We do not seek to undermine your faith; but we shall
> teach you science, whether it undermines your faith or not."

one always touches the divine. These views have received their best expression in the writings of men like George Davis Herron, Walter Rauschenbusch and Shailer Mathews. (2) The influence of modern Biblical criticism and the diversity of Protestant sects, which made elaboration of a common theology difficult, have led to emphasis on the moral and spiritual elements in the gospels as conveying the essential doctrines of the historical Jesus. The influence of German theologians like Schleiermacher, Harnack and Ritschl have contributed to this development. (3) Theologians who have given up the world as utterly lost and have preached social indifference have devoted their energies primarily to the writing of books to spread the light of Christianity among infidels or to strengthen convictions already acquired rather than to the development of a critical theology.

On the other hand, illuminating work in the history of religion has been done by C. H. Toy, G. F. Moore, Arthur C. McGiffert and Rufus Jones. Moore has written the best study extant on Judaism; Jones has treated the mystics of early Protestantism with fresh and sympathetic insight; in various works on the development of religious thought, McGiffert has defended his conception of religion as the progressive revelation of moral truth.

Strictly philosophic religious thought takes a number of different forms. It is well to note the views of (a) the functionalists or behaviorists (King, Ames, Coe); (b) the apologetic Christian dogmatists (Sheldon, A. K. Rogers, Leighton); (c) the so-called "experimentalism" of William James and his followers; and (d) individual philosophers like Royce, Santayana, Felix Adler, and Whitehead.

FUNCTIONALISTS OR BEHAVIORISTS

The behaviorist interpretation of religion holds that primary to all belief and even personal religious experience lies the social life of the group, expressed in religious observances and rites. The efforts of man to control and adjust himself to his environment gives religious institutions an instrumental character in strengthening the social bond, and the religious institutions invest the necessary activities of daily life with a deeper meaning. Religious experience expresses the dominant values and needs of the community; and as these values and needs change, there is a corresponding shift in the beliefs, legends and cults in which these values and needs find expression. The history of religions is really the history of the social systems in which they are found, and since the social systems change continuously, it belongs to the essence of religion to develop different theologies and practices in the course of time. There is no such thing, then, as the true religion. As social conditions change, social interests change, and with them the religious activities which idealize these interests.

Now the emphasis of this school upon the priority of ritual over belief, and the influence of social tradition on the religion of the individual is in line with the thought of Robertson Smith and Durkheim. In this they have been confirmed by the findings of recent anthropology. But from this it does not follow that *today* doctrine is no essential part of religion. It may be true that religion is an expression of human needs, but what the functionalists seem to forget is that one of those needs is the desire to know, and that sheer intellectual curiosity about the origin and government of the world we live in is as genuine a need for many people as the desire for good crops, victory over the enemy, or what not. No religion, especially today when so many conflicting faiths exist side by side, can really continue for long without some system of belief which it regards as objectively true. To interpret the life of imagination and thought as merely a means of environmental adjustment is to misconceive the instrumentalist doctrine that action is involved in the verification of truth as if the doctrine meant merely that all thought exists for the sake of action.

Characteristic of the extreme functionalist position is the manner in which religion is identified with the social interest. Ames defines religion as "a participation in the ideal values of the social consciousness,"[11] overlooking the fact that social consciousness is a vague phrase that includes ideals and values that may be in open conflict. In claiming that "the man who enters thoroughly into the social movements of his time is to that extent genuinely religious, though he may characterize himself otherwise,"[12] he has stated neither a necessary nor a sufficient condition of historical religion. According to this view, a communistic atheist is religious and the followers of Christ who withdrew from the world and all its social movements and lived alone in the desert were irreligious. Nor is there any place in the functionalist interpretation for motives which enter into the conception of religion as a holiday from everyday care, as personal contact with the supernatural, or as worship of the sublime.

APOLOGETICS

The philosophy of the apologetic Christian dogmatists takes the form of a rational defense of traditional Christian doctrines on the basis of an idealistic or spiritualistic metaphysics. The two types of religious philosophy that prevailed in the recent past were a diffuse Hegelianism and a

---

[11] Edward S. Ames, *The Psychology of Religious Experience* (1910), p. 356.
[12] *Ibid.*, p. 358.

more orthodox personalism. The first started with an analysis of ordinary experience and claimed that reference was involved to an all-inclusive Absolute which was called God. The second, represented by B. Bowne, sought to establish the real personality of the God of faith and prayer by arguments persuasive to those whose need for a "personal companionship with a personal God" was stronger than their sense of logical validity. Latter-day apologists, still grappling with the problem of God's relation to the world, have attempted to escape the old difficulties of evolution by fiat of will, with a doctrine of immanence and creative continuity in which God's transcendence is revealed in the spiritual life of persons—an eclectic solution more puzzling than the original difficulties.[13] Most apologists imagine that accepting both horns of a dilemma is the best way out between them. With few exceptions all philosophic defenders of revealed Christianity employ the same arguments from design based on a psychological *a priori* theory of probability which lends itself just as cogently to a proof of the existence of the elves and fairies of folklore as to the existence of the God of the Scriptures. The same theory of interaction, adhering to the old anthropomorphic conception of cause, subordinates mechanism to purpose, purpose to personality, personality to a community of selves—a community in which, in order to save the argument from the atheism it logically points to, God is arbitrarily assigned an exceptional position.[14] The same pathetic juggling with the problem of evil either denies the facts that raise the problem, or, admitting that evil is evil, refuses to take the consequences as they affect the power or goodness of a God defined to be omnipotent and all-loving.

Of all apologists for Christian dogma the most ingenious and stimulating is W. H. Sheldon of Yale University. He is the inventor of a new ontological proof for the existence of God, based upon a modification of the scientific conception of statistical frequency and upon the Leibnizian notion of compossibility. Sheldon bases his argument on the proposition that "all that is not self-contradictory is real. In the beginning all possibilities are real."[15] The only rational world would therefore be a world of absolute chance, one in which all possibilities are equally real. This is another way of saying, as Peirce pointed out before him, that such a world is one of absolute law or necessity. Chance no longer means *anything may* happen but *everything must* happen. In such a universe an individual is bound to appear which includes within itself the whole of

---

[13] J. A. Leighton, *Religion and the Mind of Today* (1924), pp. 278ff.

[14] Arthur K. Rogers, *The Religious Conception of the World* (1907), pp. 161ff.

[15] "Necessary Truths and Necessary Being" in *Jour. of Philosophy*, Vol. 26, No. 8 (1929), pp. 197ff., and "Another Form of the Ontological Proof" in *Philosophical Review*, Vol. 32, No. 4 (1923), pp. 355ff.

the existing world as well as its conditioned possibilities, and which turns out, in a merry deductive game, to be all-powerful, indestructible, free, conscious, good and creative—in short, the God of Christianity.

Sheldon's starting point can easily be challenged. To attempt to account for all things is to forget that demonstration is possible only because we assume certain indemonstrable propositions and indefinable term as ultimates. And if this is just what Sheldon denies, it can be shown that there exist significant alternatives to "the world of absolute chance in which everything must happen," so that the necessity for the existence of such a world and no other could be defended only by a vicious infinite regress. Another way of putting this is to question Sheldon's conception of possibility as prior to and determining actuality. But even granting Sheldon his world of absolute chance in which a God *must* sometime happen, it does not follow that such a God *has* already happened or *will* happen in any finite time. And according to his own principles, when such a God does happen, at some future time he must just as necessarily disappear, since all possibilities must be realized in infinite time. Unorthodox theology and cold consolation after all!

EXPERIMENTALISM

The main source of James's influence on American religious thought comes from his great book on the varieties of religious experience.[16] With the supreme courage of genius, James utterly discards the kind of religious experience which we have in the Bible and the great sacred books of the East. He is not interested in the great streams of religious experience which constitute the history of Brahmanism, Buddhism, Judaism, Christianity, and Mohammedanism. Assuming the old fashioned view that these religions were founded by individuals who expressed their own experiences, James regards these great streams of experience of mankind at large as secondary, and of little importance.

William James was the first among American philosophers to renounce the attempt to establish on logical grounds the comforting certainties of traditional religion. But in the psychological justification he offers of these beliefs he swings to the opposite extreme and opens the doors wide to all sorts of personal claims based on a strange conception of experiment and a still stranger one of truth. The two distinctive traits of James's point of view are a defense of the will to believe and the empirical evidence he presents for supernatural experience.

James's defense of the "right to believe at our own risk any hypothesis that is live enough to tempt our will" is really a restatement of the volun-

---

[16] *Varieties of Religious Experience* (1902).

taristic position that under certain conditions a man may choose to believe whatever is congenial to him. Now traditional philosophy has regarded a *resolution* to believe as indicating an *absence* of genuine belief, and James has advanced no argument to lead one to abandon this view. Genuine belief may take two forms: Either it is the inability to see that there is any alternative, in which case we have naive belief; or it is the result of the thorough consideration of all the elements involved in a situation and the logical necessity of drawing conclusions as to the degree of evidential force in favor of our hypothesis. Owing to the absence of adequate information, our beliefs may be suspended judgments or blind guesses— but surely there is nothing *religious* about such judgments. Where a man says he will vote for candidate A rather than candidate B, admitting that he does not know the merits of either, or that one is as good as the other, his belief in candidate A cannot be regarded as being of a profoundly religious character. At bottom James's right to believe is vitiated by a thorough skepticism, and can be legitimately advanced only by one who believes that, as far as the larger issues of man's religion are concerned, all beliefs are equally true or equally false.

Out of piety to James, Dewey has made a gallant attempt to save the "right to believe." Since in any case the refusal to act or believe is itself a choice, where there is no evidence or equal evidence for a course of conduct, one consequence of *any* action we undertake is to put us in a position to acquire more relevant evidence or to check on what we have, and hence prove or disprove the validity of the action undertaken. This is quite true, but it is not James's meaning, for why defend the *right* to do what we always do and *must* do as a matter of *fact*? If Dewey's interpretation were true, James's theory of the "right to believe" would be part of his descriptive psychology, not of his philosophy of religion, where its intent is to influence action.

James tries to fortify his justification of the dogmas of religion by empirical evidence drawn from the realm of the psychology of abnormal experience or what the Germans call para-psychology. An examination of the testimony of various abnormal persons who claimed to have been in direct contact with deity seems to James to afford proof of what he himself calls "piecemeal supernaturalism." To those who believe, as most readers of popular science do, that the essence of scientific method is to begin with the facts, James's procedure seems scientific. But then how can cosmic order or uniformities of nature be proved by miraculous exception?

Unfortunately few psychologists other than Leuba[17] have gone over

---

[17] James H. Leuba, *The Psychology of Religious Mysticism* (1925).

the material, correlated it with the findings of experimental and clinical psychology, and shown its utter inconclusiveness to establish the objective existence of what is "revealed" in the state of ecstasy or illumination. What is seen in such states can be duplicated by the use of drugs or nitrous oxide, and by the more familiar ways of fasting, physical gyrations, etc. Consequently, any claim made for the "validity" of what is experienced cannot be defended by an appeal to the *psychology* of religion, especially when this type of experience is not universally accessible. And it is well to bear in mind how hazardous it is to introduce a supernatural explanation simply because we do not know of a natural one.

The very concept of religious *experience*, however, is too facile and too much in harmony with current adoration of the term to serve any specific explanatory purpose. Its vagueness reinforces the general tendency of American philosophers to elevate all questionable assertions on religion into the results of religious experience, very much as the older theologians elevated every dogma into an intuition of the human mind or into a direct revelation of the religious consciousness. The difference in words connotes no difference in method.

Even more dangerous is the use of the word "experimental" in religious writing, likewise due to James, which makes people imagine that they are bringing religion closer to science. In reality it indicates serious confusion as to what scientific experiment means. In all religious circles this experimental cry has been taken up. "There is nothing essential to salvation or to the spiritual life of man," writes Rufus M. Jones, "which cannot be proved and verified as effectively as the facts of the light-spectrum are verified."[18] Wieman attempts to build an entire religious philosophy on the "experimental way of life by which vital truth is sought concerning God."[19] The following is typical: "We may approach the Christian Doctrine of the Divinity of Jesus in either of two ways. We may begin with a high dogmatic of the nature of God, drawn from philosophical sources, and then seek to show that Jesus corresponds to that conception. And since He very likely does not, we shall, in order to have our argument come out right, probably have to desert Jesus presently for a doctrine of the eternal Logos, who is more amenable to theological manipulation. Or we may begin by sitting at the feet of Jesus and letting Him tell us and show us about Himself and about God. The first way is a priori, the second experimental; the first issues in a

[18] "Why I am a Quaker" in *Twelve Modern Apostles and Their Creeds* (1926), pp. 121-122.
[19] Henry N. Wieman, *The Wrestle of Religion with Truth* (1927), pp. 245-246.

philosophy of the Divine Being, the second may issue in the Christian religion."[20]

An experiment in science is a definitely prescribed procedure to test the validity of an hypothesis by ascertaining a certain state of fact. It is essential that it be repeatable and that there be unanimity on the part of all trained observers as to what are its results. If a person is not convinced of the existence of Neptune, which is not visible to the naked eye, an atronomer will give him definite directions as to how, where, and when he can see it. How can religious experimentalism demonstrate the existence of a God, or for that matter of anything outside the immediate emotional state of the observer, with the same universal cogency as science or with anything remotely similar to it? No definite tests have been formulated; and as for the consequences of experimental ways of *living,* insofar as they bear on the allegedly objective truths of religious doctrines, the evidence is notoriously contradictory. To save a difficult position, "religious experimentalists" resort to the preposterous notion of a *personal* truth, so that the conflicting results of "religious experimental living" are reconciled by holding that a certain doctrine may be true for one person and its contradictory true for another. Such truth has nothing to do with science.

Despite the intellectual abuses which have arisen from the failure to distinguish between the fact of religious experience and its object, many treatises on the psychology of religion contain much genuine insight into the phenomena of religious life, and in that respect contribute to the work of the anthropologists in making us understand the social expression of religion which we call *cultus.* James Bissett Pratt's *The Religious Consciousness* (1920) contains an adequate and comprehensive account of both the personal and social aspects of religious life, marred only by the timid and half-hearted manner in which the harmful practices and excesses of institutionalized religion are treated. This is especially evident in the treatment of revivals. *Why Religion?* (1927) by Horace M. Kallen, an independent follower of William James, rejects James's emphasis on the character and personality of the religious leader and does justice to the influence of funded communal tradition, the organization of church institutions and ritual practices, and various social and private ends religious behavior serves. Kallen admits the presence of the supernatural on the basis of alleged mystic experiences; but it is also admitted to be a thoroughly atheistic conception of the supernatural, for it is

---

[20] Rev. W. Cosby Bell, "What Do We Mean by the Divinity of Jesus?" in *Forthright Opinions within the Church* (Record of the 54th Church Congress of the United States, 1928), p. 247.

defined as a "mode of vibrant energy, not accessible to the ordinary sensorium."[21] One might accept this and deny that it has any essential relation to religion. If the supernatural is conceived of on the model of an electric generator, the systematic attempt to harness its energy and revitalize the human organism might well become a part of a non-religious social hygiene. But it is the faith, belief and worship that grow up about a church or organized attempt to establish contact with the supernatural in which the essence of historic religion is to be found.

Individual Philosophers

ROYCE

Instead of viewing religion as do most members of the psychological school—as a matter of subjective feeling; or as do the behaviorists—as compensatory fulfillments of certain material needs,—one may view religious phenomena as the communal expression of social loyalty. It is Josiah Royce's great insight to have recognized the community as the central fact of most religious worship.

In his book on the problem of Christianity there is almost no reference to Jesus. Christianity begins with Christian communities which develop the tradition as to the character of Jesus,—just as the Jewish tradition developed the character of Moses and the Prophets, the Mohammedan tradition developed the character of Mohammed, and the Buddhist tradition developed the ideal character of Buddha. Royce was deeply steeped in the theology of Saint Paul, but he gives all of his characteristic doctrines a social interpretation, so that everything becomes subject to the spirit of the beloved community. Christianity, for him, was completely the religion of loyalty. The "Beloved Community" is "the true source, through loyalty, of the salvation of man."[22] He justified theoretically the orthodox practice (if not the orthodox profession) which implies that it was not Jesus who was the founder of Christianity but Christianity which generated the ideal of Jesus. The ideal of Jesus has certainly been developed by the Christian church. There are many phases of the actual history of Christianity, however, which Royce ignores, but they are not always relevant to his fundamental thesis. Although Royce recognizes the social character of religion, he does not carry this analysis very far into the actual *content* of specific religious activities. His own

---

[21] Horace M. Kallen, *Why Religion?* (1927), p. 312.
[22] *The Problem of Christianity* (1913), Vol. I, p. XXVI.

personal conception of religion is evangelical and individualistic, but his social interpretation of the teachings of St. Paul on original sin and atonement is more symbolic of the unity of the social body than concretely illuminating as it affects individual action. He has no conception of the meaning of Christianity to the Roman world because he ignores its significance for the individual soul.

Yet this very emphasis on the social nature of the religious rite and belief, and disregard of the question of individual freedom and responsibility, gave Royce tremendous strength in his exposition of what, after all, is the essence of spiritual religion. In such a religion our personal tragedies are seen and felt as mere incidents in a world-drama; salvation consists in the peace and release from the urgent poignancy of our personal difficulties, achieved by intellectual absorption in the spectacle of that drama and emotional detachment from our own petty roles in it. But the concrete historical tragedy of the human race is lost sight of in Royce's account. Nowhere in his *Problem of Christianity* or in his other religious writings is there an explicit attempt to determine just what Christianity did and what it failed to do for the salvation of humankind.

On the problem of mysticism the influence of Josiah Royce's criticism (to the effect that the mystic is precluded from saying anything by the negative character of his teaching) has proved very decisive. At least three men, however, directly or indirectly his disciples, have tried to answer this criticism by pointing to the positive effects of mystic experience in invigorating the moral life. These men are William Ernest Hocking,[23] the gifted and lamented pupil Bennett,[24] and Rufus Jones.

Bennett claims objective validity for the experience of the divine presence not through ecstacy but through an overwhelming sense of the increase of power. He admits, however, that it is convincing only to one who has lived it through and not to those who have not had the experience.

Jones's conception of the mystic experience of the divine claims to be of the affirmative type of St. Paul and St. John as against the negative type of mysticism which came from neo-Platonism through the pseudo-Dionysus. This affirmative experience of God Jones connects with the revival of human dignity in the Renaissance and with the Protestant (also Hussite) conception of a church of the faithful, of a spiritual kingdom chosen by grace and built by persons who have direct divine ordination rather than ordination through priestly hands.

The experiences to which Rufus Jones testifies are hardly of the kind

---

[23] See pp. 280ff *infra*.
[24] C. A. Bennett, *A Philosophical Study of Mysticism* (1923).

to be regarded as cogent evidence by a naturalist or a physician. Nevertheless, Jones's interpretation of the history of the Quakers and of the general Evangelical movement in modern times is illuminating and impressive.

Impressive also is the rigor with which Jones avoids the two extremes of dualism and pantheism, of either entirely separating spiritual reality and temporalities or of completely identifying them so that no distinction remains. Values such as beauty are a part of the world. The processes of evolution in the long run weed out the non-moral, the Dinosaur type of being. Moral purpose is thus developed with increasing clarity in forms of human experience that extend, as Kant taught, beyond actualities.

SANTAYANA

A richer conception of the content of religion is offered by Santayana's *Reason in Religion*. He discards theologic dogmas as to God's existence as superstitions but retains those values of conventional ritual and belief which make of religion a poetry of social conduct, a heightening of the spirit in which the consciousness of the ideals of our common life expresses itself. Religion, for Santayana, serves to liberate man from worldliness. Its essence is piety, as a sense of the continuity of the human adventure in which we are but carriers, from wave to wave or generation to generation, of something more precious than ourselves; spirituality, as a sense of the wider possibilities which give meaning and direction to human effort and free us from the charnel-house of the actual; and charity, as the intellectual energy of sympathy which enables us to comprehend even those things which may at first seem antagonistic or even hateful to us.

ADLER

A still different type of religious philosophy from that of Royce is presented by Felix Adler. Adler began with a book characteristically called *Creed and Deed* (1877), but went on to develop what he called the religion of duty, as a substitute for the religion of his fathers from which he separated himself. The religious conception of the world from which he starts is deepened and purified by the metaphysical implications drawn from the doctrine of the categorical imperative, which he accepts, with Kant, as the fundamental fact of ethical life.

The great truth which Adler sees with unsurpassed clarity and courage is the existence of humanly ineradicable evil, the inescapable frustration which results from our mortal finitude and makes the search for perfect happiness so pathetically vain. Neither in love nor in work, neither in society nor in solitude, neither in the arts nor in the sciences will the world of actuality permit us to attain perfection. The flowers of our hopes always wither and the fruits of our efforts are never free from the canker of disappointment. Adler is too enlightened to share the orthodox belief that all of the atrocious evil of life will be compensated in some "hereafter." He is too honest a thinker to take seriously the childish belief that by a few mechanical inventions or politico-economic changes we can create a heaven on earth where men will be happy forever afterwards. We know little of the conditions of our own happiness and much less as to what will make others happy. Certainly we have no guaranteed assurance that the blind forces of nature that crush man and brute, the just and the unjust, will permit the existence of the human race forever.

Despite the fact that modern philosophy blinks at these facts and calls anyone who insists on them pessimistic, there is nothing here to dampen courage or blunt the zest of life. An enlightened naturalist like Lucretius would say that the play of light on the waters is no less beautiful because our boat is likely to be wrecked by a storm. Moreover, the fearless understanding which is called philosophy, even if it cannot eliminate evil, can rob it of its terrors. But Adler is not a naturalist. To him evil is transcended by becoming the occasion for the recognition of an eternal supersensible world of which all human beings are even now members. The arrows of misfortune thus become beams of spiritual light piercing the dark clouds of our mortal existence.

The arguments by which Adler attempts to prove the reality of this supersensible universe seem to me entirely unconvincing—possibly because I cannot accept the Kantian metaphysics with its "reality-producing functions of the mind." But it is not necessary to subscribe to the truth of a philosopher's metaphysical arguments to find his vision suggestive and illuminating—any more than it is necessary to believe in the geography of Homer or the astronomy of Dante. For genuine philosophic work, like genuine poetry, is an exercise of the imagination and as such frees us from the charnel house of petrified complacencies. Thus, though Adler's starting point, and perhaps the influence of his vocation as an ethical preacher, lead him to adhere to the traditional legalistic conception of ethics, best represented by the Old Testament or the Stoics, the result of his experience and reflection is to undermine the traditional view of ethics as authoritatively fixed for all time and conditions and as ascetically contemptuous of human desires.

Adler's fundamental respect for human personality makes him instinctively eschew the method of authority, and he gives his teaching largely in the form of results of his own experience. "Let others consult their experience and see how far it tallies with that which is set forth here." But once the necessity of experience is admitted, it becomes impossible to maintain the traditional view that all ethical truth has already been revealed. Hence Adler rightly insists on encouraging a certain "intrepidity of soul to venture forth on voyages of discovery into unknown ethical regions, taking the risks but bent upon the prize." This recognition of the element of risk is of inestimable importance. It means that we must face life without any absolute guarantees and rely instead on our own courage. The risks of moral adventures are as grave as life and death; yet without them there is no genuinely human life, but only a slavish adherence to mechanically rigid rules which choke the currents of ever-changing life.

History amply shows that all search, metaphysical no less than empirical, after absolutely infallible guides to human conduct has proved to be a chasing after the wind leading only to the overcrowded graveyard of human hopes. This lesson of history means not despair but the wisdom of living and working with the imperfect, and above all the necessity of assuaging that fierce moral fanaticism which so often makes life needlessly intolerable.*

WHITEHEAD

The religious philosophy expressed in the later writings of A. N. Whitehead is defended as being perfectly compatible with the recent development of mathematical physics. Theologians, e.g., Henry N. Wieman, have not been slow in making use of it. Whitehead's God was originally a footnote introduced into his philosophy to cover an important metaphysical difficulty and then was amplified into a philosophy of ultra-organicism in *Process and Reality*. Starting out from an original bifurcation between eternal objects (universals) and actual occasions (particulars), God is regarded as the principle of concretion or realization, which explains why, out of infinite antecedent possibilities, existence bears the character it does. "God is not concrete, but He is the ground for concrete actuality."[25] The principle and ground of rationality, God Himself is ultimate and irrational. He does not create but continually exemplifies in existence the order of existence actually revealed. "In this aspect, he is not *before* all creation, but *with* all creation."[26] But in order

---

* A more detailed critique of Felix Adler's *An Ethical Philosophy of Life* (1918), appears in M. R. Cohen, *The Faith of a Liberal* (1946), pp. 78-84.

[25] *Science and the Modern World* (1925), pp. 249-250.

[26] *Process and Reality* (1929), p. 486.

to avoid pantheism, God is also conceived as the principle of limitation of *values,* as the selective activity which embodies in the actual world certain values from an antecedent continuum of aesthetic experience.[27]

What about negative values—or the problem of evil? Whitehead tries to solve this problem by showing that evil already involves good, that evil is parasitic and cannot by itself develop into anything concrete. It is like fire which, left to itself, can only live by consuming other things, until it eventually consumes itself. Good, on the other hand, remains intact, establishing its independence of evil. Good can become better without having been previously bad or subsequently growing worse. Good is the principle of order and concretion; evil the principle of disorder and disruption. Evil is temporal and local, revolt against the aesthetic order of that segment of the continuum of eternal objects which strives to realize itself into actual occasions. God, then, is eternally active and in strife with evil.

There is nothing new in this doctrine, nor are any of the traditional theologic difficulties solved. Creation by fiat is abandoned for a God who is substantially immanent and ideally transcendent. The attempted solution of the problem of evil does not answer the objection that good and evil are logically strict correlatives, and if they are not to be studied as phenomena empirically, then consistency demands that they be given the same ontological status.

It seems clear that Whitehead has abandoned his earlier analytic realism and that his God is only a terminological substitution for Hegel's Absolute. His attitude to the development of the doctrines of historic Christianity confirms this. If his God, like all other religious absolutes, is the "one systematic, complete fact, which is the antecedent ground conditioning every creative act,"[28] then logically He can no more serve as a principle of explanation for the *particular* ingressions of eternal objects than can the older notion of God's will for daily occurrences. And since it is admitted that the quest for the rationale of that "systematic complete fact" is forever unattainable, it makes partial truth *necessarily* false, and novelty, plurality and relative independence illusions. Even more than in Hegel, this religious philosophy strikes the note of social anthropomorphism. "Every entity is in its essence social and requires the society in order to exist. In fact, the society for each entity, actual or ideal, is the all inclusive universe, including its ideal forms."[29]

In effect, Whitehead represents a return to the Puritan individualistic

---

[27] *Religion in the Making* (1926), p. 105.
[28] *Ibid.,* p. 154.
[29] *Ibid.,* p. 108.

phase of religion which has been neglected in recent decades. By expanding the notion of environment or society to include the entire universe Whitehead comes to stress the relation of the individual to the whole world of being and thus to emphasize the partiality or inadequacy of one's relation to a particular religious or secular community. Thus, Whitehead's great influence on contemporary religious thought in America is his challenge to the religion of social mysticism and good deeds expressed by Jane Addams and John Dewey.

Perhaps it is significant that this challenge is made by the two least American of American philosophers, Whitehead and Santayana. Their influence upon the future of American religious thinking remains to be seen. As yet, the main stream of American religious thought—so far as America has produced any distinctive religious outlook—continues to move within the context of good works, neighborly compassion, and social service, viewed as forms of collaboration with God.

Chapter VIII

AESTHETICS

General Theory

IN HIS PRESIDENTIAL ADDRESS before the American Philosophical Association in 1908, Hugo Münsterberg referred to aesthetics as the most neglected field in the scene of American philosophy. Since then, the situation seems to have been completely changed. In recent decades, more books have been published on aesthetics and the theory of art than on any other philosophical topic, and this change corresponds to an extensive movement in our educational institutions and our public life to give greater attention to art appreciation. In their report to President Hoover on the State of the Arts in American Life, Messrs. Keppel and Duffus give impressive figures of the large attendance at art schools, the increased number of museums, picture galleries and art exhibits, and, they might have added, the increasing endowments for music and the ever growing number of music clubs. And this movement, it is claimed, has materially influenced our daily life. More harmony and simplicity are seen in women's costumes, and manufacturers are paying more attention to the artistic effects in their products. Art commissions, architects, and landscape gardeners are playing a larger role in American life than ever before. Yet the report of Messrs. Keppel and Duffus clearly states that a great deal of this interest is extremely superficial, that those for instance who visit museums concentrate on external facts rather than on the essential values in the works themselves, and that Americans as a rule care more for objects because they are old or by certain well-known masters than because they are inherently beautiful or appropriate for the purpose for which they are used.[1]

Nor need this surprise those who know that though external condi-

[1] F. P. Keppel and R. L. Duffus, *The Arts in American Life* (1933), pp. 78-79.

tions may change rapidly, in the ethos of a people old traditions are not so readily wiped out.

Americans' neglect of art was a by-word from the days of the genial and liberal Sydney Smith, to those when our own more strident Theodore Dreiser wrote *Hey Rub-a-Dub-Dub*. The tradition that American indifference to fine art has driven great artists like Whistler, Henry James, E. A. Abbey, and Jacob Epstein to foreign lands was still strong even in the years immediately after the First World War.

Whatever the cause is, there can be no doubt that the development of the fine arts amongst us has not shown the energy and pre-eminence of our industrial enterprise.

It has become usual to attribute the relative backwardness of the fine or liberal arts in America to the Puritanic spirit which in recent times has been known as Comstockery, and it is true that even before coming to this country the Puritans abominated organ music and the theatre as well as all games, festivals and pageants associated with the nobility and the Catholic Church. It is not true, however, that Puritanism alone will explain the prevailing American attitude, since to some extent we see the same phenomenon in other colonies and states that were not predominantly Puritan. One must also take into account the hardness of American pioneer and frontier life, which in some parts of the country lasted up into the twentieth century. There was no room for the piano or oil painting in the covered wagon or in the log cabin. In a society in which the conquest of nature is the first task and the making of money the chief mark of success or distinction, there is little inducement to devote one's self to poetry, to painting, or to music in the measure that is necessary to achieve genuine greatness. The dominance of what might be called the businessman's attitude of life must be considered as another important element.

In addition we must take into account the fact that where the arts do not find continuous patronage and where people who have just acquired wealth regard the possession of works of art as a claim to distinction, there is necessarily a great deal of meretricious work without any basis in real taste. In this atmosphere people are asked to admire objects because they are expensive or because they are recommended by some aristocrat in Europe rather than because of any inherent character of the object itself. Thus a great deal of American art consisted of the cheapest kind of imitations. French chateaus were brought over here almost bodily and adorned with almost barbaric opulence. Greek temples were copied for banks or courthouses, and placed in streets in which they could not find any appropriate background. One need not, therefore, be surprised to find a man like Mark Twain, who was naturally close to the pulse of American life, constantly repeating the statement that certain forms of art, music or painting could not be great art because he enjoyed them.

But as against this we must remember that in our seaboard towns and cultivated estates we have had a continuous history of more than three centuries, and communications with England and France were extensively developed during the early part of the eighteenth century as part of our commercial relations. Moreover, those who complain against Puritanism and insist that America has no time for the fine arts also maintain that colonial houses and furniture were superior precisely because they had no pretensions but were simple and perfectly adapted to their functions. The fact is that the great masses of the people who came to this country came here because of economic pressure and brought relatively little of the Old World art with them; what they did bring has not always thrived in the new environment.

It is the combination of all these factors which has brought about a spirit of admiration for the practical man and has glorified the virtues of industry and thrift so as to make thoughts of fine arts and leisure almost unrespectable. In a country where the prevailing absorption is in the problems of the material world; where mankind is engaged in a hurried effort to conquer and build up a great continent; to clear its fields and forests; to open its mines; to build roads, houses, and bridges, and provide for the daily necessities and comforts of the common life, it seems almost shameful to indulge in music, dancing, and the other arts usually associated with the privileges of leisure. And while it is true that great poetry, painting or music arises from an inner urge, it does need encouragement and appreciation to enable people to pursue artistic endeavor over the hard places which all great work involves.

If America is notable for the absence of hereditary and hence sharply drawn class distinctions, it is all the more significant to note the wide chasm between the art of the people and the art of the cultivated elite. Gilbert Seldes' book on *The Seven Lively Arts* shows vividly how far from the popular taste and enjoyment are our classical music, painting and other traditional fine arts.

Accredited art is something we are supposed to get acquainted with by going to Europe, visiting its galleries or studying with its masters in music, painting or sculpture. A young and courageous American philosopher once said to me that it would be well if Americans did not write so much on the fine arts. What do they know about them? What acquaintance have they with the great masters of painting and sculpture?

He obviously was not thinking of the profound insights in the field of aesthetics of Immanuel Kant who spent all his life in the provincial town of Koenigsberg.

Under the circumstances it is not to be wondered at that our writing on aesthetic theory and philosophy of art is, if not snobbish, somewhat divorced from the mass of daily experience of the common man. In its genteel tradition it shows itself in subservience to the English standards in literature and to continental standards in music, painting, sculpture and architecture. In recent years, this has led to an extreme reaction which combined with a spirit of nationalism has made many people swing to the opposite extreme and in the spirit of Walt Whitman stress greatly, and often with a fervor more nationalistic than discriminating, our native achievements in the realm of the fine arts.

Under the influence of this nationalistic fervor, we are prone to forget that human nature is not confined by political boundaries and that civilization while it assumes different dialectic forms in different times and places is something common to humanity. We need not emphasize the necessary international character of science. Even in literature it is well to remember that the most important French writer of the last two centuries was a Swiss citizen, just as the most influential political figure in France, the one who aroused its imagination most, was a Corsican. Its anti-revolutionary ideology was formulated by an Italian (De Maistre) and its dominant philosophy borrowed by Voltaire and Condillac from England. Indeed, is not the French language that which the Gauls borrowed from the Latins? Only an accidental decision determined whether Lessing should belong to German rather than to French literature. And shall we say that Wordsworth and Tennyson and Browning have had no influence on American literature because they were English?

Great art is great precisely because it is universal rather than local and the poet is an individual human being, so that as patriotic a man as James Russell Lowell said, "Nature made me a man before she made me an American."

One often hears judgments of this type: this music is good, or this is excellent painting, but it is not distinctively American. But why must art in America be different from that of other people so that nothing which is European can respond to our human needs? Why cannot there be elements of art which like elements of science are of universal appeal? Bach, Mozart, Beethoven did not try to be German, nor Rossini or Verdi to be Italian. They were devoted to their art which they regarded as quite independent of political considerations.

There can be no doubt that something is lost when people deliberately turn away from their local habitat and local conditions, that they lose thereby a certain intensity and organic foundation. But the mere worship of local particularism,—the emphasis on local separatism,—is also deadly. There is, doubtless, a great deal of genuine poetry in Walt Whitman's admiration for what is distinctive in the American scene; but there is, doubtless, also in it a great deal of fustian, just as there is in those who think they can achieve greatness by cultivating differences from classic art. The cult of modernism, of undue worship of Indian architecture or Negro-African songs, is an artificial cult that finds justification only in a sophisticated intellectual formula, and is supported by the counter-snobbish attitude that one is a superior person by admiring the new rather than the old, just as some regard it as a virtue to wear the new fashionable garments rather than the old ones, which may be in fact much more beautiful. It is not so important that art be national as that it be good art, and at no time did the art of any country flourish by setting up a dead Chinese wall against intercourse with other countries in matters of art. Why, therefore, speak of borrowing from other countries as plagiarism, theft of style, etc., when in fact every great artist has borrowed freely from all available sources?

The fact is that American artists have been for the most part as much European as American. In the field of painting and sculpture, for example, one may mention painters like Copley, in the eighteenth century, and later the Hudson River School, Winslow Homer, Whistler, E. A. Abbey, and Sargent, mural painters like La Farge, illustrators like Vedder and Rockwell Kent, and sculptors like St. Gaudens, French, and Jacob Epstein. On the side of technical analysis and historic learning, Berenson's studies have had great influence abroad and entries in all important catalogues have been changed through his judgments as to authorship and authenticity. Nevertheless, American reflection on the philosophy of art and aesthetics, while it has been developing along rather original and vigorous lines in recent years, is hardly yet fully naturalized in American thought.

When in 1908 Professor Münsterberg referred to aesthetics as the most neglected field on the American philosophical scene, American philosophers were primarily interested in defending the established order of moral values and in the main were interested in an analysis of the nature of knowledge; and yet there was implicit in the idealistic movement of American thought an aesthetic philosophy which had early in the nineteenth century been adumbrated by Schelling and which was developed along different lines by Münsterberg himself and later by Baldwin and Whitehead.

Münsterberg's analysis of the nature of those values which center about the concept of beauty follows rather closely the traditional idealistic conception of the self and its relation to the cosmos as a work of art. Indeed, the coherency theory of truth found support and plausibility by taking the concept of the cosmos literally.

The world is a work of art which the true self creates. Josiah Royce, with his keen sense of the evils and disharmonies of human existence, could not proceed along the line which his more robust though less sensitive colleague did. While Münsterberg's ambitious philosophic system proved barren and left no heirs in the field of American thought, his specific analysis of some of the aesthetic categories and, more specifically, his contention that every work of art must display a certain marked isolation, has held its own and has been illustrated in diverse ways by Mrs. Howes, Langfeld and Mrs. Wembridge. The isolation of a work of art, its relative independence, harmonizes with the idealistic conception that every reality is an organism, in the Kantian sense. This conception, however, hardly agrees with the romantic conception that a work of art should be suggestive and carry us on without any definite goal.

More rigorously epistemologic is the view of reality expressed by Baldwin, who makes it identical with "the entire experience of a consciousness capable of grasping and contemplating it as an aesthetic whole."[2] Accepting the subjectivistic analysis of the nature of true existence, Baldwin has no difficulty in rejecting both the rationalistic and voluntaristic forms of idealism. Perception as such is real, and aesthetic perception is not a pleonasm but a perfection of the act which, according to the Berkeleyan analysis, is identical with true being. The aesthetic perception, to be sure, grasps the whole, the transcendental whole. But each empirical aspect is a part of the whole and is integrated in the genetic process.

Baldwin consistently maintains the point of view of aesthetic contemplation, believing that a synthesis is not possible while motives remain in opposition and only by their effective removal can place be made for a vital union and synthesis. Baldwin also believed that art is post-logically a return to a present analytic consciousness and that we realize the real in achieving and enjoying the beautiful. To Baldwin, the inherent dualism of fact and idea, of means and end, of self and not-self, of singular and universal are absorbed in the synthesis of immediate contemplation. All this has architectonic sweep and attraction but little concrete content.

Alfred N. Whitehead has approached the problem of aesthetics from

---

[2] J. M. Baldwin, *Genetic Theory of Reality* (1915), p. 303.

an analysis of the nature of symbols. But more recently, in his *Adventures of Ideas*, he has sought to get at the essence of the matter more directly through the concept of harmony applied to our perceptions or, in his own term, prehensions.

Defending the nobility and absolute value of the idealistic tradition in art because it is based on a transcendental reality which it in part expresses, Whitehead believes that beauty is a human adaptation of the several factors on an occasion of experience. He defines the perfection of harmony in terms of the subjective form and in the aesthetic experience the past is a factor determined by the spontaneity and novelty which comes into being, novelty being the subjective aim of the occasion and the harmony is enriched and strengthened by the presence of contrasts. Art, as defined by Whitehead, is possible because subjective form is partly dictated by the qualitative character of the objective elements in the content which express the Eros of the universe. Every qualitative factor in the universe is a qualification of subjective form so that there must be an infinite variety of them. Mathematical forms, by their very nature, cannot qualify subjective form.

Some part of the objective content may be termed beautiful because it contributes to beauty as the perfection of subjective form, but beauty can be realized by it only when there are favorable subjectivity and spontaneity. Unfortunately, however, this supreme fortune is an ideal not for this world. Actually we think of the suitability of an aesthetic object to some actual judge, a cultivated man, or the general judgment of mankind.

In regard to his analyses of the nature of symbols, we may say that a work of art consists of something before us and not in the artist's intentions which may or may not have been realized. A representation of Hope by a beautiful figure will be beautiful while it represents Hope or anything else, but an ugly figure cannot be made beautiful by what it represents in the artist's intentions.

The idealistic contributions to aesthetics represent a sort of afterglow, an Indian summer of a movement that seems to have lost its grip on the American intellect. A much more vigorous handling of the problems arising in reflecting on the nature of art has come from the reflections of George Santayana, followed, though with characteristic independence, by John Dewey.

Santayana points out that man differs from his brother animals in that he has a view of the stream of life of which he is a part. In the life of reason art is a successful imprint of man's ideal on the flux of life (on nature). In this respect there is no distinction between fine and industrial arts, the distinction being rather that which St. Thomas drew between the liberal and the servile which offer no joy *per se*.

Santayana began his reflections in a little book on *The Sense of Beauty*, in which he followed in the main the psychologic tradition of the British school. But the peculiar turn which he gave to his definition of beauty, to wit: that it was pleasure regarded as the characteristic of the object, while rather crude taken literally, really anticipated further discussion of *Einfühling* or empathy. His definition of beauty as pleasure objectified seems at first a *Machtspruch*. In the first place, we are pleased by many things which we do not regard as works of art, for example, by being aided in achieving what we want, by being helped over difficulties, as well as by touching soft objects, tasting savory food and the like. On the other hand, there are also many works of art with which we do not generally associate the word pleasure, for example, the interior of a cathedral which impresses us with a feeling of sublimity. Surely the greatness of a tragedy such as *King Lear* is not predominantly associated with the amount of pleasure which we receive from reading it.

In the feeling of admiration which we have for great works of art there is even less consciousness of being pleased than there is in meeting an old friend or receiving a compliment. Admiration is a state in which we think more of the object than of ourselves. And sometimes when we admire something sublime we may even feel our own littleness in comparison with the greatness of the object. Professor Singer has even ventured to call attention to a certain divine discontent with ourselves which great works of art arouse in us.

There is, however, no reason why we should think that the state of admiration for works of great art is essentially simple rather than a complex of psychological elements. One may, therefore, maintain a hedonistic theory, such as Santayana's, to the extent of insisting that there is an element of attraction or fascination without insisting that this necessary element is also sufficient or exhaustive of the situation.

The late Henry Rutgers Marshall introduced the element of harmony, recognizing the distinction between the pleasure that we get from localized bodily sensations and the pleasure from things that are beautiful. He distinguished between the two by insisting that the latter represents not a pleasure which we feel as localized in any one organ of our body, but a pleasure which is suffused by the fact that all the elements are so harmonized that no one bodily feeling stands out sharply in our attention.

There is only a short step from this point of view to that of Santayana's theory that beauty is pleasure objectified. When the pleasure from an object is such that we are not aware of any bodily sensation, and yet feel pleasant at the sight of the object or the hearing of music, it does not require much violence of language to say that the pleasant feeling is in our minds entirely sunk in the vision of the object.

A more detailed and characteristically Germanic development of the fundamental idea here involved is the theory of Lipps which is now generally known as empathy. We feel into an object when we completely adapt ourselves to see it under conditions in which all of our energies are harmoniously adapted to its contemplation. In the light of modern developments of the theory of empathy we can see the force of Santayana's teaching that an object is judged beautiful when it arouses certain pleasant motor or kinesthetic sensations which form a measurable whole but suffuse the object because the sensations themselves are too faint to stand out by themselves in consciousness. That is why through the lower senses we do not get aesthetic pleasure for in them we are more aware of our bodily organs than of the object. It is important here that empathy be distinguished from sympathy. In sympathy there is awareness of one's self. In empathy there is no consciousness of one's self.

Much more substantial, however, and deservedly more influential, was Santayana's volume on *Reason in Art,* which is directed to social theories of art rather than to the nature of aesthetic perception. Discarding traditional theories as to the nature of beauty, Santayana boldly recognized that the essence of all art is the embodiment of what he calls reason in nature, that is, the transformation of the external world in a way to make it congenial to our organisms. (The modification of the organism itself is of course a part of this process.) In this volume Santayana's use of the term *expression* is equivalent to Ducasse's aesthetic connotation that is meaning. There is an object present and an object suggested. For aesthetic contemplation there must be no sharp distinction between the two. The second must suffuse the first. Beauty is thus due to an association of ideas.

From Santayana's point of view, the distinction between the fine arts and the industrial arts, while still important and sharply drawn, becomes secondary to the emphasis upon rational construction as the essence of all art. A construction is rational not only because means are successfully adapted to the end, but because the ends chosen express a vital or organic function. Santayana thus remains a moralist. Art is not its own excuse for being. Its justification is in increasing human happiness. The finer arts do not, to be sure, add utilitarian comforts, but they liberate the mind by assuaging the pressure of blind impulse. Through the fine arts, as through the work of all intelligence, we conquer by attaining a height in which our own earthly fate is only one of a number of objects. This view, to be sure, makes the fine arts rather frail as contrasted with organic or vital impulses. Art hovers lightly over life, and yet the specific energy which goes into the arts serves the human purpose of enhancing life by changing the environment in accordance with our ideas and makes for that harmonious development of the specifically human life which is called civilization or the life of reason.

John Dewey's democratic approach opposes glorified snobbery in art and maintains that genuine art has its roots in human nature. His belief that art is a way in which experience is heightened because embodiment clarifies the idea contrasts rather sharply with the philosophy of Santayana in which art is a holiday of religion, a heightened form of human experience. And yet Dewey and Santayana together have exposed the hollowness of the once dominant snobbish theory of fine art. Both these philosophers, each in his own way, fully demonstrate the intimate connection of art with industry and with the daily experience of the common man.

Almost all of what Dewey has written might be viewed as, in the larger sense, a philosophy of art, for the experimental theory of knowledge, the view that knowledge is always practical, means not necessarily that knowledge is always subordinated to certain ends of the bread and butter variety, but that in knowledge we are always active and productive. Dewey never tires of analogies which reduce the whole of what used to be called nature or reality to certain acts of the human organism. Whether or not he believes in a realm of being independent of our knowledge, the fact remains that his primary interest as a philosopher is moralistic; that is, as one interested in the issue of human conduct viewed as the application of intelligence to the problems of life, mainly social life. Education, which has absorbed so much of his attention, is simply one phase of this art or the use of intelligence. The strong point in Dewey's approach, however, is precisely the corrective which his view brings to the old idealistic view according to which we first have an ideal and then we more or less successfully embody it in the material before us. Dewey rejects this separation of means and ends. The significance of art is precisely in the fact that in doing things our ideals or visions are developed, articulated and clarified. Art and education thus become synonymous with growth.

Dewey places great emphasis on the activity of the aesthetic observer as well as on the activity of the artist. The full appreciation of music as well as of painting demands that we follow the structure involved. But this activity of the observer is associated with a moralistic subordination of immediate enjoyment as merely instrumental.

Dewey, to be sure, removes or distinguishes between the artistic vision and that of the practical man. The former involves some psychic distance from ordinary desires. This is parallel to his theory of knowledge. Moreover, perception is not knowledge, nor is its characteristic of knowledge exemplified in seeing apples as food. It is rather important to see them as a part of a system of laws, the artist seeing this as color and shape removed from personal hunger.

Leo Stein, a disciple of Santayana, is contemptuous of the distinction between the fine and other arts. He insists that such a distinction should never have received any currency because all arts are the results of deliberate work and should never be divided on such a meaningless basis.

He entirely subordinates artistic activity to aesthetic requirements and insists that it is the aesthetic object which has real importance; for aesthetic experience enables us to see things and serves to unify the self; to make knowledge of self available and to further its development.

In his *A B C of Aesthetics* he states that the aesthetic object has a structure that is knowable not ineffable, the only whole that man can know is the whole of practice and this is a transitive whole. But the mere fact that we can recognize a moment as transitive is evidence for the reality of a more comprehensive, though thinner, vista. Though the whole world is trouble for every creature, man is sometimes able to make monuments that endure. The true aesthetic self is a public self though the present one is little and wretched. Aesthetic experience is that form of knowledge by which we grasp organic wholes and make them humanly intelligible. "We would have a much stronger impulse to make that [the material] world beautiful if it were habitually seen."[3]

If Santayana and Dewey succeeded in focusing our thinking about art on the human efforts and desires embodied in artistic activity, the relation between the art object and the effort that went into it has been variously viewed by other American philosophers.

According to Professor De Witt H. Parker,[4] art is the expression of a wish. We create something which makes the world more in conformity with our heart's desire. This may be conceived narrowly if we identify Parker's view with the general current of psychoanalysis when we think of art as an imaginary substitute for reality. But one does not need to draw the contrast between art and reality too sharply. The very desire to improve the world and to make it conform to our heart's desire is the natural outcome of our organic constitution.

Theories of art fail when they seek a single simple formula for the

---

[3] *ABC of Aesthetics* (1927), p. 235.
[4] *The Analysis of Art* (1926).

essence of art. These simple traits like intuition, expression of feeling and others are also true of what is not art and do not exhaust what is art. Yet a description must recognize that art is organic and that its roots are many.

As works of art generally arouse our admiration, the term "art" has become an honorific one and denotes that which is beautiful. A poem is not only the expression of feeling, as an ordinary letter might be, but exhibits a form of words that fit into each other and constitute a certain pattern. So is a musical composition artistic, not because it expresses the feeling of the composer who might have expressed his feeling more directly and fully by banging his fist on the table, but because it has melody or harmony of an admirable character.

So with painting and architecture; a house is beautiful not only because it expresses the feeling of the architect or owner, but because the lines or masses exhibit certain attractive forms or patterns.

In criticism of Parker it may be urged: (1) It is not certain that wish-fulfilment is always an element, much less the sole distinctive element in art creation. (2) The beholder may not know the mind of the artist. Who can tell Mozart's state of mind when he created his Don Giovanni or his quintets? And if we had such knowledge what light would it throw on the merits of these works? (3) The feeling of the beholder of the complete work is independent of the process which led to its completion. Very often the enjoyment of a work of art requires the elimination of the machinery which produced it.

Professor C. J. Ducasse criticizes Parker on the ground that imaginative creation is not of the essence of art. When we contemplate works of art we always have a real object before us and our image of it or the meaning we read into it is not always the same as that which the artist had in mind before or even during the creation of it. When we dream and take our fantasies for reality, we are not engaged in aesthetic contemplation.

Ducasse takes the expression of emotion as the primary fact in art, for in art an object is created which in a unique way corresponds to something that was not an object at all, namely, to a feeling.[5] It is not merely a work of skill for the sake of exercising the skill, but rather for the sake of expressing a feeling. He insists that it is not of the essence of art that it should communicate feeling. But unless it does so a work of art would be of little interest to anyone except the artist himself.

Ducasse insists that art expresses emotion, but admits that there need be no emotion before the objective expression. Not expressibility but

[5] *The Philosophy of Art* (1929), p. 108.

indicability seems to be the real condition. And he admits that willy-nilly the subject matter makes its own contribution to the feeling finally objectified by the work in which that subject matter was introduced.[6]

Moreover, he admits that we have images of only a small part of what we create, and whatever feelings we wish to express are of no avail unless they are outwardly embodied. More important, however, is the admission of Wundt in *The Heterogeneity of Ends*, that what we want to express is changed by the execution and it is only at the end of the process that we attribute an integral intention to ourselves, whereas in fact the intention is subject to the achievement.

The expression of emotion is not always art. Banging the table, yawning, spitting in disgust, or even writing an abusive letter, is not necessarily a work of art. A skillful sonnet may have less emotion than a heartfelt appeal for a job or for charity. Moreover, it is rather dubious to suppose that the artistic designer of the facade of a bank building transmits thereby his own feelings or any of his own emotions. Ducasse admits that a piece of Mexican lace is a work of art, but what emotion does it express except a wish to create something, either because it is paid for or because it has a particular form? If it were made by machine instead of by hand and we could not tell the difference, would our aesthetic attitude be different?

When we analyze his specific illustrations we find that skill is always involved and our admiration of such skill seems very close to what is ordinarily meant by admiration of beauty. Skill, however, is something quite distinct from feeling. And certainly it is clear in the creation of lace, rugs, statues, etc., that the feeling of the worker may be entirely irrelevant to the aesthetic perfection of the result.

A somewhat different approach to the problem of art and emotion is taken by Irwin Edman, whose contributions to the field of aesthetics are now beginning to make themselves felt. For Edman, art is intensification, clarification, and interpretation of experience. The work of art is a foretaste of what an ordered world might be. Art reveals our data with greater clarity, intensity and purity than they exhibit to the routine practicality. The characters in a novel have more clarity and urgency than the people we meet in our daily contacts. This does not mean that artistic idealization is a process of making things about us more attractive. Balzac's idealization of parenthood in *Père Goriot* makes it indeed somewhat repulsive. But idealization emphasizes certain views generally unattended to in ordinary daily life. It thus gives us essential insights into the world we live in.

For Irwin Edman, art is a form of discovery or revelation. We appre-

---

[6] *Ibid.*, p. 91.

ciate natural beauty more if we have analyzed its elements through works of art. The local farmer is apt to see his Swiss or Adirondack mountains as so many areas of accessible or inaccessible timber or pasturage, presenting various problems with respect to travel and transportation. The painter selects certain features to form his picture and ignores irrelevant elements in the actual scene. Hence, one who sees the picture can more readily appreciate the harmony of line and color than one who has to go through the process of selection that the artist has completed. The precise observation of the object does not mean that the artist cannot or does not take liberties in changing certain features. Indeed, he must do so if he is to form a coherent picture. But if he is to produce something of interest to the spectator there must be some revelation to the latter. The artist must teach us to see a world that would otherwise pass us by.

In general, the American current in aesthetic theory runs to concentration on the problem of artistic creation and away from the hedonism that focuses on the beauty of the object. In other words, a philosophy of art has crowded out a philosophy of aesthetics. Those who wish to generalize may say that our age noticeably lacks the capacity for contemplative enjoyment and goes in for art activity out of restlessness rather than for the creation of objects which will afford relief from the fretful efforts of life's struggle. Thus, our artists have been largely dominated by the wish to produce things which are novel and which will attract attention, rather than those which are motivated by the vision of beauty.

Undoubtedly theories about art and aesthetics have occupied a relatively minor role in American reflective thought. And yet that role may assume vivid proportions if we consider American attitudes towards specific artistic activities and then examine the aesthetic theories in which those attitudes are criticized or clarified. For purposes of our present sketch a brief glance at three such fields—architecture, music, and literary criticism—must suffice as a supplement to the foregoing rather abstract observations.

Thinking about Architecture

If reflective thought were always proportionate to our practical experience, or to the material opportunities that life offers us, we should rightly expect America to make extraordinary contributions to the world's body of ideas on the architectural arts. For nowhere else has there ever been such an amount and such a variety of building activity. Not only has the whole of our vast continent been built up *de novo,* on virgin soil, within a relatively short historical period, but nowhere else are structures so readily torn down to make room for new ones. Nor have our architects been devoid either of native ingenuity or of adequate professional training. The curricula of their professional schools have been highly commended and used as models abroad. Nor has American ingenuity and practical resourcefulness been anywhere more marked than in the way it has met the great diversity of needs and problems set by modern materials, engineering methods, and the practical demands of homes, offices, railroad stations, hospitals, and the like.

Europeans, as well as the Japanese, have not only copied our methods of construction, but they have actually sent for our architects to design their hotels and apartment houses. At least one American, Frank Lloyd Wright, has become a major prophet of the new art in Germany, Holland, and elsewhere; while it would be difficult to name any building of the past century much superior in point of sheer beauty to some of those produced by Henry H. Richardson or Bertram G. Goodhue. Yet, in the field of reflective thought, we have brought forth nothing comparable to the work of men like Ruskin or Le Duc, nor even Geoffrey Scott's *Architecture of Humanism.* Whatever the cause of this seemingly national disinclination or ineptitude for general reflection, which was already noted by DeTocqueville, only ignorance or wilful blindness would dismiss as utterly worthless what America has contributed in this field.

In architecture, as in every other phase of American cutural life, the effects of the Civil War were thoroughly devastating. The ensuing era of Western expansion, railroad building, and the general mobility of that time, caused our people to look upon ordinary buildings as temporary devices. Taste was determined largely by *nouveaux riches,* who cared more for lavish expenditure than for the sources of permanent satisfaction.

Into this scene came a band of courageous pioneers trained in the *Beaux Arts* and enthusiastic for the cult of classic beauty. The greatest genius of them all was Richardson, who, to be sure, deviated from the strictly classical forms for a Romanesque which impressed him in southern France and which was more suited to his native genius. But with the construction of the Boston Public Library and the Chicago Fair of 1893, the strictly classical form triumphed and Charles F. McKim became its leader. The dominant attitude of this period is perhaps best illustrated by the following incident: When someone was expounding to students the need for a well-grounded plan as the first requisite, McKim interrupted: "The first thing is beauty."

No doubt many of the buildings produced under this impulse were really beautiful, but two criticisms soon developed: First, the beautiful Greek temples and Roman baths were scattered against an alien and unresponsive background of office buildings, storehouses, factories, and the like, with seldom enough space in front of them to enable one to get a full view. Second, the resolution to adhere to traditional forms of beauty led to the sacrifice of the purpose for which buildings are erected. Thus, almost all of the great public libraries of this period have relatively little room for readers, and the places for books are so distributed that it takes an interminable time for readers to get at them. In the end, economic pressure for tall buildings prevailed, and McKim's firm capitulated and began to build many-storied apartment houses trying vainly, by emphasis on horizontal lines, to maintain a pretense of the classic form. However, such efforts were doomed, and since the First World War and the Tribune Competition of 1922, the tendency has been to emphasize vertical lines,—a new Gothic.

The romantic revival of Gothic reached America through the work of Pugin and the writings of Ruskin. While it has never dominated the field, it has always maintained a place for itself in the building of churches and some colleges. Its great proponent in this country has been Ralph Adams Cram, a follower of Cardinal Newman. In England the pre-Raphaelites and William Morris have been its leaders. More Catholic than Rome, Cram wishes to return to the Middle Ages, and will have none of the sixteenth-century architecture used by the Roman Church. Only Gothic can express Christian piety and aspiration. Cram does not compromise with anything modern. He is opposed to democracy, favors the old guild system, and sighs for the return of the times when "noble and honourable lineage gave right of precedence."[7] In his intemperate zeal for Gothic, Cram forgets that Christianity existed for many centuries before Gothic architecture was dreamed of; his position is made somewhat ridiculous by the suggestion that if we take him seriously we should have to abandon all modern machinery and return to the custom of living in walled towns. Nevertheless, it is well to remember that not only do the very tall and costlier buildings in New York City perforce display elements of the Gothic, but its most imposing church is the Gothic cathedral of St. John the Divine. Indeed, so strong is still the vogue of Gothic that this form was imposed on the Law School of Yale University—it is said against the protest of the faculty because of the resulting dark rooms and expensive upkeep,—thus lessening funds for research.

A more sober and scholarly defender of the Gothic style was the

---

[7] *The Gothic Quest* (1915), p. 23.

late Professor A. K. Porter, whose researches in Lombard architecture have been of outstanding importance in throwing light on the origin of the Gothic form. Porter was an intellectual and a cosmopolitan who felt that the touchstone of art is intellectuality.[8] But wisely, he insisted on the dangers of what he called "paper architecture," that is, planning a building on paper and not paying sufficient attention to how it looks when built.

As far back as the eighth decade of the nineteenth century, voices began to be raised in favor of a distinctly American style of architecture. Why should we imitate the English and other foreign styles, when our scenery is so different? This idea, germinating in the mind of Louis Sullivan, led him to accept the skyscraper, so abhorrent to the followers of the genteel tradition. Sullivan became obsessed with the idea that Ruskin preached under the heading of Truth. In his own mind, however, it became the dogma that the form of a building must follow and express its function. Like most prophets, Sullivan was more vehement than coherent, and it is often impossible to get any precise meaning out of his fervid and magniloquent phrases. But the spirit back of Sullivan's attitude is that of American independence and democracy *à la* Walt Whitman. Let us give up the effort to make a steel building look like a work of masonry. Tall buildings should have steel pillars.

Sullivan's views could not prevail against the classic tradition and the cult of genteel beauty. But the dogma of functionalism has become an accepted article of faith, even though literally it leads to obvious absurdities. A modern office or commercial building may have a great many different functions which cannot all be indicated in its exterior design. Why, indeed, should they? Sullivan himself almost invalidated his theory when, starting from the idea that a bank is a place for the safekeeping of money, he began to build banks modelled on the old-fashioned strongbox. This was a triumph of dogma over reason, for people very obviously do not do business in strong-boxes. Indeed, in his own ornamentation work Sullivan himself does not employ the dogma of functionalism. The beautifying of a building is not the same as giving information to the outsider as to what goes on within it. The latter can be done more expeditiously in other ways. Indeed, the whole theory of functionalism is simply a continuation of Ruskin's hopeless confusion between moral and artistic categories.

During the early years of the 20th century the American scene was covered with temples, cathedrals, and baths of the classic design from the boards of the Eclectics, whose approach to the field was determined

---

[8] *Beyond Architecture* (1928), p. 10.

by their firm conviction that form rather than idea should control architectural productions. This school, dominating American architecture at the time, looked upon life as essentially static and consequently there was little of either meaningfulness or appropriateness in its work. Having turned to the long-deserted symbols of cultures no longer existing for both inspiration and pattern, the work of these men was not only sterile in every artistic sense, but wholly out of harmony with the sprawling American scene.

The enthusiasm with which this building activity was carried on and the acclaim with which each new building was received, serves as another instance of the lack of background and tradition in American art at that time. For centuries the Renaissance ideal of art as pure form had held a position, usually dominant, which had led to an almost complete separation of art from the life and environment of the people. Not realizing that they were applauding forms of the most ancient vintage, the people, heretofore little concerned with the more abstract elements of beauty, accepted as masterly productions all things bearing the stamp of academic approval. This lack of architectural consciousness in the mind of the general public was hardly calculated to inspire American architects to create forms of architectural expression of a newer, more modern and convenient design. In consequence, we still have the spectacle of marble façades and gilded domes casting their shadows over some of the vilest slums imaginable.

While the *Beaux Arts* architects were preoccupied with their formal problems, the masses of the people, rural and urban, were living under housing conditions seldom short of appalling. During and immediately following the Civil War the larger cities of the North were flooded with Negroes seeking the supposed freedom of that section. This sudden influx of destitute persons, lacking industrial and commercial training and possessing no resources whatsoever, created an acute housing problem. In Washington the situation was met by the construction of "alley dwellings," many of which are still in use. Chicago and the city of New York, lacking facilities to care for the waves of migration from the South and from Europe, encouraged the real estate operators in their construction of the early tenements, soon to become the symbol of a real estate era of commercialism which still continues to wring both money and life from those so unfortunate as to have to live in its products.

In the latter part of the nineteenth and the early part of the twentieth centuries there came into vogue the "dumb bell" tenement, so called because it was constructed somewhat in the shape of a dumb bell to contain as many family units as possible without sufficient, if any, thought to ventilation, sunshine, cleanliness, privacy, or any of the other considerations which make for comfortable dwelling places. The Eclectics, so preoccupied with the problems of formal design, failed completely to take notice of these conditions, and it was this non-social viewpoint of the school and the complete separation of its architectural plans from the world of the ordinary citizen which led people to turn with relief to the work of Frank Lloyd Wright and his associates.

Struck by the incongruity between the products of the prevailing styles in architecture and their surroundings, Wright turned from the Eclectics and began a career in original designing which has made him not only the foremost American architect, but almost the only one whose work in the field has had appreciable influence abroad. His work is to be found in many American colleges, in hotels and office buildings in Tokyo, sport palaces in Germany, and commercial structures throughout Holland. While other leaders of the field in America have to a large extent confined their activities to the designing of commercial and industrial buildings, such is not the case with Wright, whose work has exerted a great influence upon private dwelling construction in this country. The popularity of Wright's creations in the field of private dwellings has come as a result of his effort to blend house and environment, or as any romanticist, which Wright certainly is, might put it, "an effort to depict the oneness of nature and man through the blending of structure and setting."

There are two outstanding examples of Wright's artistic and socially-conscious approach to architecture,—the Robie House in Chicago and the Unity Temple in Oak Park, Illinois. The Robie House, later nicknamed the "prairie house," is perhaps the most daring production of any architect in the field of private dwelling designing. In it are expressed the ideas of Wright regarding utility and compatibility of structure and setting, as well as the dogma of Sullivan that form follows function, a doctrine which had for many years been in disrepute and considered somewhat plebeian in contrast with the doctrines of classic beauty in the Eclectic movement.

Wright, student of, and one-time assistant to, Sullivan, has never forgotten the form-function edict of the master. Therefore, when designing the Robie house, he set himself the task not only of blending structure and setting, but of giving example to his belief that architecture should portray the forces, social and economic, which are at work in a society. That he was successful in both aims is testified to by the immediate and widespread adaptations which were made of his production. The house is long, low and narrow with the vertical accents on the window groups and chimneys. These windows are used extensively throughout the entire house to bring the exterior and interior spaces into a seeming whole, in contrast to the usual distinct sense of separation of these two spaces. The eaves and porches are unusually wide and long; the roofs of the latter are hung by cantilevers from the house in order to give the openness for ventilation which is so essential in summer and the maximum amount of light at all times.

Both interior and exterior are centered about the massive chimney stack, thereby unifying the interior and exterior of the house. The interior is handled as one unit of space, and the space from one room flows into that of another without any impression of separateness or enclosure. Fireplaces and the staircase are the only things separating the living from the dining room. The effect is one of harmony with the outside surroundings, appearing as the background for the interior arrangements through the huge and unobtrusive window groups, and of great space and decorative harmony within. The openings leading to the outside areas are so arranged in conjunction with the window groups as to emphasize the exterior-interior unity. There is almost no artificial ornamentation in the house, the desired ornamental effects having been achieved through the skilful use of various building materials.

Another outstanding example of Wright's work is the Unity Temple in Oak Park, Illinois. The Temple, completed in 1906, utilized a new method of construction and presented a radical departure from the usual religious designs. The Unity Sect, modern and almost completely unattached to the past, could have chosen no more appropriate design than that by Wright. The building is a single monolith, the concrete having been poured into moulds, while the four hollow piers which support the flat roof serve as heating ducts. The flat roofs, the outside walls severe and completely unadorned, and the massive features of the walls, create a spirit of solemnity seldom achieved by the classic structures of other schools.

Mention should perhaps be made of two other major contributions of Wright to the field of architecture,—the Midway Gardens recreational center in Chicago and, more important still, the Imperial Hotel in Tokyo, built upon expanding piles of reinforced concrete which reach down to the layers of soft mud over which the entire city is built. In 1923, when almost every structure of any size was demolished by the earthquakes of that year, the Imperial, resting on its flexible foundation, came through as almost the only building in the city by a foreign architect to escape heavy damage or complete destruction.

Possessing a keen sense of the architect's social responsibility as a recorder of the social and economic forces which are changing and remolding contemporary society, as well as the responsibility of the architect in matters of health, comfort and beauty, Wright has been able to blend the various elements, setting and materials into a coherent unity. Through the unification of exterior and interior and the execution of ornamentation through a discriminating utilization of materials rather than by artificial methods, he has brought a naturalness to homes which has stressed more and more the closeness of man and his surroundings. To this aesthetic accomplishment he has added the utilitarian values of good lighting, good ventilation, and the elimination of much unnecessary construction, as in useless wall, to say nothing of the sheer comfort which is found in his creations.

The Eclectics, with all their classic artificialities and pseudo-classic modifications, still dominated the field of architecture, insofar as the skyscraper was concerned, until 1925, the date at about which the effects of the Saarinen design for the Chicago Tribune Competition began to be felt. Louis Sullivan, in opposition to the Eclectics, had said that a skyscraper should be a "proud and soaring thing." He believed that inasmuch as any modern office building must almost of necessity be tall, all horizontal features should be subordinated to the vertical. He felt that the true skyscraper should always give the impression of soaring above everything about it. The Eclectics, for all apparent purposes, seemed to forget that the lines of their beloved classic structures were essentially horizontal in outline, an effect wholly out of harmony with the skyscraper. They consequently approached the skyscraper as essentially a column consisting of a base, shaft, and capitol. Two outstanding examples of this approach are the New York Municipal Building and the Metropolitan Life Insurance Company Building in New York. In the former, the steel skeleton is completely unexpressed, and despite the care with which all details were executed, one is left with an impression of heavy masonry forms rather than of soaring height. In the Metropolitan Building, derived from the campanile of St. Mark's in Venice, the architects, N. LeBrun & Sons, were somewhat more successful than the McKim firm was with the Municipal Building. There was an obvious effort to give the effect of solid masonry, but there was sufficient treatment of the vertical elements to make this building somewhat more impressive as a skyscraper than is the case with the Municipal Building.

As a medium for the skyscraper the Gothic fared much better than the Classic, for the simple reason that the vertical and not the horizontal is accentuated in both the Gothic and the skyscraper. An outstanding example of an almost perfect adaptation of the Gothic to the skyscraper is the Woolworth Building in New York. From a distance the building is impressive, largely due to the excellent manner in which the tower is executed. The terra-cotta sheaths sharply accentuate the steel structure, and this medium of Gothic expression comes as closely as any in its class to expressing the Sullivan ideal of the skyscraper. However successful the Woolworth Building has been in its own class of architectural expression, there are several major objections to the use of Gothic in this or any other skyscraper. It seems somewhat incongruous to observe on the Woolworth Building, or any skyscraper for that matter, the pointed arches and pinnacles, when these are all stone forms used for vertical emphasis by the Gothic architects, whereas in the Woolworth Building they are ornaments. Not only does the Woolworth Building fail to denote or even suggest its function, but the limitations of the Gothic style have interfered with the functions of the building in many ways, not the least of which is the elimination of almost all exterior light for the offices behind the arched cornices.

In 1922 the Chicago Tribune opened a competition to all who cared to enter for a design for the new quarters of the Tribune. Declaring themselves in search of "the most distinctive and most beautiful office building in the world," the editors were swamped with entries of almost every description. First place in the competition was won by the firm of Hood and Howells with a Gothic design correct in all details, the product of which is wholly devoid of any connection with the world of today. Neither of the two mediums, steel or stone, is dominant, and the buttresses and crowns seem strangely out of place on any skyscraper, much less on "the most distinctive and most beautiful office building in the world."

Second place in the competition went to Eliel Saarinen, a Finn. Upon the publication of the various designs which had been submitted, there was an almost unanimous agreement that the design by Saarimen should have been placed above that of Hood and Howells. Here was a man with a modern design for a modern world, one who had faced the problems involved in designing and constructing a skyscraper and who had come to the conclusion that beauty can be attained in the skyscraper only through an observance of the functional requirements of the building. Saarimen had stripped the skyscraper of all artificial ornament and decoration for mere decoration's sake. He had faced the primary problem of space and eliminated the wastage inherent in both the Classic and Gothic designs. He had considered the problems of light and ventilation and had, among other things, eliminated the arched cornices and flying towers which had always presented lighting problems to the offices directly behind them. Everything in the design was calculated to stress the vertical steel construction, to achieve the Sullivan ideal of the soaring skyscraper.

Within recent years there has gathered a storm of criticism and attack against the skyscraper as an artistic creation. The point has been made that vertical lines on the outside of a building are really misleading. Not only are the interiors of buildings non-vertical in any appreciable degree, but little or no effort has been made to unify the exterior and interior of a building other than in the work of Wright,—whose efforts have largely been utilized by individuals and institutions rather than by the business world.

Although never executed, the Saarinen project has exerted a profound influence throughout the field of American architecture. Since 1925 any skyscraper with any pretensions to modernity has displayed obvious influences of the Saarimen design. However, despite the undoubted progress it has made, the present state of the skyscraper is not one to bring much joy to the heart of the critical onlooker. Because cities are not built about skyscrapers, skyscrapers almost of necessity must come after the city has shown considerable growth, and the modern skyscraper has brought on the congestion which is characteristic of our large cities of today. This congestion has already crowded transportation facilities far beyond their normal capacity, not to mention the strain put upon restaurants and other facilities for serving the public. Skyscrapers have also not proven as profitable as was originally thought. Valuable space is taken up by interior shafts, thereby reducing rental income, and in the taller buildings the problem of vertical transportation has as yet not been adequately met. The speed of elevators is limited to a maximum of about 15 miles hourly for physiological reasons, and in buildings like the Empire State and the R.C.A. movement between floors at the extremes of the buildings takes some little time.

Few indeed are the skyscrapers that are sincerely modern. Many of those hailed as landmarks in the progress of the skyscraper are little more than Gothic and Renaissance creations with a modern façade and a few symbols of the modernistic style spread most conspicuously about. These can hardly be called sincere efforts to meet the problems, much too numerous to admit such evasion, which have been raised by the advent of the modern skyscraper and are still unanswered.

Musical Thought

The amount of attention America devotes to music is most impressive. In our public and private schools, college and universities, millions get some instruction in music, and the number who attend the various concerts (many free) in our large cities is truly amazing. In the fourth decade of this century[9] we already had about 5,000 music clubs with a total membership of over 300,000, and the number of our music teachers was in the neighborhood of 200,000. There were over 24 establishments devoted entirely to the publication of musical works, and in the New York Public Library alone there were at least 49 current American musical periodicals. In quality too, some of these periodicals—the *Musical Quarterly* furnishes an excellent example—compare favorably with the best found anywhere, as do some of our conservatories and some of the orchestras in many of our larger cities.

All this effort has already brought forth a large number of native composers and augurs well for the future of American music. Yet, when we examine the body of American thought on music (as contained in its writings) we cannot escape the impression of marked thinness. Too much of it is of a missionary or pedagogical character, giving elementary information with a view of inducing people to appreciate "good" or classical music. We have legions of books on the appreciation of music, on the biographies of our composers, and on the history of music. But too little of our reflective thinking makes a significant contribution to the understanding of the nature, the function or the meaning of music as a phenomenon of human life. With the exception of De Witt Parker and Irwin Edman not one of our philosophers has written on the philosophy of music, although the influence of Plato, Aristotle, and Hegel might have been expected to make of music a standard topic of philosophic reflection. Indeed, even the great vogue of Hegelian philosophy in America during the later decades of the last century and the first of the present century did not produce a solid exposition of Hegel's excellent treatment of music.

There are those who argue that this thinness of reflective thought on music is due to the fact that most Americans are not genuinely or vitally interested in music, and that the efforts of the musical propagandists affect only the thin surface of our national life. Not only have we brought forth no great composers comparable to the leading French, Italian, German, or Russian masters; but our people do not play or sing as much as the European people do. During the First World War our army abroad was known as the great silent army. Not only have the conductors of our leading orchestras almost without exception been born and trained abroad, or at least trained abroad, but a large portion of their audiences has been composed of those who are foreign-born or

---

[9] *Cf.* John Tasker Howard, *Our American Music* (1931), especially at pp. 619-669; also F. P. Keppel and R. L. Duffus, *The Arts in American Life,* p. 173, and Augustus D. Zanzig, *Music in American Life* (1932), pp. 10, 11, 242.

descended from recent immigrants. Certainly the communities which, like those of the South, are most markedly native, do not lead in our national musical life.

Such views naturally do not pass unchallenged. Even some Europeans are beginning to outgrow the widespread view that musically America is still a colony to which surplus talent is to be exported. Our composers and writers on music have been recently displaying a marked musical consciousness and feeling of independence. They contend that as America is a newcomer to this field it is unfair to compare the works of our beginners with those of the great masters of the past, that we are making rapid progress, and that already our composers of the present day need not feel inferior to their contemporaries of other nations.

Questions of relative artistic eminence and natural artistic traits are always difficult and perhaps interminable. Nor should we uncritically accept all plausible historical explanation. It is doubtless true that musical art could not be expected to flourish under the harsh conditions of our colonial life or of a sparsely settled agricultural country, which the greater portion of the United States continued to be until the latter part of the nineteenth century. Nor, some would add, can art be expected to thrive under our too strenuous industrial pace. All this, however, will not explain why music should have been relatively neglected, while literature and the other arts began to be cultivated here. We must add to our account that for various reasons music was not in a flourishing condition in seventeenth and eighteenth century England, whence came the larger part of the immigrants who established the original pattern of our national culture.

The Puritans were not only unfriendly to games and fine arts for their own sakes,—an attitude frequently still found among our too practical businessmen and public leaders,—but for religious reasons they were especially hostile to music. The Pilgrims, dominated by the severe Calvinistic doctrines, were even more opposed to music than the Puritans. They had led in the burning of church organs in England, and it was not until 1692, after a decade of violent discussion in which music was labeled as ungodly and disorderly, that music was introduced into their religious services; choirs were not used until slightly before the middle of the eighteenth century.

I do not hold that all this fully explains the decline of music in England and the colonies any more than it explains the recent rise of a vigorous school of English music and musical criticism. It does, however, help us to understand the central fact in American musical life: the extraordinarily great chasm between popular and cultivated music. The latter is a foreign importation for the delectation of a cultivated class, while the former is of lowly origin, so that responsible critics or writers think it beneath their dignity to be concerned with such phenomena as ragtime or jazz. When the growth of our wealth and leisure in the nineteenth century permitted the cultivation of the fine arts, teachers and performers had to be imported, and those who desired to perfect their musical training went to Europe. Interest in music thus became a badge of wealth and social superiority, appealing to a class which, under our money economy, lacks the tenacious continuity of tradition characteristic of other aristocracies. Indeed, orchestral music and opera could hardly have developed in this country as they did without the influx of the liberal and cultivated Germans who came here, especially in the years following 1848; and cities like Cincinnati, St. Louis, Chicago and Milwaukee provided audiences for music of the highest artistic merit.

Despite the prestige which such music has gained through the universities and large private endowments, it has had a hard road and still does not have sufficient patronage to support it. Meanwhile our popular music has centered about the song, the band and the dance. Scottish and Irish popular songs have continued to hold their own here, and the very popular plantation songs of Stephen Foster clearly show that they derive from the Celtic element of our heritage and only their words have anything to do with Negro experiences. Indeed, the Negro spirituals themselves show little that can be traced to Africa and much that has been molded by the music as well as the religion of the white masters. Still, our popular songs are not the creations of highly trained musicians, and have, therefore, received little attention from our professional teachers. This, however, has not prevented American popular tunes from spreading to Europe. Also, recent social conditions have made for modern dancing and have found in jazz a most suitable ally not only in America, but in Europe as well. Thus, while our jazz and popular tunes are spreading over the entire world and are the objects of experiment by the leading foreign composers, our own respectable critics and writers on music generally dare not depart from the genteel tradition of a class that is too conscious of its superior taste. Those who have tried to uplift the public taste have employed a philosophy that is too largely oriented toward the celestial apex and too little toward the natural base of musical art. On the other hand, those who are in sympathy with popular taste and inclined to glorify it as modern, vital, or democratic, do not, with few exceptions, like Carl Engel, have the historic or comprehensive knowledge and detachment which is the essence of genuine philosophy.

As might be expected in a democratic country, there have not been wanting literate defenders of popular jazz. After all, Henry F. B. Gilbert, a highly regarded Boston composer, tried to put rag-time and Negro elements into his symphony. In *The Seven Lively Arts*, Gilbert Seldes takes the liberal position: Let those who enjoy Beethoven do so, but let us not forget that there are those who enjoy the more popular forms of art, and let us have the best of that. Hiram M. Kelley shocked his Harvard friends by finding some real positive merit in popular music, and in his *Tin Pan Alley*, Isaac Goldberg has written a sympathetic history of jazz, indicating why popular music enters the heart and ensnares the feet, though it has not the quality of endurance. Its sad wailing note is truly expressive of the thin American optimism. According to Goldberg, jazz has educated people to the possibilities of richer rhythmic harmony and counterpoint.

Between the modernists and jazzists there have been passages at arms. Paul Rosenfeld agrees with Daniel Gregory Mason that jazz is not music at all, and Mr. Goldberg refers to modernists like Cowell as the persuasive advocate of "the new harshnesses in music."[10] But there have been mutual borrowings. While the modernist Cowell has adopted elements of jazz, Gershwin has elevated rag-time into a musical medium of distinct potentialities.

The musical tradition of America is largely one of confusion. Our timid beginnings were dominated by the already successful German romanticists, who, through the work of Schumann and Mendelssohn were already dominant in England when the music of America passed from the sponsorship of P. T. Barnum into the hands of our pioneers like Professor J. K. Paine, whose compositions were faithful reproductions of the already accepted works of the German romanticists. When the teaching of music first became an accepted and honored part of American life professional eminence required study abroad. The music which developed in these circles was thus based entirely on European, principally German, models. Naturally the ideas and standards of musical criticism were thus similarly conditioned. Many of the gifted young men who went abroad to study brought back with them the latest European developments. Thus Wagner, Strauss, Debussy, Stravinsky, and Schoenberg successively found in America early and enthusiastic followers. German romanticism, the orderly classicism of the French schools, especially of Franck and D'Indy, and the impressionism of Debussy competed with each other on American soil. Thus, in our musically formative years, we find our pioneers working amid a confusion and under an inferiority

---

[10] Isaac Goldberg, *Tin Pan Alley* (1930), p. 15.

complex from which our native composers have yet to recover completely.

"Art" according to Daniel Gregory Mason, "is a coral reef, and the greatest artist is only one more insect, owing his virtue more to his attachments than to himself. Hence it is no small matter that there is in American music no main reef, but only a confusion of tendencies."[11] It is no great wonder, then, that in this melting-pot of races, cultures and creeds, each with its own special musical heritage, no dominant school of American music has emerged. Nor,—our snobbish critics might realize this,— is any dominant school likely to emerge for quite a long time. All great national schools of music have been built upon a long tradition of folk music, a medium which through the centuries has emerged as a unified form of national folk art expression. And at this early date one could hardly expect a unified folk music in this land of ours, so vast and so diverse. "What is American, as a meadow in Kent or Surrey is English? A New England hill pasture? A Southern plantation? A Colorado canyon? The fierce turmoil of Chicago? The careless easy life of New Orleans? The nervous glitter and clamor of Broadway? A mesa in New Mexico or a mountain in California or Oregon? . . . All of these things are American, but no one of them is exclusively American, and no one appeals to all Americans."[12]

The first of our composers to meet and completely assimilate the German romanticism was Edward MacDowell, who belonged by training and personal predilection to the romantic school of Liszt and Raff. He was greatly affected by the Celtic Renaissance through the writings of Fiona Macleod and his romanticism was of the tender kind which loves woodland notes, wild roses, murmuring brooks, and the sea and winds of the darker moods of the Maeterlinck mysticisms which were illustrated in the non-melodic forms of Debussy. As expressed in his teachings and writings, MacDowell's fundamental concept of music is expressionistic and music is the language of the emotions. At times he goes so far as to say that from his viewpoint music is not an art but a psychological utterance; he finds more of the essence of music in a song he heard one night in the streets of London than in the ambitious works of Strauss. (From this point of view he refers to Mozart's sonatas as "filigree work".) MacDowell, however, was too accomplished a craftsman to ignore the importance of form and intellectual element in design. There can be no musical expression without form, but the form must be inherent in the

[11] *The Dilemma of American Music* (1928), p. 3.

[12] Daniel Gregory Mason, *Tune In, America* (1931), p. 139.

content or "idea;" hence, old forms must change from time to time, and outworn forms, like the contrapuntal fashions or the laws of canon and fugue, should be abandoned.

In the field of aesthetic values, MacDowell believes that music has four stages: descriptive, suggestive or symbolic, declamatory or expressive, and the higher suggestiveness.

Contrary to common objections against program music, MacDowell believes that music may delineate actual occurrences by means of onomatopoetic sounds and he cites many illustrations from the works of the masters to give weight to his position. Music can imitate any rhythmic sound or melodic figure occurring in nature, such as the songs of birds, the sounds made by the galloping horse's feet, the moaning of the wind, and the like, and men of diverse conditions and nationalities will understand. Increasing the intensity of sound will suggest vehemence, approach . . . decreasing intensity will suggest placidness, withdrawal. Against those who urge that music cannot describe things, being able only to represent the emotions which they arouse in us, MacDowell points out that in Beethoven's *Pastoral Symphony* the birds and the storm are very plainly indicated; but it is not possible for the music to be an expression of the emotions caused by them for the very simple reason that no emotions are caused by the cuckoo and the thrush, and those caused by the thunderstorm range all the way from depression and fear to exhilaration, according to the personalities of the individual listeners. But while music may thus express ordinary material relations and in fact does so in Chinese speech, this is not the highest mission of music, for ordinary material relations may be expressed by words. The latter can also better serve to suggest or symbolize material objects as is done in the last movement of the *Pastoral Symphony*, in the opening of Raff's *Im Walde* and in numerous well-known works. The realization of this leads to declamatory music, of which Wagner's operas are splendid examples. But the highest order of music aims at causing the listener to go not only beyond the actual sounds heard, but beyond the representation of anything material, and Wagner's music is thus often spoiled by the intrusion of materialism. In its highest or suggestive stage, music suggests what in spoken language must forever remain unsaid.

MacDowell also has some very pertinent comments on nationalism in music. The vital element in music is personality and the nationality of a composer is, like his clothes or business, external to that personality. Characteristics of so-called Russian, Bohemian, or any other purely national music may be duplicated by anyone who takes a fancy to do so. We have seen the Viennese Strauss family adopting the cross rhythms of the Arab School of musical art. Moszkowski, the Pole, writes Spanish dances; Cowen, in England, writes a Scandinavian symphony; Grieg, the Norwegian, writes Arab music; while to cap the climax, we of America have been offered the pattern of a national musical costume by Dvorak, a Bohemian. However, masquerading in the so-called nationalism of Negro clothes, cut in Bohemia, will not help us. Nationalism, or the anti-foreign cry, has had a devitalizing influence in France, as elsewhere. MacDowell pointed out that music which is tied down by the conventionalities and moods of its time and place can never appeal but to the particular time and moods which gave it birth. What we need is the vitality and undaunted tenacity of spirit which would enable us to make music the universal language of the soul.

MacDowell's immediate successors, seldom more than tolerant of his works, have, without exception, failed to produce anything which compares favorably with his better compositions. While it is true that MacDowell was isolated from the vast body of American native and folk music, it is also true that his successors, utilizing these mediums extensively, have not been able to do as well in music with native materials as men like Whittier, Clemens, and Whitman were able to do in the field of literature. Today we have a changed attitude on the part of the public toward things American, and with the works of George Gershwin and Victor Herbert competently bridging the vast areas which formerly existed between the classical and popular music in this country, we are producing a new harvest of native composers, composers who are close to and familiar with the American scene, a scene which Americans are no longer ashamed to claim as their own. The fruits of this harvest remain yet to be judged, but what we find lacking in similarity to classic models will be compensated for in the vigor of the compositions and their authenticity as segments of our multicultured American scene.

As to the controversy regarding program music, there are two issues which are not always clearly defined. The first has to do with the question of the legitimacy of imitating natural sounds, or in general representing certain features of nature. The second is the question of the superiority of pure music, meaning by that music divorced from any other function, such as that which it ministers to in marching songs, hymns, and the like. It is the prevalent opinion of those who favor pure music that there is something superior in the sonata or symphony precisely because it is not subservient to the drama, to religious service, or to any other function than musical need.

According to this view, which is well expressed by Parker, Wagner was mistaken in thinking that music should be wedded to the other arts to achieve its highest mission. Now there can be no doubt that in opera in the effort to produce an attractive ensemble the purely musical element is neglected and even poor singers are chosen for reasons other than their musical gifts. But in general it is difficult to know what is meant by saying that pure music is higher. The music of song, the music that makes people march or dance, or the music of religious service certainly stirs more people more profoundly than any symphony. Artistically or aesthetically, the latter is more developed. Whenever music is wedded to some other purpose it must yield something to the larger whole of which it forms a part. It may also be admitted that in song the value of the words is more often enhanced by the music than the music by the words. Still in the Chorales or the Passion of Bach, and in the operas of Wagner, the music would lose a good deal of its aesthetic value if completely divorced from its external use.

On the other hand, those who defend the autonomy of pure music have a valid point in insisting that music is not a portrayal of anything objective. Rather it is a refuge from events and things and involves something more primitive than thoughts. It is for this reason that music can form a defence against the capriciousness of life and the despair engendered thereby. It is for this reason that music can harmonize or tranquilize the heart, soothing while it excites. This direct appeal, not mediated by any representative vision, is what makes music significant, whether one views music classically as a path to serenity, providing us with a taste of ideal unity, or accepts the romantic view of music as a solace in hours of defeat and a joy that brings us a world in which the troublesome and the irrelevant are excluded.

Unfortunately, some of those who see most clearly that music must have an independent aesthetic value of its own apart from any pictorial or representative context that composers or program makers can confer upon it fall into the mystical view that appreciation of music does not involve thought. The error of mystics like Eaton[13] is that they associate thought with rigid and external expression of it. But thought in fact, whether in music or in mathematics or religion, may liberate us from such rigidities and give our emotions organization and substance. And certainly musical appreciation involves the thought processes that are involved in musical memory and expectation, in the recognition of phrases and forms, and in apprehending the organization that makes the difference between a musical composition and its discrete elements.

Lawrence Gilman, who for many years wrote the program notes for

[13] Ralph M. Eaton, "Music or Poetry," in *Musical Quarterly*, Vol. IX, Oct. 1923, p. 443.

several of our large metropolitan orchestras, naturally did not share the high and mighty condemnation which has been heaped upon program music by purists like W. J. Henderson. And indeed he makes out a strong case against the purists on the basis of a careful study of the great classic composers from Haydn to Wagner, who abound in instances of representation of the moods induced by wind, water, fire, and other elemental phases of nature. In this respect Mr. Gilman only follows the point made by our poet-musician Sidney Lanier, who called attention to the fact that those who glorify pure music are bound to disparage the music that has entered into the great songs which have so stirred mankind. Here, as elsewhere, the aesthetes seem to forget that in the arts purity is often synonymous with poverty.

Carl Engel, certainly no friend of program music, says that Wagner's technical mastery of modulation, variation and orchestration, would have been of little avail if he had not thereby produced results of unparalleled musical characterization, of unfailing psychological effect. Whether it be fire or water he tried to depict, whether it be the dark and clammy caves of Niebelheim, or the bright cerulean abode of Lohengrin, his elements are unmistakable, his colors true. The imitation of natural sound by music is possible and legitimate, though not always important.

Even more of a purist and typical of the classical tradition with its unbending rigor is Daniel Gregory Mason. Descended of a family that has done a great deal for musical education in this country, Mason is a composer of some distinction who studied under Paine at Harvard and D'Indy at Paris. Of the later composers, he admires only Brahms, and is inclined to look rather critically at men like Grieg and Tschaikowsky. César Franck is the only composer outside the classical (really romantic) German music of the nineteenth century for whom he has great respect. This is probably due to the influence of D'Indy, although he does not seem to have absorbed any of D'Indy's own departures from the classical tradition. Mason is idealist enough to believe that our intuitions constitute in fact the only essence of the world spirit which is projected and symbolized in sky, stars, sun and earth; and that while painting, sculpture and poetry represent objects and arouse emotions through association, only music gives us directly the substance of the emotions themselves.

Mason points out that as consumers Americans want the best that money can buy. "We live in an age," he asserts, "compared with which that of Beethoven is barbarous, primitive, childish," [14] and yet he concludes, in all the froth surrounding the top layer of our still socially-minded music supporters, there is little of a real or substantial nature,

---

[14] D. G. Mason, *The Dilemma of American Music*, p. 31.

and as producers, our musical activities are still in the educative or taste-forming stage. Mr. Mason also believes that nothing has done more to hinder the progress of music in America than the phonograph and similar devices, all of which have eliminated one of the most important factors in developing an appreciation for music, personal participation through which is built up, according to Mr. Mason, "the intimate sense of the soul of musical expression—melody."

Mason believes that this Gilded Age, which insists that through the medium of the radio, the phonograph, and the loud-speaker it has unveiled music, has done little but deflower it. His idea as to the receptivity of the average American to the classical masters is demonstrated in his praise of Bach for anticipating Mr. Ford's dictum that the producer must give the public what it should have because the public has no conception as to what it ought to have. All this, according to Mr. Mason, has come about becauses we are still leading our musically uneducated horses to the trough in the hope of making them drink, when their sole contribution is to muddy the water.

A sober effort to take musical criticism away from the traditional high-falutin' lingo and to make it say something definite and significant was initiated in this country by the late Oscar Sonneck, who built up the unrivalled musical section of the Library of Congress and made the *Musical Quarterly* one of the best musical reviews printed anywhere. Sonneck introduced the unfortunately sounding term "musicology," but, with his emphasis on the fact that music as a human phenomena is worthy of being studied for the sake of understanding it, he has shown that accurate scholarship with regard to music can lead and help in a more discriminating and intelligent criticism. Sonneck pioneered in putting the study of the history of American music on a sound basis and showed that minute philologic study of texts can help to secure better performances and can make musical criticism more responsible.

Oscar Sonneck's disciple and successor, Carl Engel, has a more joyous—if not more light-hearted—temperament. He stands above the plain where classicism and modernism dispute the field and tries to find causes for the various changes in musical taste. Beauty depends on the appeal to our senses; but as the latter are apt to become dulled, they crave variety, and that which is at first melodious may become obvious and eventually odious through repetition. The progress of music then consists in the gradual assimilation by the ear of more and more complex sonorities. There is thus a distinction between mere changes of style and real progress. The steady progress has been from plain chant to modal polyphony and chromatic polyharmony and the like, and this progress has been correlated with certain fundamental changes occurring in various periods.

Carl Engel thus occupies a middle ground in popular musical literature, avoiding both the narrow bigotry of the classicists, who will tolerate no innovation, and the blind indiscriminateness of the progressives who hail and praise everything new and revolutionary. Good music must really please us. It must be rich in inventive thought. Good jazz is preferable to the unpardonable maltreatment of the classics by the multitude of amateurs. Laws of the new music such as Schoenberg's are as yet unrecognized by our formal aesthetics; but that there is something in it is shown by the fact that others have found the way to imitate his effects. This, of course, does not prove that such music will last, that is, that the pleasure will be found to be stable. There is certainly need for new combinations of sounds to overcome the effects of monotony or what Engel calls "arrested hearing." But to be able to hear more the ear must be progressively trained from one level to another.

The leading protagonist of modernism in musical criticism was Paul Rosenfeld. His critical writings evince a persistent effort to get at the realities rather than the polite conventional trappings of musical experience. Possessing a rather wide acquaintance with the various types of music, Mr. Rosenfeld shows a rather narrow intolerance in his contempt for the older generation of musicians. Rather undiscriminating in his enthusiasm for almost all the moderns, especially non-Americans, he has made it rather hard to gather his precise ideas because all his praise and blame is expressed in moral rather than in musical terms. Indeed, at times he, like other moralists, almost completely ignores the artistic character of the work under discussion,—all this in his zeal to denounce the personal morals or political views of the composer under discussion. In general, Rosenfeld has used a varied rhetoric and praised the moral categorical imperative of the modernistic school, namely, those who affirm life and do not deny it; but just exactly what the affirmation of life means in music we are not clearly told. The music of Saint-Saëns, for example, is denounced as official-minded,—as fearing untrodden paths. While we may grant that that formal composer was not highly original in power or ability to stir us, still his music does possess an individual loveliness and is still very agreeble to many. Is not this life? It seems somewhat arbitrary to say that such music "makes the power of feeling in you, the unborn worlds of which it performs midwifery, appear the black devil. So it assists materially the powers of states that are eager to lull the unsatisfied sense of justice, the unsatisfied sense of truth, the unsatisfied need of creation in man; eager to smother all revolutionary impulse of any sort, and thus preserve themselves in unchanged power."[15]

Rosenfeld must be taken seriously because he represents a very large and popular movement in American reflection on music. This movement notably calls itself modern and thinks itself scientific because it uses popular psychologic terms and all sorts of *a priori* assumptions regarding the relations between race or social conditions and musical qualities that are hardly calculated to withstand critical inspection. Is the quality of the musical output of a man like Mahler to be explained by the latter's Jewish background? It does not seem that the assumed timidity or self-distrust of the Jews is a quality of all their musical work. Empirically, the academic test of vitality—whether the artist says "yes" or "no" to life—hardly supports his case. Not all experimentalists succeed in producing good music; and surely many of those who did produce good music (for example Bach, Mozart and Beethoven, at least early Beethoven) did not trouble about breaking with old forms.

Literary Criticism

When the young men of William and Mary in 1776 founded the society of Phi Beta Kappa, and pledged their devotion to *literature*, they doubtless took that word as the equivalent of what the French call *belles lettres*—to denote writings of a broad human interest, and of a certain dignity of style. That very little, if any, distinguished literature had then been published in America was irrelevant. To those young men, literature was not limited by political boundary. They were brought up on the classic tradition which conceived of the arts of civilization as the common heritage of mankind, though moulded largely by the ancient Hebrews, Greeks, and Romans. This classic tradition is still the background and largely the substance of our teaching of literature as a fine art.

Just as our language, like our law, remained English in substance though modified by local conditions, so our literature remained within the English tradition. This does not deny the influence of France and Germany, but that influence was no greater in the United States than in England. Most of the American scene in the early days was not favorable to the cultivation of literature. Indeed, Governor Berkeley proudly boasted that there were no printing presses in his colony of Virginia.

---

[15] Paul Rosenfeld, *Musical Chronicles* (1917-1923), p. 205.

Apart from tracts on religion and politics, which were not confined to New England, little American writing previous to the nineteenth century is of more than local historical significance. Certainly we had no poetry worth considering before the nineteenth century. The Declaration of Independence may have set the fashion to twist the lion's tail. But no significant independent literature can be created by resolution.

We generally regard American literature as having begun after our Declaration of Independence, and one might suppose that critical reflection as to the nature of literature came later. But this would ignore the fact that the theory of literature was part of what educated Americans learnt from the classics as well as from the critical writings of men like Dryden, Addison, Pope, Burke, and later, Dr. Samuel Johnson. Lord Kames' "Elements of Criticism" was not only imported but also reprinted in this country in many editions, and abridged versions of it were used as text books in many of our colleges. When Coleridge published his *Biographia Literaria*, in 1817, an American edition appeared in the same year. The latter event is significant, because Coleridge was the first English critic to show the influence of German thought. The movement known as Transcendentalism, was largely indebted to him, as well as to the French interpretation of German philosophy in Cousin's *The True, The Beautiful, and The Good*. George Ticknor and Henry Wadsworth Longfellow did a great deal to familiarize Americans with the literature of other countries, although neither of them produced any literary criticism or developed any theory as to the nature of literature. And while the literary criticism of James Russell Lowell shows considerable competence and good sense, it is difficult to put one's finger on any outstanding contribution which he made to our understanding as to the role of letters in modern life.

While American attitudes towards literature thus had their origin as colonial manifestations of English and Continental thought, distinctive American characteristics appear at an early point in our literary development. We may pass over as not literary, in the narrow sense, the writings of Roger Williams in the seventeenth century and Jonathan Edwards in the eighteenth and the whole body of theologic or theologic-political writings of which these were representative. Still we need to remember that the doctrines of tolerance to which Williams gave expression came to play a large role in moulding the distinctive patterns of American thought. And the hard thinking of Jonathan Edwards exercised a vital influence on later American religious thought. Within the realm of *belles lettres* we may perhaps find the first distinctive American note in Benjamin Franklin's *Poor Richard's Almanac,* first published in 1732.

Here we have what was to become a standard refrain in American literature, the theme of the poor boy who by his own efforts and shrewdness rises to eminence.

One may say that the defense of the underdog is an ever-recurrent theme of early American literature in the novel and in poetry. In the 1820's in the writings of James Fenimore Cooper we find the Romantic motive which had appeared in Europe at the end of the eighteenth century applied to the American Indian. In *The Deerslayer* and *The Last of the Mohicans* the American Indian is glorified as a hero instead of being portrayed as the enemy of the white man. The same Romantic element is applied to the story of the persecuted French Canadians in Longfellow's *Evangeline.* Washington Irving in the same way found his heroes among the Dutch in New York and later among the Moors and the Spaniards. Hawthorne's *The Scarlet Letter* and *The House of the Seven Gables* portray the old life of New England in a way to broaden our sympathy for society's outcasts and to see the limitations of respectability. Harriet Beecher Stowe's portrayal of suffering Negro humanity in *Uncle Tom's Cabin*, which first appeared in 1850, and was subsequently translated into at least 23 languages, is a further development of the democratic theme in our early literature. Bret Harte's tender portrayal of human loyalty, gentleness and sacrifice among prostitutes, gamblers and border ruffians in such stories as "The Outcasts of Poker Flat" and "Tennessee's Partner" shows him as a defender of those elements which society customarily rejects. And when we come to Mark Twain we find, again, a persistent protest against orthodox religion, traditional morality, and conservative politics. It is Huck Finn, the uneducated boy who steals things that is the hero, rather than the boy who goes to Sunday school. William Dean Howells and Jack London both recognized that our treatment of wage earners was often no better than that formerly accorded to slaves, and that religiosity has not stopped savage conduct.

The aloofness of Henry James's essential snobbery makes it difficult to think of him as part of the same scene that produced Walt Whitman or Mark Twain. And yet through all his major books from *Roderick Hudson* to *The Ambassadors* and *The Golden Bowl* there runs a deeply ironic criticism of all the narrow moral values which traditional America held sacred. Thus, in *The Ambassadors,* a good conscientious New Englander is made ashamed of condemning an adulterous relation which has served to refine and elevate the young woman involved. James proved to be the forerunner of later critics of American morality.

In the writings of Frank Norris, Theodore Dreiser, and Upton Sinclair, the realistic novel became a powerful vehicle of criticism directed against the traditional morality, with its complacent contempt for the social outcast. Sinclair Lewis writes in almost the same key, as he satirizes the respectable complacency of dull provincialism so lacking in refinement, artistry and vision. With his effective use of mimicry, he succeeds in depicting the monotonous standardization of our Main Streets and Babbitts. As for Willa Cather, her theme was peculiarly American. The frontier people of the plains are displayed for what they are, sympathetically, with no effort to satirize their crudities and bad manners, but rather to depict the struggle against fate and circumstances.

Poets too show revolt against convention, and faith in the common man, from Whitman and Edgar Lee Masters to Sandburg and Amy Lowell. Edgar Lee Masters may be said to represent joyless Whitmanesque acceptance of the democratic way in his effort to make poetry out of the machinery and daily grind of American life. Sandburg is a tortured lover of humanity; Amy Lowell, a modernist poet, preoccupied with structure, form, musicality, suggestibility. Yet she has faith in democracy, and in pioneers, even when they are not the originals of the Mayflower nor even pure Anglo-Saxons.

Here, then, we may find a pattern of American literature that has continued and richly developed over a period of more than two centuries, challenging accepted superiorities and defending the human dignity of the oppressed and outcast. What type of literary criticism has this tradition aroused?

It would probably be fair to say that self-conscious American literary criticism begins with Ralph Waldo Emerson. As a critic he had fine perceptions, although he was interested only in the play of thought—not in form or in passion. In his first book on *Nature*, in 1836, and in his Harvard Divinity School address in 1838, he sounds not only the note of American independence but of human independence, the right of each individual human being to his own vision of beauty and truth. The full significance of this faith becomes clear only if one recalls the character of Emerson's background at Harvard College, with its recitations in Latin and its rigid theology according to which all important truths had been revealed in the Bible.

This emphasis upon independence explains why the austerely chaste Emerson welcomed the flamboyant and voluptuous Walt Whitman. Whitman had a good deal of newspaper braggadocio but he did have a strong and sensitive feeling for the realities of life, and if he did not always raise it to poetic heights he did make men feel ashamed of their illiberal reticences and share to some extent his enthusiasm for the flesh and blood which is the substance of our life. Let us turn to this wealth of American life, he urged, instead of singing of kings and generals. Its greatness should produce great literature.

With Walt Whitman there begins what we may call the democratic theory of literature, the view that it should reflect the life of the common people and eschew the pretty conventions of the elite classes. The preface to his *Leaves of Grass* and his *Democratic Vistas* contain in his own characteristically vibrant prose almost all that later writers have written on this theme, at times with undue length.

Equally apart from the genteel tradition of New England was the contribution of Edgar Allen Poe in the field of literary criticism. Poe was not a great critic. He was petulant in his lack of appreciation of Molière or Fielding and overvalued superficial effects such as those of Macaulay. His famous essay on the poetic principle gave defiant expression to the modern romantic conception of poetry as essentially thrilling or exciting, and hence incapable of being sustained for any length. This led him to deny the possibility of any epic poetry. To maintain his thesis he ignores the *Odyssey,* and the *Divina Commedia,* characterizes the *Iliad* as a series of lyrics, and denies poetic merit to the *Aeneid* and *Paradise Lost.* No wonder that the text-books on literature did not take him seriously.

Apart from Emerson, Whitman, and Poe, literary criticism in America remained a strictly academic province and a part of the genteel tradition throughout the nineteenth century. As our older American colleges were in origin closely connected with various religious denominations and the students were boys and girls who had to be brought into contact with the world's best or approved thought and feeling and protected against anything that might disturb their faith, there was no room for new ideas or doubts as to the old ones. Moreover our plutocratic society did not hold the career of academic teaching in great honor—at least not before a professor was elected President of the United States and a New Deal administration began to appoint professors to offices of importance. Under such circumstances academic tenure was not secure when the teacher's orthodoxy was in question. Furthermore, in a country of great economic and political opportunities the cloistered life did not attract men of originality, initiative and daring. One need not, therefore, be surprised to find academic teachers of literature devoid of independent judgment and suffering seriously from excess timidity. For the most part they were men brought up on earlier text books and generally unprepared to bring the content of their lessons into intimate contact with the soil of common human experience. Indeed, since students of literature regarded themselves as a superior class there was the ever-present danger that this superiority would be tarnished by the recognition of values characteristic of the lower classes who lived outside of the genteel tradition.

Literary criticism was thus entirely academic and completely dominated by what were considered authoritative English critics. Indeed, even in our own day it was only when an Englishman and a Frenchman wrote on Irving Babbitt and Paul Elmer More that general attention was directed to them in this country.

Meanwhile, the reviewing of books in our newspapers was largely in the hands of newspaper reporters from whom no special competence or familiarity with the field was expected. Even today most book reviewing is done as an odd job by sub-editors, assistants, and special writers in the intervals between their regular assignments. So far as the newspapers are concerned, it is easier to write favorable or non-committal than unfavorable reviews and it enables the newspaper to get along better with advertiser-publishers. Even today in our leading newspapers book reviews are often mere abstracts, on the theory that most people like to talk about books they have not read.

The *North American Review* (1815), the *Atlantic Monthly* (1857), the *Nation* (1865) and the *Century* (1870) were some of the earliest American efforts at sustained scholarly criticism. Later the *Yale Review* (1892), the *Sewanee Review* (1892), the *New Republic* (1914), *The Virginia Quarterly Review* (1925) and various other periodicals embodied real attempts at serious criticism conscious of its aims and responsibilities. Even the academic contributions to these publications are sometimes alive and truly critical.

The expansion of American commerce at the end of the nineteenth century, the greater familiarity with foreign literature, as Americans, especially school teachers, began to travel abroad in large numbers, and as courses in foreign literature began to be given in most American colleges, all tended on the one hand to break down the narrow provincialism of the academicians and on the other hand to increase the number of competent writers for our periodicals and thus reduce the chasm between them.

The First World War especially served to make us more familiar with French, Russian, and Scandinavian writers who did not share the traditional American conception of the proprieties of literature written largely for women and children. The greater freedom in sex relations brought about by the automobile and other modern conditions, stimulated by the War, and the subsequent prosperity of the prohibition era, all gave currency to an anti-Puritanic crusade which coincided with the English reaction against Victorianism.

And yet underneath the revolt against traditional Puritanic moral codes that characterized so much of the literature of the first four decades of the twentieth century, there persisted one of the essential doctrines of the Puritan philosophy, the idea that art must be subordinated to morality. We see this in Frank Norris's work on *The Responsibilities of the Novelist and Other Literary Essays* (1903), with its insistence that a great rascal cannot be a good painter, a good musician, or a good novelist. The essential Puritanism of Upton Sinclair manifests itself through his view of art as an instrument for social reform. His is an economic interpretation of literature, in which the theme of great literature must necessarily be a class struggle between the proletariat and the bourgeoisie à la Marx.

Another form of inverted Puritanism is found in the literature of escape through which there runs the pathetic hope that by human effort we can actually overcome all the insufferable hardships of life. With James Branch Cabell, for example, perhaps the most significant representative of the new element brought into our literary field by the gradual economic recovery of the South, dreams are a relief from the drabness of life, and art helps men to realize what they would like to be.

In revolt against the prosaically respectable literary standards of the genteel tradition, there arose the school which, with the aid of Freudian psychology, began to insist on new conceptions of the function and content of literature. The anti-Puritanic rebellion joined to the old popular materialistic philosophy a quite naive acceptance of the dogmas of psychoanalysis as the ultimate scientific revelation. This led to the substitution of repressions for the older difficulties of unfavorable environment as the boundaries to achievement. Sherwood Anderson, for example, an apostle of Freudianism in American literature, was overpowered by psychoanalysis. He exemplified a materialistic or animalistic mysticism. In his novels, man attains his true or spiritual goal by reverting to the primal animality. At bottom, Anderson was an inverted Puritan, tremendously concerned with salvation.

Through these tendencies in twentieth century literary criticism runs the cult of strong or violent emotions, as against the values of order and serenity, and this cult was supported by the popular philosophy of progress and the contrast between the dynamic and the static.

On the journalistic side, the herald of this movement was James Huneker, primarily a musical critic but an omnivorous reader of various foreign literatures with an uncanny eye for new writers bound to make their mark. Huneker was not a man of great analytic powers but he had a sense which enabled him to discriminate justly between matters of passing interest and those of relatively permanent value. He thus was able to treat Ibsen and Shaw as dramatists dealing with the more permanent traits of men and women and their relations to each other rather than as authors of mere isms to be expounded by exegetes.

One of Huneker's proteges and disciples was Henry Mencken who began his career as a writer on the *Baltimore Sun* and wrote a book on Nietzsche which threw defiance at the adherents of the democratic view of life. It is typical because the leaders of the revolt of the masses are generally aristocrats. In any case Mencken, a considerable scholar (as shown in his book on *The American Language*) whose contempt for the mob is shown in the term which he coined, the "booboisie," nevertheless led the attack on the academic tradition with its puritanic code as to the proprieties of literature. Without much aesthetic finesse he decried the anaemic character of past American literature and extolled the rather rough stuff of Dreiser *et al*.

For a while the pathetic Randolph Bourne was the leader of the sacred band of rebels, and with his death the leadership passed to Van Wyck Brooks. It was natural, that in the heat of controversy, the rebels were less than just, and some of them have since recognized this fact. Against the assertion that to say "No" to our natural instincts is the essence of morality, these men assumed that to say "Yes" is the essence of vitality. In their protest against narrow standards, they argued for a freedom without restraints, which reflection shows to be destructive anarchy, for without some kind of self-restraint there can be no mastery. Freedom without any regulation deprives us of all opportunity to achieve anything; we need an ordered world to attain our heart's desire. While the older tradition may have overemphasized the orderly conventions of human society, the assumption that great literature can be produced by riotous display of sex or other emotions is an old fallacy, as the literature of the Restoration period amply shows. The avoidance of certain subjects may be a matter of taste rather than of timidity.

Moreover, the new school was deplorably deficient in learning. No student of Dryden will agree with Brooks' characterization of him as bovine. And the rather indiscriminate condemnation of Howells completely ignored his frequent emphasis that literature must liberate itself from conventional rules and make more intimate contact with life. Also, the denouncers of Puritanism forgot that Henry James had preceded them and, with bitter irony, had shown the devastating character of the New England conscience against the civilizing effect of the more urbane French code.

The limitations of the new school of literary criticism stimulated and offered a target for the reaction known as humanism. It is characteristic of this school that humanism, the humanity of man, is not only opposed to the naturalistic view of man as an animal and physical organism but is also opposed to humanitarianism. This is not a mere accident. In the sharp contrast between the human and the animal, the former is identified with the negation of the latter, so that the only truly human trait is to say no to our impulses, no matter how generous.

Despite Babbitt's exaggerated horror of Rousseau and all his works, he falls into Rousseau's chief error, which is precisely the overlooking of the fact that all human conventions which constitute civilization are the outgrowth of natural or organic needs.

One is tempted to dismiss the humanists as too deficient in the milk of human kindness, or as being too devoted to dogmas which make the milk of human kindness sour. Their learning, too, is far from impeccable. More acknowledged not only his ignorance but his incapacity to read those moderns in whom Huneker delighted and who broadened his vision. And for all his admiration of the classics, Babbitt ignores the fact that Rousseau was a child of eighteenth century classicism which systematically belittled (in line with Xenophon's Cyropaedia, Plutarch's Life of Lycurgus, and Caesar's glorification of the strength of the relatively uncivilized Belgians) the value of civilization and refinement as against the primitive strength of those uncontaminated by the refinements of civilization. The humanists insist on the indispensable need of authority to bring order into the chaos of the arts. But they are not at all agreed as to which authority is to be accepted. Paul Elmer More appeals in the end to the authority of a superrational intuition. This he calls the reason of common sense, but obviously it is not at all common, else this world would not contain such wide differences of opinion and taste.

When More puts the values of property higher than those of the life of his fellow men, as when he glorifies certain queer Oxford Dons and ignores the necessity of cleansing our civilization of the outrageous injustices which mar it, he is expressing the narrow views of a privileged clique and need not be taken very seriously as a profound thinker.

In the end, humanism is a refusal to accept the Copernican revolution and a clinging to the old anthropocentric universe. It has little content or revelation as to the nature of things or even as to human nature or the specific art of literature. In their zeal for morals the humanists forget the aesthetic values of literature and do not throw much light on it. They lack catholicity of taste and make a virtue of their inability to appreciate new forms of art. But a growing age, or one of intellectual expansion, where there is a strongly felt dissatisfaction with the old standards and a constant experimenting with new forms, cannot be confined to the older aesthetic traditions.

Nevertheless, the humanistic school has not been without meritorious service to the cause of sanity in literature. Thus William Crary Brownell, for many years considered the leader of the American school of humanistic criticism, steered a middle ground between authoritarianism and impressionism. The critic must give his impressions, but the impressions are not worth much unless they are those of a cultivated man who has submitted his impressions to reason. Quite in line with the classical views, Brownell regarded the function of the critic of literature to be the revelation of the principles embodied in the work of art. Not only must he ask what the author's conception was and how he carried it out, but he must also question the value of that conception itself. How far does the artist realize the potentialities of the art itself? This involves not only analysis of the personality of the artist and the characteristic social conditions under which he worked, but also judgments on the aesthetic values that the various arts are capable of realizing. Mere impressionism will get us nowhere and just as no one can make scientific observations without some provisional hypothesis, so no one can pass literary judgments without some system of values implicitly assumed; the more conscious these assumptions are, the more critically we are likely to view our own bias.

According to the Marxist system of values, literature necessarily does and ought to express the class struggle. This movement in literary criticism would bring back the old practice of criticizing literature on the basis of the political views of the author. Writers are condemned for sociologic rather than theologic error. The literary critic is assumed to be an expert on sociology, economics and political "science." According to Bernard Smith's *Forces in American Criticism** (1939), the important thing about Howells, for instance, is not whether he had much vision, but whether he was for or against the present economic order. Thus economics determines ideology.

The whole school of literary criticism that is swayed by economic determinism has simply followed in the wake of the nineteenth century deterministic view that prided itself on being "scientific." Where Taine stressed race, the milieu and the moment, the new school stresses the bias of the ruling economic class of the period. If we know a certain number of social forces, so runs the theory, we can deduce or predict the form literature will take at any given time. Actually however it is not

* Reviewed in M. R. Cohen, *The Faith of a Liberal* (1946), at p. 213.

sufficient to assert that there must be a relationship between the forms of literary expression and the kinds of economic systems. For there would be no point in saying A depends upon B if it were equally true that it depends on everything else in the same way. To prove that a direct causal relation prevails between the two surely requires more evidence than mere sequence or even correlation. To challenge the assumption of direct causal relation (i.e., that one is the necessary and sufficient condition of the other) is not to deny all connection whatsoever. There is surely a connection between flowers and the soil in which they grow. But different flowers grow in the same soil, and the same kinds of flowers may grow in different soils. It seems plausible to assume that certain social conditions will have some influence in determining what forms of literature shall become fashionable and thus be the objects of imitation. Yet from no amount of knowledge of the environment, of the race and local conditions, can we deduce the kind of poem that will be produced tomorrow in California, Moscow, Paris, Jerusalem, or Timbuctoo. We can predict only mass phenomena of a recurrent type, not individual events. Could any one predict from the life of Cervantes that he would write precisely the kind of book that is *Don Quixote*? The tides of genius are unpredictable. Henry Adams and Brooks Adams were brothers, Jefferson and Marshall relatives from the same social class, yet how different their points of view!

The Marxian group of literary critics might well be called neo-Puritanic, since they are hostile to the idea of literature for the sake of enjoyment and insist that it must be judged by the writer's conformity to the proper doctrine. These critics generally do not express actual popular taste. The best that they can claim is that the masses are mal-educated—that they should read what will enlighten them rather than that which is an opiate. But whether mankind at last would be better off by foregoing the pleasant books for the sake of dry and bitter economic tracts is at the best very dubious. Delight in literature may be an end in itself.

Consideration of the Marxian theory of causality leads us to the allied doctrine that literature should express "life." This is a typical instance of a class of propositions that are in one sense truisms but in practice are the source of all sorts of question-begging conclusions and even downright absurdities. When writers contrast "life" with the occupation of the historian or scholar in his study they are forgetting that the latter occupation probably demands greater vitality than outdoor activity. For the Marxians, "life" means the kind of life in which they happen to be interested. Yet great events do not always make great literature. Public issues are of undoubted importance, but serious students must not forget that great literature is concerned also with those vital issues of our inner personal life and those enrapturing super-personal cosmic vistas compared with which the issues of public life are pale and relatively inconsequential.

The whole controversy over humanism and the interrelated controversies over the Freudian and Marxian approaches to life and culture have left us with a juster appreciation of the function of literary criticism and aesthetic criticism generally. Just as critical reflection on life helps to make explicit what is implicit in it, so it is with critical reflection on that part of cultural life represented by literature. To make explicit what in works of art is implicit may be regarded as analytic, but such analysis requires not only wide and refined sensitiveness but also an intellectual equipment of ideas. The critic must understand what the artist tried to do and why he succeeded or failed. The critic can serve as a guide if he has the insight that enables him to see more in the book than the reader would see without that aid. We profit by the remarks of a connoisseur of paintings, who makes us notice elements in the picture which we ordinarily would pass over, just as a geologist or a botanist makes us notice more things about mountains and places than are visible to the untrained eye. A clarified vision can be an aid to richer enjoyment, just as repeated hearing of a symphony increases our enjoyment by enlarging our capacity for appreciation. Our enjoyment of books as well as of other works of art depends upon our capacity to discriminate and to appreciate the content.

From a larger point of view, criticism is a preparation for improved artistic work. For while the critic may not himself be a great creative artist he must know something of the process of creation, just as the author or artist must be something of a critic when in the course of his work he must choose his materials and means, reject what is unsuitable and adapt the more fitting. This will explain why periods of great creative energy in literature, such as the Athenian, the Florentine, the Elizabethan, or the classical German of Goethe and Schiller, have always been preceded by the cultivation of letters through the analytic studies of grammar, rhetoric, and the elements of literary criticism.

There is thus some rational ground for hope that the rapid development of responsible criticism in literature and in the arts generally during the first four decades of the present century may mark the necessary preparation for a significant period of creative artistic achievement in a land that has been tamed and remains to be enjoyed.

Chapter IX

GENERAL
PHILOSOPHY

THAT PHILOSOPHY MUST ALWAYS REFLECT the general conditions of the time and place in which it arises, is today a widespread and unquestioned dogma. But is it not one of those pieties to which men always pay an introductory homage and which has little actual effect on their subsequent proceedings? It is well to note that both the pious dogma and its practical disregard are equally justified. It would be vain to assert that philosophy as a human activity is uninfluenced by the conditions of the life which gives it birth; but have we any genuine knowledge of the complex and elusive causes which produce philosophic genius? It would be rash to pretend that we really know what kind of a philosophic reflection will inevitably appear under a given set of historical conditions. Hence, scientifically sober historians almost instinctively avoid explaining individual philosophic doctrines by means of general political, geographic, or economic "forces." Environmental trends and social traditions may explain why a certain philosophy did not or did find wide acceptance, but not how it came into being. Creative imagination, supreme courage, and unfailing passion for truth, the essential qualities of great philosophic achievement, are the gift of the gods ("accidental variations," if one prefers modern terminology), and are present or absent in all sorts of times and places. Moreover, the attention of great philosophy is not absorbed by local and temporary conditions of the market place, but is directed more to the ever present issues of life and death, and on the total cosmic scene of which they are a part.

We must distinguish, then, between philosophy as original vision and philosophy as organized doctrine or tradition. The vision of the great seers is brought home to the great mass of humanity by a large number of intellectual middlemen, commentators and expositors who form sects or schools that live by and for the perpetuation of these traditions. It is the careers of these traditions that enter into and constitute the general intellectual history of any country or epoch.

The prevailing other-worldliness of American philosophers seems to be the only explanation for our failure to develop an original and vigorous political philosophy to meet our unique political experience. No one has yet convincingly pointed out any direct and really significant influence on American academic philosophy exercised by our colonial organization, by the Revolutionary War, by the slavery struggle, by the Civil War, by our unprecedented immigration, or by the open frontier life which our historians generally regard as the key to American history. The fact that, excepting some passages in John C. Calhoun,[1] none of our important philosophic writings mentions the existence of slavery or of the Negro race, that liberal democratic philosophers like Jefferson could continue to own and even sell slaves and still fervently believe that all men are created free and equal, ought to serve as a reminder of the air-tight compartments into which the human mind is frequently divided, and of the extent to which one's professed philosophy can be entirely disconnected from the routine of one's daily occupation. Indeed, it would seem that most of our philosophy is not a reflection on life but, like music or Utopian and romantic literature, an escape from it, a turning one's back upon its prosaic monotony. But, as we said before, though genuine philosophy never restricts itself purely to local and temporal affairs, the history of philosophy, as part of the history of the intellectual life of any country, is largely concerned with the life of various national or local traditions, with their growth and struggles, and the interaction between them and the general currents of life into which they must fit, with the general conditions, that is, under which intellectual life is carried on.

The main traditions of American philosophy have been British, that is, English and Scotch; and the Declaration of Independence has had no more influence in the realm of metaphysical speculation than it has had in the realm of our common law. French and German influences have, indeed, not been absent. The community of Western civilization which found in Latin its common language has never been completely broken up. But French and German influences have not been any greater in the United States than in Great Britain. Up to very recently our philosophers have been mostly theologians, and the latter, like the lawyers, cultivate intense loyalty to ancient traditions. Though our clergy long ago ceased to be the nation's leaders, they have continued their grip on the American colleges, including even those that do not openly profess to be denominational.

---

[1] The keen treatise on *Liberty and Slavery* by A. T. Bledsoe, the most versatile of our early Southern philosophers, and the references to the ethics of slavery in Wayland's *Moral Science,* can hardly be considered as derogating from the statement in the text.

In our early national period French free-thought exercised consider-able influence, especially in the South; but the free thought of Voltaire, Condillac, and Volney was, after all, an adaptation of Locke and English deism; and its American apostles, like Thomas Paine, Joseph Priestley, and Thomas Cooper were, like Franklin and Jefferson, characteristically British—as were Hume and Gibbon in their day. This movement of intel-lectual liberalism was almost completely annihilated in the greater portion of the country by the evangelical or revivalist movement. The triumph of revivalism was rendered easier by the weakly organized intellectual life and the economic bankruptcy of the older Southern aristocracy, as reflected in the financial difficulties which embarrassed Jefferson, Madi-son, and Monroe in their old age. The second French wave, the eclectic philosophy of Cousin and Jouffroy, was at bottom simply the Scotch Realism of Reid and Stewart over again, with only slight traces of Schelling.

Why has American philosophy in the past made so little impress on the world's thought? The close connection between the college and the seminary partly explains the intellectual anemia of our philosophy, and the hostility of the social and economic milieu to intellectual enterprise may be regarded as an important factor which contributed to the subor-dination of philosophy either to practical pursuits or to practical religious consolation. But whatever the causes, the fact can hardly be disputed that American philosophy has, in large part, been a branch of Christian apologetics. Though living in a political democracy our clerical philos-ophers were the courtiers of a celestial monarchy who, as they could not openly revolt against the throne, could only engage in factional or sectarian disputes. Their complete absorption in traditional theologic issues seems to be the only explanation of the astounding fact that, in the face of our unique political experience, we, until very recently, have almost nothing in the way of original contributions to political theory, apart from some pages in Calhoun. In spite of confident dogmatic asser-tions to the contrary, history shows that great and stirring events do not always arouse great thoughts.

The Beginnings of Philosophy
in America

Writing in 1879, Stanley Hall drew a disheartening picture of the dismal unenlightenment that then characterized philosophic teaching in

American colleges. The minutiae of sectarian doctrines and the zeal for narrow orthodoxy prevented free inquiry, which is the life of philosophic endeavor. There was little true appreciation of the world's great historic streams of reflective thought; and the contemporary evolutionary philosophy which was stirring men's minds outside of the colleges was either complacently rejected or else sterilized by being harmonized with the Scripture in the manner of textbooks on gospel harmony. But a change had already begun, signalized by the election of a layman to the presidency of Harvard College and by the opening of our first real university, Johns Hopkins. As the American colleges began to expand and as training for the educational profession became an important consideration, teachers of philosophy began to be selected with some regard for professional training and competency rather than exclusively for piety and pastoral experience.

An increasing number obtained such professional training in Germany, where, if they did not always get much fresh wisdom, they did generally learn the meaning of scientific accuracy in experimental psychology and philologic accuracy in the history of philosophy. It was through these men that the idealism of Kant and Hegel, as developed by the British writers such as Green, Bradley and Bosanquet, replaced the older Scottish common-sense realism as the basis of our academic philosophy. The older school could not hold its own before the superior dialectical skill and technical equipment of the new generation. However, the ascendency of German terms and mannerisms in our philosophic teachings and writings was only apparent for, in substance, philosophy in America has followed the modes prevailing in Great Britain.

The first serious attempt to introduce German philosophy into this country came with an American edition of Coleridge's *Aids to Reflection* (1829), bearing an introductory essay by President Marsh of the University of Vermont. The apologetic tone of this essay showed how powerfully the philosophy of Locke and Reid had become entrenched as a part of the Christian thought of America. Some acquaintance with German philosophy was shown by New England radicals like Theodore Parker, but in the main their interest in things German was restricted to the realm of belles-lettres, biblical criticism, and philology. Though some stray bits of Schelling's romantic nature-philosophy became merged in American transcendentalism, the latter was really a form of neo-Platonism directly descended from the Cambridge Platonism of More and Cudworth. Hickok's *Rational Psychology* (1849) is our only philosophic work of the first two-thirds of the nineteenth century to show any direct and serious assimilation of Kant's thought. Hickok, however, professes to reject the whole trancendental philosophy, and, in the main, the Kantian elements in his system are no larger than in the writings of British thinkers like Hamilton and Whewell. The Hegelian influence, which made itself strongly felt in the works of William T. Harris, was also potent in Great Britain.

In 1835 De Tocqueville reported that in no part of the civilized world was less attention paid to philosophy than in the United States.[2] Whether because of absorption in the material conquest of a vast continent, or because of a narrow orthodoxy which was then hindering free intellectual life in England as well as in the United States, the fact remains that nowhere else were free theoretic inquiries held in such little honor. Despite the multitude of sects, the Scottish common-sense philosophy introduced at the end of the eighteenth century at Princeton by President Witherspoon spread until it formed almost the sole basis of philosophic instruction. Here and there some notice was taken of Mill and Positivism, and Edward's *Freedom of the Will* continued to agitate thoughtful minds outside and inside of the colleges, but in the main both idealism and empiricism were suspected as leading to pantheism or to downright atheism. The creation of the earth before man was a potent argument against Berkeleyan idealism or denial of matter. The Scottish common-sense realism was a democratic philosophy in the sense that it did not depart widely from the popular views as to the nature of the material world, the soul, and God.[3] It did not rely upon subtle arguments, but appealed to established beliefs. It could easily be reconciled with the most literal interpretation of the Bible and could thus be used as a club against freethinkers. Above all, it was eminently teachable. It eliminated all disturbing doubts by direct appeal to the testimony of consciousness, and readily settled all questions by elevating disputed opinions into indubitable principles. It could thus be authoritatively taught to adolescent minds, and students could readily recite on it. Unfortunately, however, philosophy does not thrive under the rod of authority, and in spite of many acute minds like Bowen, Mahan, Bledsoe, and Tappan, or powerful minds like Shedd and Hickok,[4] American philosophy before the Civil

---

[2] One gets the same impression from Harriet Martineau's *Society in America* (1837) and from the account of Philarète Chasles, *Anglo-American Literature and Manners* (1852).

[3] It is interesting to note that Jefferson was converted to it by Stewart.

[4] Soldier, lawyer, minister, publicist, and editor, as well as professor of mathematics, Albert T. Bledsoe deserves to be better known. His *Philosophy of Mathematics* is still worth reading. So also is Shedd's *Philosophy of History*, which illustrates the independence of the evolutionary conception of history from the thought of Spencer and Darwin. For sheer intellectual power, however, and for comprehensive grasp of technical philosophy Hickok is easily the foremost figure in American philosophy between the time of Jonathan Edwards and the period of the Civil War. He left, however, no influential disciples except Seelye and Bascom.

War produced not a single original philosophic work of commanding importance. To the modern reader it is all an arid desert of commonplace opinion covered with the dust of pedantic language.

The storm which broke the stagnant air and aroused many American minds from this dogmatic torpor came with the controversy over evolution which followed the publication of Lyell's *Geology*, Darwin's *Origin of Species*, and Spencer's *First Principles*. The evolutionary philosophy was flanked on the left by the empirical or positivistic philosophy of Comte, Mill, Lewes, Buckle, and Bain, and on the right by the dialectic evolutionism of Hegel. The work of John Fiske, the leader of the evolutionary host, of Chauncey Wright, who nobly represented scientific empiricism, and of William T. Harris, the saintly and practical-minded Hegelian, united to give American philosophy a wider basis. With these the history of the modern period of philosophy in America begins.

John Fiske:
The Philosophy of Evolution

To understand the profound revolution in religious and philosophic thought caused by the advent of the hypothesis of organic evolution, we must remember that natural history was, after Paley, an integral part of American theology. The current religious philosophy rested very largely on what were then called the evidences of design in the organic world; and the theory of natural selection rendered all these arguments futile. The mass of geologic and biologic evidence marshalled with such skill and transparent honesty by Darwin proved an overwhelming blow against those who accepted the biblical account of the creation of man and of animals as literal history.

Modern physical science had dispossessed theology from its proud position as the authoritative source of truth on astronomic questions. If, then, the biblical account of creation and its specific declaration, "According to their kind created He them," were to be disregarded, could Protestant Christianity, relying on the authority of the Bible, survive? These fears for the safety of religion proved groundless, but there is no doubt that the evolutionary movement profoundly shook the position of theology and theologians. Not only was the intellectual eminence of our theologians seriously damaged in the eyes of the community as a result of the controversy, but theology was profoundly altered by the evolutionary philosophy. As a religious doctrine the latter was in effect a revival of an older deism, according to which the world, instead of being specially created and governed by divine interventions or occasional miracles revealed to us by supernatural authority, was the manifestation of an immanent Power expressing itself in general laws revealed by natural reason and experience.

In the realm of pure philosophy Spencer and his disciple Fiske brought no new ideas of any importance. Their doctrine of the relativity of human knowledge was a common possession of both English and Scottish writers, and their agnosticism, based on our supposed inability to know the infinite, had been common coin since the days of Kant, Mansel and Hamilton. But the idea of universal evolution or development, though as old as Greek philosophy and fully exploited in all departments of thought by Hegel, received a most impressive popular impetus from the work of Spencer, and stirred the popular imagination as few intellectual achievements had done since the rise of the Copernican astronomy. Just as the displacement of man's abode as the centre of universe led by way of compensation to a modern idealism which said, "The whole cosmos is in our mind," so the discovery of man's essential kinship with brute creation led to the renewal of an idealistic philosophy which made human development and perfection the end of the cosmic process travailing through the aeons. Thus, instead of doing away with all teleology, the evolutionary philosophy itself became a teleology, replacing bleak Calvinism with the warm, rosy outlook of a perpetual and universal upward progress.

This absorption of the evolutionary philosophy by theology is clearly brought out in the works of John Fiske (1842-1901). In his main philosophic work, the *Outlines of Cosmic Philosophy* (1874), which he originally had delivered as lectures in Harvard in 1869-71, he followed Spencer so closely in his agnosticism and opposition to anthropomorphic theism that he brought down the wrath of the orthodox and made a permanent position for himself in the department of philosophy at Harvard impossible. Yet his own cosmic theism and his attempt to reconcile the existence of evil with that of a benevolent, omnipotent, quasi-psychical Power should have shown discerning theologians that here was a precious ally. In his later writings, Fiske, though never expressly withdrawing his earlier arguments that the ideas of personality and infinity are incompatible, did emphasize more and more the personality of God; and his original contrast between cosmic and anthropomorphic theism reduced itself to a contrast between the immanent theology of Athanasius and the transcendent theology of Saint Augustine. By making man's spiritual development the goal of the whole evolutionary process, Fiske replaced man in his old position as the head of the universe even as in the days of Dante and Aquinas.

What primarily attracted Fiske to the evolutionary philosophy was precisely that which makes that philosophy so popular, the easy way in which it could serve as a universal key to open up a comprehensive view on every subject of human interest. Despite his services to popular science, Fiske was not himself a scientific investigator. His knowledge of biology was second-hand, neither extensive nor very accurate, and even less can be said about his knowledge of physics. But he was widely read in history, in which he was always primarily interested. The evolutionary philosophy appealed to him above all as a clue to the tangled, complicated mass of facts that constitutes human history. Like Buckle, Fiske wanted to eliminate the marvellous or catastrophic view of history and reduce it to simple laws. In his historic writings, however, he does not seem to have used the evolutionary philosophy to throw new light on past events, and in his actual historic representation his dramatic instinct gave full scope to the part of great men, to issues of battles, and to like incidents.

The extent to which Fiske as a philosopher was dominated by traditional views is best seen when we ask for the ethical and political teaching of his evolutionary philosophy. Only a few pages of the *Cosmic Philosophy* are devoted to this topic, and the results do not in any respect rise above the commonplace. He naively accepts the crude popular analysis which makes morality synonymous with yielding to the "dictates of sympathy" rather than to the "dictates of selfishness." The conception of evolution as consisting of slow, imperceptible changes—thus ignoring all saltations or mutations—is made to support the ordinary conservative aversion for radical change. The philosophy of Voltaire and the encyclopaedists is sweepingly condemned as socially subversive; and against Comte it is maintained that society cannot be organized on the basis of scientific philosophy, not even the evolutionary philosophy. Statesmen should study history, but men cannot be taught the higher state of civilization; they can only be bred in it. Just how the latter process is to take place we are not told. Fiske left nothing of a theory of education. He belittles the importance of social institutions and concludes by making social salvation depend upon a change of heart in individual men— quite in the tradition of the Protestant theology which he had inherited.

Fiske was not an original or a logically rigorous thinker, and his knowledge of the history of science and philosophy was by no means adequate; but he was a remarkably lucid, vigorous, and engaging writer who had no fear of repeating the same point. His *Cosmic Philosophy* went through sixteen editions, and this, as well as his other books, which sold by the thousands, undoubtedly exerted wide influence. Thus, he greatly aided the spread of the Berkeleyan argument that all we know of matter is states of consciousness, and at the same time of the argument (really inconsistent with it) for a psychical parallelism, to which mind and matter form parallel streams of causality without one causing the other. But above all, he made fashionable the evolutionary myth according to which everything has a function, evolves, and necessarily passes through certain stages. Thus he also introduced a new intellectual orthodoxy according to which the elect pride themselves on following the "dynamic" rather than the "static" point of view.

The pietistic philosophy which gained complete control of the American college and of dominant public opinion did not completely break all communication between America and foreign liberal thought as represented by Comte, Fourier, and even Proudhon, or by Bentham, Grote and Mill. Even the writings of the arch-skeptic Hume continued to be reprinted in this country; and the vitality of the sensualistic or quasi-materialistic tradition in the medical profession is evidenced by James Rush's *Analysis of the Human Intellect* (1865). Despite, however, the presence with us of men of such first-rate scientific eminence as Joseph Henry, Benjamin Peirce, or Nathaniel Bowditch, scientific thought was not sufficiently organized to demand a philosophy more in consonance with its own procedure. Even in Great Britain, where science was earlier and better organized by means of the Association for the Advancement of Science (1832), Mill's effort to revive Hume's attempt to introduce the experimental method of natural sciences into mental and moral questions found acceptance very slowly. Toward the end of his life Mill testified that for one British philosopher who believed in the experimental method twenty were followers of the *a priori* method.

Empiricism was certainly not the dominant characteristic of Anglo-Saxon thought in the period when Coleridge, Hamilton, and Whewell were in the foreground. Slowly the scientific mode of thought spread, however, and found in Mill's *Logic* its most convenient formulation.

Chauncey Wright:
The Start of Scientific Empiricism

Chauncey Wright (1830-75), a computer for the *Nautical Almanac*, who had made notable contributions to mathematics and physics, had, like most of the thinking men of his day, been brought up on Hamilton.

But his reading of Mill converted Wright completely; and while never a disciple of Mill to the extent that Fiske was of Spencer, he was in a fair way to re-enforce and develop Mill's logic in a most original manner when an untimely death cut him off. All of his papers, published mostly in the *North American Review* (1864-73), fill only one volume. But if the test of a philosopher be intellectual keenness and persistent devotion to the truth rather than skill in making sweeping generalizations plausible, Chauncey Wright deserves a place in the history of American philosophy with the foremost. Unlike Fiske, Wright knew at first hand the technique of biologic as well as mathematical and physical research, and his contributions to the discussion of natural selection were highly valued by Darwin. But he rejects the evolutionary philosophy of Spencer, not only because of its inadequate grasp of modern physics, nor merely because, like all cosmogonic philosophies, it goes beyond the bounds of known fact, but primarily because it is metaphysical, that is, it deals with the general laws of physics as abstract elements out of which a picture of the universe is to be drawn. To draw such a picture of the universe is a part of religion and of poetic or myth-making art. It does not belong to science. For whenever we go beyond the limited body of observed fact we order things according to our imagination and inevitably develop a cosmos as if it were an epic poem with a beginning, middle, and end.

The scientist, according to Wright, is interested in a general law like gravitation not as a description of the cosmos, but rather as a means for extending his knowledge of a field of concrete fact. Metaphysics speculated about universal gravitation before Newton. What Newton found was a law which enabled him to deduce the facts of the solar system and led to the discovery of many more facts which would not otherwise have come to light,—the existence of the planet Neptune, for instance. If the philosopher wishes to be scientific, let him discipline himself by carrying on an original investigation in some department of empirical science so as to gain a clear idea how knowledge is actually used as a basis for discovering new truths. Anticipating the instrumentalism of Dewey, as well as the pragmatism of James, Wright points out that the principles of modern mathematical and physical philosophy are rather the eyes with which nature is seen than the elements and constitution of the object discovered, that general laws are finders, not merely summaries, of truth.

Wright does not underestimate the value of religious or metaphysical philosophies, though they may be full of vague ideas, crude fancies, and unverified convictions; for they "constitute more of human happiness and human wealth than the narrow material standards of science have been able to measure." But scientific philosophy must be clearly distinguished from these. The motives of science arise in rational curiosity or wonder, while religious and metaphysical philosophies arise from desire not to discover new truths, but to defend our emotional and vital preferences by exhibiting them as entirely free from inconsistency. Logical refutation of every opposing philosophy affords us satisfaction but does not convince our opponents—because the choice of ultimate metaphysical dogmas is a matter of character (or temperament, as James later said) and not of logic.

Wright's own choice, which he does not pretend to demonstrate, is for the view attributed to Aristotle that creation is not a progression toward a single end, but rather an endless succession of changes, simple and constant in their elements, though infinite in their combinations, which constitute an order without beginning and without termination. This distinction between elements and their combinations enabled him to unite the belief in the universality of physical causation, which is the scientist's protection against the refined superstitions of teleology, with the Aristotelian belief in accidents, which keeps the scientist from erecting his discoveries into metaphysical dogmas. Scientific research must postulate the universality of the casual relation between elementary facts and cannot make use of any teleology, since there is no scientific test for distinguishing which facts are ends and which are only means. But there is no evidence that any law like that of gravity is absolutely exact or more than approximately true, or that it holds beyond the observable stars. The inductive or empirical character of the actual laws of science explains the reality of accidents or phenomena which could not have been predicted from any finite human knowledge of their antecedents. The rise of self-consciousness, the use of the voice as a means of communication, or the properties of new chemical combinations, all illustrate phenomena which are subject to law, yet unpredictable. Though life is subject to the law of conservation of energy, nothing characteristic of life can be deduced from such a law.

Wright's penetrating and well-founded reflections on the nature of scientific method did not attract widespread attention. The vast majority come to philosophy to find or to confirm some simple "scheme of things entire." And, though all scientists are empirical in their own field, most of them demand some absolute finality when they come to philosophy. Wright's profound modesty and austere self-control in the presence of glittering and tempting generalizations and his willingness to live in a world subject to the uncertainties of "cosmic weather" will never attract more than a few. Yet the character of his thought, though rare, is nevertheless indicative of a tendency toward scientific philosophy, the negative side of which was more crudely and more popularly represented by

Draper's *History of the Intellectual Development of Europe* (1863) and in the many articles in *The Popular Science Monthly*. But at least two great American philosophers were directly and profoundly influenced by Chauncey Wright, and those were Charles Peirce and William James.

William T. Harris and the
Varieties of Idealism

To the modern reader the writings of William T. Harris—even his last and most finished book, *Psychologic Foundations of Education* (1898) —sound rather obsolete and somewhat mechanical. But the position of the author, who from 1867 to 1910 was regarded as the intellectual leader of the educational profession in the United States, who for over twenty-five years edited *The Journal of Speculative Philosophy*, and who was the chief organizer of the Concord School of Philosophy,[5] gave his writings an amount of influence far beyond what the reader might expect. Sweetly generous, devout, and enterprising, Harris was an ideal apostle of philosophy to the American people, calling upon them to enter the world's great intellectual heritage and assuring them that the truths of religion— God, freedom, and immortality—have always been best protected by true philosophy and are in no need of the ill-advised guardians who, by discouraging free inquiry, transform religion into fetishism.

Just as the work of Chauncey Wright may be summarized as an attack on the pretentiousness and inadequate scientific basis of the Spencerian evolutionary philosophy, so the work of William T. Harris may be summed up as an attack against agnosticism. On its psychologic side Harris' argument is directed against Spencer's assumption (derived from Sir William Hamilton) that we cannot conceive the infinite. Against this Harris clearly points out that Hamilton and Spencer are confusing the process of conception and the process of imagination. It is true that we cannot form a picture or an image of the infinite, but neither can we form an image of any motion or process as such. This, however, need not prevent us from grasping or conceiving any universal process of which the imagination fixes the dead static result at any moment.

On the objective side Harris reaches the same result by the dialectic

---

[5] The Concord School, of which Bronson Alcott was the nominal head and Harris the directing genius, thus represented the union of New England transcendentalism with Germanic scholarship and idealism. As such, its history is a significant incident in the intellectual life of America.

argument that the finite particular cannot be the ultimate reality. Particular things are given in sense perception, but the scientific understanding shows us that every object depends on other things to make it what it is; everything depends upon an environment. Science in its development must thus emphasize dynamic processes, and its highest point is reached in the discovery of the correlation of all forces. But the moment we begin to reason as to the nature of these processes or activities, we are inevitably led to the idea of self-activity; for since every finite object gets its activity from some other object, the ultimate source of all activity must be that which is not limited by something else, and that is an infinite or self-limited activity. Thus the stages of sense-perception, understanding, and reason lead to atomism or materialism, pantheism, and theism respectively.

With the simplicity that comes from undiluted sincerity Harris repeats this argument over and over again, finding in it the clue to fruitful insights in all fields of human interest. It is the weapon with which he refutes all empiricism, which bases truth on the knowledge of particulars. All such philosophy, he says, stops at the stage of understanding and fails to note that a particular fact possesses whatever unity or character it has only in virtue of some universal. Time, space, and causality cannot, therefore, be derived from particular experiences, but are, as Kant maintained, the *a priori* conditions of all experience.

In social philosophy Harris follows Hegel rather closely with a characteristic New England emphasis on the freedom of the will. Thus the state is "a social unit in which the individual exists not for himself, but for the use of that unit"; but social order is to be secured by free choice rather than by external authority. Like his master, Hegel, Harris intellectualizes religion and art, the function of both being to reveal ultimate or philosophic truth, religion in the form of dogmatic faith, art by sensuous representation which "piques the soul to ascent out of the stage of sense perception into reflection and free thought."

Like all Hegelians and most believers in the adequacy of one system, Harris frequently thinks he has gained insight when he has translated a fact into his own terminology[6]; and the allegoric method of interpreting works of art and great literary masterpieces, notably Dante's *Divine Comedy* and Goethe's *Faust*, easily lent itself to that result. Still the general result of Harris' theoretic as well as his practical activity was undoubtedly to broaden the basis and subject matter of American

---

[6] Harris, for instance, believed that he found a new insight into the nature of light when he characterized it as "a point making itself valid outside of itself." See the similar account of gravity in *Psychologic Foundations of Education*, p. 22.

philosophy. His *Journal of Speculative Philosophy* (1867-93), the first journal in the English language devoted exclusively to philosophy, made the thought of Plato and Aristotle as well as that of the German philosophers accessible to American readers. When it was objected that America needed something more original, he justly replied that an originality which cherished its own idiosyncrasies was despicable. His conviction that a worthy originality can come only through deep acquaintance with the best of ancient and modern thought stands justified by at least one fact. The most original American thinkers, Peirce, Royce, James, and Dewey, were also the most learned, and their first philosophic papers appeared in *The Journal of Speculative Philosophy*.

The definitive triumph of the idealistic movement may be dated from the founding in 1892 of *The Philosophical Review* under the editorship of Jacob Gould Schurman and James Edwin Creighton. As the review has always been open to scholarly contributions in all the various fields of philosophy, the character of its contributions during the first decade of its existence bears ample evidence to the complete dominance of the Kantian and Hegelian idealism. The old Scottish philosophy could not hold its own before the superior finesse and technical equipment of the new school.[7] At bottom, too, it realized the necessity of an alliance with the new rationalistic philosophy in the fight for a theistic and spiritual view of the world against scientific positivism and popular materialism.

At Harvard Francis Bowen continued for many years to oppose dialectic Hegelianism as well as the "mud philosophy" of the British empiricists; but his assistant and successor, the gentle and classical-minded G. H. Palmer, turned in the main to the Hegelian idealism introduced at Harvard in 1869 by C. C. Everett.

At Princeton James McCosh, the leader of the Scottish school, poured forth an interminable list of books defending common-sense realism and attacking without excessive refinements all its opponents, including the Hegelians with their "thinking in trinities." But most of his attention had to be devoted to rendering the new evolutionary philosophy harmless to the cause of orthodoxy. His successor, Ormond, so expanded the realism of his master with Berkeleyan and Kantian elements as to make it lose its historic identity.

---

[7] This increased technical interest necessarily led philosophy to become less popular and somewhat narrow in its aims. Hence popular thought came to draw its inspiration either from the vague but sweeping generalizations of Spencer or other popularizers of science, or from mystic culture — theosophy, spiritualism, or "new thought" — which except in the writings of Horatio Dresser have nothing to do with the philosophy treated in this chapter.

A similar development took place at Yale. Noah Porter had studied in Germany under Trendelenburg, and his great text-book on *The Human Intellect* (1868) showed a painstaking, if not penetrating, knowledge of Herbart, Lotze, and Wundt, as well as of the British empiricists. But he remained substantially an adherent of a Scottish intuitive philosophy. Like McCosh, but with greater urbanity, he directed his energy mainly against popular agnosticism and materialism. His pupil and successor, George Trumbull Ladd, while professing to be eclectic and independent, follows in the main the method of Lotze,[8] and in the end bases his spiritualistic metaphysics on epistemology quite in the Kantian fashion. A leader in the introduction of modern physiologic psychology into this country, Ladd stands for a philosophy that criticizes the procedures and fundamental ideas of the special sciences. But his primary interest in philosophy is to make better Christian citizens. His idealism is a branch of modern Christian apologetics, justifying the ways of God and defending the church and the established moral and social order.

Its most distinguished and also its most influential leader the idealistic school found in Josiah Royce at Harvard. To understand his development, however, we must first take some note of Charles S. Peirce.

Charles S. Peirce: The Logic of Science

If philosophic eminence were measured not by the number of finished treatises of dignified length but by the extent to which a man brought forth new and fruitful ideas of radical importance, then Charles S. Peirce (1839-1914) would be easily the greatest figure in American philosophy. Unrivalled in his wide knowledge of the methods and history of the exact sciences (logic, mathematics, and physics), he was also endowed with the bountiful but capricious originality of genius. Few are the genuine contributions of America to philosophy of which the germinal idea is not to be found in some of his stray papers.

Peirce was too restless a pioneer or explorer to be able to settle down and imitate the great masters who build complete systems like stately palaces towering to the moon. He was rather of those who are always trying to penetrate the jungle that surrounds our patch of cultivated

---

[8] A more direct follower of Lotze was Borden P. Bowne, one of the keenest of American metaphysicians.

science; and his writings are all rough, cryptic sketches of new fields, without much regard to the limitations of the human understanding, so that James found his lectures on pragmatism "flashes of brilliant light relieved against Cimmerian darkness." Overt departure from the conventional moral code and inability to work in harness made it impossible for Peirce to keep any permanent academic position, and thus he was deprived of a needed incentive to intelligibility and to ordinary consistency. Intellectual pioneers are rarely gregarious creatures. In their isolation they lose touch with those who follow the beaten paths, and when they return to the community they speak strangely of strange sights, so that few have the faith to follow them and change their trails into high roads. Peirce was fortunate in that two powerful minds, Josiah Royce and William James, were able to follow some of the directions from his Pisgah heights and thus take possession of rich philosophic domains.

When Royce and James, however, tried to arrange to have Peirce lecture to their Harvard students, President Eliot, widely known as a courageous champion of academic as well as of other kinds of freedom, refused to allow Peirce to enter any room of Harvard University, and James and Royce had to hire a private hall. Less than thirty years after this incident Harvard University, at considerable expense, arranged for the publication of Peirce's *Collected Papers* in ten volumes, the first six of which have already appeared under the editorship of Charles Hartshorne and Paul Weiss. This contrast between the scorn for the living and the glorification of the dead is not only dramatic but significant. At least it may serve as a symbol of the truth that academic America can, like Rome, erect monuments to, and sanctify, those that it has burned—except that New England does not wait centuries thus to atone for its past errors.

There can be no doubt that Peirce's intellectual gifts were to an irreparable extent spurned by the prevailing hostility of his generation. He was endowed with a mind that was extraordinarily subtle, free, and fertile in general ideas, and his training gave him a knowledge of the whole field of science that was unmatched among philosophers in its extent and depth. The son of one of America's greatest mathematicians, Benjamin Peirce, and brought up as it were in a laboratory, Charles Peirce himself made noteworthy contributions in diverse fields of science, in logic and mathematics, in photometric astronomy, in geodesy and gravitation, and in experimental psychology as well as philology. For many years he was engaged in the United States Coast and Geodetic Survey, and one of his researches on the pendulum received unusual attention from the International Geodetic Congress to which he was the first American delegate. He was, therefore, predominantly concerned with a philosophy of science.

Here, indeed, was the ideal teacher for any young, active mind that was ready to receive ideas and to devote life's best energies to developing the wealth of their implications.

But, alas! The very untrammeled nature of Peirce's mind, which made him so valuable in the field of thought, made him intolerable to officials whose demands for practical team work could not brook his essential capriciousness and outright waywardness. For only a few years, at Johns Hopkins, was an academic career opened to him. And there not only did he show an unparalleled power to fructify active minds, but his own thought was clarified by the impulse to coherent intelligibility which good teaching stimulates. Deprived of this needed opportunity and stimulus, he became more and more self-involved, fragmentary, and almost willfully obscure. In his later years he lived entirely as a recluse, shut up in his garret with his rope ladder pulled up after him. His work thus suffered from the absence of intellectual intercourse between him and those who, like Peano, Frege, and Russell, were working in the same field. He thus lost the impulse to check his own fanciful opinions (as, for instance, his spiritual interpretation of ladies' perfumes) and became crabbedly and captiously opinionated about things beyond his knowledge, as in his references to the higher criticism of the Bible and to Claude Bernard. He thus sometimes failed to complete his knowledge on essentials, for example, in regard to Leibniz, who blazed many of the trails along which Peirce and other modern logicians have been proceeding.

What Peirce has left us consists only of fragments of a great system along logical lines on which he was working, not continuously, but by fits and starts from diverse angles. Even if he had lived to finish it, it would have been caviar to the general. For he was essentially a pioneer who lived with new and strange ideas; and he wrote for those willing to think for themselves and find out the truth, not for those who wish philosophy ladled out to them. "There are philosophic soup-shops at every corner, thank God!"

Despite, however, the unfinished character of Peirce's philosophy, his many variations and even contradictions, one great principle remained his polestar—and that was the reality of general ideas or universals. In this he was opposed to the general nominalistic tendency of all modern philosophy to believe that only particular things in time and space are real. Repelled by the abuses of later scholastic realism, and on the other hand by the suicidal character of the idea that all general terms are mere sounds or marks devoid of any objective meaning, modern philosophy has for the most part adopted a disguised form of nominalism that is called conceptualism; that is, it has given universals a dubious existence by placing them "in the mind only." But abstract predicates, relations, and laws are asserted not only of the mind but of objects in the natural or physical world. We say *things* remain identical, are equal in length, or change according to the law of multiple proportion. It is therefore irrelevant to the truth or falsity of such objective statements to drag in ideas which exist only in individual minds to which the objective world is "external." If the chemical law of multiple proportion is true, it was true before any human beings came on the scene. Moreover, if there is one thing that Bishop Berkeley *did* prove, it was that the difficulty concerning universals is in no way removed by placing them in the mind. The basic opposition to the conception of universals as real parts or phases of nature comes from the inveterate "practical" or materialistic prejudice in favor of the tangible objects of our sense perception, so that we tend to think of abstract "humanity" or "triangularity" as if it were an additional man or triangle. It is this latter view that is readily refuted by asking: Where is the general man or general triangle that is not anything or anywhere in particular? But the question *where* literally applies only to concrete objects in space. True universals or laws of nature are not additional objects, but the conditions of objects' being what they are. Thought, to be sure, is required to apprehend the universal relations which constitute the meaning of things. But our individual thinking only brings before us, and does not create or determine, the character of the objects thought about. The truths of mathematics and logic, Peirce insists, have to be discovered, and are no more subject to our fiat than are the truths of astronomy. A false inference remains false even if we cannot resist the tendency that makes us wrong.

Peirce's realism has important consequences. Theoretically it leads to the study of the character of objects apart from the psychologic processes that may go on in the individuals who think about these objects. Peirce thus anticipates the science of phenomenology by which Meinong, Husserl, and their disciples revolutionized German thought. It will, I think, be found that Peirce has more substance and less pedantic machinery than the German movement. Realism also leads Peirce to make significant contributions to the important but previously neglected problem concerning the nature of significant signs, the basis of any adequate philosophy of language that can be an aid to logic and to social science.

The practical consequence of Peirce's realism is his sharp distinction between what is useful and what is true. The founder of pragmatism insisted that theoretic science can aim only at knowing the truth, and consideration of utility is foreign to it. Anyone who subordinates the pursuit of truth to any other end, even if it be the welfare of others, ceases to be a scientist to that extent—even if it be claimed that he becomes something better. If the physiologist or pathologist, when cutting up an animal, thinks of how many human lives may be thereby prolonged (into happiness or misery), he will be devoting so much less needed attention to the problem before him. The solution of these problems of science depends primarily on critical care and not on philanthropic motives. As a logician Peirce is rightly jealous of the integrity of scientific procedure. He is impressed, as all honest men should be, by the extent to which practical interests corrupt our reasoning power and make us ignore logical consequences in favor of desired conclusions that are in no way justified by their premises. The backward state of philosophy is due to the fact that its devotees "have not been animated by the true scientific Eros," but have been "inflamed with a desire to amend the lives of themselves and others." "Exaggerated regard for morality is unfavorable for scientific progress." For morality, "the folklore of right conduct," is essentially conservative and thus hostile to free inquiry. Morality is necessary for the good life but is not the whole of it.

Excessive preoccupation with what are regarded as matters of vital importance is the essence of illiberality and leads, according to Peirce, to the American worship of business, which kills disinterested science and makes for barbarism. Science is degraded if turned to potboiling, "whether the pot to be boiled is today's or the hereafter's." Absorption in science has a much higher value. The pursuit of truth like that of beauty gives us the divine spark of blessedness. Peirce's pragmatism asserts that the meaning of an idea is to be found by considering all the *possible* practical consequences that would follow from believing the proposition that embodies it. But the deduction of practical or other consequences is a matter of science.

Science, according to Peirce, is a method of banishing doubt and arriving at stable ideas. Commonly we fix beliefs by reiterating them, by surrounding them with emotional safeguards, and by avoiding anything which casts doubt upon them—by "the will to believe." This method breaks down when the community ceases to be homogeneous. Social effort, by the method of authority, to eliminate diversity of beliefs also fails in the end to prevent reflective doubts from cropping up. Hence we must finally resort to the method of free inquiry and let science stabilize our ideas by clarifying them. How can this be done? Early in his life in Cambridge Peirce came under the personal influence of Chauncey Wright, and in a little club of which Wright was the strongest spirit he first developed the doctrine of pragmatism. The Newtonian experimental philosopher, as Wright had pointed out, always translated general propositions into prescriptions for attaining new experimental facts, and this led Peirce to formulate the general maxim of pragmatism that the meaning of any concept is to be found in "all the conceivable experimental phenomena which the affirmation or denial of a concept could imply."[9]

In his earlier statements of the pragmatic maxim Peirce[10] emphasized the consequences for conduct that follow from the acceptance or rejection of an idea; but the stoical maxim that the end of man is action did not appeal to him as much at sixty as it did at thirty. Indeed, if we want to clarify the meaning of the idea of pragmatism, let us apply the pragmatic maxim to it. What will be the effect of accepting it? Obviously it will be to develop certain general ideas or habits of looking at things. As Peirce accepts the view that the good must be in the evolutionary process, he concludes that it cannot be in individual reactions in their segregation, but rather in something general or continuous, namely, in the growth of concrete reasonableness, "becoming governed by law, becoming instinct with general ideas."[11]

In this emphasis on general ideas Peirce's pragmatism differs sharply from that of his follower, James, who, like most modern psychologists, was a thorough nominalist and always emphasized particular sensible experience. Peirce's belief in the reality and potency of general ideas was connected in his mind with a vast philosophic system of which he left only some fragmentary outlines.[12] He called it synechistic tychistic agapism (from the Greek words for continuity, chance, and love). It assumed the primacy of mind and chance and regarded matter and law as the result of habit. The principal law of mind is that ideas literally spread themselves and become more general or inclusive, so that people who form communities or churches develop distinct general ideas. The nourishing love which parents have for their children or thinkers for their own ideas is the creative cause for evolution. Stated thus baldly these views sound fantastic. But Peirce re-enforces them with such a wealth of illustration from modern mathematics and physics as to make them extraordinarily suggestive to all whose minds are not closed against new ideas.

---

[9] *Monist*, vol. xv, p. 162.

[10] *Popular Science Monthly*, 1878-9; reprinted in C. S. Peirce, *Chance, Love and Logic* (1923).

[11] These phrases (from the article on *Pragmatism* in Baldwin's *Dictionary of Philosophy*) strongly suggest the central idea of Santayana's philosophy, but the writer does not know whether Santayana was ever acquainted with Peirce's writings.

[12] See his articles in the *Monist*, vols. i, ii, and iii, reprinted in C. S. Peirce, *Chance, Love and Logic* (1923).

Peirce was one of the first modern scientific thinkers to lay hands on that sacred cow of philosophy, the belief that everything happens absolutely in accordance with certain simple eternal laws. He was too well acquainted with laboratory methods and the theory of probability to share the common belief that the existence of such universal laws is demonstrated by science. "Try to verify any law of nature and you will find that the more precise your observations, the more certain they will be to show irregular departures from law." The Platonic faith that nature is created on simple geometric lines has undoubtedly been a powerful weapon against those who would have supernatural interferences interrupt the work of science. But there is no empirical evidence to prevent us from saying that all the so-called constants of nature are merely instances of variation between limits so near each other that their differences can be neglected for practical purposes. Impressed by the modern theory of gases and the statistical view of nature as developed by Willard Gibbs and Maxwell, and perhaps also influenced by Wright's doctrine of "cosmic weather," Peirce came to believe in the primacy of chance. What we call law is habit, and what we call matter is inert mind. The universe develops from a chaos of feeling, and the tendency to law is itself the result of accidental variation which has grown habitual with things. The limiting ratios which we call the laws of nature are thus themselves slowly changing in time. This conception of the universe growing in its very constitution may sound mythologic. But it has at least the merit of an empirically supported rational alternative to the mechanical mythology. In many respects it anticipated the philosophy of Bergson. In the hands of James this tychism became a gospel of wonderful power in releasing men from the oppression of a fixed or "block" universe, but in the hands of Peirce it was a philosophic support for the application of the fruitful theorems of scientific probability to all walks of life.

What has Peirce to offer to our present generation? Any attempt at a definitive answer now would be premature. We can only say that men like James and Royce have been nourished by fragments of his philosophy, and that our present generation has caught up with him and is in a better position profitably to develop more of his fruitful ideas. Certainly in the field of exact science, in logic and mathematics, those who, like Russell, have worked along his lines have molded our most advanced thinking.

There is, however, one general observation which the history of philosophy justifies us in making with considerable confidence. Anglo-

American philosophy since Locke has, on the whole, been unduly centered about man's psychologic nature and moral duties. Such concentration on human affairs has always made philosophy narrow and illiberal —witness the Roman and later Greek periods. For it impoverishes philosophy to minimize those cosmic interests which have always constituted its life-blood. And our view of the human scene becomes narrow, unillumined, and passionate if we do not rise above its immediate urgency and see it in its cosmic roots and backgrounds. Plato is reputed to have written over the door of his academy: Let none ignorant of geometry enter here; and, later, Spinoza showed the high serenity which comes from bringing to the discussion of human passions the spirit in which the mathematician discusses lines and circles. Recent revolutionary developments in mathematics and physics have stimulated men's imaginations to a remarkable extent, and have invited philosophy to re-enter its neglected domain. To aid in this, no philosopher offers more direct help than does Charles S. Peirce. Though he has been dead for many years, he was in live contact with the forces which have molded modern mathematics and physics; and perhaps the very fact that his ideas are not completely articulated may make them all the more serviceable in the necessary task of reorganizing our general views of the cosmos so as to make them more in harmony with recent experimental discoveries. Blessed are we if the immolation of our being can weld together the smallest part of the great cosmos of ideas.*

Josiah Royce and the Idealist Tradition

Of the later and more liberal movement to defend the theistic or Christian view of the world on the basis of dialectic arguments that could profess a wholehearted acceptance of modern physical and biologic sciences, Josiah Royce (1855-1916) was by far the most brilliant mind. But he was too big to remain completely within a tradition. His devotion to the study of the logic of modern science and his zeal for the truth, which was as strong as his devotion to the doctrine of idealism, led him to continual revision of his views; and while he always remained in the bosom of the idealistic faith, his work was partly instrumental in pre-

---

* *Cf.* Introduction by M. R. Cohen to C. S. Peirce, *Chance, Love and Logic* (1923).

paring the way for the reaction against idealism which began to take place even in his own day.*

Unlike most of America's distinguished philosophers, Josiah Royce was not brought up in New England. He was born in a mining town in California and received his philosophic education in the university of his own state, at Johns Hopkins, and at Göttingen, where he studied under Lotze. Many diverse elements stimulated his subtle and acquisitive mind to philosophic reflection, the theistic evolutionism of the geologist Le Conte, the fine literary spirit of E. R. Sill, and his own reading of Mill and Spencer, as well as of the great German philosophers, Kant, Schelling, Hegel, and Schopenhauer.

In 1882 he went to Harvard, where his prodigious learning, his keen and catholic appreciation of poetry, and the biblical eloquence with which he expressed a rich inner experience, won immediate and lasting respect. His singularly pure and loyal, though shy, spirit attracted a few strong friendships; but his life at Cambridge was in the main one of philosophic detachment. As a citizen of the great intellectual world, however, he closely followed its multitudinous events; and his successive books only partly reflected his unusually active and varied intellectual interests.

In his earliest published papers he is inclined to follow Kant in denying the possibility of ultimate metaphysical solutions except by ethical postulates, but in his first book, *The Religious Aspect of Philosophy* (1885) he comes out as a full-fledged metaphysical idealist. The term idealism has been applied in modern times to so many different things that it has pretty nearly worn out all definite meaning. As applied by Royce, however, it means, in the main, the view that the nature of the universe is not at bottom alien to our thoughts and moral effort, and that its true inner character progressively reveals itself in the process of our thinking. This brilliant book at once made a profound impression, especially with the arguments that the very possibility of error cannot be formulated except in terms of an absolute truth or rational totality which requires an absolute knower. Like the parts of a sentence, all things find their condition and meaning in the final totality in which they belong. The world must thus be either through and through of the same nature as the mind, or else be utterly unknowable. But to affirm the unknowable is to involve one's self in contradictions. Royce delights in these sharp antitheses and the reduction of opposing arguments to contradictions.

In his next book, an unusually eloquent one entitled *The Spirit of*

---

* Cf. "The New Realism and the Philosophy of Royce" in M. R. Cohen, *Studies in Philosophy and Science* (1949) at p. 133.

Modern Philosophy (1892), the element of will rather than knowledge receives the greater emphasis. The Berkeleyan analysis of the world as composed of ideas is taken for granted, and the emphasis is rather on the nature of the World Mind or Logos. Following Schopenhauer, he points out that even in the idealistic view of the world there is an irrational element, namely, the brute existence of just this kind of world. The great and tragic fact of experience is the fact of effort and passionate toil which never finds complete satisfaction. This eternal frustration of our ideals or will is an essential part of spiritual life, and enriches it just as the shadows enrich the picture or certain discords bring about richer harmony. The Absolute himself suffers our daily crucifixion, but his triumphant spiritual nature asserts itself in us through that very suffering. This profoundly consoling argument, which both elevates us and sinks our individual sorrows in a great cosmic drama, is, of course, an expression of the historical Christian wisdom of the beatitude of suffering. But it offended the traditional individualism which finds its theologic and metaphysical expression in the doctrine of the freedom of the will. If each individual is a part of the divine self, how can we censure the poor wretch who fails to live up to the proper standard? It is significant of the unconventionality of Royce's thought that he never attached great importance to the question of blame or the free and intentional nature of sin. The evils uppermost in his mind are those resulting from ignorance, from the clumsiness of inexperience rather than from willful misdeeds; and, unlike most American philosophers, he rightly saw that the religious conscience of mankind has always regarded sin as something which happens to us even against our will.

Against the complacent belief of the comfortable that no one suffers or succeeds except through his own sins or virtues, Royce opposes the view of St. Paul that we are all members of each other's bodies and that "no man amongst us is wholly free from the consequences or from the degradation involved in the crimes of his less enlightened or less devoted neighbours, and that the solidarity of mankind links the crimes of each to the sorrows of all."

It is difficult to say in what respect Royce's philosophy was typical of America—he was so thoroughly a representative of the humanistic tradition that developed its ideal before modern nationalism was born, and of the liberalism which originated in the European Enlightenment and is still alive in this country. Indeed, it may be said that a philosophy of absolutism is more European than American in its temper. But what is most significant is that the unity of the absolute becomes in Royce's later writings the unity of a community, indeed, the unity of a federal republic, in which the parts or provinces have their own spheres of supremacy. This comes out most clearly in his book on Race Problems, and in the lecture on Provincialism. National unities are too vast and may oppress us into a dead uniformity unless we can also cultivate the consciousness of the dignity of our local community. We may see in this the traditional liberalism of America which favors federalism and state autonomy instead of simple nationalism. But I think there is something even more significant in Royce's later writings, and that is an analysis of the inadequacy of individualism and the recognition of human solidarity, the ignoring of which has led to the bankruptcy of liberalism in Europe.

For the elaboration of the social nature of our intellectual as well as of our moral concepts, Royce was largely indebted to suggestions from Peirce. In his earliest books we find no direct reference to Peirce. We can only conjecture that he owed to that man of genius the emphasis on the social nature of truth and the formulation of the ethical imperative: Live in the light of all possible consequences. But with the publication of the two volumes of *The World and the Individual* (1901), Royce's indebtedness to Peirce becomes explicit and steadily increases thereafter.

The main thesis of that book, the reconciliation of the existence of the Absolute Self with the genuine individuality of our particular selves, is effected by means of illustrations from the field of modern mathematics, especially by the use of the modern mathematical concept of the infinite as a collection of which a part may be equal to the whole. Peirce had done this before him in a remarkable article entitled *The Law of Mind*, in the second volume of *The Monist*. In generously acknowledging his obligation to Peirce, Royce rightly felt his fundamental idealistic position to be independent of that of Peirce; but it is noticeable that all of Royce's references to the logic of mathematics are in full agreement with Peirce's view of the reality of the abstract logical and mathematical universals, and it may well be questioned whether this can be harmonized with the nominalist or Berkeleyan elements of Royce's idealism.

His subsequent works fall into two distinct groups, the mathematical-logical and the ethical-religious. Of the former group, his essay on logic in *The Encyclopedia of the Philosophical Sciences* is philosophically the most important. Logic is there presented not as primarily concerned with the laws of thought or even with methodology, but after the manner of Peirce as the most general science of objective order. In this as in other of his mathematical-logical papers Royce still professes adherence to his idealism, but this adherence in no way affects any of the arguments which proceed on a perfectly realistic basis. In his religio-ethical works he follows Peirce even more, and the Mind or Spirit of the Community replaces the Absolute. In his last important book, *The Problem of Christianity* (1913), all the concepts of Pauline Christianity are interpreted in terms of a social psychology, the personality of Christ being left out except as an embodiment of the spirit of the beloved community.

The World and the Individual is still, as regards sustained mastery of technical metaphysics, the nearest approach to a philosophic classic that America has yet produced. Its publication was the high-water mark of the idealistic tide. Royce's previous monism had aroused the opposition of pluralistic idealists like George Howison and Thomas Davidson.[13] But with the beginning of the twentieth century, idealism itself became the object of organized attack by two movements known as pragmatism and neo-realism. The former was due to the work of James and Dewey; the latter to the spread of renewed and serious interest in scientific philosophy, especially in the renaissance of mathematical philosophy best represented by Bertrand Russell. It is, however, an historic fact that Royce contributed very largely to the effective spread of these new philosophies, to pragmatism by his ethical (as opposed to intellectual) idealism and by his emphasis on the practical aspect of ideas, and to neo-realism by his teaching and writing on mathematical logic. His profound and loyal devotion to the ethical interests of mankind did not prevent him from regarding the question of human immortality as "one for reason in precisely the same sense in which the properties of prime numbers and the kinetic theory of gases are matters for exact investigation." In this way he continued to represent, against the growing tide of anti-intellectualism, the old faith in the dignity and the potency of reason which is the corner-stone of humanistic liberalism. His study of mathematics showed him that reason can be a source of insight even in matters of religion, can simplify men's moral issues, undermine sanctified illusions, and clear the vision for the sight of the eternal.

Though Royce's own deep personal loyalty in all relations of life gave the unmistakable flavor of living insight to all his ethical writings, his work in logic will prove even more important; for it represents not only an achievement but also a basis on which others can continue to build. The greatest obstacles today to scientific study of ethics and social

---

[13] Howison and Davidson both owed much of their impulse to philosophy to W. T. Harris. Howison proved one of the most successful and inspiring teachers of philosophy that America has as yet produced. Within a short period three of his pupils, Bakewell, McGilvary, and Lovejoy were elected to the presidency of the American Philosophical Association. Davidson did not write much on technical philosophy, confining himself for the most part to books on education. James called him "a knight-errant of the intellectual life" (*Memories and Studies*). In a letter to the writer, Professor Höffding calls Davidson "one of the most beautiful figures in modern philosophy."

philosophy, of things as they ought to be, are dogmatic scepticism and stingy positivism—whose confident assumption that there can be no science except of actually existing particular things, will be found to rest on the traditional antiquated logic. The realistic logic which Royce and others brought to light cuts the ground from this discouraging prejudice. The world of actuality is not the sole reality. Indeed, there could be no science at all if logic did not apply to a wider realm, if we could not study hypothetical entities like frictionless engines, or perfect conductors, which do not and perhaps cannot actually exist. The new realistic logic, a study of the order according to which all entities of whatever kind behave, emancipates us from the debilitating doubts which naturally follow the traditional view that logic deals with the laws of thought, and that the way we think is, therefore, the only thing which we can know. It enables us to tread our way through an ever-changing world, by revealing the threads of identity which run through all changes and which form the tracks along which science moves in exploring the abiding nature of things.

Although with the passing of Royce idealism lost its most powerful figure, still as far as numbers and influence are concerned the idealistic tradition continued to be the strongest force in American academic philosophy. This may be ascribed to the fact that the idealists are generally more eager to justify the traditional humanistic values of religion and morality than to make specific contributions to philosophy. Most of the followers of Royce are objective or absolute idealists who repudiate the adequacy of the ordinary hard distinction between mind and matter, subject and object, and yet maintain that the nature of knowledge logically involves the existence of an absolute or eternal self as knower. Variants on this doctrine, represented in the past by the pluralistic or personal idealism of Howison and Davidson, who conceived the whole universe to be ordered on the model of a democracy or republic of free spirits, have left no direct influence upon contemporary idealists.

Although a close follower of Royce, W. E. Hocking shows more pronounced leanings towards mysticism than his master. Starting from a consideration of the facts of duty and value, Hocking maintains that their existence can only be intelligible in a world which has an intrinsic meaning. Since meanings independent of some mind are mere abstractions, reality must be mental. The brute arbitrary aspect of things acquires rationality in the light of our insight into the way meanings are organized into a cosmic, absolute Self. This absolute Self or One eludes cognitive analysis and its unity can only be grasped in the mystic experience. "The infinite is measured by the infinite; and the unknown by the unknown."

The mystic experience represents one pole of the rhythmic law of alternation between practical activity and the synoptic vision of the unsensed Whole which gives life meaning. Adequately understood, these aspects of experience imply one another. This mystical strain in idealism is developed in the writings of C. A. Bennett, a student of Hocking.

Most of Hocking's positions are re-statements of certain aspects of the idealism of Royce. They lack, however, the strong dialectic backing, perhaps more dazzling than convincing, which Royce gave them. To argue from the existence of meanings to the necessary presence of consciousness can only be done when idealism is begged at the outset. To assume that the quest for some unity of knowledge points to the existence of some monistic all-embracing invariant reference, called a Self or God, is to confuse a regulative ideal with a constitutive form, and to introduce a hopeless ambiguity in the connotations of terms like God and Self. To argue that some kind of alternation is necessary to save oneself from the morass of pettifogging detail and the emptiness of contemplation of the "one and all," is to overlook the possibility that such an experience need not be supernatural but may represent points of relative emphasis, activity, and detachment, in the course of natural life.

More independent students of Royce are G. P. Adams and J. Loewenberg. Adams is interested in saving the autonomy of values from both the ever-encroaching naturalistic reduction of values to the intent and object of some biological or social drive, and from the Kantian interpretation which preserves the autonomy of ethical values at the cost of their natural efficacy. An idea that something is good, just like an idea that something is true, must mean more than that someone entertains it, more than that it is a mere event deriving its validity from its very existence. Just as an objective order of ideal relationships must exist so that valid truth may be distinguished from the invalid, so an objective order of ethical values, equally compelling and universal, must exist in order to distinguish between the really good and the imagined good. Since what is judged to be good is not an unattainable abstract ideal but some concrete existence, and since the test of what is good depends upon the judgment as to what is actually true, the system of objective truths as well as the system of objective values are different aspects of a deeper, underlying reality. From this Adams skillfully deduces the familiar idealistic doctrines that all knowledge is mediate and that a definite unity pervades will and mind, and ends up with the (self-refuting) proposition that the truth is the whole. The two assumptions upon which the whole argument rests are (1) that logical, scientific and ethical propositions are self-evidently of the same structure and order of objectivity, and (2) that the consistency and social consequences of an ethical proposition which defines what a naturalist means by ethical objectivity, are not sufficient to satisfy the human need for security and freedom. Both may be vigorously challenged.

J. Loewenberg has dipped most deeply into the sources of Royce's own earlier inspiration—the philosophy of Hegel. Although his fundamental positions seem to be more Kantian than those of other members of the school, e.g., his emphasis on the element of opacity in knowledge and his distinction between the logic of discourse and the logic of existence, he has succeeded in applying the "problematic" and "paradoxical" method of the Hegelian dialectic to a fresh analysis of the nature of "judgment" and the character of "the Given" in such a way as to outflank the traditional controversies between subjectivism and realism.

Another idealist strongly influenced by Hegel through Royce is Mary Whiton Calkins. Accepting the Hegelian position that Ultimate Reality is an Absolute Self, she interprets it in a much more definite personalistic way. The Absolute Self is conceived of on the model of the natural self and in a vain effort to settle the problem of evil is endowed with the attributes of infinitude, goodness and sympathetic participation in human affairs.

Another group of Neo-Hegelian idealists influenced more directly by Bosanquet is the Cornell University school led by Creighton, Thilly, Hammond, Cunningham, and Albee. Greater importance is attached to historical rather than to analytical studies. The history of philosophy is regarded as the indispensable propaedeutic to the approach of philosophical problems; the evolution of thought is taken in the traditional Hegelian fashion, as necessarily making for progressive clarification of ideas. Creighton, a close follower of Bosanquet, holds that the task of philosophy is to interpret experience in such a manner as "to show its relations to the ideals and purposes of a rational self-consciousness." Despite its voluminous output, most of the literature of contemporary American idealism is devoted to a reiteration of a standpoint rather than to forthright attempts to meet the analytical difficulties raised by Moore, Russell, and Dewey against the coherence theory of truth and reality.

A variant of philosophical idealism which reflects the influence of Hugo Münsterberg as well as that of Bosanquet is represented by W. M. Urban. He stresses the continuity of the classical tradition of *Philosophia Perennis* or the quest for the forms of philosophic intelligibility, against modern doctrines which break up concrete reality into values that are not constitutive to existences and into existences devoid of values. Value and existence cannot be dichotomized into two ultimate surds, since

some things are pronounced to be what they ought to be; value and
existence cannot be identical, since everything would then be valuable
and the normative character of ethics, aesthetics and logic would disappear. Consequently, value and existence are related in such a way that
although they are not identical, they are not separable. The way they
actually fuse can only be revealed by some kind of mystical experience.
In the sense in which Urban uses the term "validity," it may well be
granted that its intelligibility depends upon reference to existence, that
the *is* and the *ought* are polar categories. But that is to tell us nothing at
all about the specific relationship existing between the facts and ideals of
daily life. Insight into the exact relationships, e.g., between certainty and
justice in law, and consistency and fertility in science, can only be won
by piecemeal analysis and experimentation rather than by mystic vision.

Royce has secured for himself a lasting place in American philosophy
not only through his brilliant apologetics for religious idealism but
through the influence which his work in social psychology and mathematical logic has exercised upon men like J. M. Baldwin, C. I. Lewis and
H. M. Sheffer. Indeed, by his ethical (as opposed to psychologic) idealism
and by his studies in logic as the most general science of objective order,
Royce fashioned some of the most effective tools wherewith pragmatists
like James and neo-realists like Holt were able to free themselves from
the idealistic tradition entirely. Baldwin's evolutionary social psychology
and genetic logic have been more influential in Europe than in America.
Lewis' masterly *Survey of Symbolic Logic* has won unqualified praise. In
his philosophical views he rejects the metaphysics of idealism and, stimulated by the early writings of Charles Peirce, takes an intermediate view
between logical realism and instrumental pragmatism. H. M. Sheffer has
clung more tenaciously to strictly logical interests and has done remarkable work in that field. Not only has he succeeded in reducing the number
of primitive ideas in Whitehead and Russell's *Principia Mathematica,* but
he has developed a theory of notational relativity to discover what the
logical "invariants" are which lie behind all attempts to show that postulate sets are equivalent or structurally isomorphic. Sheffer's influence on
the younger generation of philosophers trained at Harvard has become
quite marked in recent years.

Although firmly entrenched in the academic tradition, idealism is
slowly receding before the newer tendencies in American philosophy
which have sprung up in the last two generations. Its procedure seems
too remote for the kinds of proof that we demand of modern science; and
though it talks eloquently about social and political issues, it has contributed little illumination to these themes. Idealism is everywhere on

the defensive. But it will continue to charm human spirits by its lyric glorification of human consciousness, and to console human frailty with the flattering doctrine that man's ideals are woven into the very stuff and texture of the entire universe.

The Pragmatism of William James

An educated European at the mention of American philosophy thinks of pragmatism; and when he thinks of pragmatism the name of William James spontaneously rises to his lips. In William James (1842-1910) we meet a personality of such large proportions and of such powerful appeal to contemporaneous sentiment that we may well doubt whether the time has yet come when his work can be adequately estimated. There are many who claim that he has transformed the very substance of philosophy by bringing it down from the cold, transcendental heights to men's business and bosoms. But whether that be so or not, the width and depth of his sympathies and the irresistible magic of his words have undoubtedly transformed the tone and manner of American philosophic writing. Outside of America, also, his influence has been impressive.

Yet despite the enormous influence which James has exercised, he has left behind him no school of technical philosophers with a definite core of unified doctrines. The specific philosophic positions of the *Principles of Psychology* as embodied in the last chapter have not been developed by any one. Dewey has generously acknowledged his obligation, but his instrumentalism is a quite different affair from the pragmatism of James. Nor would James have agreed to the crude biological materialism which the behaviorists have developed from the suggestion thrown out in his essay, *Does Consciousness Exist?* Only in the philosophy or psychology of religion has James wielded a continuous and profound influence. It was here that his temperamental preference for the unique and colorful could be most readily adapted to the extreme emotionalism of traditional American evangelical religion. Professional philosophers, however, have invoked his name more often than his teaching. They soon realized that the doctrine of radical empiricism, to which his pragmatism was only ancillary, really left the most important philosophical issues untouched; insofar as it held that immediate experience was already categorized and that consequently no specific analysis of experienced connections was necessary. Even his later anti-intellectualism found no echo among his students despite its popular literary vogue.

It is instructive to note at the outset the judgment of orthodox philosophers, boldly expressed by Howison:

Emerson and James were both great men of letters, great writers; yes, great thinkers, if you will; but they do not belong in the strict list of philosophers. . . . Mastery in logic is a cardinal test of the true philosopher, and neither Emerson nor James possessed it. Both, on the contrary, did their best to discredit it.[14]

As a criticism this is hardly fair. James certainly elaborated definite doctrines as to the nature of mind, truth, and reality. In his *Radical Empiricism* and in *The Meaning of Truth* he even showed considerable dialectic skill. Moreover, it may well be maintained that he did not seek to discredit logic in general, but only the logic of "vicious intellectualism." Nevertheless, Howison's opinion is significant in calling attention to the distinction between philosophy as technique and philosophy as vision. From the professional point of view it is not sufficient that a man should believe in free will, absolute chance, or the survival of consciousness beyond death. To be worthy of being called a philosopher, one must have a logically reasoned basis for his belief. James was aware of the importance of technique, and was, in fact, extraordinarily well informed on the substance and main tendencies of all the diverse technical schools. But he was wholly interested in philosophy as a religious vision of life, and he had the cultivated gentleman's aversion for pedantry. His thoughts ran in vivid pictures, and he could not trust logical demonstration as much as his intuitive suggestions. Hence his philosophic writings are extremely rich in the variety of concrete factual insight, but not in effective answers to the searching criticisms of men like Royce, Russell, and Bradley. James was aware of this and asked that his philosophy be judged generously in its large outlines; the elaboration of details might well be left to the future.

"The originality of William James," says one of his European admirers, "does not appear so much in his cardinal beliefs, which he took from the general current of Christian thought, as in the novel and audacious method by which he defended them against the learned philosophies of the day."[15] This, also, is not true without qualification. James took almost nothing from current Christian philosophy. Nor do any of the great historic Christian doctrines of sin and atonement or salvation find any echo in his thought. Orthodox Christianity would condemn James as a confessed pantheist who denied the omnipotence of God. But though James is far removed from Christian theology, he gives

---

[14] *Philosophical Review*, vol. xxv, p. 241, May, 1916.
[15] Théodore Flournoy, *William James*, p. 16.

vivid utterance to the ordinary popular Christianity which believes, not in a God who expresses himself in universal laws, but in a God to whom he can pray for help against our enemies, whom we can please and even help by our faith in Him. This is due to James's deep sympathy with common experience rather than with the problems of the reflective-minded. But the modern sophisticated intellect is certainly tickled by the sight of a most learned savant espousing the cause of popular as opposed to learned theology, and by the open confession of belief in piecemeal supernaturalism on the basis of spiritistic phenomena. James's antipathy to the Hegelian and Roycean attempts to prove the existence of the Absolute certainly plays a more prominent part in his writings than does his antipathy to popular unbelief. But the method of the absolutist he rejected, not only because of its insufferable pretension to finality of proof, but mainly because it is in the way of one who prefers an anthropomorphic universe that is tingling with life through and through and is constantly meeting with new adventures.

The union of religious mysticism with biologic and psychologic empiricism is characteristic of James's work from the very beginning. He grew up in a household characterized by liberal culture and mystic Swedenborgian piety.[16] The teacher who made the greatest impression upon him, Louis Agassiz, was a pious opponent of Darwin but a rare master in the art of observing significant details. More than one American naturalist caught the fire of his enthusiasm for fact. The companionship of Chauncey Wright and the writings of Renouvier weaned James from his father's religio-philosophical monism. The empirical way of thought of Hume and Mill proved most congenial to one who was *par excellence* a naturalist and delighted in the observation of significant detail.[17]

James began his career as a teacher of physiology and gradually drifted into psychology. His *Principles of Psychology* (2 vols., 1890) contains the substance of his philosophy. Having, despite the influence of Agassiz, become converted to Darwinism, he was led to adopt as fundamental the view of Spencer that thought is something developed in the course of evolution and must, therefore, have a biologic function. The great idealistic argument against the old associationist psychology of Hume, Mill, Bain, and Spencer was to the effect that the sensational elements can at most account for the qualities of things, but not for their

---

[16] His father, Henry James, Sr., was a Swedenborgian philosopher and a cultivated gentleman of ample means, who united to genuine originality of thought a remarkable insight into human character and a delightful freshness and pungency of language.

[17] James studied art and was a proficient draftsman before he finally decided to study medicine.

relations or connections; and when it was once granted that the relations between things were of a non-sensational or non-empirical character, very little of the world was left to the empiricist.

James early became convinced of the force of this argument and, following certain suggestions of Peirce and possibly Hodgson, tried to save empiricism by making it more radical, by giving the connecting relations themselves a psychologic status on a par with the things they connect. Thus he thought to restore the fluidity and connectedness of our world without admitting the necessity for the idealist's transcendental glue to hold together the discrete elements of experience. Radical empiricism thus becomes a metaphysic which holds the whole world to be composed of a single stuff called pure experience. This sounds monistic enough, and James's adherence to the view of Bergson re-enforces this impression. Nevertheless, James insisted that the world as experienced does not possess the degree of unity claimed for it by Royce and other monists, but that things are essentially many and their connections often external and accidental. At times James professes the dualistic realism of common sense. "I start with two things, the objective facts and the claims." But ideas and things are both experiences taken in different contexts, so that his position has not inaptly been called neutral monism, and thus assimilated to the philosophy of Ernst Mach.

It has been claimed that this view eliminates most of the traditional problems of metaphysics, such as that of the relation of the mind and the body, and also eliminates the need for the Spencerian unknowable and Royce's or Bradley's absolute. At this point, however, James's philosophy becomes extremely obscure, for he fails to tell us just exactly what he means by experience. When he speaks of pure experience he certainly means to exclude concepts and logical deduction. Yet as the latter processes somehow exist and their claims are not altogether denied, the term *experience* must be stretched to include them also. But when the term *experience* is thus stretched to include everything, the crusade in its favor becomes meaningless for want of opposition. James cryptically tells us that it is something to be lived rather than to be defined.

The exigencies of controversy, as well as James's generous desire to give all possible credit to Peirce, have led the public to regard pragmatism and James' philosophy as identical terms. To James, however, pragmatism was but the method of philosophic discussion,—the vestibule to his radical empiricism. The controversy which arose about pragmatism enables James to elaborate from different approaches his account of the nature of truth. The meaning of ideas is to be found in their particular experimental consequences. Abstract ideas are not copies of things but their substitutes or derivatives, evolved in the process of evolution to enable us to deal more adequately with the concrete stream of immediate experience. An idea is, therefore, true if it enables us to deal satisfactorily with the concrete experiences at which it aims. An idea is said to work satisfactorily if it leads us to expected facts, if it harmonizes with other accepted ideas, if it releases our energies or satisfies emotional craving for elegance, peace, economy, or any kind of utility.

So anxious was James to overthrow the view that the truth of an idea consists in its being an inert copy of reality, so anxious to substitute for it the more activist view that an idea is true if it works or leads to certain results, that he neglected to indicate the relative importance of these results. This led to a great deal of misunderstanding and caused considerable scandal. Those brought up in the scientific tradition and trained to view the emotionally satisfactory consequences of ideas as having nothing to do with their scientific or theoretic value were scandalized by James's doctrine of the will or right to believe anything the acceptance of which made us more comfortable. This was in part a tragic misunderstanding. Most of James's life was a fight against accepting the monistic philosophy simply because of its aesthetic nobility. He rejected it precisely because it was "too buttoned up and white chokered, too clean-shaven a thing to speak for the vast slow-breeding, unconscious cosmos with its dread abysses and its unknown tides." It is true, however, that absorption in the psychologic factor, personal or aesthetic, which actually does make some people prefer a narrowly classic universe and others a generously romantic one, made him obscure the distinction between the causes of belief and the evidence for the truth which we believe.

We may all start with a biased or emotional preference, but that is neither evidence nor guaranty of our arriving at scientific truth. Like other violent opponents of intellectualism, James himself falls into the intellectualistic assumption that we must either wholly believe or wholly disbelieve, just as one must either go to church or stay out. He ignores the scientific attitude of suspended judgment and the fact that men may be compelled to act without being constrained in judgment. We may vote for X or Y and yet know that owing to the absence of adequate information our choice has been little more than a blind guess. His interest in vital preferences and his impatience with the emotionally thin air of purely logical argumentation led James, towards the end of his life, to the acceptance of the extreme anti-logical view of Bergson that our logical and mathematical ideas are inherently incapable of revealing the real and changing world.

James's interest in philosophy was fundamentally restricted to the psychological aspect of things. He therefore never elaborated any systematic theory of morals, politics, or social organization. His temperamental preference for the novel, the unique, and the colorful re-enforced his traditional American liberalism and made him an extreme individualist. He attached scant value to the organized or fixed channels through which the fitful tides of ordinary human emotion find permanent expression. This shows itself best in his *Varieties of Religious Experience* (1902). He is interested in the extreme variations of religious experiences, in the main, in the geniuses or aristocrats of the religious life. The religious experience of the great mass, or even of intellectual men like Chief Justice Marshall, who go to church without troubling much about matters of belief, seems to James "second-hand" and does not solicit his attention. Neither does the whole question of ritual or ceremony. He is interested in the beliefs of extraordinary and picturesque individuals. Hence his book on religion tells us almost nothing to explain the spread and vitality of the great historic religions, Buddhism, Confucianism, Judaism, Islam, and Christianity. This extreme individualism, however, is connected with an extraordinary democratic openness and readiness to admit that it is only the blindness in human nature that prevents us from seeing the uniqueness of every individual. Unlike any other philosopher, William James was entirely devoid of the pride of the intellect. He was as willing as Jesus of Nazareth to associate with the intellectual publicans and sinners and learn from the denizens of the intellectual underworld.

James's position in the history of metaphysics is still a matter of debate, but as a seer or prophet he may fitly be put beside Emerson. Like Emerson, he preached and nobly exemplified faith in one's intuition and the duty of keeping one's oracular soul open. In spite of a note of obscurantism in his attitude to logic and "over beliefs," there is no doubt that the main effect of his work was to raise the American standard of intellectual honesty and courage: Let us stop this miserable pretence of having at last logically proved the comforting certainties of our inherited religion. Let us admit that we have no absolute assurance of the complete success of our ideals. But the fight is on. We can all take our part. Shame on the one who sulks and stays out.

James created a vigorous and healthy stir in the stagnant air of American philosophy but left no permanent currents of doctrine or even of method. He shattered the smugness of the genteel tradition, called attention to the "dread abysses and unknown tides" of an unconscious cosmos, and made everyone feel the high adventure of the philosophical enterprise. But with the possible exception of H. M. Kallen, he left not a single philosopher behind who regards himself as a faithful disciple. And it is difficult to see in what way Kallen utilized the substance of James's teaching. James seems to have been what the chemists call a catalytic agent in American philosophy.

John Dewey and His School

The tendency to class James and Dewey together, noticeable among those who have read neither too closely, is misleading in that it emphasizes their common opposition to doctrines and overlooks the independent elements in their respective philosophies. Doubtless their agreement in the face of absolute idealism and atomic realism is thoroughgoing and significant; but in many respects, they are temperamentally and doctrinally at opposite poles of the philosophic sphere. James had his roots in British utilitarianism; Dewey in neo-Hegelianism. And while both follow Peirce in asserting that the meaning of any truth is to be found in its consequences, James insists that these consequences must be particular, Dewey that they must be always more than particular,—that they must be general social leads to activity. For one, the rich immediacy of sensation gives knowledge; for the other, knowledge is never immediate. Dewey and his followers are essentially moralists, interested in philosophy as an instrument for social betterment. James is a spiritualist, interested in what constitutes well-being rather than well-doing. Dewey glorifies the function of the intellect in the transformation of reality; James trusts more to intuition as a revelation of reality. Thus to James as to his English colleague, Schiller, pragmatism is a method whereby the values of the old supernaturalism may still be maintained, while Dewey's pragmatism or instrumentalism is a method for eliminating such concepts as God, free will, and immortality. For the latter, philosophy must henceforth be scientific and practical, not apologetic.

John Dewey is unquestionably the pre-eminent figure in American philosophy; no one has done more to keep alive the fundamental ideals of liberal civilization; and if there could be such an office as that of national philosopher, no one else could be properly mentioned for it. The incomparable charm of William James's style has perhaps attracted more readers than the more closely-knit technical arguments of Dewey. Yet, it is a fact that Dewey is the only American to have established a new philosophic school,—still known as the Chicago school. Whenever we meet with any apostles of the new philosophic dispensation called pragmatism or instrumentalism, we may be sure to find them using the arguments, metaphors, and phrases coined by John Dewey. That which in James is a matter of vision and intuitive suggestion becomes in the hands of Dewey a well-organized argument that can be learned and taught, expounded and defended, used as a justification for educational policies, or as a battering ram against sanctimonious complacencies. Thus, the number and the aggressive enthusiasm of Dewey's disciples, not only in philosophy but in related realms, is rapidly increasing.

Clearly this extensive influence is due not only to rare personal qualities as a teacher, but also to the degree to which some aspects of his thought correspond to the prevailing American temper of the age. His doctrine that all our ideas are, and ought to be, practical, i.e., instrumental for reforming the world and making it a better place in which to live, appeals powerfully to popular utilitarianism, to the American worship of visibly practical results, of which Theodore Roosevelt was such a conspicuous representative. In a country where so many great deeds in the conquest of nature are still to be performed, the practical man's contempt for the contemplative and the visionary is re-enforced by the traditional American puritanic horror of idle play and of that which is uselessly ornamental. And although Dewey in his later years has developed a theory of art which is anything but puritanic, the incidence of his thought as a whole has been interpreted by his followers as a justification of the ways of energetic America. To many of Dewey's disciples, as to our preachers of the gospel of success, nature is like one of the prudent heroes of Samuel Smiles' *Self Help*. It never indulges in any play or riot of exuberant activity for its own sake. It generates intelligence only to help in the serious business of life.

As a "come outer" of the idealistic church Dewey carries with him the air of sober disillusion, but a philosophy which views external nature as just so much material to be transformed by our intelligence, appeals, independently of the intent of its founder, to the thin optimism of an industrially prosperous people, which sees success as the sure reward of intelligent effort and finds no inherent obstacle to the establishment of a heaven on earth—though it will not do for practical people to inquire too curiously what should constitute such a heaven. Dewey's confidence in the power of human intelligence to change our environment is so strong that his attention is rarely solicited by the incurable evils which, in an imperfect world, every child of mortal man and woman must face before reaching the crowning agonies of death. His most distinguished disciples, like Professors Bode and Addison Moore, do not hide their contempt for a philosophy that can serve as a consolation, or can admit that there are evils against which our only remedy is some form of wisely cultivated resignation. Dewey himself takes these evils for granted, since thought arises, in a sense, because of the essential precariousness of life. But in the absence of any explicit consideration of the part they play in the whole of man' life—emotional, religious and artistic,—it is not clear always that Dewey regards them as the important and inescapable features of the background of major human activities.

The American temper, however, to which Dewey appeals, the temper which is known and likes to be known as practical-minded and distrustful of all forms of other-worldliness, is only a part of our national trait. It may be dominant in our industrial life and even in some of our churches which are trying to replace theology and religion with "social work." But there is another America, God-fearing and evangelical or vaguely spiritualistic, which, though less noticed in our urban press and literature, is still perhaps the most dominant force in our country, as our Sunday legislation and the episode of the prohibition amendment may indicate. If we judge merely by the number of adherents, there can be no doubt that our distinctive national philosophy is not pragmatism but the diluted and Americanized form of theosophy or neo-Platonism which manifests itself in the various forms of New Thought, from Mrs. Eddy's *Science and Health* to R. W. Trine's *In Tune with the Infinite*, and which crops out in our Pollyanna literature. The books of no other intellectual or semi-intellectual movement find so many millions of readers among our tired men of affairs, as well as among those who hunger for the newer mystic visions to save them from the dreary emptiness of worldly success, and who know from experience that salvation comes not solely through our own conscious efforts but depends on the grace of powers beyond us.

It is curious that the America which believes in faith above visible works gets no recognition in Dewey who comes from the rural state of Vermont, but finds dignified expression in William James who can be regarded as Celtic or European as much as American. In fact, however, we are dealing with a fundamental difference between two temperaments, which the older Henry James would have called the moralistic and religious. Dewey is essentially a moralist. His philosophy is full of the sense of responsibility, of tasks to be achieved, and of the possibilities of philosophy in helping us to perform them more efficiently. Everything in his universe has a job or function and ought to be up and doing. The otiose observer,—the one who idly admires the flowers of knowledge for their own sake rather than their consequences,—is the cardinal sinner. James, on the other hand, is essentially religious in his interest. His attention is attracted by that which makes things objects of love or worship rather than merely useful or instrumental. He is less interested in conduct than in the quality of life and our ultimate fate and well-being. Moral holidays solicit his attention more than the day's work. His frank belief in supernaturalism arises not so much out of a reasoned theory of what really exists, as out of a sympathy with those who feel how little our conscious thought can shape our individual destinies, and how seldom the works of our hand can completely satisfy our heart's desire.

With the austere self-control of the trained scientist, Dewey is willing to restrict his philosophy to that part of the cosmos for the handling of which he is technically equipped—the world of visible human conduct. Unlike James, who had a more rigid scientific training, Dewey is willing to abandon all interest in the mystery of the universe at large. He manifests no sense of the dark and unfathomable seas of being, wherein the world of human conduct occupies but an infinitesimal portion of time and space.

Despite the complexity of his sentences, which a too conscientious regard for accuracy causes to be overloaded with qualifications, Dewey is essentially one of those philosophers who, like Spinoza, impress the world with their profound simplicity. He is entirely free from that human complexity which makes James capable of banishing the soul and even consciousness as psychologic entities, and yet capable of believing in subconscious minds, Fechner's earth spirits, and the like. Dewey is a thoroughgoing and consistent naturalist, i.e., one who accepts without question the method and the results of the natural sciences, especially Darwinian biology.

Dewey began his philosophic career under the influence of Harris, T. H. Green, and Bosanquet, and in his early writings, e.g., his *Psychology*, he showed himself a master of Hegelian dialectics. In his youth he was an idealist, of the orthodox neo-Hegelian school, which professes to combine modern science and ancient religion in one harmonious system. Reflection, however, led him to find an incurable incompatibility between the diluted supernaturalism latent in idealism and the biologic or naturalistic account of the origin of consciousness which one gets from modern experimental psychology in such works as Spencer's, or James's *Principles of Psychology*. Whether because the consequent break with the idealistic school came too late in his intellectual life to enable him to ignore his former views and to throw himself unreservedly into the development of his new insight, or whether because the temptation of controversy and the prospect of securing the triumph of a righteous cause were too irresistible in the quiet monotony of academic life, the fact remains that an inordinate proportion of Dewey's philosophic writings is polemical in character. This cannot but be regarded as a great loss to philosophy, since philosophers, like others, are generally more fortunate in giving us the substance of their own vision than in denying the vision of others.

That intelligence arises in the process of organic life and in the furtherance of it, that the structure of our ideas can be understood only in the light of the transformation of our environment which they affect, is the central theme of Dewey's philosophy. When he applies it to current public issues it leads to a fresh reassertion of the liberal or Hellenic element of civilization, viz., that action should be illumined by the freest intelligence. In the fields of education, where his essentially psychologic philosophy finds most direct application, it means not only an intelligent appreciation of our environment but a liberalizing of human capacity. But when he addresses his fellow-philosophers, he tends to emphasize the practical character of ideas in a way to do scant justice to their theoretic or contemplative function. From the scientific point of view pragmatism can establish its inherently just claims only by actual analysis of our leading scientific ideas. But such an analysis requires deliberate detachment and long patient labor which can be sustained only by a love of intellectual play for its own sake. The conditions of American philosophy today do not favor such laborious undertaking. Philosophers like others are expected to show immediate results. Dewey is by the natural subtlety of his mind and immensity of his liberal knowledge eminently qualified to make pragmatism an achievement rather than a promising program. And in his later years he turned more directly to the analysis of fundamental concepts, philosophy and art, introducing by the scope as well as the standpoint of his inquiries, significant modifications of his earlier views.

When, as in his *Democracy and Education, Experience and Nature,* and *The Quest for Certainty,* he is not engaged in controversy, the rich sensitiveness and ingrained honesty of Dewey's mind show themselves at their best in the natural responsiveness to all sorts of diverse elements, in his habitual avoidance of sweeping or unqualified generalizations and of artificial dilemmas by which easy intellectual triumphs are obtained at the cost of just discrimination. But when the spirit of combat is upon us, it becomes practically impossible to devote much attention to saving what is valuable in the enemy's cause. Thus, when he insists that thinking arises as an effort to control our environment so as to get out of trouble, he is undoubtedly emphasizing an important and often neglected truth. But the zeal of controversy leads him and his disciples to assert this, not as a general but as a universal or exclusive proposition, and thus to deny the

Aristotelian view that philosophic knowledge arises from natural wonder or curiosity, from the desire to know just for the sake of knowing. Professor Moore is especially vehement in denying that there is a fundamental desire to know, co-ordinate with, rather than subordinate to, other desires. But no one who has ever watched unspoiled children can deny the tremendous reality of the desire to know, not in order to throw light on the object of our desires but for its own sake. Nor should this desire be dismissed as childish. The history of science shows clearly that when this idle and unfettered curiosity about the world is indulged as a joyous pastime, it leads to such momentous results as the discovery of mathematics by the Greeks or of modern physics in the sixteenth and seventeenth centuries. On the other hand, when Stoic philosophers rigidly insist that our thoughts should be directed to the ends of ordinary human conduct, they dry up the springs of intellectual vision. This is mentioned not only to show the very serious danger to American philosophy from this neo-Stoicism, but to illustrate how the controversial attitude cuts us off from the more adequate performance of its own task, to wit, the analysis of the nature of knowledge. For the tendency of philosophy is to stretch terms like "practical" to include everything, even the purely theoretical; but the tendency of controversy is to restrict terms so as to leave room for assailable alternatives. If the Holy Sepulchre be everywhere one cannot effectively preach a crusade to redeem it from the infidels.

That thought arises because of the desire to get out of trouble is certainly true, if "desire to get out of trouble" is stretched to include what it does not ordinarily connote, such as the love of intellectual play, of the impulse to imitate, as when philosophers rush to adopt an idea like natural selection after it acquires éclat in biology. Knowledge is experimental—aye, if we recognize with Peirce that there are mental, as distinct from physical, experiments, and that pure mathematics is full of them. The truth of general propositions is to be tested by their consequences—certainly; but if this is to mean anything definite and not a mere shifting of the difficulty, we must have a real clue as to what consequences make a proposition true. The old-fashioned assumption that there are certain absolute particular facts and that these of themselves can confirm or deny general beliefs, is one that a clear-minded man like Dewey cannot accept. For what we should consider the fact in a given case is never independent of previous assumption. Thus, when Dewey rejects God, freedom, and immortality on the general ground that philosophic concepts can no longer serve as sanctions, he opens himself to the *ad hominem* argument that his alternative concepts—experience, evolution, and democracy—are also sanctions resting on no really superior evidence. The consequences of accepting one set of categories are assuredly different from the consequences of accepting the other. But that which determines people to accept one or the other set of initial assumptions makes them differ also as to which set of consequences they regard as preferable, and the pragmatic test of truth does not in fact settle philosophic issues. Latterly, by his emphasis upon philosophy as a critical consideration of methods of criticism, Dewey has made clearer the role which philosophy must play in testing all assumptions, so that the pragmatic method again appears to be a way of determining what it is that we really mean.

Though essentially a moralist, Dewey does not give us a clear answer to the fundamental ethical question, what is good? In trying to make the world better, what is to be the test as to which of two alternatives *is* the better? The reason for this failure comes out clearly in his essay on "Nature's Good" (in the volume called *The Influence of Darwin on Philosophy*). He is so averse to the old classical formulas for the *summum bonum* that made no particular difference in specific cases, that he falls back on a very naive ethical atomism: every situation has its own good. But that is to dodge the whole difficulty. For, not only does life fail to divide itself into a convenient number of disconnected "situations," but in every actual ethical problem, as he himself points out, there is a conflict of rival considerations. If, e.g., class exploitation is to be regarded as evil and rejected, it is to be rejected not only when it affects Mr. A or Mr. B, on the fifth or the sixth day of the month, but as a general rule to control all judgments in particular cases.

When Dewey and his disciples insist that philosophy must serve human weal and welfare, they assert something which no one can or wishes to dispute. Compassion for human suffering is at the bottom of all that is noble in human effort. But the significant question really is, wherein does human weal consist? When they exclude from human welfare the philosophy which is naught but a distant vision, and can serve only as a consolation, or intellectual pastime, they seem to me to be falling into a most grievous error. For not only do consolations and pastimes—the essence of religion and fine art—most directly minister to human welfare by bringing us relief from anguish and offering us positive joy, but no human work could long prosper without them. A foolish use of pastimes and consolation may indeed dull the edge of industry. But the humblest human wisdom has always recognized the dullness of naught but work. Vacations and holidays, wherein we can completely forget the routine of our daily tasks, are necessary, even in the interests of the narrowest kind of industrial efficiency. Nor would the pragmatist be inclined to overlook this obvious point, if it were not for the zeal to contrast sharply the spirit of the new as against the old philosophy. They are also misled by the phrase "making the world a better place to live in," which suggests mastery of the environment rather than of our own desires. But as long as human desire outruns human capacity, even as the range of our vision exceeds the field of our reach, the way of happiness must include not only the mastery of nature but also the mastery of our own selves. The latter cannot be attained without the fearless examination of the limitations of human capacity due to the fact that we live in a world that is not expressly designed for human comfort. That is why no philosophy that lacks a cosmic outlook can hope to do full justice to the specifically human problem.* Even if it were true, as Dewey contends, that the fate of the cosmos has no bearing on the specific issues of education, morals, or politics, it would still not be devoid of the profoundest human interest. In seeing human fate as part of a great cosmic drama, men arise above their petty limitations and learn to look upon their passions and achievements with that measure of aloofness which is essential to any vision that can be called philosophic and to any civilization that can be called liberal.

Though some degree of impartiality is necessary to render his account even intelligible, the philosophic critic knows that complete impartiality is unattainable, and that he must leave to the discriminating reader the task of discerning and correcting the distortion resulting from partisan bias. But if this account of Dewey fails to bring into proper relief the great positive achievements which make him one of the great figures of recent philosophy, the failure is due to the fact that Dewey's own vision is not being reported as much as the general tendency in American philosophy of which he is the most distinguished representative. The kernel of pragmatism can win the hearty agreement of all thinking men. But it is difficult to emphasize properly such fundamental agreements as one has habitually taken for granted. One may share as a matter of course Dewey's scorn for those who in indolent piety continue to worship at empty shrines. But one cannot grow enthusiastic at the sight of a really first-rate mind crusading against those for whom time is erecting proper sepulchres. The multitude will not be fed by exhorting to work those who will be unproductive in any case. Nor does the interest of agriculture demand discontinuance of all worship. Rather ought we to look for new objects more worthy of human adoration. For the human need to worship is

---

* A fuller critique of Dewey's identification of philosophy with problems of humanity will be found in the essay, "Some Difficulties in John Dewey's Anthropocentric Naturalism," in M. R. Cohen, *Studies in Philosophy and Science* (1949), especially at pp. 139-163.

fundamental; and those most absorbed or skilled in producing the material necessities, the Sancho Panzas or the Huck Finns, always recognize the inherent superiority of those who can see visions, even if the latter be no better than those of Don Quixote or Tom Sawyer. For, where there is no vision the human spirit perishes from suffocation.

As one who has been brought up in the humanistic tradition, Dewey loves to see things in their historic vistas. His own interest in the clean and dexterous manipulation of ideas is so strong that the keenness of his arguments must arouse breathless admiration even in those who disagree with the purposes for which he uses them. One might readily quote him to the effect that philosophy is vision, imagination, reflection, and that sympathetic understanding and the free play of ideas are superior to skill in the accumulation of external products. He is, therefore, perfectly sincere in protesting that when he speaks of the practical character of ideas he does not mean that they should minister to ends of the bread-and-butter type. But a philosophy must be judged by its emphasis and general tendencies rather than by the character and intention of the founder. And the main tendency of his crusade on behalf of the practical is undoubtedly to disparage and leave no room for purely theoretic studies like the theory of prime numbers, which for all their glory have not, and perhaps never will, find any application to the specific problems of conduct. This attitude, as has been said, is more pronounced in some of Dewey's untrained enthusiastic disciples than in Dewey himself. But even he repeatedly expresses his dislike for "contemplative surveys of existence" or analyses of "what is past and done with." His greatest fear is lest philosophy should lose touch with that which for the moment absorbs the multitude, and he is never weary of trying to eliminate "otiose" or purely contemplative thought—forgetting in his plea for philosophy as a guide for action that mere contemplation is itself a most intense kind of action, preferred to all other forms of action by great and richly experienced minds, like Plato, Aristotle, and Dante. Indeed, it is difficult for enthusiastic devotees of the idea of universal evolution to avoid altogether the genetic fallacy of confusing the organic origin of knowledge and its present human value. But though vision may be an outgrowth of touch, it is certainly different and no longer restricted to the tangible.

Dewey's philosophy is distinctively urban, industrial, and entirely public. There are no nooks in his universe which the soul can call its own. It is full of the sense of men hurrying to work, struggling against all sorts of material difficulty and the stupid selfishness of their fellow-beings, and finally succeeding by dint of superior intelligence in the manipulation of things. It is pervaded also by a noble indignation that there should be so many parasitic idlers and unused palaces, so much class exploitation. His writings which emphasize the artistic impulse have begun to show a sense of the natural sunlight and open fields, wherein even now the children of men sometimes play in utter abandon. But as yet there is no sense in it of the loneliness of the individual human soul, facing the indifferent earth, sea, or sky, or the eternal procession of the stars that ever mock man's vain pretension to exalt himself as the master of the universe.

No sensitive spirit can fail to be stirred by Dewey's eloquent plea that we help our fellow men in the bitter struggle for a better world. But surely, an empirical philosopher has no reason to feel that he can easily obtain adequate knowledge to solve all the problems of politics, economics, social hygiene, and other difficulties which have troubled mankind for thousands of years. Dewey is aware of this but boldly asserts: "Better it is for philosophy to err in active participation in the living struggles and issues of its own age and time than to maintain an immune, monastic impeccability."[18] But why should philosophy deliberately choose to fall into error when it can save itself by suspending judgment, by recognizing that the practical necessity for making a choice does not remove our ignorance? Nor does wisdom require us to be frightened by epithets such as "monastic," "ivory tower," "escapist," or "compensatory." It is wisdom to leave a room that is filled with suffocating smoke, and in dark ages monasticism kept alive the remnants of civilization. And monastic impeccability may be far more justifiable both for philosophy and social sanity, than adding to the already large fund of error about issues that our fellow men think important.

Philosophy according to Dewey "must deny and eject that intelligence which is naught but a distant eye, registering in a remote and alien medium the spectacle of nature and life."[19] I venture to assert that relatively few sensitive and reflective minds have gone through this world without often feeling alien in its fetid air and needing to escape for a while into a rare and higher atmosphere. "My kingdom is not of this world" is an important element in a truly human life, a redemption from deadly worldliness. And most people do require quasi-monastic conditions in their study in order to engage in concentrated intellectual work which is not possible in the hubbub of crowds. The wisdom of humility requires that the philosopher should not unduly exalt the importance of his special vocation. But neither should he envy the man of

[18] *Essays in Honor of William James*, p. 77.
[19] *Creative Intelligence*, p. 66.

action, the one whose maxim is: "For God's sake, stop theorizing and do something practical!" Nor is there much weight to the argument that philosophers are economic parasites unless they direct their reflection towards practical objectives. We have as much a right to philosophize as to pray, to hear music, or to be spectators at dramatic performances. No one is really paid for philosophizing. Some, though not all, philosophers have been employed as teachers; but I should be surprised to learn that any got excessively rich thereby. The upkeep of philosophers is far from being such a staggering burden on society as to demand serious attention.

Though Dewey would hardly subscribe to Emerson's idealistic Platonism and the doctrine that the oversoul is everything, he shares Emerson's benign attitude in regard to the unconquerable natural ills which have dogged human existence throughout the ages. He rejects the view that our appetites and desires are the manifestations of unruly nature. For that would make democracy impossible.[20] "Man is capable, if he will but exercise the required courage, intelligence and effort, of shaping his own fate. Physical conditions offer no insurmountable barriers."[21] But, if that were the case, why has not mankind exercised its intelligence to remove the stupid cruelties which darken the lives of men and women in our day as much as ever, in countries that are at peace as well as those at war? If the cause is not in nature, human or nonhuman, what is there left but to invoke a supernatural source of evil? We are told to have faith in the active tendencies of the day.[22] But these tendencies may destroy all the values of civilization. As a temporalist Dewey puts the Golden Age in the future rather than in the past. Such hope strengthens men, and it cannot be refuted. But the philosopher who piously visits the cemetery of human hopes may well shake his head. And this attitude is not dismissed by calling it a counsel of despair. There is strength as well as solace in fearlessly looking at things as they are. But in the end no philosophy is really humane, or avoids needless cruelty, unless it recognizes the inevitability of human suffering, defeat, death, and destruction and provides some anodyne through wisely cultivated resignation.

So long as human beings lack omniscience they will lack omnipotence and will therefore have to face insuperable difficulties and evils. The acceptance of the inevitable, ceasing "to kick against the pricks," seems to me the great wisdom of the old religious teachers who, despite their supernaturalisms, had keen appreciations of the problems of actual living.

---

[20] *Influence of Darwin on Philosophy*, p. 59.
[21] *Reconstruction in Philosophy*, p. 49.
[22] *Ibid.*, p. 212.

This does not deny that all human beings do and should pursue what may, in the broader sense, be called economic ends, i.e., the increase of the means for the desirable kind of life. But human beings also have a craving not only for worship, but for subordinating themselves so as to avoid the intolerable distraction which often arises when we have to decide on the basis of imperfect knowledge. Indeed the history of such movements as Islam or Calvinism shows how submission can liberate human energies. No man is as happy and energetic as the one who is a glad slave to his beloved, whether it be a person or a great impersonal cause. For this reason it would be hazardous to deny that human beings have probably derived as much happiness from accepting their lot as from efforts, so often tragically vain, to improve it.

I am familiar with the argument that if we abandoned all forms of resignation and strenuously devoted ourselves instead to the improvement of actual conditions there would be no need for resignation. But this seems to me wishful thinking requiring much more evidence than has ever been offered for it. Doubtless there is such a thing as unwise submission. But who will deny that there is also an unwise obstinacy in refusing to accept our limitations and thus wasting life in efforts that are fruitless if not worse? We in America are especially in need of realizing that perpetual motion is not the blessed life and that the hustlers may not be the only ones, nor perhaps even the first, to enter the kingdom of heaven. This is not an argument against the necessity of effort and work. But we can still afford a doubt about any moral system that is too social and does not recognize the just claims of rest, of vacations from the strenuous life, of retreats or escapes if you like, from the depressing horrors of the human scene and its brutal struggles. Like other intellectual workers the philosopher must break away from the crowd, even as Jesus, filled with compassion for the multitude, retires alone to the mountain to pray. Why should philosophy deny us any private nook in this wide universe which the soul may for a while call its own?

It would be idle for anyone to undertake today a definite judgment on Dewey's philosophical achievement. The seeds of instruction which he has planted in the soil of American culture are still to flower in the future. There is no doubt that history will record that in an age of waning faith in human reason, he was one of the few who rallied those who believed in the cause of liberalism based on faith in the value of intellectual enlightenment. But it may wonder at his failure to attach sufficient importance to the fact that despite its extreme worth, human intelligence is frail, pathetically impotent in the face of great physical stress or vital impulse. Important as are the intellectual differences between men, we are all of the same clay as the insane and the criminal, even as the most potent and enlightened emperor, Marcus Aurelius, is father in the flesh to the unspeakable Commodus. Such reflections may be useless and unpleasant, but no philosophy can claim to be the liberating truth unless it faces them resolutely.

Of those who share Dewey's general position only a few can here be mentioned. An influential thinker among pragmatists who approach the problem of truth and knowledge from an examination of the nature of evidence is George Herbert Mead. Evidence, for Mead, is that which can be perceived by others under similar conditions. It is consequently social and objective, not personal or private. Universals reflect the character of the activity of the community of minds re-creating a common environment. Error is subjective only in the light of the wider social experience which gives it its proper status in an organized system of objective socio-natural perspectives. Individual perspectives transcend their own privacy by being part of other perspectives. From this point of view Mead derives a social behavioristic interpretation of speech and communication. Mead's writings reveal how strong the hereditary strain of absolute idealism still is in some of its pragmatic descendants. By substituting human purposes for the cosmic plan of the Absolute Ego and retaining the organic developmental view, Hegel's philosophy becomes sufficiently naturalized to be almost indistinguishable from some varieties of modern pragmatism.

To the pragmatist's interest in ethics and social affairs must also be set down the added stimulus American thought has received in approaching questions of social and legal philosophy. Men like J. H. Tufts, H. W. Stuart, M. Otto, T. V. Smith and H. W. Schneider, have urged concentration upon ethical and social problems, more, however, for purposes of social control than for the possible light their study might cast upon the nature of the social process or the development of a much needed methodology for the social sciences.

The secret of the vitality of experimental pragmatism lies in the diversity of the motives which have entered into it. It speaks the language of experimental science and offers a method of approach to social problems which seems liberal and informed, and to some, a diffuse humanitarianism as a substitute for religion or theological dogmas. It has evolved a theory of education which seems adapted to the democratic era,—a theory which proclaims the development of personality and the disciplined release of the child's creative impulses to be the chief goal of the educational process. Emphasizing methods not results, general attitudes rather than specific proposals, the pragmatic philosophy has revealed a remarkable elasticity in its doctrines. This has made it very difficult for critics to find a common philosophical platform for all of its adherents and very easy for people uncertain of the direction of their own thought to claim affiliation with pragmatism. A promising aspect of this indeterminateness of doctrine might have been a tendency towards the abandonment of all conventional philosophical labels—were not the pragmatists so keen upon labelling themselves.

Similar to the view of James and Dewey in accepting the evolutionary philosophy as basic, and keeping even closer to Darwinian ideas, is the philosophy of J. Mark Baldwin. Baldwin began as a psychologist of the orthodox type; but availing himself of the views on social consciousness propounded by Royce in the early nineties, he produced a system of evolutionary social psychology with a very elaborate technical terminology and analytic scaffolding. This emphasis on technical apparatus makes his great three-volumed treatise on *Thought and Things* (1906-11) one of the most obscure books written in America, but for all that it seems to have met with appreciation in France and Germany, where it has been translated. An intelligible summary of his later views is to be found in his *Genetic Theory of Reality* (1915), in which he develops this theory of pancalism, viz., that the aesthetic consciousness is primary. In this respect, as well as in his emphasis on the importance of the play impulse, Baldwin is unique among American philosophers.

The New Realism

Activated by a desire for a philosophy that should be in harmony with the method and results of modern logic and natural science, there arose the school that originally called itself the New Realism. Stimulated by the earlier mathematical philosophy of Bertrand Russell and the common-sense realism of G. E. Moore in England, as well as by the realistic aspects of Royce's logic and various suggestions of Woodbridge, a group of six philosophers published a joint manifesto repudiating subjectivism in epistemology and nominalism in metaphysics (*Journal of Philosophy*, 1910). This was followed up by a cooperative volume entitled *The New Realism** and by numerous separate publications on the part of the contributors.[23]

The new realism is regarded by its protagonists as primarily a doctrine

---

* Reviewed in M. R. Cohen, *Studies in Philosophy and Science* (1949), p. 109.

[23] See E. B. Holt, *The Concept of Consciousness*; W. T. Marvin, *A First Book in Metaphysics*; W. P. Montague, *The Ways of Knowing*; R. B. Perry, *Present Philosophical Tendencies*; E. G. Spaulding, *The New Rationalism*; and varied contributions to periodical literature by W. B. Pitkin.

which treats of the relation between knowing and the objects of knowledge. It contends that the constitution of things is independent of the fact that they are sometimes known, and the school engages in sharp polemical attack against all forms of subjective idealism. This pre-occupation with the theory of knowledge and with the resulting problems of the nature of consciousness and the status of error tended to obscure, even in the minds of the neo-realists themselves, what the most fundamental and distinctive doctrine in their position really was, viz., the belief in the objective existence of logical and mathematical entities. The actual opponents of neo-realism are not so much the traditional schools of idealism but rather the psychological empiricists and other defenders of nominalism. There may be very little theoretic difference between a position which regards everything in terms of the subject and one which regards everything as objective, since the same laws and relations might hold between "experiences" as between "independent reals." In other words, the distinctions between the different classes of entities might be the same in the two systems. Between a view, however, which insists that the propositions of logic and mathematics are as objective as those of physics, and a view which denies to objects of thought the ontologic status of the objects of sense, the issue is significant and laden with momentous consequences. Consequently, the problem of the reality of universals or "the things of thought" is the central problem which the neo-realists have raised; so that it is not so much Berkeley's subjectivism as his nominalism that presents the significant alternative to the neo-realist position.

Nominalism, or the denial of the objective existence of relations and abstractions, is based on the conscious or unconscious assumption of the ancient dogma that only a whole can really exist and that which is a logical part can have no independent existence. Now the other cardinal doctrines of the new realism, that the existence of an object in no wise depends upon our consciousness of it, and that the derivative products of analysis are no less real than the original whole analyzed, would be utterly impossible on a nominalistic metaphysics. It is not an accident, therefore, that the one positive argument which all of the neo-realists find themselves compelled to use in support of their epistemological thesis is the non-mental character of the propositions of logic and mathematics. This confirms their position that the theory of knowledge cannot be fundamental but must yield priority to issues of fact or theories of being.

The promise, however, held out by this revival of the Platonic insight into the nature of universals has not been realized. Logical entities and physical things both have being independently of consciousness. What then is the ontologic difference between logical entities and physical things? The neo-realists have answered that sensible things located in time and space have *existence,* while all other possible or impossible objects of thought have *subsistence.* This, like most dichotomous divisions, can hardly be expected to be of much use, for it puts too many things in the negative class,—in this case, in the class of subsistents. It is surely of importance to distinguish between possibles such as "honest politicians" or the "square root of minus one," and impossibles such as "round squares," or "the third root of an equation of the second degree." The neo-realists have failed to do this, and their failure can be traced to the fact that they have developed no theory of meaning. This facile distinction between existence and subsistence faces insurmountable difficulties in analyzing the status of space and time, which are supposed to be the differentiating criteria of the two realms. Further, it prevents the neo-realists from meeting the fundamental requirement of a constructive philosophy, *viz.,* a systematic classification of the types and levels of existence, or more formally, a doctrine of categories. Such a doctrine, adequately developed, would remove a great many of the difficulties which some of the neo-realists find in the existence of error and hallucinatory objects.

One of the noteworthy achievements of the neo-realists is to have impugned the claim of the theory of knowledge to be logically prior to all other philosophical disciplines. Far from being the queen of the sciences capable of issuing permits to all others on the basis of an *a priori* inquiry into the nature of possibilities and limits of knowledge, epistemology itself can only function if it assumes that we are already in possession of valid knowledge drawn from such sciences as logic, psychology, etc. It turns out that the "possibility" of mathematics, physics and metaphysics is far less questionable than the possibility of epistemology, and that free from its baneful influence the various sciences can proceed independently in their inquiry, returning to epistemological questions only after the science is relatively complete. In view of this attitude towards the theory of knowledge, why then, it may be asked, is so much of the neo-realistic literature devoted to epistemology? The answer must be sought in the several different theories of consciousness held by the various members of the school, and the failure of critics to realize that the distinctive neo-realistic doctrines of error are contained in the objective relativism faintly indicated by Holt and Pitkin.

Since the neo-realists, influenced by F. J. Woodbridge's admirable papers on consciousness, believe that true knowledge is a direct perception of the object and not of an idea or image of it, the existence of non-mental illusory objects calls for explanation. From the fact that, in beholding an illusory object one sees what is not there, and what cannot therefore be constitutively the external object, it has been argued that no objects existing independently of the mind are directly known in sense perception. Holt attempts to meet this argument by showing that many physical processes of copying, by cameras and other instruments, reproduce the same distortions and reduplications as take place when the eye beholds two parallel lines converging in the distance. There is, therefore, every reason to suppose that the distortion or reduplication is not due to consciousness but to the physical relation between the sense-organs and the objects. Thus the relativity of secondary qualities, and phenomena like the production of negative or complementary after-images, are paralleled by the action of instruments like the thermometer and the receiving set or mast of a wireless telegraph system.

Against the argument that the outside world contains only primary qualities and vibration rates, and that the secondary qualities must be aroused in the mind by specific nerve energies, Holt counters by thoroughly refuting the specific nerve-energy theory and producing a new hypothesis which attempts to deduce the secondary qualities from the frequency interval of nerve pulses or vibrations, thus reducing them to a genuine part of the objective order. This receives fuller statement in his remarkable theory of neutral monism according to which the stuff of experience is composed of subsistent entities that are neither mental nor physical. Depending upon the logical relationship in which these entities are ordered, we get either consciousness in all its aspects and observations, or material things. Just as the same point can be the intersection of many lines, so the same neutral entities can without contradiction be members of different classes which logically define an electrical field, an illusion, a true perception or what not. Error is given the same objectivity and ontologic status as truth.

The great difficulty with the neo-realistic theory of error is that in proving the objectivity of hallucinatory perception as well as the objects of valid perception, the difference between perceptual truth and error remains unexplained. Error cannot be explained on the ground that the condition of its perception depends upon the organism, for that is true of any perception, true or false. The presence of consciousness does not differentiate between true and false perception; nor can one say, as we have seen, that error is uncaused. Consequently, the neo-realist is driven to the admission that sense deception is due not to the mere fact of perception but to an *inference* based upon perception. The error consists not in seeing the railroad tracks converge in the distance, but in taking the vision of that convergence as a reliable indication that the tracks are convergent in all other perspectives. Error is mistaking a judgment relative to the meaning of possible future consequences based upon present sense appearance. If this be so, the neo-realist must surrender the doctrine that genuine knowledge is purely immediate. The immediacy that enters into knowledge is of universals whose meaning is in their consequences. When these are correctly drawn, we have knowledge; when not, error.

Although neo-realism arose as a reaction to certain doctrines in technical philosophy, it was not without promise for the development of ethics and social philosophy. The great confusion and futility of social theory in the past can be traced in large part to the attempt to build up a social philosophy on a nominalistic logic. Nominalistic logic must inevitably lead to atomic individualism and to a psychology of moments or "states," as is evidenced in the history of ethics from Antisthenes to Bentham or Spencer. By emphasizing the reality of universals or "organizing relations," by recognizing the latter as real causes in integrating human activities into the institutional wholes that define social behavior, neo-realism could have supplied a much-needed analysis to moot questions of the larger life, such as legal rights and obligations. Unfortunately, not only have the neo-realists neglected to trace consequences for social theory; but, impelled by its subsistent doctrine, neo-realism has developed a theory of absolute simples or logical monads which threatens its insight into the very logical continuities and connections which on other occasions it has emphasized. The theory of absolute simples is the logical correlate of the atomic sensation of nominalism, and suffers from the failure to note that simplicity is always relative to a specific complex. What is simple in one context may be very complex in another.

Before going on to treat of the school of critical realism which is the movement in revolt against the extreme objectivism of the neo-realists and the functional voluntarism of the pragmatists, it might be well to inquire why so much of American philosophy is preoccupied with the nature of knowledge and its relation to "reality" or "experience." Even the repeated broadsides against epistemology on the part of leading figures like Dewey, Woodbridge and Sheldon, have failed to produce a marked shift in interest. Not only have the philosophy of law, history, and, until recently, natural sciences, been neglected, but they have hardly been recognized as philosophical disciplines. One of the reasons for this is the independent development of different domains which formerly were part of philosophy, *viz.*, sociology, psychology, etc. Secular philosophy tending to dissociate itself not only from ethics and theology but from the content of the special sciences, seemed to have been left with no subject matter upon its hands but the nature of knowledge itself.

More important still, the conditions of university teaching in America which require a high degree of specialization on the part of pupils and teachers make it impossible for a man to teach the whole field of philosophy and bring his subject into intimate relation with the fundamental problems of the various branches of the physical and social sciences. Few teachers in any department of a university have the time and courage to poach upon another's preserves, and teachers of philosophy are especially timid about venturing into fields demanding specialized knowledge. Hence they, too, have regarded themselves as specialists—specialists of a very modest but highly formal science of epistemology. The older ideas of philosophy as a kind of universal knowledge or a way of life have fallen into desuetude.

Perhaps a contributing cause of the narrowness of professional philosophical interest has been the fact that philosophers generally do not see the wider implication of philosophic issues in the manifold problems arising in law, politics and education. But no matter what original causes explain why American philosophers fall to splashing in the epistemologic bog, the reason why they have continued is their failure to distinguish between the logical question of the validity of knowledge and a psychologic account of its "givenness." The origin and nature of knowledge as such is a serious issue and no philosophy can be complete without it. But logically it is impossible to raise questions about the possibility of knowledge without assuming that we are already in the possession of valid knowledge.

It should be borne in mind that although concentration upon the problems of knowledge in the abstract is particularly acute in America, it has been a growing trait of modern philosophy as a whole. It began with a metaphor of Locke's which Kant made the basis of his whole critical philosophy: before embarking upon the sea of knowledge we should examine the instruments of knowledge. A little reflection shows how misleading is the analogy involved. We can examine a ship before it sails, but it is impossible to examine the mind or faculty of knowledge before it actually knows something. If the fruitfulness of a philosophic problem is to be measured by the light that it casts on other scientific problems, it would seem that the problem of the relation of knowledge in general to its object as such must always remain a barren one. Why, indeed, should a worker in any field of physics or ethics expect help from one who is a specialist on knowledge in general but not any special domain of it? In truth, one of the most powerful motives for keeping epistemology alive was its development in the form of subjective or Berkeleyan idealism as a specific antidote to the achievements of modern science. With Bishop Berkeley it was a clear case of fighting the "atheistic mathematicians." But his modern followers are more subtle. They pretend to accept the results of science, but render it harmless by showing that it is all a transaction in our mind. In view of the tenacity with which subjectivism is held even in scientific quarters, some realistic theory of knowledge is bound to arise and be of some service as a purifying and counteracting force, let alone its direct value in dealing with certain problems of perception.

Critical Realism

The latest phase of realism calls itself "critical realism." It is represented by the writings of Durant Drake, A. O. Lovejoy, J. B. Pratt, A. K. Rogers, George Santayana, C. A. Strong and R. W. Sellars. The official pronouncement of the school is contained in the cooperative volume entitled *Essays in Critical Realism.** Critical realism differs from the "new realism" in marking a return to what is essentially the position of the old realism, according to which perception is an event involving three terms: the existent, the perceived datum and the percipient. When the mental event takes place which we call perception, what is perceived is not the outer physical event but an essence or sense-datum which refers to something always transcendent to the act of perception. Thus the star I see when I gaze at the sky is a twinkling colored datum which cannot be identified with the actual astronomical star, for that may have disappeared many years before its rays reached the earth. In veridical perception the sense datum or character is the same as the characters of the physical object; in illusory perception it is different. The familiar difficulty with this view is that it converts the *datum* known into a screen which forever separates the knower from the objects claimed to be known, so that either the mind knows only its own ideas as in Locke, or else a complex of essences which, because they are generically different from physical objects, cannot render them completely intelligible. If it requires an idea or image to see anything, then it should require another

---

* Reviewed by M. R. Cohen in *New Republic*, Vol. 32, p. 8 (Literary Supplement, Sept. 27, 1922).

image to see the original image, and so on *ad infinitum*. In neither case is direct contact established with the object of knowledge. Consequently, if the neo-realists have difficulties in explaining *error*, the critical realists have difficulties in explaining *truth*, since once it is maintained that perceptual data, not things themselves, are the direct objects of knowledge, what evidence can we have that these data truly correspond with or represent those things? Direct comparison between things and perceptual data, on this hypothesis, is out of the question.

The modifications introduced by some critical realists in the course of discussion, which explain perceptual data not as cognitive counterparts of physical things but as signs and indicators of natural connections, really align them with the pragmatists who regard sense-data to be representative functions of natural affairs. The tendency is observable on the part of the critical realists to unduly exaggerate their differences with the pragmatists and in the interests of polemics to overlook the fact that the only crucial question between them on this score is whether sense-data are necessarily psychical or not. The critical realists affirm that they are.

But this further question as to the nature of the sense-data splits the school of critical realism wide open. Lovejoy, Pratt and Sellars believe that the essential content of what is given in perception expresses the character of the mental existent; while Santayana, Strong, Drake and Rogers believe that the essences are universals, psychically conditioned but not psychically constituted, manifesting themselves in perception as a result of certain mysterious activities on the part of the body. The differences on the metaphysical status of the sense-data are much more fundamental than the agreement on the general structure of the knowledge relation. The first group, with the exception of Pratt, who is an idealist, shares the metaphysics of pragmatism; the second group, with the exception of Rogers, who is also an idealist, holds to the subsistence doctrine of neo-realism. As far as the specific epistemological difficulties are concerned, however, neither of the two critical realistic interpretations of the "datum" is adequate. In the first case, it is admitted that a mental existent, whatever that is, can be directly known, since essences are characters of such existents. But if essences are never characters of physical objects, and are directly perceivable, all we have left is a world of mental existents known in a way that cannot be explained by the triadic formula of critical realism. In the second case, if in perception self-contained essences are grasped which are not themselves existent, how can we go on from the vision of these essences to the assertion of the existence of objects which have them? And if it is answered that the essential characters of the datum are the same as the essential characters of the physical objects which are existent, how can that be known in terms of the critical realistic position?

The only solution of the epistemological predicament is to avoid (1) reducing the mental and physical to each other; and (2) dividing them into two mutually exclusive classes. Before specific questions can be put as to the relations between knowledge and its objects, there must be an analysis of the various orders and levels of existence as well as of the different types of relations. This will make it unnecessary to classify data, meanings or propositions in purely negative terms, such as subsistence, and will make possible detailed specification of the various contexts in which one can ask "where" and "when" of the qualities, real and illusory, of sense perception.

George Santayana and the Life of Reason

An outstanding American philosopher, who has kept himself distantly aloof from the din and strife of party controversy, is George Santayana. His systematic neglect is an eloquent commentary upon the ways, traditions and environment of American philosophy. His *Life of Reason* is the only comprehensive, carefully articulated, philosophy of life and civilization which has been produced on these shores. More than any of his contemporaries he has cultivated the ancient virtues of detachment, avoiding both the blind partisanship of the apologist and the impatient zeal of the reformer. The only emotional absorption he shows is that of the philosophic poet freely rendering the most significant aspects of human experience as they appear to one interested in the life of reason. The immediately pressing problems of life in a precarious natural and social order do not disturb the spectator of all existence who views man's natural dignity and proper joy to lie "in representing many things without being them; and in letting imagination, through sympathy, celebrate and echo their life." His is an attitude of enlightened Epicureanism, which holds that man's abiding happiness is to be sought in freedom from the cares and fortunes of the physical world and in the cultivation of the mind's inward landscape, whose choicest flowers are art, pure science and philosophy. True philosophy cannot be merely a doctrine of ways and means to improve the conditions of life, nor can the true philosopher be a prophet, rebel or pillar of society. "It is not easy for him to shout, or address a crowd; he must be silent for long seasons, for he is watching stars that move slowly and in the courses that it is possible though difficult to foresee; and he is crushing all things in his heart as in a winepress, until his life and their secret flow out together."[24]

The distinctive feature of Santayana's philosophy is his perfect fusion of the two *leit-motifs* which have given rise to such dissonances in modern philosophy—naturalism and historic idealism. For him as for Aristotle "everything ideal has a natural basis and everything natural an ideal fulfillment." Rejecting all supernaturalism in metaphysics and morals, he still accepts in the spirit of Hellenic naturalism those reasonable restraints upon impulsive life which, by harmonizing conflicting desires, order and dignify man's numbered days in this world.

Santayana's thoroughgoing naturalism has no place for the soul or other super-empirical entities; mind is the natural outgrowth and function of the body. But this does not mean that values and ideals which are the life of the mind are reduced to the sway of the body and the exigencies of natural struggle, for, although the *existence* of ideals depends upon the motion of "atoms in the void," their *validity* is distinct therefrom. Santayana avoids the genetic fallacy of identifying value with origin and refuses to admit that that which has survived is necessarily the best. "Modern Greece is not exactly the crown of ancient Hellas." Nor does he confuse physics and morality by entertaining the Hegelian fancy that ideals are forever real in the warp and woof of nature. Qualities and values are the passing appearances of a dance of atoms indifferent to human hopes and fears. Grief and joy with their lyric cries may arise necessarily in the flux of matter, but disappear leaving traces only in the realms of memory and truth. Love is earthly in its origin but divine in its aspiration. The true life of reason steers between the servile worship of the actual present, and the romantic self-idolatry which imagines that the universe exists to subserve human interests.

Santayana's affinities are clearly classical. His philosophy of civilization is a sustained and brilliant attempt to trace the ways in which in the fields of art, society, religion, science and common sense, human effort, conditioned by material structures and natural law, finds expression and fulfillment in ideal forms. It contains an illuminating analysis of the passions and insight which enter into traditional wisdom and which make the life of reason not only a career for individual men but a social heritage as well. Santayana has little sympathy for any form of dissidence,

---

[24] *Character and Opinion in the United States* (1920), p. 37.

and some of his judgments upon anti-authoritarian movements are arbitrary. The different varieties of German philosophical idealism are denounced for their romantic madness in attempting to legislate what kind of a universe this should be; rebels and reformers are viewed as pathetically mistaken in subordinating the solid goods of comfort and peace to nebulous freedom.

Santayana's social philosophy emphasizing cultural continuity and the importance of social institutions as disciplining mechanisms of human impulses, is essentially aristocratic. Yet, though personally hostile to contemporary international democracy, he grants that, like every other vital impulse it contains an implicit morality of its own. His philosophy of religion is not an apology for superstition, but an interpretation of the role which religion plays in emancipating man from worldliness and softening the inescapable tragedies of life by instilling an element of resignation in the hearts of believers. Although he acknowledges that religious dogma has often debauched morality and hindered science, he views its excesses with an easy indulgence.

Santayana's theory of art is thoroughly Aristotelian. Human passions and objective forms, freed from the stress of immediate action and given reflective expressions, acquire a beauty and significance inherently delightful. The business of art is not to control the world; but its visions of beauty, suggesting man's true good, may inspire a new attitude towards life.

In his approach to science Santayana avoids both the glorification of scientific results by those who have an eye for only its material uses, and the cheap and easy denunciation of those who hold science responsible for the fact that traditional values have failed to flourish in modern industrial life. Not only is science for Santayana a source of useful insight; in extending man's vistas and opening up new perspectives, it frees his imagination from the narrow confines of the actual and saves him from an uncritical exaggeration of the human foreground. He realizes, however, that science cannot take the place of sensitive vision in discovering the proper ends of human life. It is not because science has not succeeded in solving its problems that men have failed to lead the good life, but because men have failed to understand their own nature. "The darkest spots are in man himself, in his fitful, irrational disposition."[25]

The later writings of Santayana betray a marked shift away from his earlier naturalism. The life of reason, which is an achievement in the world of trial and error, has been supplanted by a life of spirituality, which is a contemplation of essence and eternity. The spiritual life is not

---

[25] *Life of Reason*, Vol. V, "Reason in Science," p. 320.

a realization of the ideal possibilities of the existent, but a renunciation of the world and of *all* existence. True to the great classical tradition which regards universals as real, Santayana has developed an extreme doctrine of essences which urges the sharp and complete separation of univerals from existence, and holds that nothing given in perception exists, so that belief in the existence of nature can only be an act of animal faith. How essences can be part of scientific theory and experiment, how ideals can inform and guide human conduct, on this latest view become mysteries. *The Life of Reason* was written by a naturalistic idealist; the volumes beginning with *Scepticism and Animal Faith* by a dualistic Platonist trying to express Plato's myths as literal scientific truths. Not only does Santayana face the traditional problems of how in his own terms he can speak intelligibly of the very existence of a natural world, but he must face the difficulties, unknown to Platonists, which come from regarding immediate sense-qualia as essences. For Plato, essences were beheld in a final vision by arduously following the suggestions of ordinary experience: they were never directly given in sense perception. What Santayana has virtually done is to hypostasize the atomic "idea" of sensationalistic psychology into a Platonic "idea", although there is no longer any ground on his new theory for believing in the existence of a consciousness which has "ideas".

Although the general public was slow to discover him, the technical phase of Santayana's philosophy brought him to the early attention of the professional philosopher. Yet his influence even here is in no wise proportionate to the power and quality of his work. One of the causes for this comparative lack of recognition is probably the richness and poetic obscurity of his style. The gleaming sententiousness of his lapidary prose presents a succession of clear-cut thought and ideas and dark sayings, but rarely sustained discursive argument. His thought must first be intuited before it can be fully understood. The chief reason, however, why Santayana has failed to establish a following, has been his departure from the customary modes of philosophizing in America. American philosophers are generally either professional apologists for revealed religion or the "higher interests" of humanity, or they are absorbed in a scientific analysis of certain general categories. To the first group, Santayana's atheistic catholicism, his aristocratic anti-puritanism and dispassionate aesthetic morality which recognizes no absolute good or evil, are anathema. To the second group, he appears to be a speculative poet who has only a bowing acquaintance with science. The vogue of epistemology, as we have seen, has made philosophy's ancient and noble task of developing a unified outlook upon the world as a whole,—still represented by Santayana—, seem unfashionable. Hence his essential loneliness. But perhaps every true philosopher, like the true poet, is essentially lonely.

Frederick J. E. Woodbridge:
Scientific Metaphysics

Frederick J. E. Woodbridge has been one of the few American thinkers interested primarily in metaphysics rather than in epistemology. But the vogue of the latter has made Woodbridge take his departure from the consideration of knowledge as a natural event in a world of space and time. That man thinks is a fact which must be affirmed even by those who are interested in explaining its possibility. The fact of such thinking implies that knowledge is *of* something other than and not created by itself. Thought involves the existence of a world which is thinkable or intelligible; it is an activity which can go on only in a world which has logical structure. This objective order which is discovered by thought is called the realm of mind, to distinguish it from the subsistent essences of the neo-realists, so picturesquely characterized by a German colleague as "*heimatlose Gegenstände*". Neither physical nor mental, the realm of mind is the organization or system of both. Knowledge of organization of nature is given through ideas. Ideas are not images or copies of things but logical meanings. They give us power to predict and control the course of things only because "the order and connection of ideas" which defines true knowledge is the same as "the order and connection of things" we have knowledge about.

Woodbridge's roots are in Aristotle and Spinoza, naturalistically interpreted. He believes that metaphysics is a descriptive analysis of the fundamental characters presented in experience, not a normative discipline of what must be. Consequently, metaphysics must forego the attempt either to deduce particular existences or to seek ethical justification for what cannot be otherwise. It must follow science, not theology.

Woodbridge differs from Aristotle and Spinoza by taking time seriously. Opposing the absorption of time into eternity, he opposes just as strongly philosophies of flux which introduce time as an essential moment of logical structures. The distinction drawn by absolute idealism between reality and appearance he regards as an evasion of the "metaphysician's experimental, inductive and objective" task of analyzing whatever traits the many aspects of the world and our activities within it do show. By his emphasis upon following the logical leads of empirical subject matter, by the influence he has exerted as editor of the *Journal of Philosophy*, and by direct personal inspiration as a teacher, Woodbridge helped American philosophers to see that method without insight is a Barmecidian feast, just as, in his earlier years, he had showed that insight without method is barren.

Wilmon H. Sheldon:
The Strife of Systems

Wilmon H. Sheldon ranks among the most competent metaphysicians in America. In his *Strife of Systems* he has made an attempt to find some principle which will enable us to envisage the entire cosmos and help organize the bewildering complexity of human knowledge according to some rational plan. In surveying the age-old controversies between different philosophic systems, he came to the conclusion that they were all true in what they assert, and wrong only in what they deny of the vision of others. Subjectivism and objectivism, for instance, are both true. One can maintain that the world is all subjective or that it is all objective, with equal immunity from refutation, and equally futile are both in attempting to throw light on the actual constitution of things. For that which is common to the nature of all things will not differentiate any one thing from anything else. Thus, to assert that all is mental is irreproachable, but futile for any description of the constitution of any actual experience.

Sheldon shows that in general the various types of idealism, realism, intellectualism, pragmatism and intuitionism are all attempts to build up the whole universe out of some undeniable but partial truths. The chief partial truths that underlie the strife of all systems are the principles of *identity* and of *difference*. The principle of identity—also called the principle of external relations—insists that a thing is what it is and not something else. It is perhaps best illustrated by atomism in physics and individualism in politics, so far as both of these insist that the ultimate nature of anything is something which maintains its own existence independent of anything else. The contrary principle of diversity—also called the principle of internal relations—asserts that a thing is constituted by its different relations to other things, for example, that an individual is what his position in society or in his physical environment makes him. The one-sidedness of even the most comprehensive systems, like those of Hegel and St. Thomas Aquinas, is due, according to Sheldon, to the assumed conflict between these two principles of identity and diversity. In the world of reality, however, these two principles do harmoniously co-exist, manifestly so whenever we see the creation of novelty out of previously existing material. Hence philosophy can become fruitful and life clarified only if we give up false antitheses and follow the actual creative processes or the principle of productive duality.

All human difficulties may be viewed as arising from conflicting needs or conflicting tendencies in things; and inventive art and wisdom are concerned with finding ways and means of harmonizing them. But the unenterprising intellect is too apt to regard difficulties as impossibilities and rival claims as absolute contradictories. Nothing is therefore more helpful to the progress of the human intellect in the removal of obstacles to human happiness than the insight which eliminates from our philosophy of life all sterile one-sidedness and devastating antagonisms.

Sheldon, however, suffers from the besetting sin of most constructive metaphysicians and occasionally claims more for his principles than he can prove. Theoretically this shows itself in his attempts to derive empirical or material facts, such as those of optics, from universal abstract principles, confusing the generation of things in time with their logical explanation. Practically, when he seeks to illustrate his principles in fields of social and religious phenomena, a narrow and illiberal political orthodoxy and a dogmatic religion make him view the present order of things as a final expression of the principles of productive duality. But these are perhaps minor matters when one considers the freshness and force with which Sheldon has tackled the fundamental problems of philosophy and the genuine light he has shed upon them.

Arthur O. Lovejoy:
Objective Temporalism

Philosophical discussion can be fruitful only when its issues are narrowed down to a point understood by all, and capable of being decided at least in part by empirical or dialectical considerations. A great deal of discussion among contemporary philosophers is a talking and writing by one philosopher to another. Few have taken it upon themselves to play the thankless role of critic in analyzing the ambiguities and removing the obscurities of philosophical debate. Foremost among philosophical critics in America is A. O. Lovejoy. Armed with extensive and accurate information and inspired with zest for the play of ideas, Lovejoy has acted as a gadfly towards neo-realists and pragmatists, often furnishing a much needed stimulus for the clarification of fundamental questions. He manifests a justified impatience towards those who while accepting a standpoint refuse to abide by its implications, to all who sing in one philosophical strain a song whose burden is completely in another. Whatever else philosophers may do, their arguments should be coherent.

Lovejoy's own philosophic position is objective temporalism. He might be very well called America's philosopher of evolution; he has produced some noteworthy historical studies on phases of evolutionary philosophy. Lovejoy's temporalism is primarily a defense of the presence and reality of genuine novelty and rich qualitative diversity in the world. The entering wedge of his argument against all eternalistic idealisms and rationalisms which deny these traits is supported by a proof that in dismissing real change from the world, idealism confuses the perception of succession with the succession of perceptions, and that in denying novelty and chance, rationalism uses as a self-evident principle the unproven dogma that there can be no more in the effect than in the cause. Once the metaphysical status of time has been assured, it is easy to show that epistemological subjectivism is false; and that the belief that there is nothing on earth and in heaven of which philosophy cannot give a rational account is a piece of metaphysical conceit.

Lovejoy subscribes to a generative theory of *sensa*, according to which the so-called secondary qualities and all other perceptual data are genuine emergents, arising from the interaction of certain types of physical existences. But as against what he calls the metaphysical behaviorism of neo-realism, he maintains that these emergent qualities are psychical, and consequently irreducibly subjective.

Lovejoy sees things sharply—sometimes too sharply—from the standpoint of his own temporalism. He defines his method as an attempt "to identify with definiteness the particular moment of existence, the relative temporal locus of each entity or process of relation referred to by any proposition". Occasionally he overlooks the fact that there are different degrees of definiteness, and that of things in transition, opposite predicates are sometimes equally true.* But as opposed to an organic type of metaphysics which systematically discounts the presence of distinctions and abstractions, the use of sharp antitheses is justified. The greatest of Lovejoy's metaphysical difficulties, however, is the status of purely logical and mathematical entities in his temporal system. Nor can he adequately

---

* *Cf.* M. R. Cohen, "Qualities, Relations and Things," *Journal of Philosophy*, Vol. 11, p. 617 (1914).

answer the argument that the qualities and characters of "real time", such as irreversibility and dimensionality, cannot themselves be characterized as temporal in the same sense as specific events.

H. T. Costello:
The Logic of Relations

Another critic of rare philosophical intelligence and insight is H. T. Costello, trained in scientific method and mathematical logic. His criticisms have the great merit not only of detecting formal flaws in the arguments of other philosophers, but of adequately restating their positions in order to see whether anything significant follows from them. This sympathetic and illuminating method is enlivened by a keen sense of humor which conveys an apposite meaning by jest more neatly than others do by labored argument. Costello is an ontological realist who believes that nature is a system of objective, logical structures; that the possibility of successfully applying universals to the control of things proves not that logic is a mere methodological device which we can accept or reject at will, but that the world has a metaphysical structure in terms of which that success can be partly construed. Consequently, he is resolutely opposed to all forms of nominalism and logical atomism, a doctrine which holds that the world is built up of an infinite number of absolutely unrelated simple facts, and which is sometimes mistakenly believed to follow from mathematical logic. Believing in the reality of universals, Costello naturally asserts the view that possibilities are objective. They are not merely a measure of our ignorance, but the actual presupposition of any attempt to understand or evaluate the world. "The greatest privilege of the human mind, and peculiarly of the philosophic and artistic mind, is to be able to rise above the world as it is, and compare what is with what might be and might have been."

Costello's relational logic is a modification of Aristotle's. His interest is not so much in the relation between qualities and things, universals and particulars, as in the systematic correlation between the qualities and universals embodied in some objective reference revealed by exhibition. All science moves on this plane of investigation into the "relations existing between relations." It has nothing to do with particulars as such. Whatever systematic connections exist—including those of causality and relevance—are to be found in this network of relations between relations.

He avoids the epistemological tangle by holding that whenever we contrast the "appearances" of a thing with its existence, we are not compelled to introduce a distinction between degrees of reality or between a mental realm in which "appearances" are located, and a physical realm which contains existing things. For the same object can have different or contradictory appearances in different contexts, and all we are concerned with are physical effects of physical causes. Truth is a property of judgment which asserts that certain relations hold of objects external to the knower. Knowledge as such makes a difference—to the knower, not to the object known. This leads him on the one hand to reject the coherence theory of absolute idealism in favor of a pluralism of logical systems; and on the other to a searching criticism of some ambiguities in the pragmatic theory of judgment which seems to confuse the conditions of knowledge, the systematic characters of things, with our knowledge of such conditions.

J. E. Boodin:
The Metaphysic of Pragmatism

That one can sympathize with pragmatism and yet not forego interest in metaphysical or speculative philosophy has been brilliantly illustrated in the works of J. E. Boodin. He calls himself a pragmatic realist but recognizes the centrality of metaphysics. Thought is not merely a methodology of behavior—its laws are also the laws of things. But the structure of things can be revealed only through the selective activity of human beings pursuing certain ends. The inference that the intellectual instruments used reflect in some way objective character can be made only after their successful application in re-ordering existence.

The world as we know it, claims Boodin, shows five distinct aspects that can systematically be explored under the head of the following attributes: stuff or energy, time, space, consciousness, and form or direction. These attributes are irreducible to one another, and define the level on which the more specific categories like causality, reciprocity, purpose, etc., function. Boodin attempts to superimpose upon a naturalistic underpinning a teleological idealism, which in the interests of man's religious needs, conceives nature to be striving towards the expression of certain ideals compatible with the enhancement of human life. These ideals operate as final causes, but whether immanently as the God of Aristotle or as expressions of the divine will of the God of Christian theology, Boodin does not say.

In his later cosmological speculations, some of these fundamental attributes appear as levels in a cosmic evolution. This evolution is not a mechanical development from the simple to the complex, for all possible phases of the universe are given at any one time. Evolution turns out to be a matter of local development in a universe whose structure remains invariant. Local development itself is not the result of chance, but of the cosmic interaction of certain lower phases in one series with higher phases already existing in another series. "Since in the universe as a whole all the levels of reality may be supposed to co-exist externally, there would thus be provided the *rationale* for the evolution in any one part of the cosmos from a lower to a higher level of existence." The religious strains in Boodin's cosmology are brought in from without. They lead him to assert belief in immortality on grounds that are really emotional rather than metaphysical. One may question whether his cosmic idealism is compatible with his pragmatic realism.

David F. Swenson:
The Problem of the Existential

Another mid-Western American philosopher of Scandinavian extraction whose philosophical qualities have not won the appreciation they merit, is David F. Swenson. He steers between voluntaristic pragmatism and intellectualism by denying any ontological significance to the *forms* of knowledge. Intellectualism, assuming that the fixed characteristics of knowledge are the characteristics of existence, eventuates in a denial either of the reality or significance of change. Pragmatism, assuming that the shifting characters of existence are characters of thought, has no room for those ideal concepts or meanings which enable us to recognize and evaluate change. Swenson fully appreciates the hypothetical character of logical universals and that whatever exists must in some way be under their sway; but that anything *should* exist cannot be deduced from them, for their necessity is relative to their own systematic connection. Contingency enters the world in virtue of its very existence and subsequent duration; intelligibility in virtue of the invariant meanings and implications in terms of which it is understood. "The given can be construed out of itself after it is given, but the giving of it can never be construed. Logical demonstration is not creation."

The existing world is one in which choice between significant alternatives is possible. But these alternatives are conditioned by the validity of logical law. To admit that man's acts take place in a world of mechanical necessity, therefore, is in no way to abridge his freedom, since in telling him what necessarily must follow if something else happens, he can determine in some way, negatively or positively, the actual occurrence of the event anticipated in the *if* clause.

Swenson's general outlook has been strongly influenced by the late 19th century Danish thinker, Kierkegaard, an original philosopher as well as a most interesting personality, little known in English-speaking countries but very popular in Germany. Uncertainty, unrest and risk are essential to human existence. From this insecurity arise fundamental beliefs that are genuinely personal, and that are not merely a matter of evidence but of adventurous assertion. We live forward but we think backward. The peace and knowledge brought by thought are continually imperiled by the dangers and novelties of sheer living. All the more does the "chief glory" of man's life lie in the sense of wonder and enthusiasm with which he faces the unknown. We literally stake our lives upon our belief in what future experience will be. Our very metaphysical assumptions, as well as the highest principles of reason, are, after all, when applied, articles of faith. Whether or not, for example, existence has logical structure cannot be settled deductively but only by living on the assumption that it has. Living is a series of crises, responsibilities and anxieties which always culminate in death. Life then for man is an ever renewed resolution to live. Only in retrospective thought are we spared this necessity for free decision. In living, thought can disclose alternatives but only passion can resolve them. "A criticism of fundamental beliefs is therefore a criticism of passions, not of knowledge . . . Passion rather than knowledge is the more adequate and concrete expression of the existential situation, since it is the mark of transition, and human existence is essentially in transition."

No more than Kierkegaard, can Swenson reconcile this romanticism and rationalism. The alternative between the completely certain and the completely uncertain is artificial, for it leaves out of account that great area which most of life includes—the indeterminate and probable, in which both regularity and chance are genuinely significant. To appeal, as Swenson does, to the duality of the ideal and real as a metaphysical sanction of the opposition between faith and knowledge is to overlook the fact that although man lives by both, faith has its tests through knowledge and knowledge its application through faith. Both are aspects of the life of reason, not warring elements within it.

C. J. Ducasse:
The Ontological Liberal

Individual philosophers who own no allegiance to school or party like stray dogs run the danger of going unnoticed. There is something irritating about a philosopher who cannot readily be classified, and he is punished by being disregarded until he sets up a school of his own. C. J. Ducasse, one of these interesting individual thinkers, has developed a theory of ontological liberalism in defense of the right to philosophical individuality. Metaphysical positions, he holds, are in the last resort purely a matter of individual taste, so that all philosophical speculation becomes either an exercise in formal consistency or insight into the sources of personality. For the critic, interest would be shifted from the philosopher's system to the philosopher's personality. The argument advanced by Ducasse is that all metaphysical positions which consistently maintain that, "To be real is to be X," can neither be proven nor refuted, for "real" is ultimately a value term, a function of taste and interest. Every position is as good as any other: all may be entertained and all may be rejected. On the basis of this liberalism, Ducasse reaches the conclusion that "individuals as such are the only absolutes to be found," a position which leads to subjectivism and nominalism, but only in consonance with Ducasse's premise.

That the words "real" and "unreal" have an honorific flavor in philosophic discourse cannot be denied. But that is because they are used in conjunction with a normative metaphysics and not given a meaning in terms of a specific context. The materialist and the Hindoo mystic may both use the word *reality* and they may both experience some elation or feeling of superiority when they utter it, but they mean by it entirely different things. We may for mnemonic convenience sum up the difference between these two philosophies by saying that they define reality in different ways. But two systems that differ only in a definition may be theoretically equivalent, i.e., they may differ only in the names that they attach to the same entities. If there is a genuine difference between materialism and mysticism it is because they differ as to whether certain entities possess given characteristics or whether certain inferences are valid. Hence, if such terms as *real* and *unreal* are discarded and technical terms substituted in our descriptions of whatever is given, the question as to whether what is given has certain qualities, or whether certain inferences are valid, can be objectively settled.

Ducasse is the author of a work on causation in which the paradoxical thesis is defended that causality is a "relation that holds essentially between single individual events"; and a book on the philosophy of art which argues for a thoroughgoing relativity in aesthetic criticism.

Edgar A. Singer and the Philosophy of Science

In the past, interest in the philosophy of science was never so keen as it is today when even the newspapers, deluding themselves and their readers, carry "scoops" on the most recent scientific discoveries. It is natural that the interest of American philosophers in science should reflect this eagerness on the part of the general public. But of those few American philosophers whose interest in science extends over many years and who possess the knowledge and training necessary for intelligent interpretation, Edgar A. Singer has been among the most suggestive. Even before Planck had struck off his famous sentence, "For the scientist only that exists which can be measured", Singer had clearly stated it as a definite proposition and drawn the implications for a general theory of measurement. In his various papers he has developed an experimental and objective theory of life and mind as forms of behavior according to which the specific laws of their functioning are compatible with the laws of mechanics but not reducible to such laws in significant explanation. An object may be a member of a class of objects whose behavior fulfills a definition of purpose, and at the same time a member of another class which can be defined and handled without reference to that purpose. As opposed to all anti-mechanistic philosophies of science which assume the existence of super-empirical entelechies or vital forces, Singer has developed the postulates of a philosophy of experimental science from which the apparently paradoxical theorem can be deduced that "a question not answerable by experiment is meaningless". Once it is realized that experiment here implies any controlled procedure involving physical or mental activity designed to test a proposition tentatively assumed to be valid, Singer's postulates give independent expression to the logic of pragmatism.

Clarence I. Lewis:
The Logic of Pragmatism

An original type of pragmatism which seems destined to exert a powerful influence upon future philosophical development in America has been elaborated by C. I. Lewis, whose work in symbolic logic has been mentioned earlier. Lewis has been influenced by Peirce, Royce, Fichte, and Dewey, but has succeeded in fusing their leading doctrines into an independent and closely-knit synthesis which promises to mark pragmatism's coming of age. In the past, the historic affiliations of pragmatism with British empiricism have made the status of the *a priori* or universal within its system rather problematic. Sometimes it seemed, e.g., in Mill, that universals were to be psychologically interpreted, thus leading to nominalism; or they would be construed as prescriptive forms of intuition, illustrated in the Kantianism of Henri Poincaré; or finally, among pragmatists who were strict in their realism, as invariant principles of natural kinds or structures, the general position of a modified Aristotelianism. It is Lewis' merit to have advanced a new conception of the *a priori* suggested by recent developments in logic. The *a priori* is a definition or a postulate. It expresses our interpretative attitude towards things, though things must be capable of being so regarded. "That is *a priori* which we can maintain in the face of all experience, come what will". Only that can be maintained in the face of any experience which is completely independent of experience, so that the laws of logic, for example, do not tell us anything which is true of things but merely about a classificatory scheme, self-contained in its own definitions. Experience can never be intractable to our *a priori* concepts, for, "if experience were other than it is, the definition and its corresponding classification might be inconvenient, useless, or fantastic, but it could not be false." But it would be meaningless, someone might retort. Not on Lewis' theory since, he continues, "Mind makes classifications and determines meanings; in so doing it creates that truth without which there would be no other truth."

A priori concepts or laws, then, tell us nothing about the material world, but are principles of procedure which we adopt towards that world. But there is no one principle of procedure or system of procedure, as Kant mistakenly supposed. There are an infinite number of possible modes of interpreting and classifying the world. There are always alternative conceptual systems by which the given can be understood. There are also an infinite number of logics, just as there are an infinite number of geometries, so that even "logical necessity" is relative to some deliberate choice on our part. It is even possible, maintains Lewis, to develop a self-consistent logic based upon the denial of the law of contradiction. The empirical, not the logical, is what the mind must accept.

What, it may be asked, has this metaphysical dualism to do with pragmatism? Simply this, that the ultimate criteria of those formal *a priori* concepts which we select from an infinite number of others, equally true and valid, are pragmatic, i.e., explicable in terms of human needs and purposes. How we categorize our experiences depends solely upon our interests. If our interests remain constant, our categories can never be proved invalid. Truth, then, aside from formal consistency, is a function of human bent or need; it is literally made by the human mind in its capacity to select from an inexhaustible series of patterns and signets that stamp which will affix the seal of "reality" upon experience.

This pragmatic conception of the *a priori* has the additional merit of rendering superfluous a metaphysical theory of experience to explain the conformity of thought to existence. The intelligibility of experience is guaranteed by our interpretations of the given. There can be no order in existence apart from our ordering. And so long as we realize that the application of hypothetical concepts to existence can only give us probable rather than certain knowledge, the absence of systematic sequence is no bar to reliable empirical truth. What is necessary for such empirical knowledge is only that our sense-presentations be *probable* indices of future sequences of possible experience. That empirical generalizations based upon past experience must be valid follows not from some objective order and connection in things but from the sole theoretical necessity that "certain presentations being given, the possibilities of further experience should not be unlimited; that is, that it should not be the case that every recognizable appearance is equally associated with, or followed by, every other." This last proposition must be true because it has no intelligible alternative.

From these positions Lewis is able to derive quite easily some of the more familiar positions of pragmatism. Truth is not the conformity of an idea with a ready made antecedent existence, but a property of ideas in virtue of which we can successfully predict and control. Knowledge is never immediate but always contains an element of the inferential; there is no knowledge by acquaintance. All existential propositions have implicit probability coefficients. The relativity of knowledge is compatible with its objectivity. Not only does knowing make a difference to objects but there could be no determinate objects, as distinct from things, without mind. Error does not give rise to a question of degrees of reality but is a challenge to improve our methods of reasoning.

It must be remembered however that these views are just as compatible with absolute idealism as with pragmatism. And on what grounds the purely Platonic conception of the *a priori* defended by Lewis, can be assimilated to the naturalistic starting point of historical pragmatism is not altogether clear. Surely an open avowal of dualism between the realm of pure concepts which possess all the forms of rationality on the one hand, and a flux possessing no objective order and consequently no rationality independent of the mind on the other, bears little enough resemblance to the Scotism of Peirce, the temporalism of James, and the emergent evolutionary naturalism of Dewey. It may well be that Professor Lewis is destined to play the part of the serpent in the pragmatist's Garden of Eden, tempting him with a conception of the *a priori* which will result in his expulsion from the paradise of naturalism into the nebulous realm of subsistence in which, Tantalus-like, one knows the general differences between *all* things without having specific knowledge of *any* thing. At any rate, the pragmatist is certain of being awakened by these interesting views from the philosophical naïveté of identifying the *a priori* either with the physically given or with its mental counterpart.

Aside from the question as to the justification of regarding Lewis' conception of the *a priori* as pragmatic, there are at least three general objections which can be raised against its validity. (1) If universals are completely separate and distinct from existence how is it possible that inferences based upon them should give valid knowledge of existence? In virtue of what traits of subject-matter can the laws of logic be applied to things such that formally valid inference from true propositions of fact always gives us other materially valid propositions? If existence exercises no compulsion upon the mind, what grounds have we for believing that existence is tractable to the mind's notions of convenience? And if it is answered that existence is so defined as to harmonize with the mind's canons of convenience, then it must be pointed out that definition does not create the subject-matter it defines but selects aspects of existence relevant to the purposes in hand. (2) If existence does not determine what system of logic is to be applied to it, leaving to the mind the power to freely choose any system from an infinite number of others, how do we know that any system so chosen is consistent? Short of ultimate exemplification of logical potulates in some subject-matter, what other proof can be offered save notoriously fallible inspection? (3) Lewis assumes an intuitive theory of meaning and not a functional one. He gives no method of determining whether alleged conceptual symbols really represent possible, transmissable meanings or whether they represent no more than nonsense syllables like "round-square". If meanings are always *of* some subject-matter, and are distinguished from one another by the consequences they effect, as all pragmatists have hitherto claimed, then whether or not a meaning is really intelligible cannot be a matter of intuition. To deny this is to forget that things do not have to *be* meanings in order to be meaningful.

Alfred N. Whitehead: Time and the Eternal

No account of the present state of American philosophy would be complete which did not mention the influence of A. N. Whitehead, the great Cambridge mathematician, upon the philosophical public, secular and lay. The modern revolutionary developments in theoretic physics have made particularly acute the question as to how the abstract scientific objects of physical theory are related to the concrete immediate flow of experience. Whitehead is one of the few men qualified by the requisite knowledge of mathematics, physics and philosophy to deal adequately with problems of this kind. The traditional mechanical philosophy had endeavored to explain the nature and relations of things in terms of a succession of instantaneous configurations of matter. In other words, the stuff of the world was regarded as composed of fundamental elements of "material points" and "instants of time". Physicists have known, of course, that "points" and "instants" are not actual facts of nature but logical limits, but yet they attempted to give a definite location to material objects as if the "heres" and "nows" in terms of which they described it, had a perfectly definite sense involving no reference to other "heres" and "nows". Whitehead maintains that there is no material element of which we can say that it exists at a given place and at a given time in any absolute sense. It is always part of a system of space-time relationships such that definite position can be assigned to it only by reference to the underlying order of this system. Consequently, we cannot make intelligible to ourselves what it would mean for an event to be completely isolated or particularized. To imagine that anything can exist in a finite region of space for a finite duration of time without essential reference to other regions of space and other regions of time in a general "ether of events", is to commit the fallacy of simple location or misplaced concreteness. Of every specific relationship which an event bears to other events and to the qualities ("eternal objects" in Whitehead's terminology) which characterize those events, it may be said that it "enters into the essence of the event; so that, apart from that relationship, the event would not be itself."

With this theory of events Whitehead is able to overcome what he calls vicious theories of natural bifurcation which divide nature into the movement of qualityless electrons, or what not, on the one hand, and variegated manifolds of sense qualities perceived by the mind, on the other. This separation then raises the question as to which realm is "really" real,—which is the cause of which,—and draws attention away from the actual character of things known and perceived. With Bergson —but eschewing his attack on analysis as such—Whitehead protests against taking scientific abstractions out of their setting and treating them as if they were antecedent existences defining "reality," and then tacking on secondary and tertiary qualities as futile "unreal" additions of the human mind. "For natural philosophy everything perceived is in nature. We may not pick and choose. For us the red glow of the sunset should be as much part of nature as are the molecules and electric waves by which men of science would explain the phenomenon. It is for natural philosophy to analyze how these various elements of nature are connected."

But whatever qualities exist in nature they are never given in atomic isolation. They depend upon the relations which events bear to one another, although they are not reducible to such relations. The center of reference for the qualities that appear in sense-perception is naturally the percipient. Qualities which appear in contexts and circumstances that do not include the human organism are still relative to some center of selective reference. Whitehead uses the term "organism" to refer to that unity of any situation which is relevant to the explanation of the specific qualities that arise in it. Within this unity there can always be distinguished an aspect, denominated subjective, in whose experience all other elements of the situation are given. By an uncritical use of the principle of continuity, it is assumed that a vague qualitative "feeling" must pervade every organic occasion just as it pervades, in more conscious form, human occasions. "The philosophy of organism attributes 'feelings' throughout the actual world."

How is any one organism, or subjective aspect of an organic occasion, to be distinguished from any other? Here, too, we must avoid a corresponding variant of the fallacy of simple location. Specific place, time, meaning and efficacy cannot be assigned to any one organism without essential reference to all other organisms. The task of speculative philosophy is now "to frame a coherent, logical, necessary system of ideas in terms of which every element of our experience can be interpreted." To such a philosophy the world must appear to be a super-organism, one great fact or totality called God, which is the presupposition of both any existent within it and any intelligible statement about it. The Hegelian Absolute is reinstated once more as the ultimate ground of the principles of ground and consequent, cause and effect, means and ideal ends. The only things genuinely novel in Whitehead's philosophy are the method and terminology with which he reaches and states the familiar conclusions of absolute idealism.

Whitehead's critique of the methodology of the natural sciences is not organically related to his systematic metaphysics. The method of extensive abstraction, developed in his earlier writings, which defines a term not by its intrinsic nature or quality but by the series of relations into which that term is capable of entering, can be used by an objective relativistic naturalism to break down the sharp initial metaphysical separation Whitehead makes between events existing in space and time, and objects or universals subsisting in a Platonic heaven. Whitehead's resort to God as the principle of concretion is an extreme expedient introduced to overcome this traditional dualism, and God's organic nature, in the light of which both events and objects acquire significance, is itself established by proclamation rather than by analysis. Personal reasons probably account for investing God with the consolatory and honorific epithets of Christian theology. However, only the future will show whether Whitehead's system or his method will exercise greater influence upon philosophy. As far as the present results of his thoughts are concerned, philosophy for him seems to have returned to where it was at the turn of the century, before G. E. Moore and Bertrand Russell broke critical ground against Bradley.

Contemporary Value Theory

The present vogue of theories of value demands a word or two about the different types of value theories and their tendency to confuse specific psychological issues with the more general philosophical problems involved. There are those for whom value has the same ontological status as the quality of truth, possessing validity irrespective of natural existence and human valuation. This Platonic strain runs through the writing of the idealists, except that they postulate a non-empirical absolute consciousness in whose minds these values lodge. Then there are the adherents of a modified Aristotelianism who make value a function of any objective fulfillment, so that whatever furthers a tendency to some end, irrespective of whether this end is approved, is valuable. Sheldon is the chief representative of this view. Finally, there is the naturalistic school which frankly defines values as essentially related to human desire and intelligence.

Among the naturalists, however, a threefold divergence has manifested itself *apropos* of the question of the possibility of a basis for objective criticism. For David Wight Prall, anything is a good which is immediately enjoyed or preferred. There can be no arguing or debating about values, since on this theory there can be no mistake in value judgments. For Ralph Barton Perry, a value is any object of any interest, which interest is interpreted as a function of a motor-affective response. The notion of "desirable," or "should be preferred" is thus devoid of significance. For Dewey, that has value which is preferred after reflection. Liking is a necessary condition in all valuation, but what is liked has value only insofar as a differential meaning is recognized as involved in it. Judgment and criticism of values consists in analyzing their conditions and consequences.

The duplicity in the discussion of theories of value arises from the fact that the purely descriptive psychology of interests, viz., what things do we desire and why, is not distinguished either from the normative doctrine of ways and means once we know what it is that we do desire, or from the analysis of the way in which the consequences of our value-commitments react upon those interests or objects originally regarded as valuable. An autonomous theory of value could best be developed if ends as such were never referred to as values and only that regarded as valuable which possessed validity for a specified end-in-view. A judgment of value could then be objective in that it enabled one to test the consequences within a definite situation of the relative validity of the different means proposed. Ends themselves would then be subject to criticism in two respects. First, the attempt to state that for which a thing was good or valid would lead to an explicit recognition of what those ends and interests were which dominate our habitual behavior, making it easier for us to entertain possibilities of alternative modes of conduct. Second, acknowledging our aim, the full meaning of that acknowledgment would then come home to us after we had considered the nature and consequences of the means necessary for its attainment.

Retrospect

The period covered by the greater portion of this survey is too near us to make a just appreciation of its achievement likely at this time. In the main it has been dominated by two interests, the theologic and the psychologic. The development during this period has been to weaken the former and to deepen but narrow the latter and make it more and more technical. For this reason the philosophers covered in this survey have as yet exerted little influence on the general thought of the country. The general current of American economic, political, and legal thought has until very recently been entirely dominated by our traditional eighteenth-century individualism or natural-law philosophy. Neither does our general literature, religious life, or current scientific procedure as yet show any distinctive influence of our professional philosophy. But it must be remembered that all our universities are comparatively young institutions and our university-trained men numerically an almost insignificant portion of our total population. In the field of education William T. Harris and after him Dewey have undoubtedly exerted potent influences, and it looks as if American legal thought is certain to be profoundly impressed by Roscoe Pound, who draws some of his inspiration from philosophic pragmatism as well as from Ward's social theories.

From the point of view of European culture, America has certainly not produced a philosopher as influential as was Willard Gibbs in the realm of physics or Lester Ward in the realm of sociology. Though Ward and even Gibbs may with some justice be claimed as philosophers, this can be done only by disregarding the unmistakable tendency to divorce technical philosophy entirely from physical and social theory. James, however, is undoubtedly a European force as are, in lesser degree, Baldwin, Royce, and Dewey. Serious and competent students in Germany, Italy, and Great Britain have also recognized the permanent importance of C. S. Peirce's contribution to the field of logic. History frequently shows philosophers who receive no adequate recognition except from later generations, but it is hazardous to anticipate the judgment of posterity.

INDEX OF
PROPER NAMES

SUBJECT INDEX

art—*cont'd*
217; and morality, 248; and Puritanism, 25, 209–10, 248; and reality, 218; and skill, 220, 221; and wealth, 209; appreciation of, 10, 208; *vs* aesthetics, 221; as expression of a wish, 218; as expression of emotion, 219; as heightened experience, 217; as pure form, 225; as reason in nature, 216; as revelation, 220–1; economic interpretation of, 56; effect of frontier on, 21, 209; industrial enterprise *vs*, 208–9; intellectuality in, 224; modernism in, 212; Old World influence on, 210, 212, 225; participation *vs* observation in, 217; philosophy of, 211, 212; social theories of, 216, 248; spontaneity in, 214; theory of, 208ff; universality of, 211–2; world as work of, 213; (*see also* fine arts, industrial arts)

asceticism: 25, 187

association: principle of, 92

astronomy: 71, 76; and evolution, 70; Copernican, 77, 190, 260; early American, 67

atheism: 181, 191, 192; and functionalism, 195; and supernaturalism, 200–1; (*see also* free thought)

authority: as method of learning, 80; in literary criticism, 251; method of, in ethical teaching, 204; oriental view of, 81

B

bankruptcy laws: 144

Baptist Churches: and revivalism, 186

beauty: and skill, 220; as perfection of harmony, 214, 215; as pleasure objectified, 215; concept of, in relation to world, 203, 213; in music as appeal to senses, 240

Beaux Arts School: in architecture, 225

behaviorism: 284, 302, 324; in law, 171, 172ff; in religion, 194–5; in social sciences, 172; metaphysical, 318

belief: as descriptive psychology, 198; essential to historical religion, 201;

right to, in historical religion, 197–8; social nature of religious, 201

Berthold v. *O'Reilly*, 142*n.*

Bible: 25, 50, 73, 139, 187, 191, 197; higher criticism of, 167, 189, 190, 191, 194

Bill of Rights: 44, 45, 118, 121, 143

biology: and evolution, 60, 81

book habits: American, 29–30

Brahmanism: 197

British influence: on American thought, 19, 49, 255

Brothers of Sincerity, 11

Buddhism: 197, 201

business: and government, 23; and law, 174, 178; man as statesman, 37; prestige of, in American community, 32, 37–9, 120; role, in journalism, 39; tradition, 67; values in, 22, 29–30, 37

C

Calder v. *Bull*, 122*n.*

Calvinism: and economic thought, 25, 88; and historical thought, 52; and human depravity, 25, 88; and political thought, 25, 115, 117–8, 121; and religious thought, 24, 26, 184, 187; and the arts, 25, 209–10, 232; in law, 168; and predestinarianism, 52; (*see also* Puritanism)

canon law: 118

capitalism: and evolution, 61; defects of, 112; defenders of, 103; philosophy of, 121

case method in law: 151ff

categorical imperative: as basis for ethical philosophy, 203–5

Catholicism: and politics, 184; and social reform, 56, 188

causation: in economics, 97; Marxian theory of, in literature, 252–3; social, 55

chance: absolute, and rational world, 196–7; and scientific laws, 274–5; in history, 63–4; Peirce's doctrine of, 76, 273–4; reality of, in universe, 318, 321

change: universal law of, 70 (*see also* evolution)